Federal Fathers & Mothers

Published in association with
The William P. Clements Center for
Southwest Studies, Southern Methodist
University, by the University of
North Carolina Press, Chapel Hill

Federal

Fathers &

Mothers

A Social History of the United States Indian Service, 1869–1933

CATHLEEN D. CAHILL

FIRST PEOPLES

The University of North Carolina Press Chapel Hill

Publication of this book was made possible, in part,
by a grant from the Andrew W. Mellon Foundation.

Library of Congress Cataloging-in-Publication Data
Cahill, Cathleen D.
Federal fathers and mothers : the United States Indian Service,
1869–1933 / Cathleen D. Cahill.
p. cm. — (First peoples : new directions in Indigenous studies)
"Published in association with the William P. Clements Center for
Southwest Studies, Southern Methodist University."
Includes bibliographical references and index.
ISBN 978-0-8078-3472-5 (cloth : alk. paper)
ISBN 978-1-4696-0681-1 (pbk. : alk. paper)
1. United States. Bureau of Indian Affairs — History. 2. United States.
Bureau of Indian Affairs — Officials and employees — History.
3. Civil service — Social aspects — United States — History. 4. Indians
of North America — Cultural assimilation — History. 5. Indians of
North America — Government relations — 1869–1934. I. William P.
Clements Center for Southwest Studies. II. Title.
E93.C27 2011   323.1197'073 — dc22   2010050773

cloth   15 14 13 12 11   5 4 3 2 1
paper   17 16 15 14 13   5 4 3 2 1

To Dennis & Pamela Cahill,

LOVING PARENTS AND LOVERS OF HISTORY

Contents   *Acknowledgments* xi   *Introduction* 1

Illustrations, Maps, Figure, & Table

Acknowledgments

I owe a debt of gratitude to the incredible group of scholars at the University of Chicago. Kathleen Neils Conzen is a gifted teacher, giving her students enough freedom to truly explore their topics but enough guidance to hone the results. Amy Dru Stanley urged me to think about the links between Indian policy and Reconstruction. Catherine Brekus offered much advice and encouragement. Ray Fogelson's suggestion about fictive kin changed the way I thought about the Indian Service. Conversations and classes with Julie Saville and Bill Novak significantly helped shape my thoughts about the nineteenth century. And without Mae Ngai's suggestion that I look into the sources at the National Personnel Records Center, this would have been a very different book.

My years in the doctoral program were among the most enjoyable of my life. The rigorous intellectual milieu at Chicago was complemented by a boisterous social life. Many close friends fostered this project at its inception: Kathy Brosnan, Tom Chappelear, Sean Forner, Danny Greene, Karrin Hanshew, Matt Lindsay, Rebekah Mergenthal, Andrew Oppenheimer, Melinda Pilling, Kim Reilly, Laurel Spindel, Kyle Volk, Amber Wilke, and many others.

Time, space of one's own, and invigorating conversations with fellow scholars are a great gift to a historian. A fellowship from the Spencer Foundation brought me to the Newberry Library for a productive and invigorating year. Along with the incredibly rich archival collections that the Newberry provided, I made many lasting friendships with colleagues, including Loretta Fowler, Rob Galler, Jim Grossman, Brian Hosmer, Rowena McClinton, Alyssa Mt. Pleasant, Lavonne Brown Ruoff, and Helen Hornbeck Tanner. It was also my privilege to hold the Michigan State University Pre-Doctoral Fellowship in American Indian Studies. My thanks to Susan Sleeper-Smith and the late Susan Applegate-Krouse, who welcomed me with warm hospitality and inspired me with their example. Thanks also to Joe Genetin-Pilawa, who kept me company in the basement of Morrill Hall. Both at Chicago and Michigan State, I had the great privilege of participating in the Newberry Committee on Institutional Cooperation's American Indian Studies Consortium (whose legacy lives on in the Newberry Consortium in American Indian Studies). The warm welcome I received from senior scholars, and the chance to share ideas with emerging ones, was invaluable for a young and impressionable doctoral candidate.

Most recently, I was honored to join the ranks of the Bill and Rita Clements Fellows at Southern Methodist University's Clements Center for Southwest Studies. The Clements Fellowships manuscript workshops are a rare and amazing opportunity for a scholar, and they would not be the same without the enthusiastic participants. I'm greatly in debt to everyone who gave so generously of their time and intellectual labor: Anne Allbright, Norwood Andrews, Jim Buss, Sarah Cornell, Edward Countryman, Crista DeLuzio, David Doyle, Dave Edmunds, John Gram, Sarah F. Rose, Jeff Schulze, and Jenna Valadez. And I'm especially grateful to Linda Gordon and K. Tsianina Lomawaima for their generous reading of the manuscript and their insightful and stimulating advice.

The marvelous and efficient Andrea Boardman and Ruth Ann Elmore made me feel incredibly welcome at SMU and helped me to be very productive. My fellow fellows, Norwood Andrews, Sarah Cornell, Raúl Coronado, and Stephanie Lewthwaite, provided good company and rigorous conversations. Michelle Nickerson and Ben Johnson shared meals, movies, babysitting, and a great deal of laughter. As acting director of the center, Ben also coordinated my fellowship, ran my workshop, and educated me in the ways of Texas. The greatest honor of my year, however, was David Weber's friendship and guidance. David was a true teacher and scholar—brilliant, generous, kind, curious, and possessing a remarkable inner strength. I treasure the time he gave to me, and I remain awed and inspired by his commitment to junior scholars. Everyone who ever knew him will miss him.

Many other institutions and organizations helped fund the research for this project. I am thankful for the Benjamin Bloom Dissertation Fellowship and the Western History Association Walter Rundell Dissertation Award, the Huntington Library–Western History Association Martin Ridge Fellowship, the Organization of American Historians Merrill Travel Grant, the Smith College Margaret Storrs Grierson Travel Grant, the Southern California Historical Society Haynes Grant, and the University of New Mexico Research Allocation Committee and Institute for American Indian Research Faculty Research Grants. Without the awards committees' belief in the merits of the project, I could not have done the archival work necessary to complete the book. I also owe great thanks to the librarians and archivists at the Bancroft Library at the University of California, Berkeley; the Huntington Library;

the Humboldt Room at Humboldt State University (especially Joan Berman); the Humboldt County Library; the Humboldt County Historical Society; the California Historical Society; Knox College; Wichita State University Special Collections; the Graduate Theological Seminary in San Anselmo; San Jose State University; the interlibrary loan office at the University of New Mexico; the University of Chicago's Regenstein Library; the Newberry Library (especially John Aubrey); the Montana Historical Society; the Michigan State University Library; and Southern Methodist University's Fondren and DeGolyer Libraries. I am especially grateful to Susie Baker Fountain, whose passion for Humboldt County history was a godsend to future historians.

This book also could not have been written without the resources of our nation's archives and their guardians. To the archivists and staff at the National Archives and Records Administration branches in Washington, D.C. (especially Mary Frances Ronan), San Bruno, Chicago (particularly Scott Forsyth), and Denver, as well as to the staff at the National Personnel Records Center in St. Louis (especially Lisa Boykin), I am eternally grateful.

My colleagues at the University of New Mexico have been a tremendous source of support and advice. I am extremely lucky to work at an institution with so many scholars in my fields of study, and I have greatly benefited from invigorating discussions with Durwood Ball, Judy Bieber, Melissa Bokovoy, Margaret Connell-Szasz, Jennifer Denetdale, Linda Hall, Paul Hutton, Tim May, Barbara Reyes, Virginia Scharff, Jane Slaughter, Frank Szasz, and Sam Truett, as well as the participants in the University of New Mexico History Workshop. I'm also grateful to Dana Ellison, Helen Ferguson, Yolanda Martinez, and Barbara Wafer for all of their support. But all work and no play makes us dull, and my colleagues have also ensured that I put my pen down once in a while. Many have also become dear friends, providing good food and great company on multiple occasions. Virginia Scharff has looked after my well-being in both intellectual and social realms while providing extraordinary hospitality. And I raise a glass to Sarah Cornell, Eliza Ferguson, Tom Leete, Sophie Martin, Nancy McLoughlin, Erika Monahan, Anna Nogar, Mary Quinn, Enrique Sanabria, Tom Sizgorich, Jason Scott Smith, and everyone else who attended the Thursday night happy hours. Many thanks also to Kent Blansett, Meg Frisbee, and Elaine Nelson for their stimulating conversations. Heather Hawkins in particular deserves great praise for her Herculean efforts while checking my notes, ordering images, and keeping up my spirits in the home stretch.

This book may truly be said to be a cooperative project, as many friends and colleagues read portions of it and made incisive and constructive suggestions. Thanks to David Wallace Adams, Willy Bauer, Brian Collier, Joe

Genetin-Pilawa, John Hankey, Margaret Jacobs, Richard John, Jacki Rand, Susan Sleeper-Smith, Sharon Wood, and Barbara Welke. Bert Ahern not only read portions and spent many hours in discussion on the topic but also very generously shared his own research notes with me. A few heroic individuals read the entire manuscript and offered invaluable advice. Brenda Child, Susan Gray, Linda Gordon, Tsianina Lomawaima, and Virginia Scharff—I cannot thank you enough.

A hearty thanks is also due to all of the panelists, audience members, and commentators at conferences of the Western History Association, American Ethnohistory Association, Newberry Committee on Institutional Cooperation, Native American and Indigenous Studies Association, Berkshire Conference on the History of Women, Organization of American Historians, Policy History Conference, and Vernacular Architecture Forum, whose thoughts on my work have been extremely helpful.

Mark Simpson-Vos, Jay Mazzocchi, Russ Damian, Tema Larter, and the rest of the editorial staff at UNC Press have been extremely helpful and beyond patient while shepherding me through the unfamiliar process of turning a manuscript into a book.

I also greatly appreciate the time and energy Bradley Marshall, Joe Marshall, Jude Marshall, and Byron Nelson Jr. devoted to talking to me and sharing some aspects of their family and tribal histories. Jack Norton and Jana Rivers Norton generously drove from Gallup to Albuquerque so that Jack could share memories of his parents and grandparents and offer his suggestions on a draft of chapter 7. As the mother of newly arrived twins, I cannot state the depth of my appreciation for their kindness for making the trip. In recognition of the struggles of the Native people in this book, a portion of the proceeds will go to Humboldt State University's Indian Teacher and Educational Personnel Program.

Friends and family opened their homes to me during research trips, and I am especially indebted to the generosity of Peggy Miles; John Hankey and Frances Hankey; and my uncles, Paul Cahill and Ed Connelly.

There were many, many more people who helped in countless ways big and small. While I cannot include them all here, I am in their debt.

Writing about families reminds me of how fortunate I have been to have such a wonderful and supportive family of my own. I hope this book makes them as proud as they make me happy. It is dedicated to my parents because without their endless love, support, and encouragement, I would never have started—let alone finished—the journey. They also deserve thanks for all of the books they provided and the family trips they planned that developed my love of history. Much love and gratitude also goes to Christine, Bill, and Ila

Disbrow and Kevin and Christine Cahill for their willingness to listen to me talk about this project for many years, for opening their homes, and for making sure I remembered to have fun. This project would not have happened if my godparents, Aunt Cathy and Uncle Ron Maher, had not given me an important graduation present: the memoir of two women who worked as field matrons among the Indians in Northern California, which piqued my interest in the subject of Bureau of Indian Affairs employees. Sally and Pete Tannenbaum set a great example, and Grandma Edie and all the Davises offered enthusiastic encouragement. Ellen Levine and Ivan Strausz were always happy to talk about writing and books while giving me enthusiastic support and a place to relax in New York.

Cecilia and Lincoln were very patient while mommy had to work and will, I hope, be much happier now that she has more time to play. Their extraordinary presence made me even more empathetic to the struggles, heartaches, and joys of the families I discuss in these pages. And no acknowledgments would be complete without expressing gratitude to my great love and partner, Andrew K. Sandoval-Strausz. I am distinctly fortunate to live my life with a man who exemplifies scholarly excellence coupled with boundless enthusiasm for all things. He shared in my exhilaration, exhaustion, laughter, and tears as I wrote this book. Without his grammatical expertise and frequent cheerleading, this project would be a mere shadow of itself. As much as his intellectual companionship means to me, however, it is the life we have built around our academic endeavors that I am most amazed by and hold most dear.

As my family and Andrew can attest, I am extremely stubborn, and therefore any mistakes in this book are mine and are probably the result of my intractableness in the face of good advice.

Introduction

In *Custer Died for Your Sins*, his 1969 manifesto, Native intellectual Vine De-loria Jr. (Standing Rock Sioux) wryly observed: "It would be fair to say that Indian people are ambivalent" about government agencies. "Some Indian people want desperately to get rid of the Bureau of Indian Affairs. Others want increased bureau services to help solve problems of long standing."[1] This ambivalence has a long history. For many Native people,[2] the Bureau of Indian Affairs has been the face of conquest, a reminder that the federal government has exercised power over Indian land and lives but has not al-ways had their best interests at heart. A joke often told in Indian country has it that the bureau's acronym, "BIA," stands for "Bossing Indians Around." On the other hand, the bureau is also the executive agency charged with fulfilling federal trust responsibilities and thus administers many services that were stipulated in treaties between sovereign Native nations and the U.S. govern-ment. Indeed, even radical critics have seen the need for some sort of federal office. The American Indian Movement (AIM) demanded that the agency be dismantled; one member, Floyd Red Crow Westerman (Sisseton-Wahpeton), even wrote a popular song called "B.I.A." with the lyrics: "B.I.A. you can't change me don't you try . . . / I'm not your Indian anymore / You belong to White man." But AIM still proposed the formation of a new federal agency to serve Indian people.[3]

Native people have not been alone in feeling ambivalent about the Bureau of Indian Affairs. Whites have also been of two minds about it. Many white policy makers have deemed the agency unnecessary, called it an impediment to the assimilation of Indians into the nation, or simply criticized it as a drain on the federal treasury. Almost from the moment of its creation, whites spoke of the agency as a temporary bureau that should gradually disappear. In point of fact, policy makers spent decades trying to get rid of the agency, whether by breaking up tribal landholdings in the 1880s or terminating the tribes' sovereign status in the 1950s. There were many moments when policy mak-ers optimistically announced that the need for federal oversight was at an end. In 1914, for example, Commissioner of Indian Affairs Cato Sells proudly reported that his educational policy of moving Indian children from federal Indian schools to local public schools offered "a splendid example of the elimination of the Indian as a distinct problem for the Federal or the State governments."[4]

Despite this long history of ambivalence, during the late nineteenth and early twentieth centuries—the most formative period of the Office of Indian Affairs (as the bureau was known at the time)—Natives and whites devoted extraordinary amounts of labor, money, and materials to the work of the agency. It is striking that despite the position of the Indian Office as the administrative arm of a conquering state, thousands of Native people took jobs in the Indian Service (the workforce of the Indian Office) in those years. At a high point in 1912, for example, the Indian Service employed more than 2,000 Indians as regular appointees—over a third of the total—as well as six times that number in temporary positions.[5] Moreover, the workforce as a whole expanded dramatically in those decades, from just over 500 employees in the field in 1869 to nearly 4,000 by 1897 and 6,000 by 1912. Significantly, a large number of the new employees were women. Meanwhile, Congress dramatically increased the Indian Office's budget appropriations. In 1881, for example, $75,000 went to Indian education; a mere four years later, the appropriation was $992,800, and a decade after that it had reached $2,060,695. In 1913 the commissioner of Indian affairs reported that since 1881 the government had appropriated more than $263 million for the Indian Service and to fulfill treaty stipulations.[6] These massive commitments indicate that although the people involved disagreed—often vehemently—about the direction of federal Indian policy, the Indian Service presented them with the possibility of shaping the agency's agenda, or at least using its resources to suit their needs.

Federal Fathers and Mothers reveals the distinctive social history of the Indian Service and presents broader arguments about governance, colonialism, and gender in the United States. After the Civil War, a newly enlarged federal government launched ambitious and aggressive efforts to control Native American populations in its western territories in order to make these areas available and safe for white settlers. If we examine how federal Indian policy borrowed from earlier Reconstruction-era initiatives and consider how the Indian Service influenced the administration of America's overseas colonies, we can see all three as part of an evolving relationship between the federal government and its wards. Although Native tribes were sovereign nations, and most had treaty-stipulated rights, the federal government generally ignored that status and began to treat them as it did its other subject populations. It was precisely because the United States disregarded tribal sovereignty that it could experiment with new modes of governance. In creating and implementing a new suite of social programs, most of them in the American West, the federal government developed a large, complex, and durable bureaucracy (Illustration 1.1).

While historians of the West have long recognized the important role of the federal government in the region, they have not always adequately connected that story to the larger national narrative of state development. Few scholars have followed up on Richard White's assertion that the West served as "the kindergarten of the American state." Elliot West and Karen Merrill have renewed the call for western historians to make the linkages between region and nation more explicit, and Merrill has urged policy historians to give the West more attention as a site of federal governance. "If historians and theorists of the state have yet to include the West in their models of state-building," she notes, "western historians have yet to consider whether federal involvement in the West follows other patterns in the nation." Only recently have scholars begun to do this.[7] William J. Novak, for example, has challenged historians of the state to redefine their models by examining government activity along frontiers; he argues that "coming to terms with the American state requires a better understanding of [its] power on the periphery."[8]

In the period considered in this book, what became the American West was the periphery of the United States; most of the land was under federal jurisdiction, either as territories or Indian reservations. Having seized the land, the federal government envisioned settling it with white Americans. This was clearly a colonial project. In classical colonial models in which a nation subordinated a territory external to itself, the primary issue was the extraction of resources and the control and subordination of Indigenous labor by a small colonial force. In the U.S. West, by contrast, as in Australia, Canada, and South Africa, the government followed a model of settler colonialism that had different imperatives and different goals. Most significant, the conquering nation sought to acquire land for settlement. As such, land dispossession was the central aim, but the colonizers who hoped to permanently settle that land also had to decide what would be done with the people who were dispossessed. While the process of conquest and dispossession had a long history, it accelerated and intensified in the decades after the Civil War. The goal that drove the federal government in this period was to take land from Native nations and place it in the hands of white settlers. Achieving this goal involved an attempt to destroy Native cultural identities, thus severing their emotional ties and legal claims to the land.

The government's method for expropriating Native land and annihilating

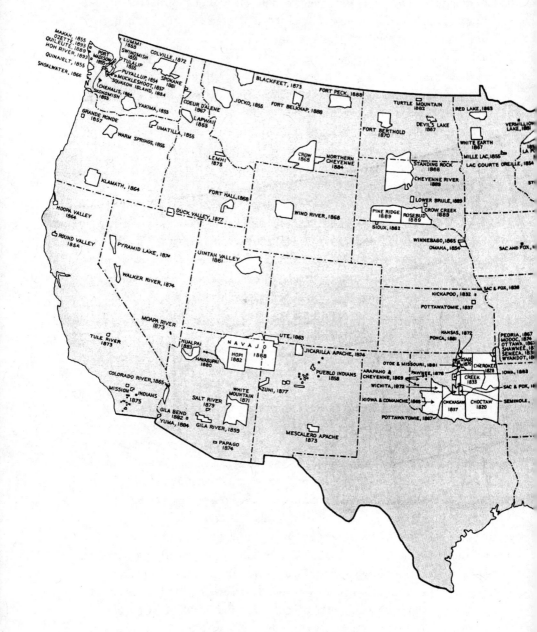

MAKAH, 1855
OZETTE, 1893
QUILEUTE, 1893
HOH RIVER, 1893
QUINAIELT, 1855
SHOALWATER, 1866

LUMMI 1855
SWINOMISH 1855
PORT TULALIP 1855
MADISON 1855
1855
PUYALLUP 1854
MUCKLESHOOT, 1857
SQUAXON ISLAND, 1884
CHEHALIS, 1864
SKOKOMISH 1855

COLVILLE, 1872
SPOKANE 1881

BLACKFEET, 1873
FORT PECK, 1888

YAKIMA, 1855
COEUR D'ALENE 1867
LAPWAI 1863

JOCKO, 1855
FORT BELKNAP, 1888

TURTLE MOUNTAIN 1882
RED LAKE, 1863

DEVIL'S LAKE 1867
VERMILLION LAKE, 1881

GRANDE RONDE 1857
UMATILLA, 1855

WARM SPRINGS, 1855

LEMHI 1875

FORT BERTHOLD 1870

WHITE EARTH 1867
MILLE LAC, 1855
LAC COURTE OREILLE, 1854

KLAMATH, 1864

FORT HALL, 1868

CROW 1868
NORTHERN CHEYENNE 1884

STANDING ROCK 1868
CHEYENNE RIVER 1888

HOOPA VALLEY 1864
DUCK VALLEY, 1877

WIND RIVER, 1868

LOWER BRULE, 1889
CROW CREEK 1889
PINE RIDGE 1889
ROSEBUD 1889
SIOUX, 1882

ROUND VALLEY 1858
PYRAMID LAKE, 1874

UINTAH VALLEY 1861

WINNEBAGO, 1865
OMAHA, 1854
SAC AND FOX,

WALKER RIVER, 1874

KICKAPOO, 1832
SAC & FOX, 1836

MOAPA RIVER 1873

POTTAWATOMIE, 1837

TULE RIVER 1873

HUALPAI 1883
NAVAJO
HOPI 1868
1882
UTE, 1863

KANSAS, 1872
PONCA, 1881

PEORIA, 1867
MODOC, 1874
OTTAWA, 1867
SHAWNEE, 1831
SENECA, 1831
WYANDOT,

HAVASUPAI 1880

JICARILLA APACHE, 1874

OTOE & MISSOURI, 1881
OSAGE 1870
CHEROKEE 1828
IOWA, 1883

COLORADO RIVER, 1865

PUEBLO INDIANS 1858
ARAPAHO & CHEYENNE, 1869
PAWNEE, 1876
CREEK 1833
SAC & FOX, 18

MISSION INDIANS 1875

SALT RIVER 1879
WHITE MOUNTAIN 1871
ZUNI, 1877

WICHITA, 1872
KIOWA & COMANCHE, 1868
CHICKASAW 1837
CHOCTAW 1820
SEMINOLE

GILA BEND 1882
YUMA, 1884
GILA RIVER, 1859

POTTAWATOMIE, 1867

PAPAGO 1874

MESCALERO APACHE 1873

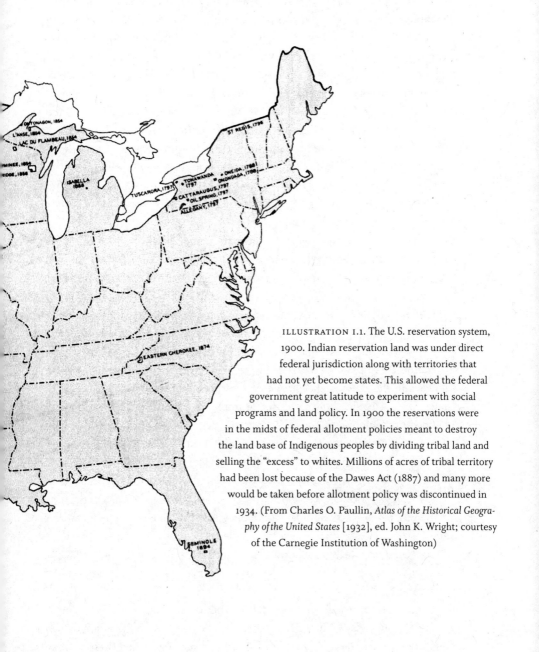

ILLUSTRATION I.I. The U.S. reservation system, 1900. Indian reservation land was under direct federal jurisdiction along with territories that had not yet become states. This allowed the federal government great latitude to experiment with social programs and land policy. In 1900 the reservations were in the midst of federal allotment policies meant to destroy the land base of Indigenous peoples by dividing tribal land and selling the "excess" to whites. Millions of acres of tribal territory had been lost because of the Dawes Act (1887) and many more would be taken before allotment policy was discontinued in 1934. (From Charles O. Paullin, *Atlas of the Historical Geography of the United States* [1932], ed. John K. Wright; courtesy of the Carnegie Institution of Washington)

Native cultures hinged upon assimilating Indian people into the citizenry. Policy makers sought to transform Native peoples' intimate, familial ties by creating a new set of relationships between the nation's Indian "wards" and government employees—the "federal fathers and mothers" of this book's title—who would guide them by offering examples of "civilized" behavior. These efforts to administer a subject population were perhaps the most deliberate instance of what scholars like Ann Laura Stoler have labeled "intimate colonialism." Stoler has demonstrated that intimate familial and sexual relationships were key aspects of larger imperial projects in which colonizing powers used "the production and harnessing of sentiment as a technology of the state." In the United States, assimilation policy centered on severing affective bonds between Native children and their families, transmogrifying Indigenous marriage relations, and restructuring Native households according to white middle-class gender norms.

The theoretical framework of intimate colonialism can help us better understand the specific characteristics of the Indian Service and the way it compares with other imperial projects. A number of scholars have taken up the idea of intimate colonialism in their analyses of how states have intruded into the lives of Indigenous people, most notably Margaret Jacobs in her award-winning book on how governments justified the policy of child removal. *Federal Fathers and Mothers* advances our knowledge of how states executed these policies by revealing the crucial role of Indian Service employees in the schools and on the reservations. As Stoler insists, it is at the micro level—in the "intimate sites of implementation" in the relationships between colonial agents and the colonized—that we most clearly see intimate colonialism at work. In these interactions, we discern the complex connections among race, gender, class, and colonial power.[9] By the same token, Novak urges historians to "look in detail at what state officials of all kinds . . . actually did."[10] This book does precisely that by focusing on the men and women who actually translated policy into practice on the reservations and in the schools while working as superintendents, principals, teachers, doctors, nurses, clerks, matrons, disciplinarians, policemen, cooks, bakers, laundresses, seamstresses, blacksmiths, farmers, freighters, mechanics, and carpenters.

Among the most distinctive features of the Indian Office was that it brought thousands of women into federal employment with the intent of having them serve as "federal mothers." Administrators imagined these women offering maternal guidance and nurturance to the government's wards. This compels us to revise our existing accounts of the emergence of what Linda Gordon and Theda Skocpol, among others, have termed the "maternalist welfare state." Decades before the establishment of the federal Children's Bureau (1912) and the Women's Bureau (1920)—events that most scholars point to as the moments when women and women's concerns entered the federal bureaucracy—the Indian Service brought large numbers of women[11] into the federal workforce to enact policies formulated in considerable part by female-dominated Indian reform groups.[12] But maternalist theories about how white women would change Indians soon collided with the reality of those women's own agendas and their experiences on the job.

Even more important for the Native people who were the ones most affected by federal policy, the Indian Office hired thousands of Indigenous employees, both women and men. This employment pattern arose from a similar emphasis on the power of example. Policy makers argued that employing people who had been educated in federal Indian schools would offer living examples of the "civilized" path they hoped all tribal members would eventually take while also serving as a defense against backsliding. The presence of so many Native workers also signaled the government's reliance on a colonized labor force. Many of these employees were unskilled, but they also included the first generation of Native professional and white-collar workers.

The government's decision to hire Indians had unintended consequences. For Native employees, work in the Indian Service was an important economic survival strategy; in some cases, it also became a political act that undermined federal efforts to "break up the tribal relations." Many Indians used the opportunity to earn a living while remaining within their communities. Others worked far from home: Pueblo people served on reservations in Northern California, Winnebago women trained children in New Mexico, and a Lakota man supervised an entire school in Oklahoma. Most unexpectedly, witnessing and participating in the government's oppression of other tribal peoples ultimately strengthened Natives' ideas about a modern intertribal Indian identity.[13] Many Native people found solidarity as members of a group identified as "Indian" both by whites and, eventually, by themselves. They then built on this shared identity to organize a national cultural and political movement.

A BRIEF HISTORY OF U.S. INDIAN POLICY
THROUGH THE CIVIL WAR

The development of Indian assimilation policy in the years after the Civil War had its roots in the longer history of Indian affairs—the political relations between Europeans in North America and the continent's Indigenous peoples. British colonial policy in North America adopted an imperial model that recognized Native tribes as sovereign nations and conceded their ownership of the land, a status that required treaties for the transfer of territory from those nations to the Crown. The founders of the United States established federal authority over Indian affairs in Article I, Section 8 of the Constitution, which placed Indian policy squarely within the bailiwick of the federal government by declaring that Congress had the power "[t]o regulate Commerce with foreign Nations, and among the several States, and with the Indian Tribes."[14] This regulation took a variety of forms, but its primary emphasis was on treaties like those that Congress made with other foreign powers. As the United States expanded its national boundaries, it continued to make treaties with the Native nations it encountered. These treaties stipulated that the tribes would cede land to the United States in return for the recognition of their sovereignty.

The federal government's dealings with Native nations over the course of the nineteenth century can be divided into three broad periods: trade, removal, and assimilation (the point at which this book takes up the narrative). Ideas about "educating" and "civilizing" Indian people ran through all three eras, but the federal government's emphasis on these concepts varied. Many early treaties, for example, included provisions for teachers and instruction in farming, and the government encouraged missionary work on reservations.[15] Between 1790 and 1834, the Trade and Intercourse Acts framed federal Indian policy. These acts were designed to uphold treaties and keep Indian friendship by attempting to rein in the abuses perpetrated by white settlers in Indian country. Laws regulated and licensed trade, especially of alcohol, and provided legal recourse for prosecuting whites who had committed crimes in Indian country. As part of this strategy of protecting tribes from its unscrupulous citizens, the U.S. government experimented with setting up "factories." These were federally run trading houses, generally sited at military posts, in which government agents monopolized commerce with the tribes as a way to protect them from illegal traders. In 1816 the superintendent of Indian trade argued that the factory system not only regulated the Indian trade but also furthered the education and civilization of the tribes who did business there. Anticipating later policy makers, he argued that the white men employed at the factories offered Indians examples of civilized living and the tools with which they could achieve it. The Intercourse Acts were rarely enforced, however, and the factory system ultimately failed as well due to fierce resistance from private trading companies.[16]

Next was the era of removal. By the 1820s and 1830s, growing pressure from white emigrants' demand for Native land in the Midwest and South initiated a series of military and legal clashes and a new policy in which the government compelled tribes to move to lands that were located west of the Mississippi. In the Midwest, tribal resistance led to conflicts such as the Battle of Tippecanoe (1811) and Blackhawk's War (1832). The defeated tribes, including the Shawnee, Delaware, and Sauk and Fox, were forcibly removed to Indian Territory. In the South, the Cherokee and other "civilized" tribes attempted to use politics and public opinion to resist efforts to take their land. Despite a ruling by the U.S. Supreme Court in 1832 that upheld Cherokee treaty rights, President Andrew Jackson forced them to leave their homelands for the newly designated Indian Territory on the infamous Trail of Tears. Because the army performed these forced relocations as well as many of the other duties necessary for implementing federal Indian policy, the government created an Office of Indian Affairs in the War Department in 1824.

In 1846 the United States provoked a war with Mexico, and two years later, in the Treaty of Guadalupe-Hidalgo, it annexed a vast expanse of territory containing scores of Native nations. In order to facilitate dealings with these new populations, the federal government transferred the Indian Office to the newly created Department of the Interior in 1849. There it became a neglected bureaucratic division in a disorganized department, what one historian has called "the department of everything else."[17] Part of this neglect was due to the fact that national concern about Indians diminished as the conflict over slavery intensified.[18]

With the outbreak of the Civil War, the nation's attention was all but removed from the territories of the West and the Indian nations there. Although reservations continued to exist in this period, their boundaries remained relatively permeable or even ignored for a number of years. The government's preoccupation with the rebellion depleted the number of troops in the West, and as a result, the tribes not restricted to reservations moved freely across many parts of the region; the Lakota Nation even succeeded in significantly expanding its territory.[19] The Native groups that were technically confined to reservations found that supplies were short, as wartime exigencies diminished the capacity of agents to provide treaty-required rations to the Indian nations with which the government had signed treaties. Some federal Indian agents even had to sell agency equipment in order to buy goods for their charges. A few agents were indifferent to the fact that the people under their care could no longer support themselves on their reservations and were also not receiving the treaty-stipulated rations of food and clothing meant to offset the loss of their previous forms of subsistence. The Dakota of Minnesota, who were overseen by a particularly strict and greedy agent, took matters into their own hands in an act that was later labeled the "Sioux uprising" or the Dakota War of 1862.[20] Many agents more sympathetically encouraged their wards to hunt off the reservations so as to avoid starvation. As M. P. Berry, U.S. special Indian agent for the New Mexico Superintendency, later reported, "I am not at all astonished at the action of my predecessors in giving to the Indians long permits of absence from the reservation, having been obliged to do precisely as they did, viz, push the Indians out on fishing and hunting excursions for purposes of economy."[21]

After the Civil War, many Americans looked at the West with considerable anxiety, with the result that Indian policy was pushed to the fore once again. Northern Republicans worried that the region might become a new South: a place of cultural conflict, a Democratic political stronghold, and a drag on the nation's newfound moral authority. The publication of the federal census of 1870 made this second regional divide strikingly visible. The census, which was conducted by soon-to-be commissioner of Indian affairs Francis A. Walker, used color-coded maps and graphs for the first time, demonstrating both the geographic breadth of the nation's territory and the scarcity of white people in the West. On Walker's map, a "line of population" ended at the ninety-eighth meridian, neatly dividing the nation in two. Beyond that line, with the exception of the populated West Coast, lay a few scattered settlements amid various Indian reservations. But the map depicted the rest as open space, an impression intensified because Walker chose not to include "Indians not taxed" in his population counts. This dramatic contrast between the population densities of the East and West was the most striking feature of this census. Created only five years after the surrender of the Confederacy, the map presented Americans with a new kind of sectional divide[22] and raised difficult questions: Who would settle this vast area? What kind of states would they form? What sort of values would they hold? As most Americans saw it, the West was already a troubling place, filled as it was with Mormon polygamists, rowdy miners, Hispanics, and Indians. The fate of the region became even more crucial in the delicate balance of national politics a few years later, when the Compromise of 1877 restored home rule and Democratic Party supremacy to the South.[23] All of these concerns about the future of the American West led to fundamental changes in how the federal government dealt with the Native people who lived there.

THE WAY FORWARD

This book adopts a three-part structure to explain the development of Indian policy in terms of the interplay between employees working on the reservations and in the schools and those serving in administration at the national level. It begins with the policy decisions that created a particular kind of workforce, continues with an exploration of the day-to-day experiences of the employees themselves, and then returns to the resultant shifts in policy.

Part I, "From Civil War to Civil Service," reveals how the Civil War, emancipation, and Reconstruction influenced the development of assimilation policy during the 1870s and 1880s. In debating the "Indian problem," reformers and policy makers placed Native people in the category of "wards" alongside emancipated slaves. Policy makers drew upon the household model of free-labor ideology in designing Indian policy; their ideas about work and gender laid the foundation for the racially and sexually diverse bureaucracy they developed. The debates over who should implement the new assimilation policy resulted in the federal government assuming direct responsibility for work previously done through subcontracting to private religious organizations.

The five chapters in part II, "The Women and Men of the Indian Service," detail the workings of this new bureaucracy and the ramifications of hiring female and male, Native and white, and married and single people to administer Indian policy. These chapters demonstrate how the everyday lives of the employees interacted with and shaped federal policy. They draw upon an extraordinarily rich and rarely used body of evidence: personnel files for scores of Indian Service employees. These files offer unmatched access to both the daily lives and longer career arcs of individual workers. (In the case of Native employees, I have followed their tribal designations as they described them in their correspondence.)[24] The section begins by examining employees as part of a national system and later focuses on a single reservation. In the process, it also illustrates the interracial and intertribal relationships employees formed with their coworkers, often as a result of the government's strategy of intimate colonialism.

In part III, "The Progressive State and the Indian Service," I return to shifts in policy that were generated by forces both inside and outside the Indian Service. In a number of cases, change came in response to the actions and demands of personnel: the Indian Office was forced to accommodate employees' desire for additional training, respond to the suggestions and criticism in internal reports, and deal with the simultaneous (and opposite) problems of rapid employee turnover and an aging cohort of workers. At the same time, outside forces that included Native resistance to full assimilation, vocal public criticism of the Office of Indian Affairs, and a changing political landscape all had ramifications for the bureaucracy in the first three decades of the twentieth century.

Federal Fathers and Mothers demonstrates the unexpected outcomes that resulted when policy makers' assumptions collided with what actually happened on the ground with the employees. When policy makers began to develop assimilation policy in the post–Civil War years, they conceived of the Indian Office as a temporary bureaucracy. In their plans, they assumed that an enormous amount of labor and resources channeled into land and education programs, coupled with interventions into Native families, would assimilate Indian people into the nation within one generation. Once that occurred, they argued, the agency's mission would be fulfilled, and it would disappear. However, as they developed those programs and hired employees to run them, they ironically created a much more permanent bureaucracy.

I. FROM CIVIL WAR TO CIVIL SERVICE

There Is an Honest Way Even

of Breaking up a Treaty

THE ORIGINS OF INDIAN ASSIMILATION POLICY

A strange but revealing exchange took place on the floor of the Senate in February 1871. During a debate on the Indian Appropriations Bill, senators from the North, South, and West engaged in a heated discussion of the following question: Which group had the United States dealt with more dishonorably, Indian tribes or African slaves? Part partisan posturing and part struggle over resources, the senators' arguments grew beyond the immediate issue — a supplemental payment of $15,000 to the Chippewa of Lake Superior for instruction in the "arts of civilization" — and became a debate over the direction of federal Indian policy more broadly.

On one side of the issue stood senators who emphasized that the United States owed Indians compensation because it had stolen their land and means of support while degrading their character through contact. Republican James Harlan of Iowa, chair of the Committee on Indian Affairs, argued that Americans "have driven the Indians before the tide of civilization, instead of incorporating them into civil society and providing for them in that way, having literally robbed them of their homes and given them to strangers."[1] Despite Indians' best efforts to support themselves, observed Harlan, white settlement had "crowded [them] off their old hunting grounds . . . where for a number of years they were able to make a living by hunting and fishing."[2] Garrett Davis, a Democrat from Kentucky, agreed, adding that not only had white men taken the Indians' land, but they had also corrupted them and transformed them from "hardy and manly" noble savages into "degenerate and ignoble being[s]."[3] For these sympathizers, it was clear that the nation owed Indians assistance and indeed was "under a moral obligation to enable the few that are left, if it be possible, to adopt the habits of civilized life . . . [and] to enable them to go to work."[4]

Opposing senators asserted that the United States' dealings with Native nations had been perfectly fair and Indian lands properly purchased. They claimed that treaties were legitimate contracts and then went on to contrast America's democratic culture and strong work ethic with supposedly despotic and indolent tribal societies. Timothy Howe, a Wisconsin Republican, took issue with his colleagues' characterization of past Indian policy as theft. "We have dealt beneficently and munificently with them," he asserted. The United States took "that which was worthless to them; land which they did not know how to cultivate, and would not learn how to cultivate . . . [and] we are paying them . . . four to seven million dollars annually."[5] If white Americans had benefited from this transaction, said Howe, it was because they were willing to improve the land through their labor. In response to Senator Davis's challenge that those who supported freed slaves but not Indians did so only because freedmen could vote for them and Indians could not, they retorted that the African American case was different because of their willingness to work. Republican senator William Stewart of Nevada proclaimed: "I have heard this argument very frequently before: that inasmuch as the Indians were the lords of creation here at one time, therefore it is necessary to make immense appropriations to them. . . . That argument has been used, and millions and millions have been expended without that discrimination which ought to be had."[6] Indeed, he contended, Indian society was hierarchical and undemocratic, akin to a system of slavery, and federal money only benefited the elite. "We have been taxing the white people, taxing the washerwoman," he thundered, to give aid to "petty despots called chiefs, who take it and make slaves of the rest."[7] This social system inhibited them from being productive, he argued, because "no man will work unless he is compelled to do it either by necessity or by some stimulants to his ambition or because he desires to acquire something. The Indian will not work from necessity while he is fed. He will not work from ambition while he is a slave to a petty chief and has nothing of his own. It does not appeal to [the] one element of human nature that induces a man to struggle for wealth or for the benefit of his family or himself."[8] Senator Howe concurred: "The Indian[s] would not work," and land was thus "worthless to them." Slaves, by contrast, were taken "from the continent of which they were the lords in the providence of God. . . . The negro had virtue enough to work, and he did work, and we made him support us, we made him cultivate this continent of ours."[9]

This debate might at first glance seem idiosyncratic, but in fact it reveals the two concerns that most strongly shaped Indian policy at a critical moment in its development. The first was the obligation of the federal government to uphold promises and protect the populations under its authority. Since the United States had taken Indian land and deprived tribes of their means of subsistence, as a great nation it was obligated to help them support themselves once again. Equally important, the senators emphasized the centrality of work. They spoke the language of free labor, emphasizing the dignity of self-support, the sacredness of contract, and the fear of dependency. These two issues were among the most important concepts in the American political lexicon in this period because the major question of the day was how to reorganize the labor system after the end of slavery. In juxtaposing the "Indian problem" with the problem of the former slaves, the senators made clear that they perceived them as two examples of the same larger question — what to do with populations who were present in the United States but did not have full rights of citizenship.[10]

Soon afterward, this same group of legislators dramatically changed the nation's administration of Indian affairs. First, Congress in 1871 ended the negotiation of treaties with Native nations, thus shifting Indian policy from a diplomatic basis to a domestic one. The country still needed a treatylike apparatus because the United States remained engaged in hostilities with many tribes; representatives of the government therefore continued to negotiate "agreements." But unlike diplomatic treaties that received only senatorial ratification, these agreements required bicameral approval. This process took Indian policy out of the realm of foreign relations and into that of domestic social policy.[11] Second, a decade later, the U.S. government accelerated this trend toward disregarding tribal sovereignty by again revising its policy toward Native nations. Specifically, administrators began to formulate new ideas of governance by disregarding treaty promises and substituting social programs. They justified this by arguing that the treaty stipulations of tribally held land and ration payments were harmful. The result was the development of a comprehensive system of social programming aimed at Indians.

The social programs of the Office of Indian Affairs have gone unnoticed by scholars who have written about the development of compensatory programs for soldiers, mothers, and public servants. These historians have demonstrated that early in the nineteenth century, the government justified its allocation of pensions and bounties for soldiers based on its obligation to those who had risked their lives defending the country. They have uncovered similar motivations at the turn of the twentieth century, when mothers' pensions and the creation of the federal Women's and Children's Bureaus were justified by the state's obligation to mothers for their role in reproducing the next generation of citizens. In all of those instances, however, the new social programs rewarded a particular group of people for services they performed for the state.[12] Discussions of federal obligation after the Civil War included another important category: groups to whom the government owed a debt for wrongs that the nation had committed against them. The development of federal policies toward freedpeople and Indians was thus a key episode in the formation of the modern state.

DEVELOPING A POSTWAR INDIAN POLICY

Before we can discuss the development of these compensatory programs, we must understand the political struggles over Indian affairs in the post–Civil War period. When President Ulysses S. Grant took office in 1869, the federal government faced serious problems with Indian policy in the West. Relocated eastern tribes increasingly ignored the boundaries of their reservations, and many western tribes, most notably the Lakota (Sioux) and Apache, had not been conquered militarily and continued to control vast areas.[13] As increased white migration and railroad-building efforts exacerbated conflicts with Indians, the government modified its approach: it responded first with military force but also began to rethink its relationship to Indian tribes. Grant attempted to initiate a new Indian policy that reflected his experiences during Reconstruction, when the army, the Freedmen's Bureau, and northern religious organizations cooperated to inculcate free-labor ideology in the freedpeople. His attempts met with a resistant Congress and led to the end of the treaty system that had been the basis for federal Indian policy since long before the founding of the United States.

In his first address to Congress, President Grant announced a new Indian policy that became known as Grant's Peace Policy or the Quaker Plan. The two names indicated the dual nature of the policy: the first aspect was directed at relations with the tribes, while the second referred to the operation of the Indian Service. The Peace Policy sought to solidify reservation boundaries and discipline Native populations. It declared that the federal government would remain at peace with all tribes who agreed to stay within the boundaries of their reservations but would go to war with all who transgressed those borders. As U.S. Indian inspector James McLaughlin, who began his career in the Indian Service in 1871, described it, "the mailed fist of the military was cuffing the untutored men of the grasslands into a sense of the beneficence of the peace policy inaugurated by General Grant." This aspect of Grant's Peace

Policy resulted in over 200 military actions against "hostile" tribes during his administration.[14]

The second part of Grant's Indian policy, the Quaker Plan, sought to quash corruption in the Office of Indian Affairs, whose employees were patronage appointees and who often used their positions for personal enrichment. At that time, the Indian Office had two primary functions: administering reservations and distributing rations. This required a staff of about 500 people. An agent, along with perhaps a clerk and a physician, staffed each reservation. The rest of the Indian Service was occupied with making contracts to buy treaty-stipulated ration goods such as beef, cloth, shoes, and blankets. This role as a supplier of goods created many opportunities for corruption, the most common of which were the "Indian Rings" in which an agent, the politician who appointed him, and the reservation trader all profited from cheating the Indians. President Grant, possibly influenced by his first commissioner of Indian affairs, Ely Parker (Tonawanda Seneca), sought to turn the administration of several reservations over to the Quaker church because the Society of Friends enjoyed a reputation for honesty and claimed a history of good relations with Indians stretching back to William Penn's interactions with the Leni-Lenapes in the 1680s. Under Grant's plan, the Quakers would appoint the reservation agent, who would then be in charge of staffing the other positions. The president also sought to transfer control over Indian affairs back to the War Department. Grant hoped that these measures would cut off the avenues of corruption.[15]

Grant's new initiatives faced considerable resistance in Congress, leading to a power struggle that set the stage for major changes in the Indian Service. Legislators fought to maintain their control of patronage appointments and objected to any loss of control over federal agencies; and in the age of Reconstruction, they were accustomed to opposing even presidents of their own party. They contested the president's plans in three ways. First, they attempted to weaken executive control of Indian affairs. Congress added a provision to the 1869 appropriations bill that created an independent Board of Indian Commissioners (BIC). The board was to be composed of a group of well-respected men, often churchmen, who would serve as unpaid advisers and inspectors for the Indian Service. It was also to share control of federal Indian funds with the presidentially appointed secretary of the interior. Grant supported the board, perceiving it as the nonpartisan group that it was.

Second, Congress tried to stymie Grant's transfer of control of Indian affairs to the army. The following year, it passed legislation that forbade army officers to serve in civilian posts. Rather than capitulate to Congress, Grant chose to keep these positions out of patronage politics by following the advice of the newly formed BIC and enlarging his Quaker Plan to include other Protestant denominations and also Roman Catholics. He would turn administrative control of a reservation agency over to a particular denomination whenever a vacancy occurred.[16]

But it was Congress's third policy—prohibiting the executive branch from negotiating any new treaties with Indian tribes—that led to a new phase in Indian policy: the era of assimilation.[17] Congress was somewhat divided on this question. Those arguing for an immediate end to all treaties lacked support, since most legislators agreed that this would only exacerbate deteriorating social conditions within some tribes and cause others to resort to violence. Supporters of the treaties wanted the government to uphold its commitments. Several pointed to the ruling in *Cherokee Nation v. Georgia* and stressed the nation's moral obligation to the tribes. "[I]t is the proud boast of our country," one declared, "that the Indians are the wards of the United States," and thus it was the nation's duty "to protect" them.[18] At the same time, they also agreed that treaty stipulations created harmful dependency and poverty. As one senator argued, Indians were "in the habit of relying upon these annual [treaty] appropriations; it begets idleness and indolence which results in good-for-nothingness to the Indians."[19] Faced with this impasse, Congress compromised by agreeing to stop signing any new treaties while still upholding existing ones. In the midst of these debates, a consensus emerged that tribes should be dissolved and Indians incorporated into the citizenry as "what they should be, a useful people" who were not dependent on federal outlays.[20]

THE RISE OF AN INDIAN RIGHTS MOVEMENT

For the next ten years, however, federal efforts were focused primarily on confining Indian nations to their reservations. The resultant military campaigns raised public awareness of Indian affairs. And as attention shifted away from the South after 1877, this military activity began to trouble people's consciences with respect to the government's treatment of the tribes. The strategies of total warfare learned during the Civil War were now directed against Indians, leading to repeated incidents of disproportionate use of force against entire communities.

During the 1870s, the newspapers covered several violent military expeditions and described Native peoples' desperate and tragic flights from pursuing troops, raising questions in the East about the wisdom of allowing the army to have charge of Indian policy.[21] One of the most extensively reported events occurred in the summer of 1877, when Chief Joseph led a band of Nez Perce from their home in Oregon's Wallowa Valley toward hoped-for asylum in Canada. The conflict had its roots in an 1863 treaty that had eliminated the Nez Perce Reservation. Some tribal members, like Chief Joseph and his band, refused to recognize the treaty and remained in their eastern Oregon home rather than move to the Lapwai Reservation in Idaho. Tensions grew as white settlers encroached on the valley, and the situation exploded when a tribal member was murdered and a group of young men from the band killed a party of white settlers to avenge his death. The federal government sent in troops to ensure order; faced with the prospect of war, the Nez Perce chose to flee toward Canada. Chronicled first by regional newspapers such as the *Portland Daily Standard* (Oregon) and the *Lewiston Teller* (Idaho), the tribe's ordeal caught the attention of the national press when Chief Joseph and his band passed through the recently created Yellowstone National Park and took a group of nine tourists captive to keep them from reporting the tribe's whereabouts to the army. The press focused primarily on Chief Joseph, offering a sympathetic account of a heroic leader guiding a desperate tribe and repeatedly outmaneuvering the U.S. military while seeking his people's freedom. Captured only forty miles from the border, the Nez Perce were sent to a reservation in Oklahoma, where many of them became sick, depressed, and even suicidal. The plight of the Nez Perce remained in the national spotlight. In 1879 Chief Joseph traveled to Washington, D.C., to make the case for his people to be sent to the Lapwai Reservation in Idaho to live with their fellow tribal members. His fame preceded him, and a large crowd of "American and foreign dignitaries" gathered to hear his speech. In the address, he offered an account of the wrongs done to his people and entreated the government for justice. Translated and reprinted in the *North American Review*, the speech generated further sympathy for the tribe.[22]

That same month, Ponca chief Standing Bear, his wife, and thirty followers left their reservation without permission in a bid to return from Indian Territory to their homeland along the Missouri River. As with the Nez Perce, their struggle also captured national attention. Their story had begun in 1865, when the Ponca signed a treaty assigning them 96,000 acres of their homeland in what would become the state of Nebraska. Three years later, however, the United States accidentally gave the Ponca Reservation to the Lakota Sioux, traditional enemies of the Ponca, in the Fort Laramie treaty. Almost everyone agreed that the Ponca tribe had been wronged, but the federal government did not believe it could change the terms of the treaty with the more powerful

Lakota; and so, despite the vehement protests of the Ponca, it removed them to Indian Territory. There, homesickness and the unfamiliar environment took their toll on the Ponca, as it had on the Nez Perce and many others. When Chief Standing Bear's son died of malaria, the grief-stricken leader decided to return the body to his homeland for burial. Standing Bear and his followers traveled north to Nebraska, where they paused among their friends on the Omaha Reservation. There, the U.S. Army arrested and imprisoned them and made plans to send them back to Indian Territory.[23]

Ironically, it was a military man, General George Crook, commander of the Department of the Platte, who set in motion the subsequent public outcry. Disgusted with having to carry out the order to arrest the Poncas, Crook approached Thomas Henry Tibbles, the assistant editor of the *Omaha Daily Register*, and asked him to do what he could for the tribe. Tibbles was a former Methodist circuit rider, abolitionist, and member of John Brown's band in Kansas, and he immediately swung into action, enlisting ministers from local Omaha churches to alert the public to the Poncas' plight. He also transcribed the speeches given by Standing Bear and others during their meeting with General Crook, publishing them in his paper and sending telegrams to newspapers in Chicago, New York, and other eastern cities, where the stories were republished.[24] The Poncas — homesick, often ill, and desperate enough to flee from the army in the middle of winter and brave all sorts of hardships — inspired tremendous sympathy among many white Americans, especially in the East, and Tibbles was able to orchestrate a speaking tour for Chief Standing Bear throughout eastern cities.

The chief's impassioned retellings of his story fanned a spark of reformist sentiment into a flame. Northerners who believed that the United States had atoned for the great national sin of slavery through the "blood and fire" of the Civil War listened to reports of western atrocities with growing alarm. After the war, they had looked upon the federal government with a new sense of optimism but worried that it could easily lose the moral high ground if other national wrongs were left unaddressed. By the end of the 1870s, a number of them began to argue that the Indian problem was as much of a threat to the newly regained national honor as slavery had been. Just as the Civil War had been necessary to purge the sin of slavery, another cleansing would be necessary to redeem sins committed against the Indians.[25]

The first voices among this new generation of reformers were women who urged Congress to maintain the nation's honor by upholding treaties. These women had been influenced by the long history of white women's work on behalf of vulnerable groups of people. Mary Bonney and Amelia Quinton of the Chestnut Street School for Girls in Philadelphia, for example, had been trying to decide whether or not to continue their petition work regarding federal Indian policy when Standing Bear's speech encouraged them to go even further. They organized a group under the name Indian Treaty-Keeping and Protective Association, emphasizing a strategy of urging Congress to keep its promises and recognize treaty stipulations. Their group continued to grow and incorporated in 1883 as the nondenominational Women's National Indian Association (WNIA). Its members initially focused on enormous petition drives urging Congress to uphold treaties, collecting 100,000 signatures in 1883 alone.[26]

Helen Hunt Jackson, a writer for popular journals, was so moved after hearing Standing Bear's story that she immediately began to research and write an exposé of federal policy.[27] Jackson made the idea of national sin and national debt explicit in her book *A Century of Dishonor* (1881). In it she traced treaty violations and argued that the federal government had failed to live up to its obligations to the tribes: "The history of the United States Government's repeated violations of faith with the Indians thus convicts us, as a nation, not only of having outraged the principles of justice, which are the basis of international law . . . but of having made ourselves liable to all punishments which follow upon such sins." Bishop Henry Whipple echoed this sentiment in his introduction to her book: "Nations, like individuals, reap exactly what they sow; they who sow robbery reap robbery."[28]

Bonney, Jackson, and others had witnessed many of the the early efforts by white women to engage in more traditional politics in support of Indian reform and other issues. In the 1820s, for example, white women in the Northeast were moved by the plight of the Five Civilized Tribes and organized massive petition drives to protest their removal from the American Southeast. Petitioning was especially suited to women's prescribed role in society as it allowed them to draw upon personal networks and use their influence on neighbors, friends, and fellow parishioners, educating them on the problem and encouraging them to sign a petition that contained a solution or a partial solution. Although their petition campaigns failed to stop the removal of those tribes to Indian Territory, they had learned important lessons about political mobilization and redirected their skills into the abolitionist movement. Women's use of the petition as a political tool in the fight against slavery was so successful that Congress passed the "gag rule" in 1836 that tabled all petitions to Congress, allowing lawmakers to ignore the petitions presented to them.[29]

The women who became active in Indian reform had also been influenced by women's use of novels and short stories as important political instruments during the early and mid-nineteenth century when they were growing up.

Female writers used the power of fiction to highlight how the political issues of the day affected families, especially women and children. As readers of serials and novels, they vicariously experienced the hopes of a white woman married to an Indian man (*Hobomok*, 1824), the terror of a family living under a drunken father (*Water Drops*, 1848), the plight of a slave mother whose children were torn from her arms (*Uncle Tom's Cabin*, 1852), and the sense of helplessness of a plural wife trapped in a polygamous Mormon marriage (*Mormon Wives*, 1856). The authors hoped these stories would arouse the sympathies of their readers and stir them to action to redress the real-life victims of those wrongs. Mary Bonny, a cofounder of the WNIA, for example, was eight in 1824 when Lydia Maria Child published her sympathetic novel, *Hobomok*.[30] Bonny was thirty-six in 1852 when Harriet Beecher Stowe released the best-selling *Uncle Tom's Cabin*. An impressionable Helen Hunt Jackson was twenty-two years old that year, and she later confided to a friend, "If I could write a story that would do for the Indian a thousandth part that *Uncle Tom's Cabin* did for the Negro, I would be thankful the rest of my life."[31] Indeed, some of the earlier activists and authors also turned to the Indian question after the Civil War. Stowe wrote several articles for national publications, while Child published "An Appeal for the Indians" in 1867, arguing that "our relations with the red and black members of the human family have been one of almost unvaried history of violence and fraud."[32]

The massive petition drives of the WNIA and Jackson's *A Century of Dishonor*, as well as articles written by both Jackson and Quinton, helped fuel a movement for reform that also incorporated male reformers. In 1883 a group of men with ties to the BIC founded the Indian Rights Association (IRA) after a visit to the Sioux Reservation. Established by Herbert Welsh and Merrill E. Gates, the IRA became a male counterpart to the WNIA. Although both groups initially emphasized upholding treaty stipulations, they soon became important advocates for setting up assimilation and "civilization" programs among the tribes.[33]

Meanwhile, change was also coming from another direction. In 1875 Captain Richard Henry Pratt, who had been assigned to guard a group of Kiowa and Cheyenne prisoners of war at Fort Marion in Florida, began his famous experiment in Indian education. Believing that the prisoners could be "civilized," he and a group of local women began to teach them to speak English and provided other basic lessons. Pratt also allowed them to work in the adjacent community, hoping, as he saw it, to teach them the value of wage labor. His efforts proved extremely successful, and he garnered attention from nationally known figures like Stowe, who wrote several articles about the experiment for the *Christian Union*. Hoping to expand the project, Pratt began to look for further educational opportunities for his students and found them in the person of General Samuel Armstrong, principal of the Hampton Institute for African Americans in Virginia. Armstrong enrolled the first class of Indian students at Hampton in 1878, beginning the practice of off-reservation education for Indians.[34]

All of these strands of reform came together in an exceptionally durable and influential institutional vehicle, the annual Lake Mohonk Conference for the Friends of the Indian. In 1883 Quaker and BIC member Albert Smiley founded the conference when he invited missionary societies and other "Friends of the Indian" to his resort hotel, the Mohonk Mountain House, located up the Hudson River from New York City, to discuss the Indian problem. Both the WNIA and the IRA were well represented, along with a number of other important organizations and individuals. The conference became an annual affair, and its participants emerged as a powerful and persuasive lobbying group in Indian policy.[35]

FROM TREATIES TO SOCIAL PROVISION

The men and women gathered at Mohonk represented a well-connected and organized group of allies. Their expertise in social reform gave them a deep pool of knowledge to draw upon, and they commanded a wide range of resources. As Theda Skocpol has argued, the ability to mobilize support was essential to the development of compensatory social programs, and that was certainly the case at Mohonk. These reformers had extensive previous experience in marshaling private and public resources as a result of their work with freedmen's education. This experience made them the most knowledgeable people in the nation when it came to thinking about how to incorporate a group of people into the national citizenry. Their expertise extended from knowing how to set up school systems and negotiate with the federal government to understanding how to influence public opinion and raise funds. The other professionals at the conference — university presidents and professors,[36] government officials and administrators,[37] ministers, missionaries,[38] and journalists[39] — also possessed important skills and knowledge. Moreover, conference participants were able to mobilize public opinion through their organizational connections. For example, in 1884 the WNIA had thirty-eight auxiliaries; by 1887 that had increased to 104 auxiliaries distributed across the nation.[40] The participants at Mohonk also held sway over an array of publications, including the abolitionist press, missionary and religious periodicals, and reform organization journals. These resources made them a force to be reckoned with.[41]

The reformers at Mohonk drew heavily upon their experiences with the freedpeople as they began to articulate a new theory of social provision and extend it to Indians. Emancipation and the end of the treaty-making system had placed blacks and Indians into a category of people whose citizenship status was uncertain, and policy makers thought of both groups as being under the benevolent guardianship of the federal government. This wardship status, as well as a sense of national obligation for wrongs committed against them, became a justification for compensatory social programs intended to prepare blacks and Indians for full citizenship by making them self-sufficient. The goal of creating citizens on a free-labor model made the imperatives of social provision very different from rewarding citizens for past or future service, as was the case with veterans or mothers. As a consequence, federal policies aimed at freedpeople and Indians went beyond social *provision* and incorporated extensive social *programming* through education, land policy, and the introduction of new legal regimes. These differences notwithstanding, the resultant policies for the nation's black and Indian "wards" did indeed constitute federal social provision because the federal government provided benefits programmatically to a legally defined group of beneficiaries, a process that increased the size and complexity of the federal bureaucracies that administered them.[42]

Many of the most prominent men[43] who helped formulate Indian policy at Lake Mohonk had played major roles in either the antislavery movement or, more often, federal programs for freedmen during Reconstruction.[44] In *The Abolitionist Legacy*, a collective biography of the abolitionists and their postwar endeavors for blacks, James McPherson argues that during the early 1880s, these white northern activists held optimistic views on the race question and insisted that Reconstruction had been successful. They continued to work for racial advancement through education and training of black leaders, emphasizing these methods as the key to the uplift of the race. What McPherson did not make note of was that many of these men applied the same beliefs to work in Indian reform. Their understanding of the experience of freedpeople in Reconstruction heavily influenced their deliberations about how the nation should treat its Indian wards.[45]

The evidence of overlap between reform work for freedpeople and Indians is overwhelming. For example, President Grant appointed Clinton B. Fisk to the BIC in 1874, and Fisk served as its president from 1881 until his death in 1890. Fisk also held the position of conference chair at the Lake Mohonk Conference for the first several years of the gathering. Fisk understood the Indian question as a new iteration of the Negro question. In 1883 he concluded his BIC annual report by explicitly linking the plight of the Indian to that of the slave: "We could not fit the negro for freedom till we made him free. We shall never fit the Indian for citizenship till we make him a citizen." It was entirely unsurprising that Fisk saw things this way, given his work during Reconstruction. In 1865 he was appointed to serve as assistant commissioner of the Freedmen's Bureau for Tennessee and Kentucky. In this position, he worked closely with the American Missionary Association, a private organization that sponsored numerous schools for freedpeople under the auspices of the Freedmen's Bureau (and subsequently for Native students under the Indian Office). In 1866 he opened a school for black students in Nashville, Tennessee, that later became Fisk University. Free-labor ideology drove Fisk's dealings with both groups of federal wards. In 1866, while he was serving as assistant commissioner of the Freedmen's Bureau, he penned the pamphlet *Plain Counsels for Freedmen*, in which he articulated this vision: "Every man is born into the world with the right to his own life, to personal liberty, and to inherit, earn, own and hold property. These rights are given to him by the great God; not because he is a white man, a red man, or a black man, but because he is a MAN."[46]

Thomas Jefferson Morgan had a similar personal and administrative history. He served as commissioner of Indian affairs from 1889 to 1893 and frequently attended the Lake Mohonk Conference both before and after his term. Morgan's frame of reference for Indian policy came from his role commanding four regiments of black troops during the Civil War; at the 1885 conference, he commented, "During the war I had between five and six thousand colored soldiers under me. I found I had to teach them, and I have watched the progress of the negro from that time with great interest. I think there can be no doubt as to the practicability of the elevation of the Indian."[47] After his tenure as commissioner of Indian affairs, he became executive secretary of the Baptist Home Missionary Society, an organization that focused much of its energy on black education in the South.[48]

Like Fisk and Morgan, other regular participants at the Lake Mohonk Conference brought their extensive experience with freedpeople during Reconstruction to discussions of Indian policy. Michael E. Strieby served as secretary of the American Missionary Association for almost thirty years, first during Reconstruction and later while the organization ran a series of contract schools for the Indian Office.[49] Edward Pierce of Massachusetts had served as a member of both the New England Freedmen's Aid Society and the American Freedmen's Union Commission. During the Civil War, he had been in charge of General Butler's black "contrabands" at Fortress Monroe, Virginia, and he was appointed to supervise the Port Royal experiment in South Carolina, where he orchestrated the famous "Rehearsal for Reconstruction."[50] He later held many political offices in his home state of Massachusetts, including serving as the secretary for the State Board of Charities from 1870 to 1874. At Lake Mohonk, as in South Carolina, Pierce emphasized free-labor ideology as the solution for the Indian problem, stating at the 1886 conference that "in all plans for the civilization of the Indian, *as of any race*, the greatest emphasis should be laid upon the necessity of his having a fixed individual home and acquiring regular habits of industry."[51]

A further perusal of Lake Mohonk attendees reveals many more individuals who had earlier worked with organizations that assisted the freedpeople; these include the Honorable A. C. Barstow (American Missionary Association), John Burroughs (American Freedmen's Union Commission), Philip C. Garrett (Freedmen's Relief and Friends Association of Philadelphians for the Relief of Colored Freedmen), Daniel Coit Gilman (American Freedmen's Union Commission), and Moses Pierce (vice president of the New England Freedmen's Aid Society and member of the American Freedmen's Union Commission).[52] Other prominent examples who appear both in McPherson's list of prominent abolitionists and on the attendance rolls for the Lake Mohonk Conference include Professor Charles C. Painter (a prominent member of the IRA and the BIC), James E. Rhoads, Rev. Dr. William Hays Ward, Rev. Dr. A. F. Beard, and Rev. Dr. William W. Patton.[53]

Thus during the 1870s and 1880s, politicians, reformers, and policy makers all drew parallels between freedpeople and Indians, making the connection time and again in discussions of Indian policy. In likening the Indian problem to slavery and emancipation, reformers also implied that it needed the same kind of solution.[54] For example, in 1885 a member of the BIC explained: "Six million negroes . . . are now a part of the whole privileged population, and surely less than three hundred thousand Indians can be absorbed or diffused and in a domestic sense settled among the 55,000,000 of our American population."[55] That same year, Merrill Gates, the president of Rutgers College and also a member of the BIC, proclaimed: "There is great mission work to be done . . . for these Indians. The spirit that settled Kansas in the interest of liberty and fair play for all men, however despised, is not yet dead in our land."[56] Walter Allen of the Boston Indian Citizenship Committee asserted in 1886: "It was argued that it would be unsafe, that it might wreck the Republic to give to the ignorant freedman, just emancipated from slavery, the rights of citizenship. But I do doubt if there is a large number of people in this broad land to-day who do not recognize that the Negroes, if they had been kept under guardianship and not given the inspirations which citizenship gives, would have been in a far worse condition to-day than they are." He noted that if Indians were given the franchise, then congressmen would be accountable to them as voters.[57]

The formulation of a new Indian policy took place at a time when America's postwar discussions were filled with concern about dependency and the balance between helpful and harmful assistance. Many people argued that "misplaced charity" repressed its recipients' will to work and made them dependent paupers. Referring to the freedpeople in 1865, one leading Republican adviser asserted that while giving charity to widows and orphans might be beneficial, it was extremely harmful to do so for "a man with full health and plenty of work." During the 1870s and 1880s, numerous northern states passed new vagrancy laws that punished beggars with time in a workhouse. Lauding new legislation in 1884, the New York State Board of Charities posited that monetary relief was an "unmitigated evil" that destroyed the "habit of industry." Thus reformers interested in Indian policy (some of whom overlapped with these other movements) strongly believed that federal assistance had to be very sparingly utilized.[58]

Reformers of Indian policy began to liken treaty stipulations to misplaced charity and argue that they needed to be modified. Policy makers placed the blame squarely on the "pauperizing reservation system" for creating and exacerbating dependency. They especially pointed to the ration system and the reservation's role in isolating the Indians from civilized communities. BIC member Merrill E. Gates articulated these concerns at the 1886 Lake Mohonk Conference: "The reservation shuts off the Indians from civilization, and rations distributed unearned tend to pauperize them."[59] Another conference goer, WNIA member Mrs. G. W. Owen of Ypsilanti, Michigan, was even more emphatic. "It keeps the Indian more dependent upon the Government and less able to help himself. The reservation system is fatal to the Indian," she declared. In order to demonstrate her point, she referred to the distinguished crowd of reformers and politicians at the Lake Mohonk Conference: "Now, we will keep all these people here and not let them go away . . . and don't let them buy nor sell anything. Now, I don't think you could get together a more cultivated crowd than we have here, but under the plan I have proposed, in what condition would they be forty or a hundred years from now?" The audience responded with "laughter."[60] Hampton Institute founder Samuel Armstrong drew an analogy between slavery and reservation policy to emphasize how both impeded free labor: "Treating the black man as chattel created a 'caste,' a social separation. . . . Treating the Indian as an Indian and not as a person is as false as slavery; it has created a separation, by way of the reservation system."[61]

But before reformers could treat Indians like former slaves, they had to confront the problem of treaties that protected tribal sovereignty. Initially, as *A Century of Dishonor* illustrates, reformers urged that treaties be upheld and corruption expunged from the Indian Office. Using copious quotations to bolster her arguments, Jackson argued: "It is sometimes said, by those seeking to defend . . . the United States Government's repeated disregard of its treaties with the Indians, that each Congress may, if it chooses, undo all that has been done by previous Congresses. However true this may be of some legislative acts, it is clearly not true, according to the principles of international law, of treaties."[62] This sentiment also motivated the women who pointedly named themselves the Indian Treaty-Keeping and Protective Association (later the WNIA).

The treaty system, however, posed a conundrum for reformers. While they wanted the government to honor its word, they also believed that treaties harmed Indians by keeping them confined to reservations (enslaved, some argued) and preventing them from freely participating in the market by limiting their ability to move around and their access to buyers and sellers. The same treaties they had recently championed prevented the creation of "civilized" behavior among the tribes because they protected tribal landholdings, endowed tribes with a sovereign political identity, and stipulated the way tribal funds would be spent (primarily for purchasing rations).

Reformers soon formulated a new strategy of replacing treaty obligations with social programs that they believed would uphold the spirit of the treaties but solve the problem of dependency. They began to argue that instead of literally upholding treaties by spending money on rations for the tribes, the government should use those same resources to establish social programs that would help bring Indians into the nation as citizens. For example, Alice Fletcher, who later served as a federal allotment agent, argued that "such portions of treaties as call for vast expenditures for annuities, food, and clothing—material things, most of which tend to pauperize the Indian—are carried out to the letter . . . while those portions of the treaties which required the education of the Indian are either ignored or only very slightly regarded, so that today the Government, according to treaty requirements, owes the Indian more than $2,000,000 for educational purposes."[63] Fletcher proposed that rations be discontinued and the funds—along with the money still owed to the tribes for instruction—reallocated to expand educational programs. This strategy would simultaneously lessen the dependency of Indians on the government and repay federal obligations.

Policy makers and their allies in Washington echoed this strategy, urging the government to initiate a series of programs that they believed would "civilize" Indians in a single generation. This proposed solution was based on land policy and education operating in tandem (somewhat analogous to the Homestead and Morrill Acts for white Americans, but coercive). Allotment, which would divide tribally held reservations into private family plots and encourage settled communities to become sedentary farmers, was the first step. Meanwhile, educational programs would destroy Native cultures and teach Indians how to use their newly allotted lands efficiently. The federal outlays necessary to set this process in motion were conceived of as temporary expenditures that would ultimately save the government money by making Indian wards responsible for themselves. In its 1885 report, the BIC suggested that "if we could take these 50,000 Indian children, and put them in schools at an expense of some millions of dollars to the United States, teaching them the trades and employments of civilized life, and then send them back to their homes, the Indian problem would be solved. In ten years the parents would have passed away."[64] The "educated" generation would then be able to socially reproduce American citizens on their privately held property, permanently ending the need for government intervention and expenditure.

In constructing these compensatory social programs, policy makers modeled the Indian Office according to the precedent of the Freedmen's Bureau and its federally funded education initiatives. Many reformers were deeply impressed by Captain Richard Henry Pratt's experiment in Indian education at the Hampton Institute, an effort that seemed to prove that formal education would assimilate Indians into the national citizenry just as it had helped integrate former slaves.[65] Samuel Armstrong, principal of Hampton, reminded conference goers:

> The very best possible relation between public and private work is
> that Government shall supply the buildings and current expenses,
> and the churches the teachers and such supplemental aid as may be
> needed. . . . The aid given by way of building funds, between 1866
> and 1870, by the National Government, through General O. O. How-
> ard, Commissioner of the Freedmen's Bureau, to Howard University,
> Hampton School, Lincoln, Atlanta, and Fisk Universities and other
> leading Southern institutions which are to-day shaping the future of
> the negro race, gave them a tremendous push to usefulness. Private
> charity did the rest, and a vast and vital result has been reached by
> this wise co-operation.[66]

While educational programs were relatively uncontroversial because many treaties already provided school funds, allotment programs that divided tribally held land ran directly afoul of treaty stipulations. Reformers nevertheless believed that the presumed beneficial effects of the new social programs justified such abrogations.[67] Even those who initially supported treaty obligations came around in the face of this substitution argument. Dr. Merrill Gates, a BIC member, opened his endorsement of the Allotment Act by stating: "When I first attended this conference and heard talk about breaking up these treaties, I questioned in my own mind whether I was among honest people. I felt that we were forgetting one or two of the commandments. But I afterwards felt that there is an honest way even of breaking up a treaty."[68] Reformers and policy makers thus concluded that temporary social programs could honorably satisfy the nation's obligations in the spirit of the law rather than fulfilling them according to the letter of the law.

CONCLUSION

The reformers and officials who returned to the Indian problem after the Civil War looked to the nation's dealings with the freedpeople as a model for policy regarding Native Americans. They argued that these two populations shared important characteristics: they were wards of the nation rather than full citizens, and the United States owed them a debt for wrongs it had committed against them. Seeking a way to repay those obligations, the "Friends of the Indian" urged the federal government to design programs that would give these wards the tools needed to become citizens while avoiding the problems of dependency created by misplaced charity. Once the programs had successfully run their course, the nation's debt would be settled. But in treating former slaves and Indians alike, policy makers had to ignore the sovereign status of Native nations as enshrined in numerous treaties.

The many connections and overlaps between the policy makers involved in freedpeople's education and Indian affairs should alert us to the importance of that ideological current in the development of federal dealings with Native people. While scholars tend to highlight the influence of anthropological thought[69] on assimilation policy, the conversations and work in which most early policy makers participated referred to abolition and Reconstruction far more than anthropology.

Recognizing that the shapers of national policy perceived these two groups as a single category of people who qualified for social provision on the basis of their status in relation to the federal government also adds to our understanding of the development of the administrative state. Programs for federal "wards" were different from other forms of social provision that scholars have studied. Unlike soldiers' pensions, in which the government rewarded people for their military service with land or money, these newer efforts sought to repay national debts through social programs aimed at educating wards in the ways of "civilization" and citizenship. For the federal government, this experiment in social programming was a new departure, a more intensive mobilization of state resources. Scholars have overlooked this particular iteration of social provision, even though it brought federal authority into new areas of governance.[70] Once policy makers agreed that the solution to the Indian question was to shift it to a domestic basis and substitute social programs for treaty stipulations, they faced the question of what sort of programs the government might implement.

Only the Home Can Found a State

BUILDING A BETTER AGENCY

On the evening of 10 October 1890, the "Friends of the Indian" gathered for the closing session of that year's Lake Mohonk Conference. The three-day event had been deemed a great success, with attendees listening to various presentations that included "The Capacity of the Indian to Be Educated," "The Choice of Industries in Indian Education," and "Indian Agents." They also had heard reports from the Women's National Indian Association and various missionary societies about their work on the reservations. In between sessions, they had enjoyed the beauty of the hotel grounds, strolling through its formal gardens, relaxing on its shady lakeside verandas, and venturing up the rocky crest of Shawangunk Ridge for panoramic views of the Hudson River valley below. Before thanking their hosts and the hotel staff for their generous hospitality, the conference goers spent a few final hours discussing the "Indian problem." In one lively exchange, they peppered the Reverend Thomas Riggs, Indian agent for the Standing Rock Reservation in South Dakota, with probing questions about the details of Dakota family life. These questions demonstrated just how fundamental the home was to the project of Indian assimilation.

> What is the condition of the houses of the Indians at the
> present time, as compared with two or three years ago?
> Do you find soap and towels and wash-basins now?
> How about chickens and pigs?
> Is the grade of house steadily improving?
> How many of the three thousand Indians at Standing Rock
> live in houses?

Do your Indians burn up the house after the death of any person?

Do these houses consist of one room?

What are you able to do about that?

How do the houses, as a rule, compare with those of the
white people?

Do they use knives and forks and plates?

Do they use tables?

Do the men work in the fields?

Do they not buy agricultural machines a great deal?

How do you think the pecuniary obligation of the Indian
compares to that of the white man in the same place?

When the head of a family dies, do the mourners carry off all
the things?

Do they have sun dances now?

Do the children stay with the widow after the father's death?

If the rations were stopped, what would they do?

How would you make them self supporting?

If the ration system were stopped, how would the agent fill up
the schools?

When these Indians get money, how do they spend it?

How do they get money?

How about houses for the Indians — does [the] government issue
lumber?

Will an Indian carpenter do as good a day's work as a white man?

Is polygamy practiced?

Do they not sometimes grow manly, under the influence of having
a family to work for?[1]

This near obsession with Native households is not surprising, considering
that these reformers had come of age during the heyday of Americans' celebration of the home as the keystone of their political, economic, and social
order. When members of the the nineteenth-century middle class coined the
phrases "Home Sweet Home" and "Home Is Where the Heart Is," they were
referring to a specific configuration of people and spaces. For them, home
conjured up visions of a happy and respectable married couple and their
children living in a permanent, freestanding, multiple-room house that was
built and owned by men and decorated and kept neat by women. This idealized home also prescribed specific duties for men and women. Husbands
would go out into the world to work and thereby support, protect, and represent their families; they would then return to the comfort of their homes

at night. Wives would use their homemaking skills to create sanctuaries for their world-weary husbands while teaching their children how to grow into proper men and women; as angels of the household, they would lend a moral sweetness to it all. Americans romanticized this idealized home in novels, songs, and plays and enshrined it in their laws.[2]

When reformers and policy makers looked at Indian families, however, what they saw did not at all conform with their ideal of home, and in their minds this fact was at the root of the Indian problem. Native cultures displayed an amazing diversity of family life and social organization. While some of their traditions had been disrupted by war, conquest, and confinement to reservations, many remained. In the Southwest, some Pueblo tribes lived in matrilineal kinship systems in which women owned the houses and passed them down to their daughters; often a mother's brother had a closer relationship with her children than did their father.[3] Such practices stood in direct contrast to the policy makers' idea that husbands must be the heads of household and owners of property. One commissioner of Indian affairs asserted, "under the rule upon which the family is constructed among civilized nations the predominant principle is descent through the father."[4] Other groups had equally foreign-seeming family structures. Among the tribes of the Great Plains, polygamy had become more common with the rise of horse culture. A successful hunter needed more wives to help process the larger number of hides he brought back to camp. Sometimes those wives were sisters to one another. White reformers did not understand the social and economic complexities of polygamy, instead perceiving it as proof of Native barbarism and disdain for women. Also, in many Native cultures, nonnuclear extended families and clans were the norm. In the Navajo language, for example, according to Left Handed, "'mother' refers to a great many other women besides one's real mother. In fact, wishing to distinguish his [biological] mother from among all these other women . . . a Navaho [sic] must state explicitly, 'my real mother,' or use some such circumlocutory phrase as, 'she who gave me birth.'" Similarly, the Crow terms for sibling and cousin often applied to all clan relatives.[5] And among the Kiowa, homes were not centers of moral education; children, especially boys, received their training in social relations and proper conduct away from home in sex-based associations like the Kiowa military societies.[6] These family structures alarmed white reformers who glorified the nuclear family, especially the moral authority of the mother within it.

Nor did the dwellings of Indigenous people look to reformers like proper homes (Illustration 2.1). Again, diversity reigned, representing troublesome abnormalities for policy makers. Plains tribes such as the Kiowa, Crow, and

ILLUSTRATION 2.1. Construction of a wigwam, 1925. In many Native cultures, women were responsible for building the dwellings. Here, Ojibwa women from Mill Lac, Wisconsin, demonstrate for anthropologist Frances Densmore how to construct a wigwam. Compare this architecture with Figure 9.1, the frame house of an Ojibwa family, the dwelling preferred by the Indian Office. (Frances Densmore, *Chippewa Customs*, Bureau of American Ethnology, Bulletin 86, plates 3 and 4 [Washington, D.C.: Government Printing Office, 1929]; courtesy of the Center for Southwest Research, University Libraries, University of New Mexico)

Blackfeet used pine or spruce poles and buffalo hides to construct tepees that were usually built and owned by the women.[7] Their architecture and spatial configurations were linked to religion and culture. For the Oglala Lakota (Sioux), for instance, the circularity of the tepee spiritually linked together the earth, sky, moon, seasons, shields, camp circles, and ceremonies such as the sun dance.[8] The circular space inside the tepee was physically unpartitioned but was carefully arranged with designated uses: the space was centered on the firepit, which was surrounded by couches and sleeping platforms for family members and guests; the family altar and sacred possessions were generally located at the back, opposite the entrance; and other places were reserved for cooking utensils, clothing, and personal property. To whites, this single space seemed undifferentiated and crowded and spoke of immorality and disease.[9] White reformers also pointed to the portable nature of Native architecture and castigated Native people for "wandering" aimlessly. In fact, those tribes that were mobile (and not all of them were) had developed dwellings perfectly suited to their economic cycles of seasonal rounds of hunting and gathering, which involved very deliberate routes tied to specific territories and family-use rights.[10] In the Great Lakes region, for example, Ojibwa women made wigwams of woven reed mats draped over bent saplings for their winter hunting camps. Individual families slept in the wigwams, but they cooked communally over a fire in the middle of the camp. In the spring, the families moved to their individual sugar bush territories, where they had left storage lodges with food caches and the sugar-making tools. At the end of the sugar season, the families traveled to their summer camps, built bark lodges, and planted their gardens before leaving to gather wild rice. When they returned after gathering rice, the gardens were ready to be harvested and cached. Soon, winter arrived, and the cycle began again.[11] To white Americans, this "wandering" way of life indicated a denial of private property, both as real estate and as commodities that could be accumulated within a home. Describing Indians in this way had previously allowed Americans to justify dispossessing Natives of their territory, but now it posed a problem for bringing them into the nation as like-minded citizens.

Because white Americans' political theory placed the household at the very foundation of society, homes that appeared to them to be in disarray were threats to the nation. As one member of the Board of Indian Commissioners (BIC) declared in 1885: "Character . . . is worked out in the relations of the family, first; then in the relations of the larger society, the State. . . . The family is God's unit of society. On the integrity of the family depends that of the State."[12] A pamphlet for the Indian Rights Association likewise proclaimed: "Only the home can found a state. Three persons . . . the father, mother, and the child—these three, and these only can build a successful commonwealth."[13] In order to make Indians into citizens, policy makers believed it was necessary to terminate their "uncivilized" customs and compel them to start living in accordance with white ideas about family. To accomplish this, the Friends of the Indian devised social programs to transform the two major components of Native homes: the family relations within them and the physical environment that encompassed and reflected those relations.[14] Moreover, the family model served as the template for the government's employment policies when it set about hiring people to staff those programs.

MARRIAGE, HOUSE, AND LAND

The marital relationship between husband and wife was at the heart of reformers' ideal of a "civilized" home because it structured a complex set of rights and duties among family members.[15] As a legal form, marriage endowed couples with a particular relationship to the state and to each other while also creating and reinforcing Anglo gender norms. The marriage contract implied that each party agreed to certain terms and accepted certain responsibilities. Marriage also established a particular and gendered relationship to property, children, and the outside political world. Women who married gave their consent to be governed and represented by their husbands; they agreed to become dependent upon them. Marriage simultaneously conferred upon husbands the privileges and duties of the head of the household. In exchange for control over the bodies and property of their wives and children, husbands were expected to provide for and discipline those dependents.

Because matrimony carried so much ideological and legal weight, policy makers employed it as a major weapon in their arsenal and designed most of the assimilation programs to encourage it. Marriage offered an ideal means by which the Office of Indian Affairs could end Indian people's supposed dependence on the government. In theory, Indians who married under the U.S. legal system would be transformed. Native men would be infused with ideas of familial responsibility, and the duty of caring for dependents would be transferred to male heads of household. This was the calculus behind the question asked of Agent Riggs: "Do [Indian men] not sometimes grow manly, under the influence of having a family to work for?"[16] In this configuration, Native women and children would still be dependents, but the object of their dependency would shift from the national government to their fathers and husbands, as was appropriate in a "civilized" society. Superintendent of Indian Schools Estelle Reel later described this objective: "The Indian must be brought to a point where he will feel the work spirit and become self-supporting, where he will have the ambition to support his family and not look to the Government for help."[17] This emphasis on male heads of household also provided a way to regulate and control female sexuality, matrilineal descent, and female property ownership—all characteristics that white Americans saw as adverse to "civilization."

Legal marriage, which required a license, also helped the Indian Office attack the "tribal relations" of Native populations. Along with other record-keeping measures, such as property deeds and census rolls, it made individual Indian people identifiable and regulatable, allowing the United States to deal with them on a separate basis rather than through their tribal leaders. It also made it more difficult for Native people to avoid government policies by hiding or giving false information to administrators. The BIC emphasized the importance of this function and pushed hard for the regulation and recording of marriage within the Indian Bureau. "The regulations for the registration of marriages, births, and deaths," BIC members argued, enabled the government "to deal directly with individual Indians in all their relations of property. . . . [I]t furnishes an authentic list of individuals, needed in breaking up the tribal organization . . . [and] it inculcates sound views of the marriage relation and of family life."[18]

Indeed, knowing who was married to whom, who owned which property, and which children belonged to which parents helped the Indian Office coerce tribal populations. For example, in order to impose the configuration of male heads of household on unwilling people, it became Indian Office protocol to distribute rations and annuities according to a family member's relationship to the husband and father rather than to individuals. In its *Regulations* of 1884, the Indian Office laid out its definition of heads of household, describing them as men who were "heads of families receipting for the amount due them, their wives, and the minor children of their families."[19] This policy was intended to overcome the kind of resistance exemplified on the Southern Ute Reservation, where Ute men and women refused to identify themselves and silently waited for the rations to be distributed individually. Administrators also used knowledge of Native family trees to force recalcitrant parents to send their children away to federal schools. Because parents would often hide their children to prevent them from being seized, an official census that administrators could compare with school records allowed authorities to ascertain which families were concealing their children. They could then coordinate that with a list of who was entitled to receive rations, using the threat of hunger to force families to surrender their children. Even this measure almost failed because of Native parents' intense resistance to child removal. Superintendent of Schools Reel reported: "So strong is the opposition to this that in many cases they [Indians] have held out against it until their families were on the verge of starvation."[20]

Land allotment, the most important assimilation program devised by reformers, was also designed to encourage proper marital relations while placing married couples in the appropriate spatial configuration of private property. In 1887 Massachusetts senator Henry Dawes, chairman of the Senate Committee on Indian Affairs and a regular participant at the Lake Mohonk Conference, guided the General Allotment Act (or Dawes Act) through Congress with the enthusiastic support of the Friends of the Indian.[21] The legislation divided communally held reservation lands among tribal members and reflected white middle-class cultural expectations of a male-headed (and -owned) farming household. Each "head of a family" received a quarter of a section, or 160 acres, the same amount white settlers could claim under the Homestead Act. Single men and women over the age of eighteen received one-eighth of a section, or eighty acres, as did each orphan under eighteen years of age. As a result, if single people married, their total household property would amount to 160 acres. All other single persons under the age of eighteen were allotted one-sixteenth of a section, or forty acres, which was chosen for them by the head of their family. Married women received no land; it was assumed that a married woman would share in her husband's property and that he would provide for her. A wife therefore did not need property of her own, as it would only revert to her husband's control under the rules of coverture. The Dawes Act also stipulated that the allotted land came under the inheritance rules of the state or territory within which it lay. Any remaining reservation land was to be sold off to finance the necessary surveying work as well as "education and civilization" programs for the tribe. For Native nations, this resulted in the loss of millions of acres of treaty-guaranteed land. Finally, while the act technically bestowed citizenship upon Indians who took up their allotments, it also stipulated that the government would hold the land in trust for twenty-five years. This paradox would be resolved later in a court case.[22] Thus allotment and legal marriage worked together to place Native families in an arrangement in which private property was owned and passed on by the male members of the household, which administrators believed was necessary in an enlightened society.

The reformers at that year's Lake Mohonk Conference hailed the passage of the Allotment Act in almost millennial terms, celebrating the beginning of a "new era," "a new order of things," and "a new dispensation" in Indian policy. "The passage of the Dawes Bill," they exulted, "closes the 'century of dishonor'; it makes possible for the people of America to initiate a chapter of national honor in the century to come."[23] But the division of reservations was only the first step in the evolution from treaties to social programs. Policy makers believed that it would not be sufficient simply to assign private land-holding to individual families. As Senator Dawes explained, "the severalty [allotment] act was only an open door to make a home," and Indians needed to be taught how to make their homes.[24]

To do so, the federal government constructed an enormous educational bureaucracy that sought to teach Indians about every aspect of "civilized" life. The Friends of the Indian believed that in this new era, the process of assimilating the government's Indian wards would require "a new strategy," "new men," and new "machinery." They agreed that the "old machinery" of the Indian Service — the patronage-driven agency system of political spoils — was inadequate to its "new duties." As one conference goer put it, "We are all agreed on this that the present Indian administration is a failure. . . . [S]ome blame the system, some the men, but the result has always been the same, that the Indian is the injured party."[25]

The question of Indian Service administration completely dominated the Lake Mohonk Conference program the year the Dawes Act passed. Participants opened the 1887 meeting with a discussion of the question, "What changes in Indian Governmental Administration are required by the abolition of the Indian Reservation System?"[26] The Friends of the Indian concentrated on the question of personnel because Indian Service employees would be responsible for carrying out the programs that would mold Indians into future citizens. Speakers enumerated three basic qualities essential to the people who would do the delicate work of Indian assimilation. First, employees had to have the special educational skills needed to teach Indians about work, family, and respectability. Second, employees must not come and go with each new election but stay in their positions for many years so as to maximally influence their wards. As General Armstrong of the Hampton Institute pointed out, "As politics now go, [there is] no permanency, but a complete and disastrous change every few years." Finally, employees had to be extremely dedicated. Dr. Edward H. Magill, president of Swarthmore College, elaborated: "This long and patient labor for the elevation of a race, to be effectual, must devolve upon earnest consecrated men and women, who gladly devote their lives to it, and whose high qualification for this service depends upon no mere government appointment."[27]

But how would such employees be found? In taking up the work of education, matrimony, and social services, the federal government was entering territory previously inhabited by state and local governments or private organizations. This posed new challenges for the federal government. The very different solutions proposed at Lake Mohonk suggest just how novel this undertaking was and how willing policy makers were to experiment. Herbert Welsh of the Indian Rights Association insisted that "the work must be done, not by official mechanism, but by Christian spirit and Christian knowledge." In other words, only churches and religious organizations could provide a reliable workforce. Others suggested governance by commission. President Grover Cleveland's idea of establishing an independent board modeled on the Interstate Commerce Commission was championed by Professor C. C. Painter, also of the Indian Rights Association. Still others endorsed the idea of a merit-based civil service system.[28]

Policy makers initially agreed to expand the contract-school system, which seemed to offer the best way around the problem of patronage. This solution, which was supported by Senator Dawes, drew heavily on the precedent of cooperation between the Freedmen's Bureau and private organizations, especially the American Missionary Association.[29] The contract-school system created educational institutions that were funded by the government but staffed and administered by religious and charitable groups. These schools theoretically avoided the perils of patronage because benevolent associations selected the employees. Senator Dawes emphasized that the contract schools would be a joint venture, reiterating that while private organizations would build the facilities and choose the teachers, the "teachers should be paid in large degree by the Government and the Government has shown its readiness to supply everything that can be done in educating [the Indian]."[30]

Over the next few years, however, the combination of sectarian and partisan tensions led to the collapse of the contract-school system and the assumption of total administrative control by the U.S. government. While churches and benevolent associations had been operating contract schools since Grant's Peace Plan and had increased their participation throughout the 1880s, the private reformers who ran them were beginning to question their role in Indian education. Many groups were stretching their resources between freedpeople's education, Indian schools, and other commitments and were feeling the pinch of constrained budgets. Moreover, the Roman Catholic Church, which had not played a role in Reconstruction education programs, was enjoying extraordinary success in capturing federal money for Indian contract schools. In 1886, for example, it received more than half of all federal contract-school dollars, and by 1890 its share had risen to 63 percent. This success angered the participating Protestant churches, which had previously spent over a decade fighting Catholic efforts to gain public funding for parochial schools.[31] The turning point came in 1891–92, when concerns about Catholics led the Protestant churches to pull out of the system altogether in an effort to pressure the Catholics to follow suit. They felt assured that a Republican-administered educational system would emphasize their Protestant values because Commissioner of Indian Affairs Thomas Jefferson Morgan was a Baptist minister, his superintendent of schools was a Methodist minister, and both men had a history of anti-Catholic agitation.[32]

These religious struggles were enmeshed with partisan political maneuvering. In 1893, just before he left office, Republican president Benjamin Harrison extended the merit service system over the positions of Indian school superintendent, assistant superintendent, teacher, matron, and doctor in an attempt to protect the Protestant character of the Indian Service. A few years later, President Cleveland, a Democrat, responded by issuing an executive order that placed the majority of the remaining Indian Service positions under civil service administration. Reflecting the general affiliation at the time of Protestants with Republicans and Catholics with Democrats, the presidential actions should be seen as an attempt to "freeze" partisan appointees and coreligionists in office.[33]

The upshot of these bureaucratic struggles over religion and politics was that the federal government became exclusively responsible for Indian Service personnel. When it did, the family model provided the framework for staffing that bureaucracy. The federal government needed employees who not only were moved by a higher purpose but also could demonstrate ideal gender and family behavior.[34] For policy makers, women's position in the household was particularly important, and this factor critically shaped the Indian Service workforce. Supporters of assimilation posited that changing the behavior of Indian men was essential for making Indian families self-reliant, and changing Indian women was imperative for the long-term success of the policy. Within the household model of assimilation, women, as wives and mothers, were responsible for socially reproducing the next generation of citizens. In 1896 the BIC insisted that "so long as the mother remains ignorant and degraded the family will have no true home and the children will grow up without proper training."[35] Anglo gender ideology assigned moral influence in the family to women, who would guide their husbands' behavior and reinforce the tenets of assimilation from within their homes. "Soften, purify, and refine the mother," insisted one reservation official, "and the task is more than half accomplished. Her genial influence will mold and inspire the children, and will civilize and elevate the father."[36]

The Indian Office ultimately developed two broad levels of educational programs: adult education and childhood education.[37] The adult education programs were administered directly through the reservation agencies, while the childhood education system became the Indian School Service, a separate branch of the Indian Service, in 1882. The Indian Office did not believe that the older generation of Indians on the reservations could be truly transformed, but it nonetheless established a few programs to teach them how to behave on their new allotments. It directed most of its energy and resources at the childhood educational programs that tried to completely remove Native children from the influence of their families and communities in order to transform them. We will return to the School Service later in this chapter.

ON THE RESERVATIONS

The two primary adult education initiatives on the reservations — the farmer program and the field matron (or female industrial teacher) program — aimed to teach Indian men and women appropriate household skills.[38] Federal employees showed Native people how to farm and keep house by modeling those skills on the reservation and visiting individual homes to provide instruction and encouragement. These homemaking lessons were based on the same household vision that structured the curriculum at federal Indian schools. The position of reservation farmer was not new to the assimilation period. Some treaties had provided for the employment of a person to teach agricultural techniques to Native men, but like many programs in the assimilation period, the difference was one of scale. According to David Rich Lewis, the number of farmers more than doubled between 1881 and 1905, and ultimately over 80 percent of reservation agencies employed at least one.[39] Farmers were hired to instruct Indian men how to use their allotments by running a demonstration farm at the reservation agency and offering advice regarding their plots and equipment. As with other Indian Service personnel, the farmer's position encompassed much more than just the technical aspects of agriculture. As one commissioner of Indian affairs explained it, the "duties of the Indian farmer are manifold. . . . [He] instructs . . . assists . . . supervises . . . oversees . . . settles . . . protects. . . . [I]n fact, he stands ready at all times to serve [the Indians'] interests as occasion demands. His duties, therefore, like those of a conscientious teacher, are without boundary."[40]

Farmers worked to turn the new reservation allotments into landscapes that fit the vision of an ideal home. Time and again, reformers described "the best sort of farm"[41] as one growing crops for market and boasting neat outbuildings, fences, orchards, and animals — all representing the productive economic role of men.[42] Fields were the male domain of the household economy, the spaces in which production for the market took place. Farmers would demonstrate how to create these landscapes and help remasculinize Native men by teaching them how to support their families through farming. "What he earns on this farm will help him learn the value of it," Senator Dawes forcefully stated. "The idea is to make something of him, to make a man of him. . . . He is to be taught self-reliance, or he will never be a man."[43]

Policy makers stressed participation in the cash nexus as essential to the male role in the household. Men were quite literally expected to wear the pants in the family. One reformer stated that the goal of government assimilation policy should be to create a farmer wearing "trousers with a pocket in them, and with a *pocket that aches to be filled with dollars*."[44] Another wrote that "if an Indian can be made to hear the jingle of dollars in his pocket, he may follow the sound into the promised land."[45] The reason for this insistence was that unlike subsistence farms, market-oriented households required money for a variety of purchases, including farming tools and machinery. Even more important to the reformers' household vision, however, was the idea that a farmer's money would be used to build and furnish a house and make it into a home.

This duty of making a home was assigned to the counterparts of these productive men: their consuming wives.[46] To help wives learn their responsibilities within the household, the Indian Office established the position of field matron. "What the farmer does for the Indian men," one commissioner stated, "the field matron accomplishes for the Indian women." It was the matron's job, another proclaimed, "to perform the numberless duties and services which transform a house into a home." This program, created in 1890, was new to the assimilation period. It grew out of the maternalist insistence of the Women's National Indian Association (WNIA) that assimilation would not prevail without a program aimed at helping Native women adjust to their new domestic roles. Notably, the Office of Indian Affairs took recommendations from the WNIA for staffing the first positions.[47]

Field matrons focused on the yard, house, and domestic interiors—the female domain of the household economic unit. These spaces were gendered female because they reflected a woman's skill in arranging and decorating, as well as making economical use of her husband's income.[48] Traveling for miles across the reservations, field matrons were expected to visit Indian women in their homes and instruct them in the domestic arts while also opening their own homes as examples of ideal households. As implied in their job titles, field matrons were to be wise mother figures who taught Indian women to "do the innumerable other things which present themselves in the life of a housewife. . . . [S]he is expected to exert her influence to improve their moral welfare."[49]

The field matron program also offers the best example of how the Indian Office's adult training programs were designed to work with an expanding childhood education system by serving as a temporary measure until the next generation inherited its homesteads. Field matrons were expected to offer support to returning boarding-school students by providing white maternal models on the reservations. When Merial Dorchester, special agent in the Indian School Service and wife of the superintendent of Indian schools, described the field matron program, she combined concern for the former students with a negative image of their mothers. To her, field matrons offered the kind of support that Indian women could not: "Often all that an Indian girl needs to keep her pure and true is to know that near her is a kind-hearted white woman ready with sympathy, advice, and help."[50]

At first, during what one reformer described as "a transition period," field matrons would teach Indian women to improvise with the resources on hand until they could buy new and better items. Policy makers were encouraged by any small sign of "progress" toward a pleasant furnished home: "A cloth spread over a board or box for a table, a wash-basin outside the door, a suggestion of an apron, a white handkerchief, or perhaps a picture cut from a pictorial paper on the wall, are small things in themselves; but these seen in an Indian settlement speak volumes," claimed the chief of the educational division of the Indian School Service in 1890.[51] Ultimately, though, the best sort of houses needed to be furnished not only with large pieces such as tables, bedsteads, windows, and stoves but also with more specialized commodities like curtains, flatware, rugs, pictures, and even pianos. Such houses, another policy maker enthused, would be places "where they can gather about them those things which make home pleasant and attractive."[52]

Reformers and policy makers fetishized commodities beyond their practical and motivational functions.[53] They believed that the mere presence of goods could inspire changes in behavior and sensibility. They argued that like a conversion process, the interaction of Native people with commodities would lead miraculously to a new way of living. Many of their examples portrayed Native women transformed by the presence of the goods in their homes. The most striking instance of this came from Mrs. Sarah Kinney, president of the Connecticut Indian Association (an auxiliary of the WNIA). She argued that it was the influence of a "decent home" with its particularly furnished domestic spaces that inspired change in one Native family.

> This woman was naturally lazy, shiftless, untidy and disorderly.
> Her husband, somewhat more fastidious, wished her to be neat
> and cleanly; to live and dress more like white people, and to make
> "white woman's bread." To all these she seriously objected. She did
> not like white people, nor their ways, and she would have none of

them. It finally occurred to this man to enlarge his house, to add on a kitchen, to buy a new stove, and then to watch for the effect. . . . For a time the woman seemed perplexed by this unusual magnificence. . . . But the right influence had reached her at last. She soon began to feel disturbed because of grease spots on the new pine floor, and a scrubbing brush was brought into requisition. Then, of course, she began to notice the difference between the clean floor and her own face, hands, and clothing. The scrubbing brush was again called for and worked wonders along those lines. By degrees she has lost many of her slovenly ways, and at last accounts she was learning to make "white woman's bread." Here, then, is an instance of one Indian woman who has been civilized through the medium of a pine floor and a scrubbing brush.[54]

In other inspirational stories, a "clean apron in the kitchen" or pictures on the walls were credited with similarly transformative powers.[55] Something as simple as a switch from tin plates to china dishes was described as producing "a marvelous influence on the soul [sic] development."[56] The fact that reformers pinned their hopes on this power of commodities reflected some wishful thinking: if the goods could perform this work so quickly and thoroughly, the task of assimilation would be an easy one. But it also explains the emphasis on consumption within their political economy.

This goal of putting Indian men and women into "civilized" homes was so important that the WNIA actually offered home building loans to "deserving applicants."[57] In 1888 the Home Building and Loan Department of the association raised $2,000 and loaned out $1,600 to applicants.[58] They also helped furnish the houses, offering smaller loans for "crockery, cooking utensils, and [to] make articles of clothing."[59] The fact that these were loans rather than charity was important: reformers feared that giving goods away would replicate the government's ration system and reduce the incentive to work and produce. The WNIA therefore designed their assistance to teach the values of credit and interest, investment and repayment. Their lessons also assumed a future universality of material items. Without these items, many other lessons would be for naught. One field matron, Anna Dawson (Arikara), described this practical imperative for goods: "It is hard to teach the serving of meals in a cabin where there are neither tables nor chairs, to teach dishwashing and laundry work without any of the utensils usually considered necessary, or to teach hygienic conditions of living where there are no towels, sheets or even a piece of cloth to clean with."[60]

But more important, goods had an influence beyond a practical pedagogical function: they could inspire emulation. As Indians began to work, earn money, and accumulate property, policy makers hoped their example would create feelings of envy that would encourage other Indians to work toward assimilation as well. Reformers maintained that successful examples of people with purchasing power would create discontent among those Indians who had not yet converted to ideas of production and consumption. They celebrated cases in which industrious Indians converted their "backward" neighbors to the ways of the market. For instance, one reformer claimed that "it was evident that the $5 a ton [of hay] secured by the industrious ones was proving an irresistible argument, one after another of the blanket Indians dropping his pride and blanket, getting a team, and going to work."[61]

Policy makers also argued that the Indians were not selfish enough, characterizing them as too generous and wholly lacking a desire to accumulate possessions. Certainly, many Native cultures were based on gift giving, and ties were cemented through those gifts; likewise, kinship obligations often required that people share among their families. Moreover, in the high-poverty communities of reservations, resources had to be shared to ensure survival.[62] But this giving away of goods and resources frustrated policy makers because it undermined Indians' ability to accumulate capital and thus increase investments or improve land. If basic necessities such as food and clothing were always shared, reformers reasoned, how could a greater participation in production and consumption be ingrained? One Lake Mohonk Conference speaker used a basic example to make this point: "An Indian woman in the old life would never keep two shawls. If she came into possession of more than one, she would divide with her more needy neighbor."[63] This impulse was not completely wrong, they argued, but misguided. It indicated Christian generosity, but as mentioned above, postwar reformers believed that misplaced charity did more harm than good. Field matron Emily C. Miller lamented the problems caused by such mutuality, explaining that "those who are better off never refuse to feed the poor and lazy ones,"[64] which reformers understood to be reinforcing the tendencies of laziness and pauperism in some while simultaneously limiting the ability of others to accumulate property.

One obvious answer to this dilemma was to make the Indians acquisitive. In 1886, for example, the commissioner of Indian affairs urged that "[the Indian] must be imbued with the exalting egotism of American civilization so that he will say 'I' instead of 'We' and 'This is mine' instead of 'This is ours.'"[65] Policy makers strongly encouraged Native men to go forth and participate in a modern and fully competitive market economy: "We must make the Indian more intelligently selfish. . . . By acquiring property, man puts forth his personality and lays hold of matter by his own thought and will."[66]

Even as policy makers encouraged this selfishness, however, they betrayed considerable ambivalence about it. After all, it sat in tension with their other goal of instilling Christianity in Native people. One speaker at the Lake Mohonk Conference encapsulated the problem: "The Indian is instinctively generous. . . . Of course we must develop the desire for possession, . . . [b]ut, in doing this, we must not crush out this natural instinct of generosity. It is to be directed in [the] wise and wholesome channels of civilization and Christianity."[67] Policy makers resolved this conundrum by returning once again to their family ideal. As Merrill Gates of the Board of Indian Commissioners asserted: "It is chiefly the affections and interests of *family life* that take out of this desire for gain its debasing element, its utter selfishness."[68] A major component of "civilized" manhood was a man's support of his dependents. Therefore, if a man was selfish for the benefit of his family, his behavior was virtuous. Of course, the success of this strategy depended on keeping people from sharing excessively with their friends and relatives. But policy makers continued to hope that even the smallest evidences of material goods could spark the desire that would lead Indians into production and consumption.[68]

APPRENTICESHIPS

The Indian Service also hired employees to fill many other positions beyond those of farmer and field matron. These positions were necessary to manage the growing volume of paperwork generated by Indian affairs, to assist the Indians in building "civilized" communities, and to maintain the physical plant of the agencies.

The Indian Office's goal of social transformation required the development of an increasingly complex bureaucratic structure. By the end of the nineteenth century, the Indian Service had developed an elaborate set of employees with specific duties — so many, in fact, that the Indian Office regularly published a set of *Rules and Regulations* that described the positions.[69] The reservation agent was the highest-ranking official at the agency. Agents were executive appointments requiring confirmation by the Senate, but they were being phased out; by 1908 all agents had been replaced by the appointed civil service position of superintendent. As had been the case during the preassimilation period, the agent, or later the superintendent, remained "the highest authority on the reservation." His (and in virtually all cases, agents were male) duty was to supervise all reservation activity. Assisting him in these tasks was a broad range of clerical employees. The administrative work of reservation agencies exploded with the emphasis on marriage and private property, which required the taking of censuses; the recording of marriages, births, and deaths; and the surveying, allotting, and leasing of reservation property under the Dawes Act. The vast amount of paperwork led to greater and more specified positions. In place of the single general clerk per agency that had been standard previously, employee rolls by the turn of the century included many different kinds of clerks. For example, financial clerks oversaw the accounts of individual Indians, leasing clerks supervised the leasing of Indian allotments, and issue clerks coordinated the issuing of equipment and rations. In addition, assistant clerks and stenographers were necessary for making multiple copies of records and correspondence for the agency files to be sent to Washington, D.C.

The maintenance of draft animals and farming equipment, the development of agricultural and in some cases industrial infrastructure, and the construction of new buildings on reservations — including school facilities, mills, electrical plants, and multiple new houses on Indian allotments — required growth in skilled positions. The most common of these were blacksmiths, mechanics, carpenters, sawyers, and millers. The Indian Service also employed men as stockmen, laborers, and freighters and in law-and-order positions.

Like the farmers and field matrons, employees hired to fill support positions were envisioned as educators. Summing up the constellation of agency positions, one commissioner stated, "The industrial training of the reservation of which the farmer and field matron are the dynamos, together with the stockman, the carpenter, the blacksmith, and many others, I regard as a matter of the first importance."[70] The industrial training to which the commissioner referred worked on two levels. White employees taught by example; the Indian Office regarded the laborers and mechanics at the Indian agencies "as teachers in their respective lines of work and expected, in addition to performing their regular duties, to give instruction."[71]

Many of these positions also served as on-the-job training for Indians. As part of the effort to instruct Native people about the market, the government hired them to work for the Indian Service. This idea had a long history in the Indian Office, stretching back to 1834, but its postwar iteration was different. After the Civil War, with the increased emphasis on assimilation, the number of Indian employees began to skyrocket. Administrators' desire to inculcate free-labor ideology, especially market-friendly work discipline and the desire for accumulation, was the principal motivation for this policy. By 1880 an Indian Office rule stated that "no work must be given white men which can be done by Indians."[72] The following year, the commissioner of Indian affairs reported that "particular effort has been made to push forward the education interests of the Service, and to advance the process of civilizing the Indian by inducing him to labor, [and] paying him therefore."[73]

Administrators hoped that hiring Indians to work in the Indian Service would further reinforce the white family model while simultaneously undercutting Native structures of kinship and authority. Policy makers used positions in the Indian Service to teach specific gendered skills. For both men and women, employment would serve as an apprenticeship in agricultural, industrial, or domestic crafts. This was especially true for adults who had not attended school. Indeed, many Native employees held positions labeled as assistantships to white employees; assistant farmer and assistant matron were two of the most common. Federal employment also served as an incentive to keep educated Indians from "returning to the blanket" and falling back into their tribal ways since, on isolated reservations, the federal government was often the only employer.[74] Meanwhile, policy makers sought to undermine the authority of Native leaders by offering employment because they believed that chiefs derived their power from distributing goods, especially government rations. Policy makers therefore attempted to give Indian men independent sources of income and goods. Indian Service positions could also disrupt noneconomic lines of authority within the tribes by introducing the federal government as an alternate source of power. In describing the Indian police forces — a source of employment for many Indian men on the reservations — the commissioner of Indian affairs noted that federal employment "makes the Indian himself the representative of the power and majesty of the Government of the United States."[75] As a result, the percentage of Native employees in the Indian Service climbed steadily throughout the last two decades of the century.[76] (We will return to this in chapter 5.)

SCHOOLS

As important as the Indian Service was, and as large and complex as its bureaucracy and hiring strategies became, it remained something of a catchall department that administered the reservations and provided merely provisional measures to help (or force) Native adults to adjust to federal policy. It was in the School Service that the government focused its energy most closely on achieving the rapid and complete transformation of Native nations. There, the battle for the hearts and minds of Native America was fought, and Indigenous children were on the front lines as students in federal schools. By imposing Anglo family roles onto Native children, especially the task of social reproduction within families, policy makers sought to ensure that the next generation of Native people would grow up learning those les-

ILLUSTRATION 2.2. Gardening at Tulalip, Washington, 1912. The Indian Service assigned federal employees to serve as surrogate parents to the nation's Indian wards, especially the Native children in federal schools. Here, a white couple, most likely a husband and wife, supervise a group of Native boys. (Courtesy of the Ferdinand Brady Collection, Washington Museum of History and Industry, Seattle [MOHAI 88.11.7])

sons in their own homes and inheriting their property in the same way that white people did. This strategy was intended to ensure that these social programs also would be temporary, ending after one generation of students had been successfully educated in the federal schools. The introduction to the 1892 *Rules for Indian Schools* optimistically declared: "It is the design of the Government to remove, by the shortest method, the ignorance, inability and fears of the Indians and to place them on an equality with other races in the United States. In organizing this system of schools, the fact is not overlooked that Indian schools, as such, should be preparatory and temporary; that eventually they will become unnecessary."[77]

The School Service administered the educational programs designed to transform an entire generation of Native children by replacing their families with "civilized" influences (Illustration 2.2). It was in the staffing of the education programs, especially the boarding schools, that the strategy of the family model became most explicit. These programs focused on academic and industrial training while constantly reinforcing proper behavior and sex-appropriate tasks for the girls and boys who, it was assumed, would grow up to live on the allotted farms. Miss Alice Robertson, a teacher in Indian

Territory, emphasized this: "[W]e have to educate [the girls] for wives and mothers. We teach them how to make pleasant homes, and the boys how to support the wives."[78]

In an insidious effort to disrupt the affective bonds between Native children and their parents, the boarding schools tried to substitute Indian Service employees as fictive kin for an entire generation of Indian children. Policy makers argued that boarding schools would replace the negative influence of a child's Indian parents with the positive influence of white parent figures. In 1885 the superintendent of schools warned that Native students returned home each evening after day school and therefore had not "acquired a distaste for the camp-fire, nor a longing for the food, the home-life, or the ordinary avocations of the white man . . . because it does not take him away from barbarous life and put him into the enjoyment of civilized life—does not take him from the tepee into the house." As a solution, he urged compulsory attendance at boarding schools, where white employees would teach students to revile their parents' culture. He acknowledged that this might be painful for Native families, but he dryly asserted that "its provisions would be the kindly cruel surgery which hurts that it may save, and would in good time cure the Indian race of savagery."[79] A decade later, the superintendent of Indian schools entitled his report "The School as a Home." The school, he wrote, "is to the child not only school, but home and community as well."[80] The commissioner of Indian affairs agreed: "When the closing hour has arrived teachers and pupils in white schools go to their homes and enjoy around the family circle those pleasures of home life which are characteristic of the American people. The Indian reservation school, on the other hand, must combine both the home and the school."[81] He highlighted the important role of the employees in creating those surrogate homes: "The Indian school is the Indian's home and the success of the present educational policy is largely due to the earnest and faithful cooperation of these patient workers in this great field."[82]

Policy makers were explicit in describing employees as parents. At Lake Mohonk in 1895, Dr. Hailmann, superintendent of Indian schools, reported that the reorganization of the School Service was having a great effect: "The matron is beginning to feel that she is more than a housekeeper, that she is a mother rather than a housekeeper; and she prides herself upon the title of 'school mother' and emphasizes that in her work."[83] The next year, the commissioner urged employees to remember that they were competing with Native parents for their students' affections, saying that because "home life is nearest the heart of the child and exerts the greatest influence upon the development of character, the Indian school should place adequate stress upon its home features, and should never sacrifice these to the more or less heartless necessities of institutional requirements." He pointed out that this could only be accomplished by the creation of loving relationships between the children and the employees because "unless the child is loved and can love unreservedly, he will never take a real heart interest in the school." He reminded the Indian Service employees that they were competing with the real parents of the children; if they were not affectionate, the "influences of school will be banished out of his life joyously as soon as he returns to the Indian home, where love again rules supreme."[84] The commissioner was essentially advocating a community-centered education within an institutional educational system. The employees were to teach everything, even that which white children learned "at the fireside and in Christian homes."[85]

The School Service systematized its schools into three basic types: day schools, on-reservation boarding schools, and off-reservation boarding schools.[86] The smallest and simplest component of the school system was the reservation day school. The day schools were scattered throughout the reservations, often far from the agencies. Students attended the schools during the day and returned home to their families at night. As a result, day schools did not need large support staffs and usually employed only two people: a teacher and a housekeeper. The teacher was responsible for classroom lessons, while the housekeeper made lunch for the students and demonstrated homemaking skills. By the 1890s, the Indian Office stated that an "endeavor is made to fill them [the positions of teacher and housekeeper] with a man and his wife," a trend that increased after the turn of the century. The hiring of married couples reinforced the idea of a family model and augmented the staff members' ability to demonstrate the ideal household and marital roles to their Native wards. The goal of the day schools was to provide elementary instruction in subjects like English and mathematics; they were also made responsible for being "a civilized home among the Indians," who would "emulate the example set" by the employees.[87] The directive of "object lessons" was fundamental to their jobs and inseparable from their pedagogy. As the School Service became more systematized, the day schools were meant to serve as feeders into the more advanced educational institutions: the on- and off-reservation boarding schools.

The boarding schools employed the family model on a much grander scale; they were always the biggest institutions and employed the largest workforces. Initially, policy makers had hoped to educate all Indian students in off-reservation schools, thus completely removing them from the influence of their parents and tribes. The first off-reservation boarding school was Richard Henry Pratt's Carlisle School in Pennsylvania, founded in 1879. By 1902 twenty-five off-reservation schools had been established. Despite this rapid increase, however, there were simply not enough off-reservation schools to educate all Indian children. Budgetary limitations led to the simultaneous development of a series of on-reservation boarding schools, which were usually located at the reservation agencies. Policy makers comforted themselves with the idea that even if students could not be sent completely off the reservation, they could at least be removed from their parents and closely monitored.

The official in charge of most boarding schools was the superintendent. Most often a white man, he acted as a father figure to all of the schoolchildren as well as to the other employees. He "had general charge . . . of the school premises," a task that was sometimes shared with an assistant superintendent. Superintendents were also responsible for the school's "discipline, for the character, conduct, and efficiency of the employees," as well as for the "moral and industrial welfare and progress" of the students. In smaller schools, the principal teacher fulfilled those duties.[88]

In many cases, the superintendent's wife was employed as a school matron or a teacher, thus completing the familial image. By 1903 this was institutionalized, and the Indian Service rules and regulations specified that superintendents' wives could occupy those posts after taking a noncompetitive civil service exam.[89] Matrons did indeed provide a motherly figure for the schools. Their official job description made them "responsible for the management of all the domestic affairs of the school," including "oversight of the dormitories." Matrons were specifically in charge of the schoolgirls and were required to oversee their physical appearance and their gender-appropriate work assignments in the kitchen, laundry, dining room, and dairy. The supervision of the male students varied. Some schools had a "boys matron," who was the counterpart to the chief matron for the girls. For other schools, the superintendent would select a male employee to supervise the boys. Sometimes this position was designated as the "disciplinarian," denoting the male employee who was required to "maintain at all times exemplary discipline, order, and good conduct" among the boys (Illustration 2.3).[90]

In order to feed, clothe, and shelter large numbers of students, schools had a team of support staff—bakers, laundresses, cooks, seamstresses, farmers, mechanics, engineers, carpenters, blacksmiths, shoe-and-harness makers, stockmen, nurserymen, gardeners, and dairymen—who provided for the physical needs of the institution. As in the reservations programs, the positions mirrored the gendered division of labor within households and were instructional as well as practical. Indeed, their job descriptions all included variations of the phrase "with the assistance of the pupils."[91] In some schools, they may have had paid assistants working under them as well as the

ILLUSTRATION 2.3. *Group of Young Indian School Boys*, Hoopa Valley Indian School, ca. 1901–6. Not all Indian Service employees were married or white, but the familial metaphor of federal parents remained strong. This typical class picture includes a white woman, probably the teacher, and a Native man, likely the assistant industrial teacher. (Courtesy of the Phoebe A. Hearst Museum of Anthropology and the regents of the University of California; photograph by Nellie T. McGraw Hedgpeth [catalogue no. 15-20885])

schoolchildren. Women most often filled the positions of cook, baker, seamstress, and laundress. They cooked and baked for the school mess; sewed underwear, uniforms, and aprons; and washed clothes, towels, and bedding. While these positions did have counterparts in the home, the sheer size of the boarding schools turned them into industrial labor. Likewise, there were counterparts to the male occupations of farming and building. Schools employed male support staff to "attend to all the outside manual labor connected with the school farm and garden, caring for the stock belonging to the school, keeping a supply of fuel on hand, making repairs on buildings, and seeing that the school property and grounds are kept in good order."[92] They, too, worked with details of male students to accomplish these goals and as a method of instruction. The primary point of schools was classroom education, and the boarding schools had large teaching forces. Their composition depended on the size of the schools and could include principal teachers, first and second teachers, kindergarten teachers, and assistant teachers. Some of the larger schools also had orchestra and band instructors, domestic-science teachers, and art instructors. Schools also employed a variety of white-collar and professional employees. Clerks and stenographers assisted superintendents with their official duties, such as keeping student records, handling correspondence, and coordinating personnel paperwork. Most schools had their own doctor or perhaps a nurse, although the agency physician could be called in if a school did not. Some schools even had hospitals.[93]

CONCLUSION

The grand theory of assimilation that reformers and policy makers formulated in the 1870s and 1880s shaped the Indian Service and influenced its operation for decades thereafter. In 1909 the commissioner of Indian affairs invoked this expansive vision of assimilation: "The personnel, the general administration of schools and agencies, the buildings in which we house the children and employees, the food and clothes we buy for the children and the tools and machinery for their instructive use, are all a part of the educational organism of the service. The farmer, the trader and even the agent are as much teachers as the persons in charge of the schoolrooms. All persons and things on or about a reservation, in or out of the service, are educational factors to be given their full weight in preparing the Indians to take a place in the civilized body."[94] This theory made the personnel of the Indian Service and the reservation landscapes into key components of a totalizing strategy of cultural change. Reformers and policy makers placed white Americans' vision of the idealized home at the center of their efforts, just as it had been at the center of the effort to make freedpeople into citizens during Reconstruction. The Friends of the Indian asserted that the home could be both the method and the manifestation of citizenship: they believed that altering the relationships and physical surroundings of the tribes would result in their transformation, while the reproduction of proper homes by the next generation of Indians would signal the success of the reform project.

The methods that policy makers developed to achieve these goals relied substantially on the tactics that scholars have described as "intimate colonialism."[95] This involved changing the fundamental nature of Native familial and social systems — the most intimate of relationships. Restructuring Native families, administrators believed, held the key to the total conquest of Native nations. Policy makers knew that the intimate decisions about how to raise children, how husbands and wives should relate to each other, and what their homes should look like were not private questions but key political concerns upon which the fate of federal Indian policy rested. And if the fate of Indian policy lay in those changes, the fate of those changes lay in the hands of the

Indian Service employees—a group often overlooked in scholarly discussions of Indian policy.

Despite all of their planning, policy makers and administrators had not really understood how individual Indian Service employees would affect the outcome of their efforts. They had lofty goals and ambitions for the personnel, believing that the example of employees would combine with the reservation landscapes and the muscle of the Indian Schools to quickly and successfully assimilate the tribes. The chapters in the next section explore the everyday experiences of the Indian Service employees and demonstrate that, unlike the sweeping ideals of fictive kinship and the quick fix set up by the Indian Office, the reality was much more contradictory, confusing, and often frustrating for all parties working in this multiracial bureaucracy.

II. THE WOMEN AND MEN OF THE INDIAN SERVICE

Members of an Amazonian Corps

WHITE WOMEN IN THE INDIAN SERVICE

In Williamsburg, Virginia, in 1901, a family disagreement became entangled in national governance. One can almost imagine the stoic resolve, or more likely the exasperated sigh, with which Minnie Braithwaite's mother met her daughter's announcement that she wanted to join the Indian Service. Earlier, Mrs. Braithwaite had been relieved to find that Minnie's plan to go to China as a medical missionary had been derailed by the College of William and Mary's refusal to train women as doctors. But now Minnie seemed determined to go west and teach the Indians.[1] Mrs. Braithwaite decided to use political influence to foil her daughter's plans, turning to her good friend and neighbor, U.S. representative Richard A. Wise. The congressman owed the family for previous political favors, and Mrs. Braithwaite hoped that he would now reciprocate by preventing Minnie's appointment. Wise amusedly pointed out that most people asked their congressmen to help them *obtain* positions in the Indian Service, not the opposite; not only that, but he actually supported Minnie in her decision. "With so many children," he teased Mrs. Braithwaite, she "could surely spare one to teach the Indians." In an apparent effort to please both women, he secured a position for Minnie, but at the worst post in the Indian Service: a school in a hot, remote, and inaccessible canyon in Yuma, California. "All appointments to it have been declined," the clerk in the Office of Indian Affairs had assured him. "She also will turn it down." But Minnie did not turn it down. "To the dismay of all," she later wrote, "I accepted and left home promptly, although dutiful daughters weren't ever supposed to be so independent."[2]

With that decision, Minnie Braithwaite joined thousands of other white women who became federal Indian Service employees during the late nine-

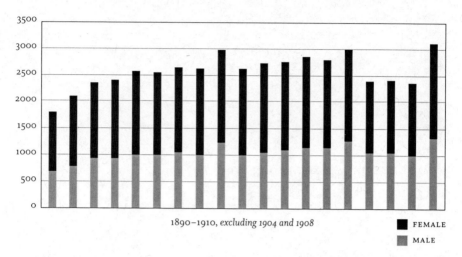

FIGURE 1. Graph of Employees by Sex in the Indian School Service, 1890–1910. The Indian Service, especially the School Service, had a highly feminized workforce that assigned women to teach gender roles and serve as surrogate mothers for Native children, making it the first maternalist bureaucracy in the federal government. (Compiled from the annual reports of the commissioner of Indian affairs)

teenth and early twentieth centuries. Assimilation programs would have been impossible if not for women like Braithwaite who sought employment in the service. The number of women in the Indian School Service grew dramatically (Figure 1). In 1869 women made up slightly less than 5 percent of the Indian Service (only 28 women out of a total of 625 employees).[3] By 1881 the service had more than doubled to 1,310 employees, while the percentage of women had tripled to 15 percent. And these numbers kept rising: in 1898 women made up 42 percent of all regular Indian Service employees and, remarkably, a full 62 percent of the 2,649 employees in the Indian School Service. Through 1910, the proportion of women held steady at around 55 to 60 percent of Indian School Service employees.[4] The available evidence indicates that most of these women were single. In 1885, just as the school system was beginning to hire women intensively and the only year for which the Indian Office kept statistics on sex and marital status, 65.5 percent of white female employees were single.[5] Compared to other federal positions, then, the Indian Service had an unusually high number of female employees.[6]

The importance of women in this agency is further demonstrated by the fact that the Indian Office appointed and promoted some of them to very high positions of authority. Alice Fletcher, for example, was appointed as special allotment agent in 1882 and served in that capacity for over a decade.[7] In 1883 Helen Hunt Jackson, reformer and author of *A Century of Dishonor* and

Ramona, was named special inspector and sent to investigate the condition of the Mission Indians in California. In 1889 Commissioner Morgan appointed Merial A. Dorchester as special agent in the Indian School Service. During the 1890s and into the twentieth century, many well-educated women came to occupy high-ranking positions in the School Service. For instance, Molly Gaither and Clara True, as well as others, served as superintendents of individual boarding schools. In 1898 a woman became the second-highest-ranking official in the Indian Office when Estelle Reel was appointed as the superintendent of Indian schools.[8]

When they took up federal employment, these white women became agents of the state and a part of the nation's colonial bureaucracy. They were there because the maternalist underpinnings of federal Indian policy viewed women as essential to accomplishing the goals of assimilation. Reformers and administrators had developed assimilation policy using a theoretical model of influence that made employees into "object lessons" who would teach through example. This use of suasion hewed closely to nineteenth-century ideas of women's sphere and literally required women to be on site in order to display proper female behavior. This combination of theory and practice meant that the personal characteristics of Indian Service employees mattered far more than in other federal agencies and led to the hiring of a unique group of civil servants.

This chapter argues that this distinctive employment pattern in the Indian Service requires us to rethink the development of the maternalist welfare state at the federal level and how it played out at the local level. It was in the Indian Service in the nineteenth century, not in the Women's and Children's Bureaus in the early twentieth century, that the federal government first incorporated large numbers of female employees as providers of social programs. The ranks of female Indian Service personnel dwarfed the number of women federally employed in the Women's and Children's Bureaus; by 1925, for example, the Indian Service counted more than 1,000 women among its personnel, while the Children's Bureau employed only 120 women and the Women's Bureau a mere 45.[9]

The sheer number of women involved in actually carrying out assimilation policy is essential to understanding the ways that the Indian Service worked as a maternalist agency. Scholars have argued that maternalist social programs have three particular attributes. First, they are designed with input from women's reform networks and female policy makers, who emphasize the important social place of women in the home, especially as mothers. Second, they are aimed at other women and children, who are perceived as in need of special guidance and nurturance. And third, they are administered by women, who are able to do the work of education and uplift by virtue of the special characteristics of their gender.[10]

Although scholars have discussed the formulation of assimilation policy and studied the lives of the people at whom it was directed, we know little about the thousands of women who did the day-to-day work of the Indian Service. This chapter focuses on the white women whom the government put on the reservations and in the schools as federal agents. It argues that the way these women understood their roles and performed their jobs was critical to the success or failure of assimilation.

FEMINIZING THE INDIAN SERVICE

The rapid growth of female employees in the Indian Service reflected changes particular to Indian policy as well as broader shifts within American society. Taking a job in the Indian Service gave single white women the ability to support themselves and choose their own path in life at a time when middle-class women were just beginning to enter the workforce in large numbers. But Indian Service work was different, because it often took women to very remote areas of the country. Their new economic and political circumstances often changed their own sense of who they were.

The work of assimilation had a number of characteristics that in nineteenth-century America were connected with women and women's sphere. As we saw in chapters 1 and 2, policy makers pushed for new programs that emphasized the role of the household and education in "civilizing" the Indians. In Victorian America, that kind of work was particularly associated with women's role as mothers, women's benevolent work, and female moral authority.[11] Moreover, advocates for female employment emphasized the importance of home interiors as sites of social reproduction. They contended that only women had the capacity to teach the childcare and homemaking skills essential to assimilation. Policy makers also linked assimilation with women's gendered qualities when they described the ideal Indian Service employee. Calling on employees to be selfless, loyal, and moral influences; to display "sympathy and gentleness";[12] and to lead the Indians by example, officials echoed the feminized language of moral suasion and moral authority. For example, General Samuel Armstrong, one of the most influential men in Indian education, used feminine qualities to describe the work: "It means drudgery and self-sacrifice; it means, too often, the devotion of but a few."[13] This emphasis on sacrifice and the heart—the language of women's benevolence and women's sphere—heightened an Indian Service employee's identity as female.

Other policy makers called specifically for female employees, arguing that they were better suited to the work of assimilation—that precisely because of their gender, they possessed the qualities necessary for moral suasion and moral authority. For example, in 1878, just as assimilation policy was being formulated, the Quaker church, which had a prominent role in work with Indians, passed a resolution calling for the creation of positions for female matrons: "The peculiar adaptation of women for this work has been too much overlooked in the efforts that have been made to civilize the Indians." The Quakers based their argument on maternalist claims about women's particular ability to do work for other women and for children, as well as their moral and sympathetic nature: "It has been found by experience that an enlightened and good woman, who will go among the Indian women, and manifest an interest in them and their children, can soon gain their confidence. She may instruct them in the proper care of their children, and in other household duties, and she will often find opportunities of imparting religious knowledge, which, being associated with deeds of love, will make a lasting impression." They envisioned female employees as good, enlightened, and religious—characteristics linked to white women in contrast to Indian women.[14]

Similarly, in their 1883 report, Helen Hunt Jackson and Abbott Kinney, special inspectors of the Indian Service for the state of California, endorsed white women as the most suitable employees for the work of assimilation, arguing that only women had the moral strength that was the foundation of civilization. They emphasized a woman's virtue as her shield and her power. "[I]n our judgment," they wrote, "only women teachers should be employed in these isolated Indian villages. There is a great laxity of morals among these Indians, and in the wild regions where their villages lie, the unwritten law of public sentiment, which in more civilized communities does so much to keep men virtuous, hardly exists. Therefore the post of teacher in these schools is one full of temptations and danger to a man." For them, a woman's authority in the service would stem not from her position as federal agent but rather from an innate moral authority. Jackson and Kinney went on to describe the particular feminine characteristics necessary for the job: "[W]omen have more courage and self-denying missionary spirit, sufficient to undertake such a life, and have an invaluable influence outside their schoolrooms. They go familiarly into the homes, and are really educating the parents as well as the children in a way that is not within the power of any man, however earnest and devoted he may be." In this formulation, women's positions rested on their inherent virtue, their "self-denying missionary spirit," and their power as women.[15]

Certainly, many white women, like Minnie Braithwaite, sought jobs in the Indian Service because they equated those positions with missionary work. Women had long been involved in organizing societies to support missionaries with prayers and supplies, and some of them had also gone out to do the work of evangelization themselves. The American foreign missionary movement was rapidly feminizing during the second half of the nineteenth century, with greater numbers of single women becoming missionaries. During the nineteenth century, women increasingly insisted that it was their duty as mothers and women to bring their moral authority to the public sphere. Their contributions and experiences in the Civil War had helped to extend their influence, making "the world their household." Ideas of perfectionism predominated, and thousands of missionaries went off to convert the "heathen." Moreover, because women were unable to become ministers, their missionary contribution had to consist of teaching, nursing, or social service. Many of the religious colleges emphasized the role of service to their students, and some "pointedly committed themselves to educating for foreign missionary service."[16]

As the foregoing quotations suggest, federal employment and missionary service often blended together for female employees. Many of them had first learned of the plight of the Indian through religious and reform organizations such as church missionary societies. Before she became an Indian Service teacher, for example, Corabelle Fellows was a missionary sponsored by the Women's National Indian Association (WNIA). She wrote that her decision to work among the Indians had been inspired by the lectures of another religious worker: "I greedily absorbed every word of the sermons on the missionary. The red man, as I had met him on the history page, seemed innately fine. He needed only a little showing how."[17] In 1884 Fellows moved to South Dakota to receive missionary training and instruction in the Sioux language at the Riggs Institute, but she was soon hired as a day-school teacher in the Indian Service. Indeed, the contract-school system encouraged that ambiguity, as teachers worked directly for religious organizations that contracted with the government to set up schools for Indian children. The missionary societies also helped blur the line. In its literature, the WNIA often conflated federal employees and its own field workers with whom it corresponded, referring to both as "mailbag missionaries."[18] In one publication, under the heading "Christian Teaching," Cornelia Taber, secretary of the Northern California Indian Association, included discussions of both federal field matrons and missionaries.[19]

Other women's motivations for taking Indian Service positions combined their sense of benevolence, their need for a paycheck, and their desire for adventure or just a change of scenery. The application of Miss Maggie Hogan of Donovan, Illinois, offers a good example of this constellation of reasons for entering the service. In 1889 she wrote seeking appointments for her whole family in the Southwest, explaining, "I am anxious to make arrangements for leaving this cold changeable climate for a milder one yet I desire a good paying position and my loved-ones with me that we may all work together to get homes and do good to others at the same time as we journey heaven ward."[20] Indeed, in contrast with the usual charge from historians of Indian policy that salaries were low and provided little material incentive, women's letters and memoirs tell a different story. A number of women very candidly admitted that the salaries available in the Indian Service motivated them to join. In her memoir, Gertrude Golden, who taught for seventeen years in the Indian Service, described leaving a job in a Michigan public school for a position at the Warm Springs Indian School in Oregon in 1901. "I was elated," she remembered. "Here was everything: a salary twice what I was getting, with the promise of an increase; a chance to study human types in which I had always been interested; opportunity to travel and see something of the country." And recalling their applications for Indian Service positions in 1909, Mary Ellicott Arnold and Mabel Reed remembered asking to be stationed in the "roughest field in the West."[21]

Thus, while ideas about women's moral authority initially opened jobs in the Indian Service to them, women were from the very start moving beyond that traditional public role in their quest to enter federal employment. While married women could rely on their husbands to apply for them (as we will see in the next chapter), single women had to negotiate the messy process of procuring federal employment themselves. While we do not usually think of women as among the hordes of office seekers who flooded into Washington, D.C., after presidential elections, they in fact actively participated in that process. Many women chose the seemingly less-political option of using benevolent and missionary societies as mediators between themselves and the Indian Office. For example, many women wrote to Amelia Quinton, national president of the WNIA, and asked her to personally present the commissioner with their request for a job. While this may not have appeared as patronage, it was: reformers like Quinton had close ties to the Indian Office, and many of them ran Indian schools under the contract system. These connections gave them great sway with federal administrators and sometimes gave them direct responsibility for staffing positions.[22]

Other women were less circumspect and employed the same kinds of openly partisan strategies used by male office seekers. Women sent requests directly to the commissioner of Indian affairs or conveyed their letters through male party operatives. Their correspondence was often direct and to the point, emphatically proclaiming their party loyalty. After President Cleveland's second election in 1892, for example, Mrs. Jemima A. Davenport of El Reno, Oklahoma, wrote to the commissioner asking for a matron position. She signaled her political allegiance by noting: "Have never made application for any Governmental position as the Antecedents of myself are Democratic." Her letter of recommendation from S. Harlow, also of El Reno, reiterated — after noting that she possessed the qualities necessary for the position — that Davenport was "a true Democrat and I don't think a better selection could be made."[23] Some women joined the crowds of male aspiring officeholders in Washington, D.C., and paid visits to the men who had the power to appoint them. Elaine Goodale Eastman, later an important author and powerful voice in Indian affairs, remembered that at the beginning of her career, she went to call on Commissioner John Atkins, "the whiskered politician from Tennessee." She suspected that he "was more amused than impressed by his naïve and youthful caller," who was proposing to create a "model day school" on the Sioux Reservation, but he hired her nonetheless.[24]

In seeking these positions, women entered into a new relationship with the federal government. Emphasizing their partisan loyalties and using politically connected go-betweens in an effort to obtain jobs demonstrated a keen political awareness that was as informed and strategic as that of their male counterparts. In addition, these women made aggressive claims about their political significance and the nature of their civic identity — this despite the fact that they would not be eligible to vote in national elections for another three decades.

Just as women began to use these strategies of personal connection to receive their positions, however, the nature of appointment was shifting from patronage to the merit system. After the Civil Service Reform Acts of 1892 and 1896 instituted the merit system for most Indian Service positions, prospective employees journeyed to the test sites, took an exam, and waited for the Civil Service Commission to inform them of their appointments.[25] Isabella C. Simmons of Cedar Rapids, Iowa, for example, took her exam in Chicago in 1893. Though offered a position at Fort Belknap, Montana, she turned it down and wrote to the commissioner of Indian affairs to negotiate for a position "nearer home in the Dakotas or Nebraska."[26] Like Simmons, many women continued to write directly to the commissioner, asking for information about the exams, Indian tribes, or the positions. Some asked more specific questions, including one woman who wrote to request that she be excused from the math section of the exam.[27] These elaborate bureaucratic procedures made the cottage industry of writing guidebooks for job seekers even more imperative. J. H. Soulé, the editor of the *United States Gazette*, periodically published a small booklet with a big title: *The United States Blue Book: A Register of Federal Offices and Employments in Each State and Territory and the District of Columbia with Their Salaries and Emoluments. Together with a manual of information and instruction for persons desiring public employment at the seat of government or elsewhere, showing who is eligible for appointment, the mode and form of application, by whom appointments are made or controlled, the tenure of office, etc., etc., etc.* As Soulé explained, the booklet was designed "to show, in plain and compact form, the patronage, working organization, and business of the Federal Government, and the means by which any deserving and capable aspirant for public employment may hope to share therein." He also noted that women "may be as freely appointed as men" and receive "like pay," but he added that the number of "suitable employments" was "limited."[28]

FROM PERSUASION TO POWER

As white women accepted their appointments and moved to their posts, the tension between the ideals they were supposed to represent as women and the federal authority they actually held became increasingly evident. Ideas about women's innate moral authority, especially their ability to fill maternal roles, had provided the opportunity for their employment in the Indian Service; but in reality, as agents of the federal government, they embodied the coercive power of the national state. This manifested itself in their power over Native people, both children and adults, who were considered "wards of the government." In this position, Indian Service employees could take a variety of actions with impunity, including entering Indians' homes, taking and punishing their children, and observing and reporting on their behavior. Women in the Indian Service had a more complicated relationship to their own colonial authority because of their sex. As a result, their new identities as federal agents required a renegotiation of gendered and racial understandings of power.

Policy makers were the first to recognize that the masculine attributes of state power were in tension with the more feminine attributes of the idealized Indian Service employee. They realized that a new alchemy of identity had occurred with the appointment of women to positions of federal authority in the service, and they struggled to find new language with which to describe those female employees. Sometimes their efforts led to curious linguistic constructions. For instance, one participant at the 1887 Lake Mohonk Conference described a woman who fit his ideal of a teacher. She was, he said, "a good strong Scotch woman, with a masculine intellect yet a woman's heart."[29] In other cases, the result was a variety of virtually hermaphroditic descriptions with classical or mythical allusions. One minister described a teacher as "a veritable female Caesar."[30] In 1908 the commissioner of Indian affairs used the terms "amazonian" and "virago-like"—both implying women of masculine strength—in order to reconcile their dual identities.[31] This descriptive confusion remained in the official rhetoric and, as we will see, in the minds of many of the female employees.

Estelle Aubrey Brown's story provides a good entry point into the way women renegotiated their identity upon entering the Indian Service. In her memoir, *Stubborn Fool*, Brown described her new federal identity as a stark contrast with the expectations for women that had constrained her at home. She had grown up in a "hamlet of the northern Adirondack foothills" in upstate New York. Her "stern father" was disappointed by "his lack of sons," and like the other members of the hamlet, he held a "smug assumption that women were not really members of the human race but merely appendages to it, to be wagged by men." Brown was different, however, as the title of her book suggests: she "wanted to do [her] own wagging." Moreover, she understood that this kind of liberty was conditioned upon economic independence. "I wanted a purse of my own," she wrote about her motivations for entering the teaching profession. Despite that prized economic freedom, Brown portrayed teaching in a county school as difficult work for low pay. Nor had she escaped male disregard for women: "For a girl, sixteen dollars a month was enough. More than one taxpayer thought it too much." Even her male students, like the boys with whom she had grown up, radiated a patriarchal attitude. "Every boy in my schoolroom owned a jackknife," she remembered, "and possessed the urge to relieve the building's barren surfaces with his own conception of phallic symbols."[32]

It was while teaching for the state of New York in 1900 that Brown heard about positions in the Indian Service. Like many others who eventually became employees, she knew little of the service or its duties: "No one had heard of the Indian Service. . . . What was it? Some kind of government missionary? I knew there were missionaries to the Indians, for as a child I had watched my mother's missionary society pack barrels of old clothes to send them."[33] Her only other knowledge of Indians came from newspaper coverage, especially of the Custer massacre. But to the adventurous Brown, who was tired of life in New York, this did not serve as a deterrent. Slightly tongue in cheek, she wrote: "For a girl, life in the hamlet was a dreary business that made even the threat of Indian atrocities in distant lands seem preferable."[34]

Even Brown, whose feminist sensibilities may have been sharpened in the years between her desire to leave home and the writing of her memoir, was not prepared for the novel identity and power her new job would entail. Years later, she constructed her narrative to highlight the contrast between the limited position of women in her hometown — even those women, like her mother, who represented female moral authority as members of missionary societies — and her power as a federal employee.

Brown described the very process of applying to the Indian Service as placing her in a liminal position between the role expected of her as a woman and the actions necessary to obtain federal employment. She initially sought a position as a clerk but was informed that the service rarely appointed women to that rank, especially if there were any eligible men. However, they told her that a great demand existed for kindergarten teachers. Although she was not trained in early childhood education, she took seven quick lessons from a woman who ran a private kindergarten in her home before taking the civil service examination in Burlington, Vermont. Brown was the only woman in the room during the two days of testing, and she passed despite her limited knowledge of kindergarten methods. She later wryly wrote: "The fact that I passed that examination was ample proof of its leniency."[35]

Like most white employees, Brown had a very limited knowledge of Indian tribes and Native cultures. Upon receiving her appointment to the Crow Creek Reservation in South Dakota, she finally told her father of her plans, to which he responded by pointing out to her that South Dakota was "Sioux" territory: "'Sioux. They're the ones that butchered Custer and his men.' I was startled. The Bureau's letter had not given the tribe I was to work with. I knew that there was a tribe of Crow Indians. I had thought that Crow Indians would be found at Crow Creek."[36] He advised her not to go, while simultaneously railing against a Republican administration that would send women out to the reservations. Thus, from the very beginning of her decision to take an Indian Service position, Brown found herself between worlds: she was the only woman in a room full of men, following the path of the U.S. military and provoking a political discussion with her decisions.

Brown's next step of accepting and taking up her appointment pushed her further into a highly unusual position for a woman. When she arrived at Crow Creek, she experienced a seminal moment in her life and self-understanding. On Brown's first day at the reservation, the agent went through the official paperwork with her. This consisted of verifying her letter of appointment, taking down her vital statistics, and administering the oath of office. While these steps were routine for the agent, they were transformative for Brown. This was a ceremonial conferral of a new and more powerful identity, one that she accepted with great satisfaction: "'Hold up your right hand.' A bit startled, I did so. When I lowered it I had sworn to support and defend the

Constitution against all enemies foreign and domestic, so help me God. In after years, as notary public at more than one agency, I was to administer that oath to other young entrants into the Indian Service, never without remembering my secret elation in that Crow Creek office. There I came of age in awareness, in the realization that I was an entity in my own right, no longer merely an appendage to someone else's life."[37]

Brown's "secret elation" was premised upon her own agency in choosing to take the oath as well as the substance of the oath itself, which was a powerful statement of allegiance, strength, and protection that legalized her role as an officer of the federal government as represented by the Constitution. Such an oath was rather an astounding act for a woman in 1900;[38] it endowed her with qualities that Americans thought of as male attributes: authority, power, and an implied identity as a citizen-soldier.[39]

Many female Indian Service employees vigorously insisted upon their federal identity in the field, perhaps because of their own insecurity in challenging men. Elaine Goodale Eastman recorded an incident in which her anxieties over appropriate behavior for men and women colored her response to a group of Indian men: "On our way back to the agency, we stopped by appointment at the school on White Clay Creek to meet in council 50 or more men of that district. They were in a thoroughly dissatisfied frame of mind, seemingly not without good reason. Whatever they may have thought of Washington sending a woman out to confer with them, their attitude was above criticism."[40] Eastman was uncomfortably aware of the incongruity of her situation, knowing that among white Americans, government negotiations were a male domain. Sending a woman to negotiate a political issue with a group of white men would have been perceived as a joke or an insult, and this assumption framed her expectations about how Native men may have perceived her. This example hints that the women themselves may have found their federal identities more useful when confronting men alone on the reservations. They compensated for the cultural disadvantages of being female by invoking their association with the federal government.

On the other hand, some white female employees were intimidated by the dual identities that their positions created for them. They did not feel comfortable making new claims to government power, and their conflicted identities left them feeling too weak to enforce their authority, either moral or federal. As a result, many women felt frustrated, confused, and disempowered as federal agents. For example, Marie Johnson, the field matron at Requa in Del Norte County, California, was angered by her inability to stop the sale of liquor to the Indians in her district. She described her difficulties in a letter to Cornelia Taber, secretary of the Northern California Indian Association:

"Breaking both state and federal laws is so evident and yet being a woman and known I cannot get all that the courts require."[41] Johnson argued that both her gender and her federal status stood in the way of the effective execution of her job. Her status as an outsider and government agent, while conferring authority upon her, also limited her ability to obtain the community's support. Her solution was to bring in a man who could work his way into local confidence in a way that she could not. "What would it cost," she asked, "to hire a man to gather evidence? He need not be a professional detective, as any man of tact could get all of the information needed."[42]

These women were not the only ones who felt this way. Some male agents also disparaged the practice of endowing women with federal authority. In 1911 the agent at Hoopa Valley reported on the work of Mrs. I. M. Hamilton, a field matron at Requa and the wife of a local rancher. He pointed out that she represented federal authority at a post far from the agency but that, as a woman, she had no means to wield that authority. "About the only federal supervision attempted over these Indians has been through a field matron stationed at Requa for some years," he wrote. "[H]er efforts are and must be confined largely to relieving individual needs among the women folks, and in reciting rather harrowing tales of the evil conditions prevailing, which she is powerless to control. This is an undertaking by no means suited to a woman, and to so entrust it means bringing federal authority somewhat into ridicule and disrespect."[43] This report should have reflected poorly on him, as Mrs. Hamilton was performing precisely the duties the Indian Office assigned to field matrons, but the agent was clearly uninterested in supporting her.[44]

In a more humorous but equally revealing narrative, Mary Ellicott Arnold and Mabel Reed, lifelong companions and field matrons among the Karuk in Weitchpec a few miles downriver from Requa, described the cold shoulder they received from local whites, who looked with suspicion on them as outsiders in the community: "We were beginning to feel very much alone in this country. When people looked at us their faces were blank. They were not openly unfriendly . . . but if anything was really unsafe we had a feeling that no one would warn us."[45] Arnold and Reed came to a solution that involved semantics and adjusting to the expectations of locals. "Mabel called to me," Arnold wrote. "'I've been thinking it over. Schoolmarms! A nice familiar occupation that everyone understands. It's bad enough for us to be women. No one thinks much of women in this country. And no one likes them. And missionaries are worse. We simply can't be missionaries. And government agents are worst of all.'"[46] Reed and Arnold used cultural ideas about women's roles to elide the fact that they were federal agents and thereby avoid the negative connotations that identity carried. In their case, the women were both frustrated by and able to manipulate their identities because of their unique position as female federal agents. This flexible situation arose because the federal government had never before incorporated women and women's work into its bureaucracy in quite this way, and no one—not the employees, the policy makers, or the public—had a fixed idea of exactly how it should be done. This uncertainty should be read alongside the wider post–Civil War expansion of the federal government, in which there were new federal responsibilities and much room for experimentation.

Female employees' newfound power was premised upon the subordination of Indian people. In accepting their appointments and swearing the oaths of allegiance, the female employees entered the colonial administration of the United States. Underlying the reservation system was the constant threat of military violence as a means of controlling Native populations.[47] The employees of the Indian Service were protected and empowered by that threat. As much as policy makers might have desired that Indian people would come to assimilation freely and of their own will, officials were not averse to using force to make them choose assimilation. Corabelle Fellows offers an excellent example of how female personnel utilized the threat of state-sanctioned violence to force Native people to comply with their instructions. She initially went to work on the Cheyenne River Reservation in South Dakota as a missionary. Yet when she was hired by the Indian Service to work as a day-school teacher at Cut Meat Creek on that same reservation, she revealed the extent to which even women empowered by the idea of moral suasion came to rely upon their federal authority. In her memoir, Fellows repeatedly revealed her reliance on federal power despite her claims that Indians were converted by her good example. For instance, she described her attempts to convert the Indians of Cut Meat Creek to civilization through the planting of a demonstration garden. In language that policy makers would have appreciated, she depicted her personal example as the means she used to discredit the power of the medicine man and tribal tradition: "Here was a small white woman in a very large hat, unlike anything in the uniform of the medicine man, and she was making as many beans come out of a little piece of ground. . . . The medicine man was second to me after that, and all of the Cut Meat Indians put complete faith in all I said."[48] As she went on with her recollections, however, she inadvertently revealed that the Cut Meat Creek community did not put their faith in her. In fact, she constantly had to draw on her access to the state's coercive power, often threatening people with time in "the guardhouse" to make them obey her.

Fellows also demonstrated the Cut Meat Creek community's attempt to incorporate specific aspects of white culture even as they rejected the totalizing project of cultural assimilation. She narrated one story that she saw as an amusing incident to be told at the expense of Yellow Hat, the man she called the chief of Cut Meat Creek. Instead, she revealed the true foundations of her authority in that community. Yellow Hat, she wrote, was constantly "begging" her for school supplies. One day, he came to her and asked for help.

> He wanted, he said, to "know what is horse in English." By the time I had given him the English words for all the common things about camp he had quite a lengthy list. At his request I had written the information down for him. He went away, grunting contentedly. . . . The next day there were no children at school. . . . I went to the Government Indian police and sent him with a message to Yellow Hat. The message he brought back [was that] Yellow Hat would henceforth teach the children all their fathers thought needful, that such was not the business of "two little white squaws." I walked down to Yellow Hat's hut alone. Inside I saw a blackboard. He had the chalk and pencils he had begged from me. His "book" from which he had taught the children that morning for an hour was the paper list of English words I had written for him. "Every morning," I said to him in his own tongue, "when the flag is raised at my school, the Great Father in Washington commands that every child shall come to school to be taught. If you refuse to let them, in three days you will be taken to the guard house." He returned not a word. . . . Next morning the children came back.[49]

Fellows asserted her authority by invoking multiple symbols of the federal government's power: the flag; an Indian Service policeman (with his uniform); her school building; the personage of the Great Father; and the seat of colonial power, Washington, D.C. Moreover, when Yellow Hat tried to counter her with a gendered argument—that the prerogative of the children's fathers should override the authority of "two little white squaws"—she rejected it. She reminded him that her identity as a woman was superseded by her identity as a federal agent, that her command was the command of the Great Father, and that therefore she could order him imprisoned.

This was not the only time Fellows used the threat of coercive power. She often disagreed with the people of the camp regarding her running of the school. In each incident, she relied on the power she could wield as a federal agent to quash the community's resistance. For example, one day she punished a pupil by hitting him, an action almost unthinkable in Lakota culture. When the father complained, she refused to compromise: "Wednesday, High Bear came in person. 'Itaska, winyn nasula' ('White-faced woman has no brains'), he said sullenly. 'I am sent by the Great Father at Washington to teach the children,' I replied. . . . 'The way of the Great Father is not your way,' I said."[50] Likewise, she recalled angering all the men of the camp by implementing the federal policy of assigning each child a surname: "I nearly precipitated civil war when I attempted to call each child in the family by the father's name. The men stormed the schoolroom, wagging their heads fiercely and vociferously repeating, 'Hecca tu sni!' ('This is all a mistake!') I had to talk fast about the Great Father at Washington and mention my own relative who sat under the same lodge skin with the Great Father and made laws concerning their names."[51] In all of these instances, Fellows reminded them of her position as representative of the federal government and thus her authority; and in the latter example, she even used her male relatives who held high office in Washington to identify herself with Congress and the "Great Father." Although Indian women also confronted white female employees, Fellows chose to discuss moments when she faced down the challenges of Indian men, thus highlighting the power white women gained through their federal authority. In doing so, she implicitly rejected the ideals of female moral authority, despite her assertions to the contrary.

We have only hints as to how Yellow Hat and the children's fathers might have described these incidents. It appears that they did want their children to learn those things that "their fathers thought needful," such as reading, writing, and a practical English vocabulary. These skills would be necessary in order to participate in further political negotiations with the federal government or in market relations with their neighbors.[52] Their reaction indicates that it was not the education that they resisted, but rather the cultural impositions that accompanied it. Although not Lakota, historian Rupert Costo (Cahuilla) had similar thoughts on the issue: "After all, the Indians were not and are not fools; we are always ready to improve our condition. But assimilation . . . with a complete loss of our identity and our culture, was another thing entirely." Regardless of the Indians' desires, however, Fellows's politicized white female identity dominated their racialized male identities.[53]

While few white female employees recognized that assimilation rested on coercion, Native people understood its foundation in violence from the start. Being "kidnapped" by government police was the way Irene Stewart (Navajo) described her entry into the Indian Office's school system. Parents at Isleta Pueblo also used the language of imprisonment when they referred to their children who were being kept at the Albuquerque Indian School as *cautivos*, or captives. Many other Native children and parents had correspondingly traumatic memories of their families being wrenched apart as federal offi-

cials implemented assimilation programs, especially the child-removal policies that filled the boarding schools.[54]

Policy makers preferred persuading parents to send their children to
school, and not all children were forcibly taken from home, but many were.
Native parents often resisted the removal of their children, the destruction
of their cultures, and the casual violence inherent in this policy of tearing
apart their families. They took desperate measures, such as hiding their children when officials came; some buried their children in sand with breathing
straws, sent them into the bushes around their homes, or rolled them up in
rugs. In other cases, administrators bribed or coerced them with promises of
food and health care, the denial of the family's rations, or even the presence
of the military. Some officials undermined parental authority by taking advantage of children's curiosity about new experiences like train rides or fresh
fruit.[55] Although Native parents were seldom able to protect their children
from all aspects of government policy, their resistance destabilized the strategy of intimate colonialism, which never operated as smoothly in practice as
it did in the conference rooms at Lake Mohonk or in the halls of the Indian
Office headquarters in Washington, D.C.

In the schools, Indian students understood quite clearly that policy makers hoped to replace their mothers with female Indian Service employees,
and they generally rejected the idea. Many former students carried traumatic
memories of harsh physical and psychological treatment experienced at the
hands of their superiors—treatment that gave the lie to the Indian Office's
language of affection. One Ojibwa girl who had attended the Haskell Institute in Lawrence, Kansas, summed up her experiences with her matron with
this question: "Ever hear somebody say, 'All Indians look alike to me, I can't
tell them apart?'"[56] Many former students remembered their school days as
being punctuated by beatings, extreme manual labor, confinement without
food, and public humiliation. Everyday classroom experiences were often
infused with casual abuse from white teachers. Irene Stewart recalled that at
the Fort Defiance School in Arizona, "The teachers were mean and strict. We
were always being punished for not knowing our lessons. Once I was slapped
in the face for gazing out the window." School records of multiple runaway
efforts and attempted arsons further emphasize the students' intense resistance and unhappiness.[57]

Certainly, some children did form strong bonds with their teachers and
matrons, but most denied the premise that strangers could replace their
own families or communities—even if the employees had good intentions.[58]
Tsianina Lomawaima interviewed alumni of Chilocco Boarding School in
Oklahoma, and many emphasized precisely this point. Looking back, Vivian,

a Choctaw alumna, said that "they tried to take the place of your home life but they can't." Noreen (Potawatomi) laughed while recalling that "the only time you saw your, talked with your matron was in a disciplinary area, you see, so you didn't *love* your matron." Albert, a Cherokee boy, recognized one of the biggest problems with substituting employees as surrogate parents: the model was based on the formation of individual relationships, but the schools were industrial in scale. "I won't say she [the matron] was motherly because you can't hardly mother three or four hundred boys at once," Albert observed, "but, she was kind, but she was firm."[59] Although policy makers hoped that "home life" at the schools would never be sacrificed "to the more or less heartless necessities of institutional requirements," it often was. Moreover, the attitudes and actions of many white female employees bore little resemblance to the nurturant ideal of assimilation theory.[60]

CONCLUSION

Female employees were absolutely essential to the work of assimilation; the federal government placed women at the very center of its "civilizing" project. Not only did white women offer a model of proper domesticity on the reservations and in the schools, but they also embodied the ideas about personal influence and moral suasion to which administrators had pinned their hopes for a quick transformation of Native communities. The tremendous number of women in the Indian Service was unprecedented and the direct result of the maternalist strategy of attempting to change every aspect of Native households, especially the drive to transform Native women and girls into the vehicles for perpetuating "civilization" in their communities. The feminization of the agency also represented a major experiment in federal governance: for the first time, the national government brought large numbers of women and numerous women's issues directly into its bureaucracy. It is no coincidence that these policies were devised as a way to incorporate the colonized populations of the nation's periphery—a development that exemplifies how the federal government increasingly used the American West to experiment with new methods of governance.

As women sought jobs in the Indian Service, their actions immediately generated a tension between the apolitical moral authority they supposedly embodied as females and the political nature of their positions. The very act of applying for and accepting appointments as federal employees involved them in political patronage, partisan dealing, and administrative maneuvering—areas not traditionally considered part of women's sphere. Newly endowed with these political identities, female employees immediately experienced tension between proper womanly behavior and the authority they could command as federal agents. The novelty of their positions left them without a precedent because no one knew what it meant to have female federal agents, and as a result, there was a great deal of confusion as to how they were supposed to act and how others should regard them.

This tension was most strikingly illustrated in their relations with their Native wards, interactions that revealed the contours of colonial power and slowly moved women into a new relationship with the state. The women and the policy makers who sent them to the reservations hoped to use women's powers of moral suasion rather than force to enact change in Native communities; indeed, this was the major rationale for employing white women in the first place. Indians, however, refused to play their assigned role of malleable subjects in this colonial fantasy. Their resistance forced white female employees to resort to threats and use of state power, thereby tearing off the mask of noncoercive assimilation and exposing the policy's inherent violence. It also began to cast doubt upon the optimistic notion that the process of assimilation would be rapid and its instrumentalities temporary.

4

Seeking the Incalculable Benefit of

a Faithful, Patient Man and Wife

MARRIED EMPLOYEES IN THE INDIAN SERVICE

When prospective employees opened their letters of appointment from the commissioner of Indian affairs, they learned which position they had been offered, where it was located, and the date they were expected to report for duty. Many letters also included brief directions to their new post. But the three or four concise sentences typed out on the page rarely prepared them for the actual journey. The first leg usually involved a train ride, during which they might carefully ration a basket of food meant to see them through their long trip. Some might transfer to a smaller rail line that would take them to a local station. Upon their arrival, a few found themselves close to their new school or agency. Many others faced a journey of a day or more over the sandy soil of a short-grass prairie, up steep mountain passes or around dry arroyos, some of them bouncing on the hard wooden seat of a wagon and others clinging to the back of a horse or a mule. Most ended their journey when they arrived at the scattered array of wooden buildings that comprised the reservation agency, but day-school personnel continued on to their small cottage and classroom, which were often located in a remote corner of the reservation (Illustrations 4.1 and 4.2).[1]

In the most distant posts, the Office of Indian Affairs intended its employees to serve as examples of "civilized" living in places where no white communities existed; it also needed to retain them in their isolated locations. To accomplish both of these goals, the agency turned to hiring married couples. In this way, the same experiment in building a workforce based on influence, example, and suasion that brought thousands of single white women

Boys Building in which
I am quartered as the mess is
full.)

ILLUSTRATION 4.1. Postcard of the Tomah Indian School. The living conditions of Indian Service employees varied from cramped rooms in small cottages to dormitories in boarding-school buildings. Compensation for regular employees included fuel and furnished rooms. This teacher was quartered in the boys' building. Also note the X on the left upstairs window where the writer wrote: "My school room." (From the author's collection)

to Indian country also filled the ranks of the Indian Service with married couples, both white and Native. (The growing number of Native couples in the service shared certain family considerations with their white colleagues; their race-specific concerns will be discussed in the next chapters.) This hiring pattern was extremely unusual at a time when married, middle-class women in the general population seldom worked for wages outside of their homes and spouses of any class rarely worked together except in their own households.[2] The employment of married couples in the service has gone largely unnoticed by historians, and those who note it at all too often dismiss it as nepotism.[3] But to ignore this phenomenon is to overlook an important window into federal Indian policy.

The Indian Office's hiring of spouses clearly reveals the results of a project of intimate colonialism. Policy makers hoped to position these employees symbolically as federal fathers and mothers to their Native wards. Once again, administrators predicated their hiring strategies upon particular assumptions, this time on the workings of white households; and once again, the differences between those assumptions and the reality of life on the

ILLUSTRATION 4.2. Employees' quarters (left) at the Zuni Day School, 1924. Married Indian Service personnel were especially attentive to their living arrangements. A report noted that "these are considered the best quarters for the day school employees in this district," probably because each of the "four small apartments" was "furnished entirely separate from the others with modern plumbing." Employees with children favored dwellings like these over the oft-provided single dormitory rooms. (Courtesy of the National Archives and Records Administration, Washington, D.C.)

reservations had a major impact on how employees put assimilation policy into practice. As the Indian Office struggled to bring its theories into alignment with reality, it demonstrated some flexibility and willingness to experiment in adjusting its procedures to fit the needs of its personnel, especially its white employees. These examples offer a vivid depiction of how Indian Service workers meaningfully influenced the shape of the nation's colonial bureaucracy.

CREATING A WORKFORCE OF COUPLES

The number of married couples in the Indian Service increased rapidly at the end of the nineteenth century, dramatically altering the demographics of the agency. Couples held positions throughout the various assimilation programs. In the boarding schools, married men often served as superintendents, while their wives worked as teachers or matrons. Out of the ninety-one boarding schools that reported in 1893, for example, forty-eight of them—over half—had superintendents whose wives were also employed at the schools.[4] Similarly, by 1898 the commissioner of Indian affairs had officially sanctioned the policy of hiring married couples in the day schools. That year, he observed that day schools were "presided over by a faithful, patient man and wife, as teacher and housekeeper, [who] provide a method of instruction for Indian boys and girls of incalculable benefit to the system."[5] Between 1889 and 1905, the number of husbands and wives employed in the reservation day schools rose markedly, as did the number of schools themselves (the reasons for which will be discussed in part III). In 1889 the federal government ran fifty-one day schools, seven of which were staffed by a spousal team.[6] By 1895 both the number of day schools and the number of employees with conjugal bonds had more than doubled: the government expanded its operations to 110 day schools and hired couples to staff 39 of them, or 35 percent of the total.[7] In 1900 the number of day schools increased to 128, and married employees had almost doubled their representation again, teaching in 64 percent of them (making it the peak year for married couples).[8] Over the next few years, the number of employed spouses hovered at around 60 percent in the day schools.[9]

For both white and Indian personnel, the number of married women in the Indian Service greatly outdistanced their proportion in the national workforce. For example, in 1885, a year in which the commissioner of Indian affairs recorded the marital status of female employees, one-third of the white women were married. Statistics for Native women followed a similar pattern but with a slightly higher percentage of married women (36.7 percent). Nationally, by contrast, only 14 percent of the female labor force was married in 1890, and few of those were middle-class women.[10]

These numbers beg an obvious question: why did the Indian Service have such an unusual workforce? To find the answer, we must ascertain how the employment of married couples fit the agendas of both the people who applied for service positions and the Indian Office itself. Couples eagerly sought the positions made available for them by the Indian Office's policies, and their determination should remind us that the desires and goals of employees played a key role in developing this unique workforce. While married employees demonstrated a wide range of reasons for requesting positions in the Indian Service, most sought steady income for their families. A number of husbands made it clear in their applications that they wanted appointments for themselves and their wives, indicating that they approved of their spouses working to increase their total household earnings. The economic benefits of spousal employment could be substantial for those families. When Charles

H. Groover of Leavenworth, Kansas, applied for a school superintendency in 1889, he also appended the application of his wife, Sarah, for the position of matron or assistant teacher at the same school.[11] That same year, when John Spencer McCain was asked to take up his previous position as the superintendent of the Siletz School in Oregon, he agreed to return only on the condition that his wife, who had previously served with him as assistant teacher, be reappointed as the matron;[12] notably, the matron position paid $500, twice as much as the assistant teacher position.[13] In 1900 Albert and Edith Kneale enjoyed a substantial pay increase when Mr. Kneale left his job as a public school principal in upstate New York for a teaching position at Day School No. 10 on the Pine Ridge Reservation in South Dakota. "The salary mentioned [in the job offer] was the same as I had been receiving, namely, $600 per year," he remembered, but the appointment also furnished his wife with an annual salary of $300, thus markedly increasing their household income.[14] Many of the applicants for the positions of superintendent and teacher had previously worked in public school systems, and the salaries and the regularity of work in the Indian Service offered an attractive incentive, since short school terms and the notorious stinginess of county school boards often translated into low pay for public school teachers.[15]

Despite these incentives, these men were unusual in an era when the elevation of the male breadwinner and the ideal of a family wage held deep cultural sway. Much of middle-class ideology and status revolved around the mother staying in the home. At the same time that these couples sought joint employment in the Indian Service, for example, labor unions were demanding that men be paid enough for their wives to avoid having to work. In her study of federal clerks in Washington, D.C., Cindy Aron found that struggling middle-class families preferred to send their unmarried daughters—not mothers—out to work in government positions to shore up their class status. Generally, only very desperate families would send a wife or mother out to work for wages, as the nonwaged position of a woman in the home was the hallmark of middle-class respectability. Married women did engage in demanding and complicated benevolent work, but such pursuits were generally predicated on a male breadwinner's salary being sufficient to support his wife's unwaged labor.[16]

While men often wanted their wives to work in the Indian Service, it is difficult to determine from their applications the extent to which the married women shared that same desire. Certainly, many single women sought positions, implying that other women did so as well, though wives may have had different considerations. When Charles Groover applied in 1889, he noted that his wife had served as a matron and taught at the Pottawatomie Boarding School for a year and a half, though he himself had no previous Indian Service experience. His wife may have suggested that they apply based on her familiarity with the work. Albert Kneale reported that both he and his wife, Edith, accepted their appointments with a sense of adventure. During the train ride from New York to South Dakota, he wrote, "we kept our noses plastered against the window. It was all new, all exciting, all most wonderful."[17] Not all women, however, responded as enthusiastically to their husbands' decisions. George Nock secured positions for himself and his wife, Mary, at the remote but well-paying Colorado River Agency in Arizona in 1887. Mary eventually agreed to move her family from their home in Virginia, but George recalled that "the words she used [to agree] cut like a two edged sword." It was not until well into their cross-country train journey that Mary relented, and George seemed relieved to write that "she was the same merry companion that she had been before the trip was thought of."[18] The difference of opinion between Mary Nock and Edith Kneale may have reflected the fact that the newlywed Kneales had no children, whereas the Nocks had two young sons who accompanied them to Arizona.

The eagerness of couples to join the Indian Service corresponded with the government's ideological and practical reasons for hiring them. Assimilation policy's ideological grounding in marriage, gender systems, and family set the stage for the hiring of spouses. Employees wanted dual salaries and good positions, while the Indian Office wanted a stable and efficient workforce. From the standpoint of policy makers, married employees offered the ideal way to present model families for Indians to imitate in their own domestic relations. By adopting this strategy, the Indian Office seems to have been drawing on the long-standing missionary procedure of hiring husbands and wives. As early as 1815, the American Board of Commissioners for Foreign Missions had recommended married missionaries because they offered a model of the Christian family and also brought white Christian women into the field to work with the non-Christian women whom male missionaries often could not approach.[19] The Indian Service, as we have seen, used the language of religious work to describe its employees, as did the commissioner who proudly proclaimed in 1899: "The little day school . . . is a center from which the missionary spirit of a faithful teacher and his wife may be exerted upon old and young."[20] Although much of the Indian Office's familial rhetoric was metaphorical—schools were homes, employees were parents, Indians were children or wards, and the U.S. President was the Great Father—here was one place where its familial model could be made more concrete.

This was unusual within the broader federal bureaucracy. While Aron's study found that married women did work as clerks in Washington, D.C., their presence within the federal workplace was frowned upon because of concerns that they were taking jobs from more deserving workers. During the 1870s, various departments prohibited the employment of more than one family member, though as a whole the government did not specifically exclude married women from employment. Aron asserts that two-thirds of the female clerks were single and many others were widowed, but she also reveals that some married women went so far as to lie about their status (claiming to be single or widowed) in order to receive appointments.[21]

Significantly, the only other federal agency that was similar in terms of the marital status and racial make-up of its workforce was the Philippine Civil Service Commission, founded in 1900. The personnel of this agency— whose goals were similarly colonial—mirrored that of the Indian Service. Not only were Filipinos given preferential hiring treatment,[22] but the Civil Service Commission also explicitly stated that it favored women married to employees over single women when filling its positions. The 1915 *Manual for Examinations* for the Philippine Service, for example, stated: "Unless otherwise specially announced [women] will not be admitted to this examination unless they are the wives, immediate relatives, or fiancées of men examined for teacher or assistant, or appointed to or already employed in the Philippine Service; or unless they have had special experience in teaching of domestic science and home economy." This policy was partially a reflection of a different bureaucratic structure in which white Americans primarily served in supervisory posts (it was also a practical way to reduce expenses), but it is striking that both colonial branches of the federal government had similar policies regarding personnel.[23]

The decision of policy makers to hire married women does not seem to have been primarily motivated by efforts to save money. If it had been, it seems safe to assume that married women would have been paid less than their single counterparts in the same positions. Indian Service salary records indicate that this was not the case, and payment varied depending upon the school or agency at which an employee was stationed. Nonetheless, there were other practical considerations that encouraged it. The Office of Indian Affairs did tend to hire married women to fill what were already lower-paying positions; for example, the day-school posts of teacher and housekeeper— jobs often staffed by a married couple—paid less than the boarding-school equivalents of teacher and matron. The difference in salary may have been justified by the fact that boarding-school employees were expected to serve around the clock, but it may also have been influenced by the marital status of most day-school employees.[24]

The Indian Office certainly did find that hiring couples was a way to attract employees and enhance family salaries while also staffing isolated positions. Day-school teachers and instructional farmers serving in outlying areas both worked with housekeepers, and the Indian Office assumed that their wives would fill those positions. Their location far from white communities and the government's desire to ensure the presence of female role models meant that it made sense to hire the wives of employees who were already on-site rather than to try to find others. In this way, the offer of two salaries does seem to have been one way the service was able to attract employees.

But the Indian Office was also learning to respond to the actions and desires of its employees and prospective employees. It valued stability in its workforce, believing that influential relationships between employees and their wards could only be developed through long terms of service and employee tenure. In spite of this aim, the service had a perennial problem of employees transferring and people turning down their appointments. This made it willing to cater to the desires of applicants, including those who pressed for spousal hires. In 1893 a reporter for the *New York Evening Post* investigated complaints by the commissioner of Indian affairs that the new Civil Service rules had resulted in "delays and hitches" in the manning of the Indian Service. The reporter found that the majority of people declining their positions were women, particularly those appointed to matron positions (nineteen out of the forty-nine selected as eligible). "Most of the cases where matrons have hesitated to accept," he concluded, "have been where their husbands were eligible for appointments as superintendents, and had not yet been reached in the certifications. These women naturally desired to be assigned [to the] same schools with their husbands, and rather than be separated, declined their first offers with a view to a later certification to a place to which both could go."[25]

The Indian Office apparently responded with a greater willingness to hire spouses. By 1903 it had institutionalized a policy of exempting superintendents' wives from competitive civil service exams for matron or teacher positions. Other than Native personnel, these women were the only employees allowed to take a noncompetitive exam. And like Indian employees, they were exempted from the age requirements of the positions.[26] But the problem of a turbulent workforce remained, and the Indian Office continued to look to spousal hiring as a solution. As late as 1911, the commissioner of Indian affairs was still complaining about the "large number of transfers, resignations, and declinations of appointment." He noted that couples' desire for a dual income offered one possible defense against such turmoil.[27] In this way, the cumulative actions of employees (and potential employees) as they sought to make government work more amenable to their needs helped re-shape the service.

ASSUMPTIONS ABOUT WOMEN'S DOMESTIC SKILLS

In developing its new workforce, the Indian Office made a number of assumptions about how white households worked—assumptions that were not always aligned with reality. Sometimes the responses of Indian Service employees revealed the agency's assumptions to be illogical or faulty, and in many cases administrators were forced to adjust accordingly. One particular point of tension involved their understanding of white women's domestic skills. Indian Office officials correctly understood that gender roles were teachable rather than inherent, and that domestic skills had economic value. However, they misunderstood the nature of domestic work and failed to appreciate the enormity of the tasks they set before female employees, especially the difficulties of creating bourgeois households under rural conditions.

Policy makers assumed that white women would have training in domestic skills by virtue of their identities as women and, particularly, as wives. If they ran their own households or had witnessed their mothers doing so, the logic went, they would surely be qualified to teach other women to do the same. As one employee later remarked, policy makers believed that "any good woman could teach every good woman what all good women should know."[28]

The Indian Office initially hired women for many of the positions after doing no more than asking them about their own experiences as homemakers and their personal character. In 1890, for example, the School Service application asked women: "Are you accounted a first-class housekeeper, cook, or seamstress[?]" Applicants were also required to sign a statement that emphasized dedication and moral conduct, with phrases such as "firm, kind, affable, considerate, and careful . . . dignified, even-tempered, above reproach in personal character . . . earnest, conscientious, patient, persevering."[29] It was only when these positions came under the oversight of the Civil Service Commission that employees began to be tested in their fields. As the Indian Office expected, many women pointed to their own experiences with sewing or cooking for their families and raising their own children. Notably, some Native women also claimed in their applications that their mothers had taught them their domestic skills. While this reinforced the Indian Office's idea that women could teach household skills because of their gender, it also undermined the office's assumption that Indian women did not teach such skills to their daughters and undercut the logic of assimilation.[30] But this assumption most often applied to white employees.

The Kneales, for instance, had no idea what Edith's housekeeping position entailed when they received their letter of appointment in 1900; Albert Kneale later recalled that there was "nothing being said concerning the duties of the position." It was not until they reached Day School No. 10 on the Pine Ridge Reservation in South Dakota that they learned what it involved.[31] For Edith Kneale and others in her position, those duties were substantial. At the day schools and even at smaller boarding schools, the job of a female teacher or matron required that she cook for all the students while instructing the girls in food preparation, helping them create their wardrobes while teaching them how to sew, and bathing them while informing them of sanitary practice.[32] This obviously was a great deal of work, and even if all women had been well prepared to perform it, the sheer weight of it may have overwhelmed them.

Many of the women, however, were ill prepared to perform the domestic work that the Indian Office assumed they would, in part because it seemed outside of their job descriptions. For example, Luther Standing Bear (Oglala Lakota), a day-school teacher himself, depicted a white female teacher critically in his autobiography. He described her as "smart enough in books" but completely ignorant about domestic skills since "she did not even know how to keep house." As a teacher of housekeeping, she was a complete failure. "At that time," Standing Bear wrote, "the Government furnished the Indians ginghams by the bolt, and the teacher was supposed to show the Indian girls how to make their own clothes. . . . But this is the method she used in making the first dresses for the girls: The girl would stoop over; then the teacher would roll the whole bolt of gingham over her head, and with a piece of chalk mark the outlines of the girl's body, after which the goods were cut out. When the dress was finished, it was a most peculiar piece of dressmaking."[33] His description hints at how sharply the expectations of Indian Office administrators diverged from the abilities of the employees. In the teacher's defense, she may have assumed that her job was to be limited to academic instruction, a role in which Standing Bear noted she was very proficient. However, on the reservation, her position also required her to be able to instruct the students in domesticity, something she was by no means prepared to do.

Similarly, when Albert Kneale and his second wife, Etta, arrived at their post on the Uintah and Ouray Agency in Utah in 1914, Etta had to learn a number of new skills, including how to cook. Her previous missionary experience both in urban areas and on the Winnebago Reservation made her seem the perfect Indian Service candidate, but throughout the duration of those positions, her domestic needs had been satisfied in a very different economy and environment. Her husband recalled: "Etta had many new and, at first, rather startling experiences. Aside from the time spent among the Winnebagos, her life had been spent in some city—in school, in the Moody Bible Institute, working in some mission. Even at Winnebago she was but one of a large force of men and women. When she had eaten, she invariably sat down at a table and the table was always plentifully supplied with food." Nor was Etta's experience unusual in the Indian Service boarding schools. In 1913 Jennie Burton wrote to the Indian Office to question her reappointment as a seamstress instead of a teacher. She noted that "it is true you offered me a position as seamstress; but having passed all my life since the age of fourteen, in connection with schools, colleges, and educational institutions, and particularly as I hire my own sewing done, how could I conscientiously undertake the making of garments and the direction of Indian girls under that work?"[34]

Other women found that their training was too advanced for the rural conditions of reservation schools. Minnie Braithwaite remembered that Mrs. Mary Foss, the newly appointed laundress at the Yuma School, expected to find modern laundry facilities and not the outdated outdoor equipment used at the school. Braithwaite recorded in her memoir her coworkers' reaction to a letter Foss sent ahead: "'Is the laundry run by steam or by electricity? How many assistants shall I have and how many workers shall I be allowed?' There was a stunned silence when this was read aloud, after which raucous hilarity exploded among the employees. There, out in the open on the canyon floor . . . stood the twelve washing machines. Water for these hand-run machines was heated in one large iron caldron and in five-gallon coal-oil cans, in which came the kerosene that filled our lamps."[35] These examples suggest that the female personnel had been hired to teach Indian girls and women to participate in a household economy in which the employees themselves did not live.[36]

The distance between policy makers' idealized domesticity and the female employees' qualifications lay in real-world socioeconomic change. Many of the female Indian Service employees were not prepared for the conditions on the reservations because they had come from households that were closely connected to the market—both a domestic labor market and a market for household goods. In urban areas, the market economy had for some time been offering substitutes for women's domestic work. Women could buy ready-made clothing from new department stores or pay a dressmaker. They could eat at the new lunch counters or hire a cook.[37] On the reservations, domestic servants were not part of the ideology of assimilation, nor were supplies easily available. As a result, many of the women were unprepared for the rigors of this work and came away frustrated by the sheer amount of labor that their positions required.[38]

Indian Office administrators slowly came to recognize that something was wrong because assimilation was not taking place as quickly as their models had suggested it would. They eventually revised their personnel requirements to emphasize professional training (as will be addressed in part III). This may also have had an impact on the civil service exams required of women holding these positions. For example, the exam for matron in 1900 tested the applicant on domestic economy, the keeping of accounts, and nursery management, while by 1915 the exam was more detailed.[39] One scholar has noted that by the 1920s, the Civil Service Commission began to require that women applying for seamstress positions demonstrate their ability to sew as part of the exam. Applicants were asked to bring "needle, scissors, thread, and an 8-by-12-inch piece of white muslin to the examination, to demonstrate hand sewing."[40]

ASSUMPTIONS ABOUT EMPLOYEES' CHILDREN

A more striking example of the contrast between the government's theoretical formulas about its employees and their actual experiences stemmed from administrators' assumptions about employee families. While the Indian Office wanted married couples, it was slow to adjust to the fact that these couples were likely sooner or later to have children of their own (Illustration 4.3). Under pressure from employees who were parents, the Indian Office attempted to address these concerns in the first quarter of the twentieth century, enacting a wide range of regulations regarding employees and their families in an effort to create a smoothly functioning colonial bureaucracy.

The office's bureaucratic ideal was one of childless couples who would spend all of their time and attention looking after their Indian wards. The *Rules for Indian Schools* of 1892 specifically stated: "No person should offer himself for a position in this service who is encumbered with the care of children."[41] A decade later, the rules reiterated: "Employees are expected to devote their whole time and attention to the duties for which they are employed." And by 1915, the civil service descriptions stridently discouraged children: "No applicant who is encumbered with the care of infants or invalids, or is in any way hampered in giving to the Government his full time and best service, should enter the Indian Service."[42]

But applicants repeatedly ignored these statements, and it is clear that the Indian Office only inconsistently followed its own rules. Administrators were certainly aware of the possibility of employees' children accompanying

ILLUSTRATION 4.3. Agent James Sanders with child with Blackfeet men, Blackfeet Reservation, Montana, 1908. Despite the Indian Office's preference that their employees not have children, many service personnel did bring their offspring with them to their posts on the reservations and in the schools. (Courtesy of the Walter McClintock Collection, Yale Collection of Western Americana, Beinecke Rare Book and Manuscript Library, Yale University)

them, since the applications required that job seekers list the number and age of the family members who would be going with them to the reservations. When in 1889 Patrick Henry Hamlin of Texas wrote in regard to the position of principal teacher, for instance, he noted that he had a "wife, 24, and child 12 a boy. If wife could be of service would bring her but not if objected to—would prefer to have all together."[43] Salena Kane (Pottawatomie) accused her superintendent of overlooking her application for a seamstress position and hiring a white woman with a young baby in contravention of the rules. In another example a few years later, the Indian Office seemed more cognizant of this issue. When Autta Nevitt Parrett (Delaware), wife of the white superintendent at Bishop, California, requested reinstatement as a field matron, the office inquired about the status of any children. The Parretts responded that although they had a young daughter, they had hired "[a] good girl as domestic help . . . [who] makes it possible for Mrs. Parrett to devote considerable time to outside matters." This argument did not sway officials.

An interoffice memo noted: "Mrs. Parrett has a baby six months old. As you know it has been the policy not to appoint to field matron positions persons who cannot give their undivided attention to their duties." Ultimately, Mrs. Parrett's request was denied.[44] It is worth noting that in both cases, Native women came out on the losing end of the decision.

But there were many other occasions when employees were hired despite having children. Photographic evidence from the Indian Schools illustrates that many employees had their children with them. Both white and non-white children appear in numerous staff photographs, suggesting that they are with their parents. Two different staff portraits from the Albuquerque Indian School portray small children sitting with the employees; their small numbers and their inclusion in the photographs imply that they had a special relationship to the adults in the pictures (see Illustration 6.1). Other children appear in photographs with the entire student body but are set off from the pupils by their clothing, placement in the images, or physical proximity to the adults who are most likely their parents. The 1888 school picture from the Fort Simcoe School in Washington, for example, depicts several light-skinned children wearing refined clothing and sitting on the grass in front of the uniformed students, who are standing. In the portrait of the 1909 Eastern Cherokee School community, several adults who were likely staff members are positioned on either side of the array of students, where they are tenderly caressing small children. A Native woman holds on her lap a small boy who, unlike the pupils, is not dressed in uniform; on the other side, another non-uniformed boy stands in front of a Native man, and a white man rests his hand on the shoulder of a young, fashionably dressed girl.[45] The Indian Service was thus clearly at odds with itself, as well as its personnel, on the question of staff children. While administrators assumed that its employees would be dedicated, childless, and able to devote all of their time and energy to their jobs, family obligations often took precedence over their Indian "wards," just as policy makers feared they would.

Indeed, many female employees were frustrated at having to choose between fulfilling their familial duties and their employment duties. Estelle Aubrey Brown, a single employee at the Crow Creek Boarding School in South Dakota, contrasted the situation of two women at her school, one who was employed by the Indian Service as a matron and one who was not. Of the former, Brown wrote: "White children were not eligible to enter classrooms for Indian pupils. Mrs. Lake's two sons were pitiful. Her duties left her little time for her own children, who shared her one small room in boys' quarters." Standing in contrast to Mrs. Lake's experience was that of the superintendent's wife, who in this case did not work: "More than many of us, she managed to display an equable happy spirit, perhaps because she was not an employee, or perhaps because she had the solace of her small son of 8 years whom she taught at home."[46] In Brown's version, the white employees' children ironically suffered from a lack of education while their parents spent long hours teaching the Indian children.

The underlying problem was that because the Indian schools were funded by either treaty stipulation or the proceeds of Indian land sales compelled under the Allotment Act, they were intended only for Native children. White Indian Service workers found it particularly offensive that their children were not allowed to attend the Indian schools and yet often did not have access to other alternatives.[47] Several boarding-school employees recalled the lack of educational opportunity for their own children. For instance, Flora Gregg Iliff and her husband, Joe, who met while working at the Havasupai Agency in Arizona, had three children when they transferred to the Chilocco Indian School in Oklahoma. It was, Iliff wrote crossly, "one of the largest in the United States. Here the children of White employees attended public school. The free schooling granted Indian children was not available to those of White blood."[48] But the Iliffs were lucky to have established public schools in their community. Most employees were not so fortunate. There were some exceptions to the prohibition on employees enrolling their children in school, but they were often based on particular circumstances and probably the superintendent's willingness to bend the rules. Thisba Huston Morgan, a teacher at Pine Ridge, remembered that sometimes Indian parents had a say in whether the white children could take classes in their schools: "Several small German children were enrolled in the school—the sons and daughters of a newly arrived employee, a German carpenter. Since they knew as little English as the Indians, it seemed natural to give them the same instructions. Some Indian parents thought otherwise, and complained to the Agent about their children having to attend school with the children of a different race. The matter was brought before the [Indian] council. . . . It was discussed in a truly democratic way." Ultimately, the council agreed to allow the German children to attend school.[49] This was also true in less-isolated posts. In 1900 a journalist reported that the Haskell Institute in Lawrence, Kansas, had "501 Indian students, besides a dozen white children of officers, admitted on sufferance but not regularly enrolled."[50] Rather than making white employees negotiate for their children's education on an ad hoc basis, Congress passed two laws that officially allowed white children to enroll in Indian Schools— one in 1907 for day schools and another in 1909 for boarding schools. White families were required to pay tuition fees, which would reimburse the funds out of which the schools were maintained.[51]

While congressional legislation allowing white children into Indian Schools addressed concerns about younger children, many employed parents still faced hard choices when they had children of high school age. With the exception of some of the off-reservation boarding schools, most Indian schools were never intended to prepare students for more than a basic education. Most white employees believed in upward mobility for their children through schooling, illustrating precisely the middle-class aspirations that administrators hoped to inspire in Indians. The lack of public high schools near most reservations, however, bred discontent. What this meant for the service was a barrage of transfer requests, rejections of appointments, and outright resignations.[52] For example, when offered a promotion to the position of day-school inspector at Pine Ridge in 1916, William Blish hesitated, writing to the commissioner, "I was much in hopes that I might be so located that we might have our daughters at home until they had finished their high school." He further explained: "They are not yet ready for college, but are beyond the place where they can be taught at home to advantage. Were I to go to Pine Ridge it would be necessary for me to send, at least, two of these girls away to school, just at the time when they most need the home, or of having my family live away from the reservation and being separated from them. The expense of either of these arrangements would be much more expensive than the increased salary could cover."[53]

Native employees shared this concern about their children's education— though, as we will see in chapter 5, with a slight twist. They often requested posts at schools where their children were students or were eligible to enroll. Many of their letters reveal that they, too, perceived education as an opportunity for social mobility for their children. When Dollie Johnson (Chinook) requested a transfer from her position as cook at the Ponca School to baker at Chilocco, Oklahoma, she explained: "I would like very much to have a change and better paying position. My oldest child will soon be ready for high school so I must prepare to help him get a good education and to do so one must have money."[54] The correspondence of Harriet Kyselka, a woman of mixed white and Anishinabe heritage married to a white man, reveals her great concern for her children's education. Requesting a transfer for herself and her husband in 1915, she noted: "I prefer Osage agency on account of the excellent public school advantages for our two children aged 10 and 13 years." A few years later, she wrote for another transfer, stating: "I have thought of Cass Lake, Minnesota, and as there are High School advantages there I could have both Madeline and Carl with me."[55]

Throughout the period covered in this book, employees' concerns about their children continued to cause major staffing problems, thus significantly disrupting the work of assimilation. In 1928 the Brookings Institution released *The Problem of Indian Administration*, its massive and critical study of the Indian Service. Based on extensive research, including numerous interviews with service personnel, the study concluded that family interests were a primary reason for employees' decisions to transfer or resign. It especially noted their complaints regarding their inability to secure good education for their children and the isolation of their positions. The report concluded: "To a certain type of employee, considerate of his wife and children, conditions of the home and access to schools mean even more than wages."[56]

LINES OF AUTHORITY WITHIN INTIMATE COLONIALISM

The workforce that resulted from the government's strategy of intimate colonialism created complex webs of power on the reservations and in the schools; this affected the implementation of assimilation programs. The lines of administrative authority often became confused because of the personal or intimate links between family members. In addition, the presence of relatives, especially children, resulted in unanticipated connections that colored employee life in the service.

One particularly charged intersection between family and administration was in the figure of the superintendent's wife. As women moved into the Indian Service with their husbands, their presence created confusion and concern among their superiors and coworkers, and a persistent trope of the superintendent's wife as agitator emerged in many depictions of the service. Indian Office policies that facilitated hiring the superintendent's wife as a teacher or matron made her a threatening figure to female employees already in those positions because she might covet their jobs. In addition, her dual identity as wife to the superintendent while simultaneously being a subordinate colleague disrupted administrative hierarchies in the schools and resulted in real or perceived abuses of power.

Accusations from unhappy personnel often revolved around the idea that the superintendent or his wife was trying to drive away an innocent employee so that the wife could then take their position. This dynamic set the tension for Minnie Braithwaite's entire memoir: the superintendent's wife, she wrote, "wanted my job and meant to get it. If one plan failed, she tried another. She always had another."[57] Other complaints focused on the unofficial influence of the superintendent's wife. In 1917 Lucy Jobin (Chippewa/m), the matron at the Chin Lee School in Arizona, received a negative efficiency report from Mr. Garber, her superintendent, charging her with disloyalty. She fired back with several charges of her own, including that he had targeted her because she didn't "toady" to Mrs. Garber. Julia DeCora (Winnebago/French), an Indian Service nurse, received a letter of support that used similar imagery: "It appears that the wife of the superintendent who has now left there, [s]ingled Miss DeCora out for slaughter. . . . [I]f that Superintendent's wife had remained at Tower much longer there would not have been any school left. She was a shame and a disgrace to the service. . . . It seems that the Superintendent was all right, but his wife was *a hellion*."[58]

An accusation that a superintendent's wife was behaving badly could also damage her husband's position. David U. Betts, principal at the Yankton School, received negative reviews from both his superintendent and a special Indian agent sent to investigate the charges. While most of the evidence revolved around Betts's behavior, the agent and the superintendent also blamed his wife for problems at the school. The agent noted that the employees were divided and pointed to the fact that "[h]is wife is inclined to do much gossiping about the employees, and that adds fuel to the feeling."[59] By 1928 the Indian Service rules included a provision stating that bad behavior on the part of employees' relatives was cause for termination.[60]

Women were certainly involved in the internal battles of the Indian Service,[61] but it is unclear whether superintendents' wives were more likely to cause trouble than others. This theme might have had some grain of truth because of the hierarchical nature of the service, or perhaps some superintendents' wives were just easy marks. Either way, the idea came to influence administrators. For example, the official who filled out the 1926 efficiency report for Jerdine Bonnin (Wyandot/m) approvingly noted that "Mrs. Bonnin is the wife of Superintendent [Leo] Bonnin. . . . She assumes no authority because of the fact that she is the Superintendent's wife."[62]

The children of employees also became complicated figures in the world of the Indian Service, although less consistently so than the superintendents' wives. In many cases, they were caught up in the same conflicts based on class, race, tribe, and authority that their parents faced. It seems as though some Native students took out their frustration on the children of their teachers. Memoirist Estelle Aubrey Brown described the sons of a fellow white employee, the matron Mrs. Lake, as "pitiful" and remembered that, although they were "housed with a hundred boys, they had no playmates. If they ventured to join the games of the small Indian boys, they merely got bloodied noses for their pains." Jennie C. Brown had similar problems at the Cantonment Boarding School, where an official stated: "She is always in trouble with the Indian boys for abusing her children, as she sees it."[63]

Other white children had more positive experiences. Julia and P. V. Tuell appear to have been less worried about their children's companions. The

Tuells joined the Indian Service right after getting married and served on several different reservations. Their first daughter, whom they named Weno-nah, was born at Vermillion Lake Reservation in Minnesota. They were later posted to the Northern Cheyenne Reservation for several years and became close friends with many tribal members. Julia, a photographer, captured the experiences of her children on the reservation. While the Tuells' children are rarely pictured with Native children, the photographs reveal their extensive interaction with the adult Cheyenne who were their parents' friends. One striking photograph, for example, shows Chief American Horse, a warrior who was at the Battle of Little Big Horn, gently holding Julia's son, Carl, and standing with her and her two daughters in front of their home, to which he was a frequent visitor. In another, Vo'estaa'e (White Cow), a Cheyenne woman, teaches the Tuells' daughter to shoot a bow and arrow. Many similar photographs exist of the Tuell children (and in at least one case, grand-children) interacting with people on the Northern Cheyenne, Sisseton, and Rosebud Reservations. The pictures, along with the anecdotal stories, dem-onstrate the close friendships that developed between the Tuell family and the people among whom they worked.[64]

But even good relations between Indians and white children could cause white parents anxiety.[65] George Nock, superintendent at the Colorado River Agency School between 1887 and 1889, recalled that both of his sons became fluent in the Mojave language. He remembered that he often saw his younger son "sitting in a group of six or eight squaws, chatting away and entertaining them, and I could not understand one word of what was going on." But Nock also reflected that each son had a very different attitude toward the Mojave people. "The smaller one," he wrote, "was constantly thinking of danger" as a result of "the whispered words of mother and myself before we arrived at the agency . . . [which] seemed to haunt him from the first to the last day, and whenever the subject was mentioned he would always say he wanted to go back East. He was only a little over four years old when we arrived at the agency." In contrast, his older son, Walter, "would go off with [the Mojave] and stay half a day at a time, and neither mother nor I would know where he was." One family story holds that the Nocks left their positions in Arizona because George Nock was afraid that Walter would fall in love with a Mojave girl.[66]

The children of Native employees had similarly complex relationships to the Native people among whom their parents were employed. Their experi-ences ranged from the development of intertribal connections to revealing the tense lines of class and tribal identity that could exist within Indigenous communities. Native children who attended a boarding school where their parents worked probably had experiences similar to those of boarding-school pupils more broadly, which scholars have described as both positive (the development of close and lasting friendships) and negative (bullying and factionalism based on tribal identity).[67] At some schools, however, all employees' children, Native and white, were educated together in a separate group from the other students.[68]

It is possible that the children of Native employees who worked away from their communities made similar friendships. During the 1930s (a slightly later period than that under consideration here), Jack Norton Jr. (Hupa but enrolled Yurok) fondly remembered his childhood on the Navajo Reservation, where his father worked as the superintendent of schools for Kinlichee, Klagetah, Tohatchi, and several day schools. He recalled learning of the shared Athabascan roots of the Hupa and Navajo languages and sitting in a "circle of old Navajo men singing."[69] Writer N. Scott Momaday (Kiowa/Cherokee), whose parents taught in the Indian Service in the Southwest during the same decade as Norton's parents, also absorbed a great deal of information about the peoples among whom they worked, especially the Navajo and the inhabitants of Jemez Pueblo. While he was unable to participate in the pueblo's sacred ceremonies, he did witness them. Later, Momaday based much of his Pulitzer prize–winning novel, *House Made of Dawn*, on those boyhood memories. Momaday has also noted that growing up in Indian country helped him retain a sense of Indian identity.[70]

The experiences of Native children were also colored by the class and tribal tensions experienced by their parents. For example, Lottie Smith Pattee (Eastern Band Cherokee/m), a boarding-school teacher, was worried about what her daughter might learn from her dorm mates if she was sent away to another Indian school. She wrote to a friend of her concerns: "You know what vile stuff she would learn to put her in with a lot of girls. She may be no better than other children but I don't want her to learn all kinds of bad things." Some of this concern may have arisen from Pattee's ideas about class and proper behavior. Indeed, she had previously expressed the hope of a transfer to Haskell Institute because there, the Indian students with whom her own children would mix were "a better class as a rule."[71]

When Joseph Estes (Yankton Sioux) and his white wife, Anna, were transferred to the positions of teacher and housekeeper at the Stockbridge Agency in Wisconsin, their children's relationship with the other students became a point of conflict between the employees and tribal members. It is unclear whether the quarrel among the children or the adults came first, but the two certainly became interwoven. An investigation of complaints against Estes revealed that Native people did not necessarily embrace Indian employees because of their shared Indigenous identity. The parents at Stockbridge complained that he used physical punishment, kept their children long after school, favored his own children, and lost his temper with parents, and that his wife cooked unpalatable meals for the pupils and made the children do her housekeeping. As one parent, Mary Hammer, testified: "It is my opinion that he is not interested in the advancement and teaching of my children."[72]

In their testimony, the Stockbridge parents especially accused Estes of punishing their children too harshly when they fought with his children. One parent testified: "My boy was accused of knocking Mr. Estes' little boy off a seat, and then he, Mr. Estes whipped him, with a rawhide." Another said his daughter was afraid to go to school because "she said that if any of the children hurt his, Mr. Estes' children, he would use the rawhide." In his defense, Estes claimed he had justifiably punished several of the boys for "employing language pertaining to sexual intercourse to my youngest daughter" and "spitting in the face, kicking and pulling my older daughter's hair."[73]

Race became an interesting and complicated part of the investigation. It is unclear how the Stockbridge parents felt about having a Dakota teacher specifically, but their agent noted that "every effort has been made to embarrass Estes in his school work and to break up his school. They have heaped insult and abuse upon him and his family and even threatened him with bodily injury." The special inspector added his own interpretation to this: "Another cause of objection to Mr. Estes is that he is an Indian. The Stockbridge people are practically white. . . . Mr. Estes' experience has mostly been with Indians and it is very probable that he failed to meet all their requirements or expectations of a teacher." The question of race, however, did not surface in the parents' official testimony against Estes. But Estes himself turned to racial slurs in his defense, writing of his Stockbridge accusers, "it seemed as though I were chained to a stake and being consumed in flames while my captors were brandishing their scalping knives and dancing in fiendish glee around me."[74]

CONCLUSION

The everyday lives of the men and women in the Indian Service held major ramifications for the results of assimilation programs. While historians have superbly demonstrated how the agency of Indian peoples affected the results of assimilation policy, they have continued to characterize Indian Service employees as mere functionaries rather than as historical actors. The experiences of these married couples, however, offer a striking depiction of how personnel also substantially influenced federal colonial policy.

The Indian Office's use of the family model to construct its workforce resulted in the employment of numerous spousal teams. Initially, it seemed as though the needs of those couples and the Indian Service neatly corresponded. As couples began their work on the reservations and in the schools, however, it became clear that in many cases, their desires actually diverged. Couples who found their hopes for their own families' well-being stymied by the demands of their jobs protested by asking for transfers, declining positions, or even resigning. This turnover in personnel was at odds with the service's goal of making employees into stable object lessons. The Indian Office tried to modify its policies toward its employees in order to address their concerns but was often unable to satisfactorily do so.

These dynamics imply that Indian Service administrators were ultimately conflicted about the role of families in their strategies of assimilation. For example, even as they asked couples to devote all of their time to teaching Indian children, they implicitly asked the same couples to neglect their own children or hire someone else to raise them. Americans were just becoming aware of the problems of working mothers, but they thought of such mothers as working-class. As a result, the Indian Office was simply unprepared for the consequences of its hiring policies. Moreover, policy makers' assumptions about what household labor entailed were premised upon an earlier producerist model and no longer matched the circumstances of many of the families they hired. Ultimately, the Indian Office's anachronistic ideas about how families worked and its failure to anticipate the complications that might arise actively impeded its use of intimate colonialism as a strategy of Indian assimilation.

5

An Indian Teacher among Indians

AMERICAN INDIAN LABOR IN THE INDIAN SERVICE

In the second decade of the twentieth century, Yavapai Apache activist Carlos Montezuma, a veteran of the Indian Service, accused Native people who worked for the government of being "Indians, but heartless of an Indian's heart. Their souls are stupid and their hearts asleep."[1] Montezuma argued that while the problems faced by Native people were principally the fault of the government, Indian employees also deserved part of the blame. "The Indian Bureau is hanging by a thread of 6,000 employees, interwoven with whom are Indian employees," he editorialized in his newspaper, *Wassaja*. "Indians have always been used by the Government to destroy other Indians, and it is the same old story here."[2]

Not all Indigenous people agreed with Montezuma. Esther Burnett Horne, a Shoshone woman who had attended Haskell Indian School and moved on to teach in the Indian Service, affirmed that "the aim of the Indian Service was to divorce our people from our heritage and to assimilate us into the dominant culture," but she added, "I was not in sympathy with this endeavor." Instead, Horne worked to subvert the goals of assimilation by teaching her Native students to be proud of their Indigenous heritage. Her own experience as a boarding-school student had taught her the importance of having Native mentors who could do this. She wrote: "I wanted to provide [my students] with the same security and sense of self that my Indian teachers, Ruth [Muskrat Bronson (Cherokee)] and Ella [Deloria (Yankton Sioux)], had instilled in me."[3]

Although they disagreed about Native people's choices, Montezuma and Horne were in accord on one point: the government was indeed trying to use Indian employees to destroy tribal identity and further the project of assimilation. The Office of Indian Affairs depended heavily upon the labor of Native people to staff its programs. From the administrative point of view, hiring Indians served both ideological and practical ends: ideologically, administrators believed that Indian wage labor could be used to teach Native people the crucial lessons of working in the capitalist marketplace; and practically, they could hire Indian workers for less money than white workers.

But if the government's agenda was so obvious, why did thousands of Indian people take jobs in the service? Indian employees had incredibly varied work experiences. They held manual and white-collar positions, and sometimes both. Some chose to spend their lives in government careers, while others moved in and out of the bureaucracy. A few employees remained in one position for so long that they became fixtures at their schools and agencies, while others moved from post to post throughout the reservation system. Like their white colleagues, Native employees were adjusting to the changes brought on by the rapidly developing modern economy; but as colonized peoples, Indians were also struggling for economic and cultural survival in a hostile world. They were subalterns in the colonial bureaucracy or, to borrow a term that Philip J. Deloria has used to describe other turn-of-the-century Native people, "Indians in unexpected places."[4]

Many Native employees, like Essie Horne, understood their work in ways that policy makers had not anticipated. They tried to use their positions to help themselves, their families, and often their communities, even as the government was seeking to tear them apart. But the influence of Indian employees was always constrained by the system within which they worked.[5] Despite these limitations, their actions offer an intriguing counterpoint to the government's rhetoric about the transformative power of work. Recovering their stories allows us to reconstruct the survival strategies of a key generation of Native people. It also exposes the impact of government service on individual lives, reservation economies, and tribal and intertribal politics.

A SPECIAL HIRING POLICY

Native employment in the Indian Service grew markedly over the course of the late nineteenth century. As the School Service developed during the 1880s, Indians in the service began to substantially increase in number as well as in variety of positions. By the end of the century, Indians filled every job in the Indian Service, from laborer to school superintendent. The Indian Office employed Indians primarily because of the perceived pedagogical possibilities of work. Policy makers thought that wage work comprised an integral part of the assimilation programs because it would teach Indians the virtues of productive labor within the free market. Administrators believed employment worked on several levels: it was instructive and taught specific skills, it was an incentive to keep educated Indians from "returning to the blanket," and it could undermine tribal authority. Echoing earlier policy makers, Commissioner William Jones urged that the government must "instill a love for work, not for work's own sake, but for the reward which it will bring."[6] While Jones meant rewards for the Indians themselves, their employment also benefited the federal government because the Indian Office often paid Native employees less than white employees for the same work.

The Indian Office had a long history of hiring Native employees, but only in limited numbers. According to Steven J. Novak, between 1834 and the Civil War, only 253 Indians worked for the Indian Service. After the Civil War, the Indian Office embarked on an ambitious employment policy that brought thousands of Indians into the service.[7] While statistics on Native employees for the earlier period of this study are available only for those employed by the School Service and not by the entire Indian Service, they are nonetheless suggestive. In 1888 the commissioner of Indian affairs reported that Indian employees constituted 15 percent of the School Service. By 1895 that proportion had risen to 23 percent and by 1899 to a peak of 45 percent. In 1912 Commissioner Valentine stated that Native employees made up almost 30 percent of all 6,000 regular employees of the total Indian Service, encompassing both school and agency personnel.[8]

Freighting and law enforcement were two of the first positions in which the government used a deliberate, large-scale policy of paying Indians as an incentive to work. The ideal of the male economic provider within assimilation theory spurred those first appointments. Commissioner of Indian Affairs Hiram Price argued that it would serve "to advance the process of civilizing the Indian by inducing him to labor, [and] paying him therefore,"[9] and by 1883 the government had instituted a rule "requir[ing] that Indians shall be employed in every position which they are capable of filling properly, and the expense for white employees shall be reduced to the lowest possible limit."[10] In his annual report, Price emphasized the efforts that had been made to employ Indian men. In the account of office expenditures, for example, he included a section titled: "To promote civilization among Indians generally, including Indian labor." This he juxtaposed with hopeful statistics charting the "results of Indian labor," which included the number of houses built and occupied, apprentices trained, acres cultivated, and animals owned.[11]

The idea of using Indian labor for freighting seems to have begun on the Rosebud and Pine Ridge Reservations in the fall of 1878, when the government hired 200 men to haul the rations from the railroad at Sidney, Nebraska, to the agencies. The men from Rosebud received 25 cents per 100 pounds, while the men hauling to Pine Ridge were paid $30 a month. A year later, according to Jeffery Ostler, "the Oglalas had carried two million pounds of freight and earned $41,000."[12] The Indian Office soon extended this program to many other reservations. The *Regulations of the Indian Office* required special hiring beginning in 1883, when a policy was enacted stipulating that "whenever and wherever practicable, transportation from railroad stations or steamboat landings to agencies shall be performed by Indians." The Indian Office also sought to encourage Native men who did not own their own equipment to become freighters by lending them government wagons and harnesses and letting them work toward ownership rather than for cash wages. This strategy was meant to ensure that the men would continue to be productively employed, and as a result, it imposed controls on how they spent their earnings. The policy also eased administrators' fears that giving Indians supplies would pauperize them, since it required them to work before equipment was issued to them.[13] The wages for these positions were low and the work often temporary, but freighting did contribute a flow (or perhaps a trickle) of cash that could mean a great deal on the poverty-stricken reservations. The enterprise continued to offer Native men a source of income as well as some freedom of mobility, though as roads and railheads moved closer to the reservations, it became less lucrative.

In a similar effort to employ Indian men in positions that encouraged productive labor and assisted in the administration of reservation agencies, Congress allocated funds for Indian police forces in 1878 (Illustration 5.1).[14] Practically, policy makers believed that the police would help uphold the reservation agent's authority, keep order, and combat the illegal liquor traffic.[15] But Indian police positions could also undermine tribal authority, as Commissioner Price emphasized when he observed: "The indirect results and ultimate influence of this system are even more important than its direct advantages. Well trained and disciplined, the police force is a perpetual educator. It is a power entirely independent of the chiefs. It weakens, and will finally destroy, the power of tribes and bands. It fosters a spirit of personal responsibility."[16] He was echoed a few years later in the debates on Capitol Hill over the Indian appropriations bill, during which a congressman noted that the Indian police served to "create a spirit of emulation and ambition" on reservations.[17] During the 1880s, large numbers of Native men worked as Indian policemen, making up "the single largest personnel classification" in the Indian Service.[18]

In 1883 the federal government added to the law-and-order apparatus on reservations by creating the Courts of Indian Offenses and the position of

ILLUSTRATION 5.1. Arthur Saxon (Hupa), Indian Service police private. Policy makers believed they could undermine and eventually replace tribal authority by employing Native men in Indian police forces. The men who worked in these positions, however, often had more complicated motives for joining the police force than federal officials realized. (Courtesy of the Phoebe A. Hearst Museum of Anthropology and the regents of the University of California; photograph by Alfred L. Kroeber [catalogue no. 15-3692])

Indian judge. Presiding over infractions by reservation residents, the judges would, policy makers hoped, serve as examples of right living. Many of the appointees were "mixed-bloods" who had already adopted some Anglo characteristics. For example, in 1893 Herbert Welsh favorably described the members of the court at Pine Ridge: "All three of the judges represent the civilized or Christian element. . . . All judges wear citizens' dress and are strong advocates of education."[19] Policy makers hoped that these men would supplant the power of traditional leaders.[20]

Despite the praise showered upon the law-enforcement employees as object lessons of assimilation, Native men had their own reasons for taking up these positions. In his study of the early Pine Ridge police, historian Mark Ellis found that among the Oglala Lakota, law officers generally came from the ranks of the *akicitas*, the cohort of "traditional Lakota law enforcement." Many men joined the agency police force in order to help their communities adjust to reservation life, to police themselves while avoiding U.S. military presence on their reservation, to secure greater access to agency resources, and possibly to gain advantage in tribal politics.[21] As we will see, other Native employees had similarly complex motives for joining the Indian Service.

The government initially focused on hiring Indian men to do unskilled work on their own reservations, but by around 1890, the Indian Service was hiring Native people who had been educated in the Indian School system. As the system grew and began to turn out graduates trained in various fields, Native men and women filled the ranks of the Indian Service in a wide variety of positions, including vocational jobs such as matrons, seamstresses, laundresses, cooks, carpenters, farmers, and mechanics, as well as white-collar and professional appointments such as clerks, nurses, teachers, doctors, and superintendents (Table 1). Historian Wilbert Ahern has found that a policy of hiring boarding-school graduates arose early in the assimilation era. Reformers urged that former students be given positions in the Indian Service as a precaution against their "relapsing at an early moment into the barbarism of the tribe." Superintendent of Indian Schools William Hailmann strongly endorsed such hiring: "The appointment of Indians as employees in all positions in which this is practicable should be not only recommended, but consistently enforced. . . . By this policy the Government will afford to Indians fresh incentives for faithful work at school, additional reasons to love and foster the school, while at the same time it will make the school a practical object lesson of life in which the two races labor hand in hand toward a common purpose."[22]

Policy makers sought to facilitate the entrance of Native people into the Indian Service by extending the existing policy of special hiring. In 1895 the

TABLE 1. A Comparison of Selected Positions in the Indian School Service, 1888 and 1905

POSITION	1888		1905	
	WHITE	NATIVE	WHITE	NATIVE
Superintendent	13	0	117	1
Assistant superintendent	1	0	14	1
Superintendent of day school	2	0	3[1]	0
Clerk	9	0	56	18
Physician	6	0	29	1
Nurse	4	0	31	2
Teacher	241	0	450	50
Industrial teacher	63	0	68	34
Matron	82	0	215	37
Assistant matron	0	7	116	49
Seamstress	63	2	113	43
Cook	63	4	144[2]	73
Laundress	53	8	88	59
Disciplinarian	3	2	23	13
Farmer	7	0	50	13
Gardener	1	0	19	6
Engineer	5	0	55	27
Shoemaker	6	1	16	20
Tailor	7	1	9	6

1. I have assumed day-school inspector in 1905 was comparable to superintendent of day school in 1888.
2. Cooks and bakers.

Notes: Comparing the number of employees in selected positions for which data were available for 1888 and 1905 reveals that Native employees were slowly moving into some of the white-collar jobs, though the majority remained in manual-labor positions. In 1888 the school service was composed of 757 non-Native employees and 137 Native employees, for a total of 894. In 1905 there were 1,814 non-Native and 602 Native employees in the school service, for a total of 2,416. While assistant positions were introduced in 1888 (and all were filled by Indian employees), they were not divided in 1905. The Indian employees filled the following positions in 1888: disciplinarian (2); assistant teacher (7); assistant industrial teacher (5); assistant matron (7); seamstress (2); assistant seamstress (10); cook (4); assistant cook (10); laundress (8); assistant laundress (7); baker (4); butcher (2); assistant farmer (2); shoemaker (1); harness maker (1); tailor (1); printer (1); storekeeper (2); watchman (10); apprentice (15); janitor (1); hospital steward (1); cadet sergeant (19); herder (2); helper (7); laborer (6). In 1905 Indian employees filled the following positions: superintendent (1); assistant superintendent (1); clerk (18); physician (1); disciplinarian (13); teacher (50); kindergartener (1); matron and housekeeper (37); assistant matron (49); nurse (2); seamstress (43); laundress (59); industrial teacher (34); cook and baker (73); farmer (13); blacksmith and carpenter (19); engineer (27); tailor (6); shoe-and-harness maker (20); gardener (6); Indian assistant (44); miscellaneous (85).

Sources: ARCIA 1888, in Report of the Secretary of the Interior, 1888, xx–xxi; and ARCIA 1905, 46.

civil service rules were amended so that "Indians employed in the Service at large" could be appointed without a civil service examination. Native applicants who desired the regular position of superintendent, teacher, manual-training teacher, kindergarten teacher, physician, matron, clerk, seamstress, farmer, or industrial teacher did need certification from the Civil Service Commission, but they were only required to pass a noncompetitive exam that theoretically gave them an advantage over white job seekers.[23]

WHY INDIANS WORKED

Historians of the boarding schools have argued that the schools prepared students primarily for work in the Indian Service. Tsianina Lomawaima, for example, posits that "despite federal rhetoric, which claimed to train young Indian people unencumbered by tribal loyalties for a place in white mainstream society, schools prepared Indian students for employment—as support staff and vocational instructors, rarely as academic instructors—in Indian schools" (Illustration 5.2).[24] Indian Office administrators did indeed perceive the boarding schools as a source of labor for the service. The number of employees with boarding-school connections lends credence to historians' assertions that the federal educational agenda played a large role in preparing students to serve in a colonial labor force. Some employees had known little else besides the Indian Service's bureaucracy, reminding us of the legacy of conquest and the tragic poverty and disruption experienced by many Native communities. Native children sent to off-reservation boarding schools frequently had lost one or both parents. Others spent years separated from their families at school.[25] The superior of Susie McDougall (Chippewa), a teacher at White Earth Reservation, noted that McDougall "grew up in the Service"; and Julia DeCora Lukecart made the same point when she wrote in a request for reinstatement: "I was practically raised in the government school and I like the work."[26] Other Native employees also emphasized their boarding-school training in their applications for positions. Describing her background, Violetta Nash (Winnebago) wrote that "being a student in an Indian School gave me an idea of the positions," and Nellie Santeo (Papago) listed her six years of experience while a student at Carlisle Indian School. Likewise, Sophie Picard, a Native woman from L'Anse, Michigan, remembered that instead of taking the civil service exam, she had been "sent from Haskell Institute out to work."[27]

There is substantial evidence, however, that a significant number of former boarding-school students did attain white-collar and professional positions in the service. By the turn of the century, many of the large off-reservation

ILLUSTRATION 5.2. Nurses at Tulalip School, 1912. Many Native employees received their training as students in the federal boarding schools, as did nurse trainees (front row, from left) Josie Cayou (Swinomish), Theresa Young (Tulalip), Myrtle Loughrey (Suquamish), Clara Jones (Swinomish), Emily Limon (Upper Skagit), and (second row, center) Annie Nason (Muckleshoot). Nurse O'Dell and Dr. Buchanan stand at the rear. (Courtesy of the Ferdinand Brady Collection, Washington Museum of History and Industry, Seattle [MOHAI 88.11.63])

schools, including Chilocco and Haskell, had established teacher-training departments "to prepare Indians to teach successfully in Indian schools," and many of their graduates went directly into the Indian Service. In 1900 the annual report of the commissioner of Indian affairs offered a breakdown of the careers of former Hampton Institute students. Focusing on those who had "been home over a year," the report noted that out of 328 returned students, 65 were serving as teachers or school employees, while an additional 54 had found employment at the agencies. Another eight worked for the federal government in non–Indian Service positions.[28]

In my sample of fifty-five personnel files of female Indian employees—drawn from a list of all 265 of the female Native employees listed as employed in the School Service in the *Annual Report of the Commissioner of Indian Affairs* for 1905—ten of the women (or 18 percent) held white-collar positions as nurses, teachers, or clerks, including one who served as the superintendent of the Grand River Boarding School on the Standing Rock Reservation.[29] Five women were employed as field matrons or female industrial teachers. The other forty served in the manual-labor positions of matron, seamstress, laundress, cook, or baker (or assistants in those positions). Three of them served in white-collar positions temporarily at one point in their careers.[30] Virtually all of these women had been trained in the federal boarding schools.[31]

By following the students beyond the schools, it becomes clear that the government's efforts to create a docile Native labor force failed. Despite the colonial motivations behind federal educational policies, Native people had their own reasons for taking jobs in the Indian Service. Indigenous employees did not necessarily share the same vision of assimilation as federal officials. They often opposed the government's attacks on their cultural identities, but they also recognized that they could use their education as a powerful weapon in their fight for survival and sovereignty. While federal policy sought to destroy tribal identities, Native employees used Indian Service employment as an economic strategy that allowed them to maintain family, and in many cases tribal, ties. Many believed that their educational experiences, as well as their racial and tribal identities, made them better qualified than white employees to serve Native communities. Luther Standing Bear (Oglala Lakota), for example, articulated a vision of an Indigenous Indian Service bureaucracy that could be empowering rather than destructive: "Indians should teach Indians. . . . Indians should serve Indians. . . . [E]very reservation could well be supplied with Indian doctors, nurses, and engineers, road- and bridge-builders, draughtsmen, architects, dentists, lawyers, teachers, and instructors in tribal lore, legends, orations, song, dance, and ceremonial ritual."[32] Indeed, in contrast to official ideas that posited that work in the service would help further the goals of assimilation, positions within the Indian Service could and did become politicized sites of resistance for Native people.

Native people took jobs in the service for a combination of economic, communal, and personal reasons. Indian people often pointed to economic survival as the most basic reason for working for the Office of Indian Affairs. Their employment choices, both off and on the reservations, were usually limited to manual labor.[33] According to their applications, a number of the Indian women in the service had previously served as domestic workers for private families, a job notorious for its difficulty, long hours, and lack of privacy. Hiring on as a laundress, seamstress, or cook for the government may have offered a more agreeable alternative. Men's opportunities were also mainly limited to menial work, such as lumbering, harvesting crops, or canning fish. By the twentieth century, some Native people were able to work in the tourist industry as guides, entertainers, and artisans.[34] For the

ILLUSTRATION 5.3. Mrs. Many Horses typing, Blackfeet Agency, Montana. Native employees served throughout the ranks of the Indian Service in every position from temporary laborer to school superintendent. Many held white-collar jobs that were more difficult for them to attain in the private sector, including clerk, teacher, doctor, and nurse. (Courtesy of the Library of Congress)

small cohort of Native people trained for white-collar jobs such as nurse, clerk, and doctor, the private sector may have been less welcoming than government work because prejudice against Indians ran high in this period (Illustration 5.3). Some skilled Native women working as teachers, nurses, or clerks in the service had previously worked not in the private sector but in the public-service sector for the U.S. Post Office or for the state as teachers or public-health nurses.[35] Professional Indian employment in the private sector is not well documented and requires more research to determine how Native workers fared in private labor markets in a racist age. We do know that African American professionals found it extremely difficult to attract white clients willing to engage their services, and thus they served a primarily black clientele. The off-reservation population of middle-class Native people who could have made up such a clientele for Indian professionals was virtually nonexistent.[36]

On the reservations, Indian Service employment provided one of the few sources of wage income in what were often poverty-stricken areas. John Brown, a Native man from Siletz, Oregon, remarked that he desired employment in the service "on account of steady work."[37] Elinor Gregg, a supervisor of nurses who worked for the service in the 1920s, recorded another reason, which she had learned from her interpreter on the Eastern Navajo agency. He told her that "he had started to study Indian medicine, but it took many years before the old man [sic] would transfer their power to their young apprentices. Willie wanted to get married and decided that he could get along better with a government salary of forty dollars a month as an interpreter. He also did some interpreting for one of the missionary churches. He could live well on sixty dollars a month."[38] In another example, during the 1930s, Virgil Wyaco, a Zuni man, worked as a temporary laborer on the Zuni Reservation, building fences during the summers. Although his experiences came slightly later than the period under study here, the seventeen-year-old Virgil described the work as a summer job that gave him money to buy clothes with which to impress girls.[39] Many other applications in the personnel files expressed similar sentiments.

Native people may also have been drawn to the Indian Service by the opportunities for promotion, transfer, reinstatement, and, by 1929, retirement pensions that were simply not available elsewhere. (Indeed, before World War I, even white employees sought well-paying Indian Service jobs in part because they offered perquisites not usually offered to employees of any race.) Indian employees' personnel files indicate that part of the appeal of service work was its flexibility, which allowed them to fulfill their family responsibilities. The service offered its regular employees a number of incentives as it began to bureaucratize during the early twentieth century. At the time, these options were highly unusual, especially for nonwhite employees; they included month-long vacations,[40] leaves without pay,[41] the possibility of reinstatement after resignation, and retirement pensions.[42] Although many employees did not know about them when they first entered the service, these incentives may have served as inducements for remaining in government employ. For instance, civil service protocol granted all employees a grace period after resignation, during which they could apply for reinstatement. White employees had one year after resignation, but the period was indefinite for Native employees. Native workers often took advantage of this reinstatement policy to move back and forth between work in the service and their other obligations, especially to family members. Lavinia Cornelius (Oneida) resigned several times to care for her sick mother, dying sister, and ailing father.[43] When her mother's health failed, Anishinabe Sarah

Wyman resigned and was reinstated twice.[44] Wyandot Naomi Dawson used the option to combine kinship obligation and a break from work. She resigned in 1909, writing of her "being needed at home, and I also require a little rest from school-room work"; reapplying in 1915, she wrote, "[I] have had sufficient rest and feel that I want to go to work."[45] Although these strategies were generally successful, for a variety of reasons, some Native employees were unable to get reinstatements.

These familial considerations remind us that kinship and community played an especially important role for Native people, and entering the service was seldom an individual economic decision. Indigenous families often pooled their resources, using the wages from labor in the Indian Service to supplement other forms of subsistence.[46] Anthropologist Alfonso Ortiz notes that the families of San Juan Pueblo in New Mexico often used Indian Service employment in such a way.

> There was really very little need for cash on a day-to-day basis. Sugar and coffee and then, occasionally, cheese and soap were the staples most often paid for with cash. Each family needed only to have one member working seasonally to have enough cash for the whole year. Typically, a family sent an older son, or in the absence of an older son the father went, to herd sheep in the mountains of northern New Mexico or southern Colorado to earn the needed cash. A few young women worked as maids on call 24 hours a day for well-to-do whites in Santa Fe. They earned, as they were eager to tell me, thirty dollars per month and were lucky to get one or two Sunday afternoons off per month to go home. A few other people worked for the BIA or in stores in nearby Espanola.[47]

For people living on reservations, Indian Service work offered an additional option in the diversity of economic strategies drawn upon by families or individuals. It was even more important on reservations with fewer employment alternatives.

Like white employees, Native people primarily emphasized their families in their Indian Service applications. But for Native employees, keeping one's family together carried greater political valence because government policy sought to destroy family and community ties in the name of assimilation. Indian personnel used the service to maintain those ties, thus undermining federal goals. In 1909 Maude Peacore (Chippewa) requested a transfer to the Seneca School in Oklahoma, explaining: "I have held the position here at Tomah School [in Wisconsin] as assistant seamstress for several years. When I came here my home was at Tomah, but now my relatives are in Oklahoma.

I would like a position in an Indian school near their home."[48] Luther Stand-ing Bear had similar motivations when he left Carlisle Indian School and returned to the Rosebud Reservation, where he accepted an Indian Service job. He left the school, he later wrote, because "I became lonesome. Finally I told Captain Pratt I wanted to go home to my people." In 1891, when his family moved to Pine Ridge, he accepted a job offer in the service there and responded to the Rosebud agent's counteroffer by saying: "But as my whole family were at Pine Ridge . . . I thought I would be better off with them."[49] Many applicants indicated that they would accept positions in nearby states but refused to take jobs that were too far from their homes. For instance, Madeline Jacker, a woman of mixed Chippewa and German heritage from Houghton, Michigan, asked several times for a position in "Wisconsin, Min-nesota or some state not far from Michigan."[50]

Other employees stressed their children's futures.[51] Unlike white families, whose offspring were not allowed to enroll at Indian Schools until the first decade of the twentieth century, Native employees working at the federal schools could keep an eye on their children who attended the same institu-tions.[52] This was the case for Jessie Morago, a Native woman from Lac du Flambeau, Wisconsin, who asked for a teaching position with the request: "I would like to get in a school where I could enroll my children; and yet not be a great ways from my home."[53] In another case, Lottie Smith Pattee (Eastern Band of Cherokee/m), a boarding-school matron, wrote to a friend: "O! I can't think of giving up my little girls. . . . I want to keep [Cora] in the same school with me and if possible to room with me. . . . I feel like this: if I separate the two girls they will grow up strangers to each other. I think that I could watch over them better than a stranger." Despite fond recollections of her own experiences as a student at the Hampton Institute, Pattee rejected the premise of child removal inherent in the boarding-school philosophy, insisting that as their mother, she could raise her children better than any surrogate.[54] By working in the same school with their children, Native par-ents preserved some oversight and perhaps hoped to ensure that the other employees treated their children well. In this way, they tried to use their employment within their commitments to their family.[55]

Many Indian applicants combined their economic concerns with com-munity needs. In 1912 Nellie Santeo, a Papago woman from the Salt River Reservation, requested a job "to help earn a living and to be helpful to my people."[56] Annie Abner, a Carlisle graduate, indicated that her Pueblo was behind her decision making. Requesting a transfer from the Albuquerque Indian School to Laguna Pueblo in 1915, she wrote: "I am taking this step not that I desire to give up the work but rather to urge my people on if possible.

It has ever been their wish, since I came from school, that I remain on the reservation."[57] Yankton Sioux author and activist Gertrude Bonnin (Zitkala-Sa), whose husband and brother-in-law were both in the service and who had also served briefly herself, asserted: "I am intimately acquainted with certain Indian employees who are prepared to enter the world at large, to compete with people in different lines of occupation, to make a livelihood and get better things, who, from a sense of duty to and by all the ties of the heart stay in the wilderness. . . . Because there are human beings there today that need their sympathy."[58]

Some white administrators recognized the vital economic role that service employment played within tribal communities. During her time on reservations in the Dakotas, Elaine Goodale observed that "the limited number of salaried positions open to Indians in government employ was no real solution, although ability to secure one of these posts was, and still is, practically the only chance to earn a decent living on the reservation." She further recorded the importance of those salaries for the entire community, although she, like other white policy makers, viewed this negatively: "The man with a regular pay check, however small," she wrote, "was handicapped by incessant demands upon his hospitality, an obligation impossible to evade under tribal custom."[59]

Native employees who remained in their own communities sometimes sought to use Indian Service employment to gain political leverage in their fight for tribal sovereignty. The career of Robert Burns (Cheyenne) offers an excellent example of this strategy. When Burns died in 1931, the Cheyenne and Arapaho General Council passed a resolution in his honor. Describing him as a "beloved friend and fraternal brother," the resolution stated that "the citizens of the Cheyenne and Arapaho Indian Tribes" desire to "express our great appreciation of his labors for and on behalf of his Indian brothers, both in person and also in his active service in Washington, after continuous service in the government for a period of thirty-seven years."[60] The resolution depicts Burns as simultaneously a valuable tribal member, a tribal politician, and a federal Indian Service employee.

As defined by white Americans, Robert Burns was a well-educated man. He had attended the agency school on the Cheyenne and Arapaho Reservation in Indian Territory for four years, spent one year taking an elementary course at Carlisle Indian School in Pennsylvania, and later attended the Methodist Episcopal College at Fort Wayne, Indiana, where he took academic courses and "received a diploma, but no degree." Returning to Oklahoma in 1887, he took a job as the agency cattle herder at Darlington, thus initiating a long career in the Indian Service. As he worked his way up from herder

to agency clerk, his salary increased as well. He entered the service earning $240 per year and by 1926 took home $1,500 annually. Burns retired in
1927 after more than thirty years in the service at the Cheyenne and Arapaho
agency.[61]

During that time, the government considered Burns a valuable asset.
He achieved efficiency ratings as an "excellent" employee during much of
his tenure, until his health began to deteriorate.[62] The agents learned that
Burns's "chief value" was "as an encyclopedia on the family history of Cheyenne & Arapaho Indians."[63] These plaudits stemmed from the government's
agenda of ordering and disciplining the seemingly unruly tribal populations
into governable units. As part of that agenda, Indian Service employees took
tribal censuses; enforced the registration of marriages, births, and deaths;
and carefully allotted property and recorded the deeds. It would have been
invaluable for office work to have a clerk like Burns, who, according to his
superior, was "a walking bureau of information regarding the family and
personal history of practically all of the members of the tribe living under
the four agencies."[64] Indeed, one of Burns's supervisors described him as an
Indian whose "ideas are advanced and [who] takes a strong stand against the
use of intoxicants including [peyote]."[65] From that angle, Burns appears to
have been everything policy makers hoped to achieve through assimilation
policy.

However, if we remember that the General Council's resolution also commended Burns for his "labors for and on behalf of his Indian brothers," he
appears in a much more complicated light. Burns was a well-respected and
active figure in Cheyenne and Arapaho politics.[66] In 1899 he served as interpreter for a delegation that successfully worked to remove their agent. During that negotiation, Burns, as an agency employee, offered key testimony
that supported the complaints of the delegates.[67] In 1928 he was chosen as
a delegate himself to convince the Indian Office to approve the tribal attorney's contract and to extend the deadline for filing claims of treaty violations against the government.[68] As Loretta Fowler, a scholar of Cheyenne and
Arapaho political institutions, has written: "Consistently, the [General] council chose delegations that contained both old chiefs and young, educated,
bilingual men. This combination was viewed as promising in terms of dealing
successfully with the bureaucracy in Washington. The older men knew the
history of the treaties, and the younger men could communicate effectively
and comprehend the legislative process and legal contracts."[69] Burns—with
his substantial background in tribal history and genealogy, his interpreting
skills, and his extensive knowledge of agency history and records—embodied
both categories.

Robert Burns's career exemplifies the economic bind in which Native people found themselves. Living on a reduced land base where their previous economies had been destroyed or greatly diminished, Indians knew that federal employment was often the only wage-labor option that allowed them to earn money while remaining in their communities. This meant, however, that their labor contributed to the continuation of the federal government's colonial agenda in their communities. While Burns could use his position to monitor and sometimes protest the doings of the Indian Service on behalf of his tribe, his knowledge also helped the government survey Indian people and administer colonial programs, such as allotment, more effectively. Nonetheless, Burns stymied the Indian Office's overarching goal of destroying tribal identity; not only did he keep his family on the reservation with their tribal community, but he also used his education and his knowledge of bureaucratic procedure to help protect Cheyenne and Arapaho sovereignty.[70]

Some of Burns's superintendents recognized his commitment to his tribal community. In their reports, we catch glimpses of his activism. Superintendent Freer described him as "thoroughly Indian," and Superintendent Scott was often aggravated by his political actions. "His loyalty to the Office is questionable," Scott wrote in 1917, recommending that Burns be transferred. "He would be more valuable at some place where his political and social obligations were less binding."[71] Scott's accusation echoed those of many other white administrators and suggested emergent tensions in the Indian Service workplace.

IDENTITY AND THE INDIAN SERVICE

As more educated Indigenous people entered the Indian Service, and especially as they began to move into skilled positions, they repeatedly asserted tribal identities, pressed the Indian Office to live up to its policy of hiring Indians, and criticized white employees. On their own reservations, Native people often made claims on the basis of their connection to the community in ways that white administrators rightly understood as assertions of sovereignty. Many Native applicants for jobs in the Indian Service cited their tribal identities or their ability to speak the language of their tribe as making them more qualified for the positions. In 1908 Ada Rice requested reinstatement as a field matron at Winnebago, noting: "I am a Winnebago Indian myself. . . . I speak their language . . . and that ought to be quite a help in visiting the older Indians and helping them in sickness, instructing in sewing, cooking and encouraging them to be clean and tidy about their homes."[72] When requesting promotion to the position of superintendent at Fort Yates, North

Dakota, in 1913, Raymond Bonnin (Yankton Sioux) presented himself to the commissioner of Indian affairs in this way: "I am of Indian descent and an enrolled member of the Yankton Sioux Tribe of Indians of Greenwood, South Dakota, and after ten years of experience in the Indian work among other Indians, I am making this application. . . . I can speak the Sioux language fluently and could converse with the Indians in their own tongue and thereby get better results not having to depend on an interpreter; that is provided I am given an agency among the Sioux. However, I am heartily interested in the advancement of the Indians in general." Others were more cautious, trying to use their tribal connection as an advantage but clearly aware that it could also work against them. Mary Paquette (Winnebago/French) disavowed her initial claims of tribal affiliation after being informed that the Indian Service did not station Native people with their own tribes.[73]

Some employees who made tribal claims were supported by their nations, who recognized their special suitability for the positions. In 1885, for example, a delegation of Menominee chiefs presented a statement of six complaints to the commissioner of Indian affairs, including a demand that the government hire Indian instead of white employees at the tribal sawmill.[74] In the case of Susie McDougall (Chippewa), tribal defenders explicitly pointed to her identity and treaty stipulations to support her. The "parents of children and other members of [the] reservation interested in education" at the White Earth Reservation in Minnesota wrote to their senator, arguing that "Miss McDougall is a member of this reservation [and] has been very successful as a school teacher. . . . [W]e wish to keep her here as her services are valuable and her people want her." Episcopal minister C. H. Beaulieu, another member of the tribe, asserted emphatically in a letter to the commissioner that "Miss McDougall is a member of this reservation and therefore has both treaty and moral rights to be employed in the Indian Service among the Chippewas."[75]

Such assertions of tribal identity were disconcerting to white administrators, who worried that such employees might place the interests of their communities ahead of their duty to carry out federal assimilation policy. Administrators preferred to have Indian employees unmoored from their tribal identities so that they could avoid having a group of educated tribal bureaucrats who might challenge superiors. The Indian Office moved to end this practice. By 1912 the School Service's "Indian Application for Appointment" form specified that "it is not considered to be for the interest of the service or the applicants to assign him [the applicant] to a position among his own people. Therefore the Indian Office looks with disfavor upon applications for appointment at home schools."[76]

Despite this new policy, the problem did not disappear. For instance, the superintendent at Tomah School in Wisconsin protested the reappointment of Lavinia Cornelius to his school, stating: "I have no doubt but [t]hat Miss Cornelius is a competent nurse but I would like to state that we have now on our school roll of employees six Oneida employees. I do not want to convey the impression that I have a thing in the world against Oneida people but long experience has taught me, that for the sake of peace and harmony it is not at all advisable to get too many Indian employees of the same tribe. This transfer will give us another Oneida employee."[77] While the superintendent's comments implied that the problem was tribal factionalism, they can also be read as his fear of being outnumbered by people with a stake in the school and the community.

Agents and superintendents concerned with the Native employees on their own reservations often suggested that the service transfer Indian personnel whom they deemed as aggressive or politically active away from their own reservations and schools. Their complaints indicated that white administrators felt challenged and threatened by Indian workers who had ties to the reservation or who spoke the language, even when those employees held little administrative authority. For instance, in 1918 the new superintendent at Quapaw, Oklahoma, recommended that Naomi Dawson Pacheco (Wyandot), a kindergarten teacher whose husband also worked as the baker, be "transferred or removed" despite her twelve years of service at the school. He acknowledged her skill in the classroom but claimed that "her disposition to find fault and to antagonize those in authority over her offset her school room work." Part of the problem, in his opinion, stemmed from her residence on the reservation and her sense of entitlement as a tribal member. "Mrs. Pacheco has been allowed to go ahead in her ways without being disciplined heretofore and being of Indian blood she has come to feel that she is secure in her position. She will be a big handicap to the administration of the new principal if allowed to remain." He tried to use her desire to remain near her family to force the outspoken Pacheco out of the service by disingenuously suggesting a transfer, knowing, as he wrote to the commissioner, that "Mrs. Pacheco's people live about four miles from the school. . . . It is probable that she would not accept a transfer to some other school."[78] Similarly, in 1915 the superintendent of the Hoopa Valley Reservation in Northern California urged the transfer of Sherman Norton, the agency's outspoken Hupa carpenter.[79] In his letter, the superintendent took the opportunity to castigate all local Indigenous labor: "there are too many local Indian employees at Hoopa, for the good of the school." Both Pacheco and Norton had irritated their superintendents by expressing their opinions about how the schools serving their communities were being run. As bureaucratic insiders, they had intimate knowledge of the schools; and as tribal members (and in Norton's case, as a parent of schoolchildren), they had a vested interest in the school's success.[80]

Ironically, however, in seeking to solve the "problem" of tribal political loyalties, administrators helped foster a modern intertribal identity, as Native employees experienced shared work concerns and discovered that other tribal communities contended with similar difficulties under the colonial regime of the federal government. While Indians' experiences in the off-reservation boarding schools helped develop this realization, working at various locations across the country in the service solidified it for many Native employees.

Many of the Indian personnel in regular positions moved throughout the archipelago of Indian Service schools and agencies across the country as a consequence of both the Indian Office's efforts to keep them away from their communities and their own desire for promotion opportunities. As they did so, they worked among people of many different nations. For example, Julia DeCora Lukecart, a Winnebago woman and younger sister of the artist and teacher Angel DeCora, began working for the service in August 1898 and retired in April 1932. She held a variety of positions, including field matron, assistant matron, matron, seamstress, cook, and general laborer. She worked at fifteen different schools and agencies, including Fort Berthold, North Dakota; Jicarilla and the Albuquerque Indian School, New Mexico; Rosebud, South Dakota; Winnebago, Nebraska; Kickapoo, Kansas; Klamath, Oregon; Pierre School, South Dakota; Vermillion Lake, Minnesota; Rapid City School, South Dakota; Wittenburg School, Wisconsin; Tohatchi on the Navajo Reservation in New Mexico; Crow Creek School, South Dakota; and the Winnebago Hospital, Nebraska. When she finally retired in 1932, she was serving as an attendant at the Shawnee Sanatorium in Oklahoma (Map 1).[81]

By the same token, Dollie Johnson (Chinook) attended Chemawa and Chilocco schools before joining the Indian Service. She began her career as a laundress in 1902 and went on to work as an assistant, cook, assistant matron, and baker. She also temporarily filled in as a teacher at the Salem School in July 1919. She passed away while working as a cook at the Kiowa Agency in Oklahoma in 1932. Overall, Johnson's career took her to eight different schools, including Red Moon, Oklahoma; Ponca, Oklahoma; Chilocco, Oklahoma; Cushman School, Tacoma, Washington; Salem, Oregon; Rosebud at the Cheyenne and Arapaho Agency; and the Riverside School at the Kiowa Agency.[82] The careers of Lukecart and Johnson were not unusual. The files of nine female Native employees who retired upon reaching the age of seventy or had served at least thirty years provide a sense of the common characteris-

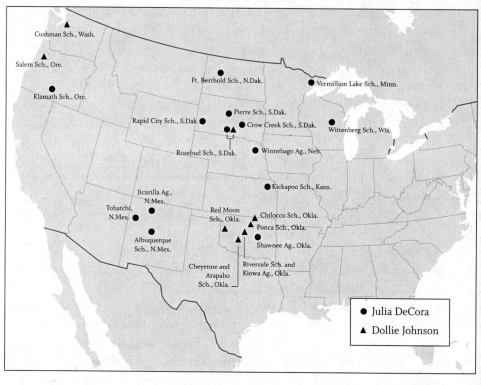

MAP 1. Movement of Indian Service Employees Julia DeCora Lukecart and Dollie Johnson. A career in the Indian Service often involved great mobility in the form of numerous transfers from post to post. This included Native employees, exemplified here by the career paths of Julia DeCora Lukecart (Winnebago/French) and Dollie Johnson (Chinook). The Indian Office hoped that keeping Indian employees off their own reservations would undermine their tribal identities, but it often had the unexpected outcome of creating sympathy between people of different tribes, thus contributing to the development of a modern intertribal identity.

tics of their occupational journeys. The women held, on average, four different job positions and worked at more than six different locations throughout their careers.[83]

As a result of their sojourns on different reservations and in various schools, many of these employees began to see the commonalities that Native people of all nations shared.[84] This was unmistakably the case for Esther Burnett Horne (Shoshone/m). Horne's intertribal experiences began with her education at the Haskell Institute, where she met and married Bob Horne, a Hupa man from Northern California. Working in the Indian Service, the couple moved through the system. Esther turned down an offer to transfer to her home reservation in Wyoming, writing: "As a product of the boarding school, I had a deep-seated desire to continue teaching at the Wahpeton Indian School [in South Dakota] and to instill in these kids a sense of their dignity and worth as individuals. . . . While I knew that I could do this at Wind River, I had a special place in my heart for these Indian kids who were far away from home." She also emphasized the importance of her Cherokee and Yankton Sioux instructors several times throughout her memoir. She hoped to provide her students with "the same nurturing and consideration that Ella and Ruth had given me." She saw herself following in their footsteps as an "Indian teacher" who could incorporate "our cultural values" into the curriculum and student life. An avid student of culture, Horne continued to learn about other tribes when she became a teacher. She remembered that her work at Wahpeton Boarding School "broadened my horizons about the varied tribal cultures. . . . There were tribes from North Dakota, South Dakota, Minnesota, Nebraska, Iowa, Montana, and Wyoming, including Sioux, Chippewa, Cree, Blackfeet, Gros Ventre, Mandan, Hidatsa, Arikara, Mesquakie, Winnebago, Cheyenne, and Shoshone" at the school.[85]

Many other Native employees experienced similar interactions with members of different tribal nations. For example, in a poignant request for a transfer back to the Chin Lee School in Arizona where she had previously worked, Lucy Jobin (Chippewa/m), confessed "that she never was so homesick in her life as she is now, and she thinks so often and so much of the Navahos [sic] that she sometimes feels as if she were a Navaho."[86] When Mrs. Dollie Johnson, a Chinook woman from Washington State, requested a transfer to the Shawnee Agency in Oklahoma, she asserted: "I understand my people and their needs."[87] Also notable were instances in which local tribal members defended the right of Indians from other tribes to work in the service due to a shared intertribal heritage. For instance, people on the Klamath Reservation in Oregon supported field matron Ada Rice, a Winnebago woman from Nebraska, because she was Native, although she was not a tribal member. They asserted that "being a member of our own race, Miss Rice is more closely in sympathy with our people and has a better understanding of our needs." They added: "We believe the opposition to Miss Rice is due to her Indian blood." Rice's Klamath defenders recognized that whites were ignoring their tribal identities instead seeing them as members of an Indian race; in response, the Klamath claimed that identity and used it to assert intertribal solidarity in opposition to white ignorance and prejudice.[88]

Indeed, whites often did treat all people with Native heritage as members of a single race. But they did so for different reasons. Distinguishing between these reasons allows us to understand the contingent experiences of Indian employees as they worked within the Indian Office bureaucracy.[89] The bureaucratic imperatives of the Indian Service led it to create a classification system that divided personnel between whites and Indians.[90] The Indian Office's project of assimilation required that it hire Indians, and its hiring policies required that it identify who was or was not an Indian. This led administrators to repeatedly emphasize employees' status as Indians rather than their tribal identity or individual personhood (Illustration 5.4). For instance, in the lists of employees in the *Annual Reports of the Commissioner of Indian Affairs*, the overwhelming majority of employees were classified as either "Indian" or "White." This dichotomy tended to flatten what were more complexly mixed identities by ascribing the identity of "Indian" to all people of Native heritage, no matter how little or how much. In a few rare instances, employees were listed as "H" (for "Half-blood"), but this was never done consistently, and most people of mixed heritage were not identified as such in the reports.

This classification then colored the evaluations that Native employees received from their superiors. Administrators couched even their praise in racial terms.[91] In 1912, for example, the commissioner of Indian affairs saluted Dakota Charles Hoffman's eighteen-year record in the service as having "especially reflected credit upon the race of which you are member."[92] Yankton Sioux Raymond Bonnin's supervisors at the Uintah and Ouray Agency backhandedly complimented him, saying, "while he is an Indian, he is thoroughly competent" and "[h]ere is an Indian man who is making good."[93] Chippewa Susie McDougall's file is filled with comments noting that she was the best "Indian teacher" in the service.[94]

The other way in which employees of various Native heritages were assigned to a single racial category was in the minds of their white coworkers, who were at best ignorant of their separate tribal cultures and histories and at worst blatantly prejudiced. While the Indian Office had high hopes for the character of its white employees, many of the people it hired to serve Indians were in fact openly racist. The myriad encounters with personal prejudice that Native people must have faced every day generally went unrecorded, but some of the personnel files capture glimpses of them. For example, in 1923 the commissioner of Indian affairs reprimanded Mr. Earl Place for addressing Miss Lucie Jobin "in insolent and profane terms." Apparently, Place defended himself with the claim that his "language was meant for 'squaws collectively,'" an explanation that the commissioner deemed a "very lame excuse." But instead of firing Place, the commissioner counseled him, saying: "You will be expected hereafter to refrain from cursing employees associated with you" as "the work of our Service should be free from coarse or harsh methods and the influence of its personnel should be refining and exemplary,

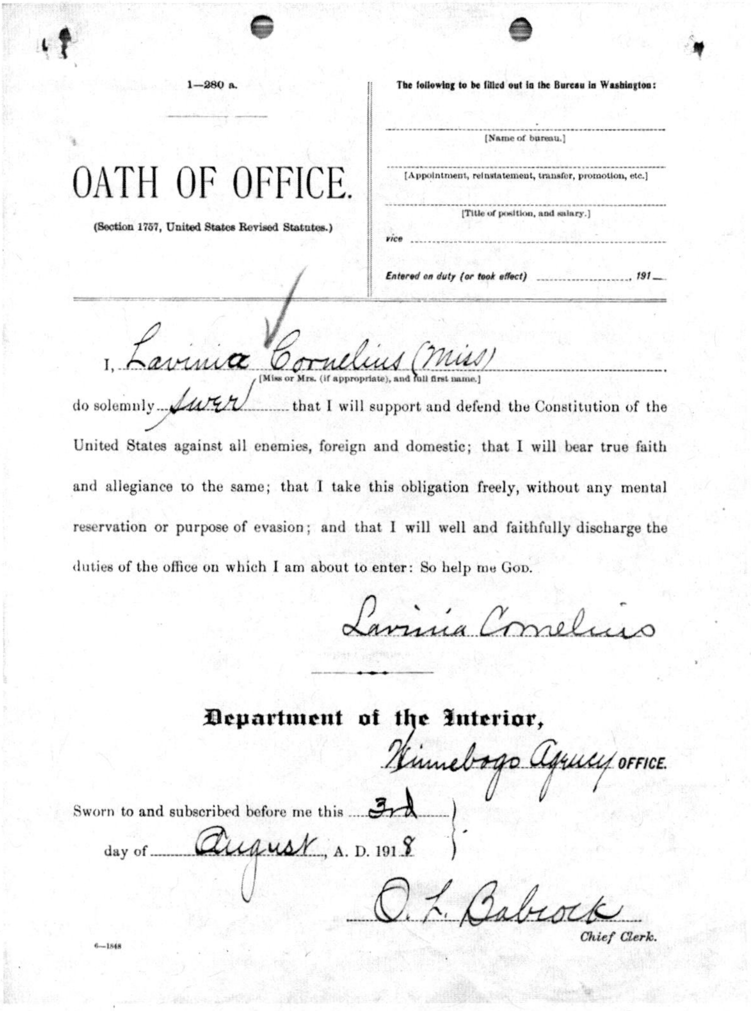

The following to be filled out in the Bureau in Washington:

[Name of bureau.]

[Appointment, reinstatement, transfer, promotion, etc.]

[Title of position, and salary.]

vice _____

Entered on duty (or took effect) _____, 191___

OATH OF OFFICE.

(Section 1757, United States Revised Statutes.)

I, *Lavinia Cornelius (Miss)* _____
[Miss or Mrs. (if appropriate), and full first name.]

do solemnly *swear* that I will support and defend the Constitution of the United States against all enemies, foreign and domestic; that I will bear true faith and allegiance to the same; that I take this obligation freely, without any mental reservation or purpose of evasion; and that I will well and faithfully discharge the duties of the office on which I am about to enter: So help me GOD.

Lavinia Cornelius

Department of the Interior,

Winnebago Agency OFFICE.

Sworn to and subscribed before me this __3rd__

day of __August__, A. D. 191 8

O. L. Babcock

Chief Clerk.

ILLUSTRATION 5.4. Indian Service oath of office. All regular employees were required to take an oath of office in which they swore to protect and defend the U.S. Constitution. For most Native and white female employees, this was a remarkable expression of citizenship, since few Native people were citizens before 1924 and women were ineligible to vote in federal elections before 1920. (Courtesy of the National Personnel Records Center, St. Louis, Missouri) especially so because we are in contact with a race whose moral and social elevation depends largely upon the guidance we furnish."[95]

Assigning a single racial category to all people of Native heritage heightened white administrators' concerns because they thought that Indian personnel would place their allegedly unitary racial interests ahead of their responsibilities to the federal government, thus subverting the goals of assimilation. They frequently questioned the loyalty of Native employees and repeatedly used particular phrases to signal their fears that the employees were being insubordinate. These accusations and phrases became a sort of racial code that was rarely applied to white employees in the same way. The files of Native employees are littered with charges of disloyalty that arose most often when employees disagreed with their superiors. Any behavior that was perceived as undermining the authority of the government or its representative—the superintendent or agent—was labeled disloyal. For example, Harriet Kyselka's superior described her as disloyal because he disliked that she and another employee were "whispering and giggling" while they worked; he suspected them of gossiping about him. When Julia DeCora disputed her superintendent's decision to fire two temporary employees who were probably Indians, the Indian Office charged that she was being disloyal for "oppos[ing] the good discipline of the school." Other charges were more literal. Lucy Jobin's principal insisted that she was "disregarding many of the rules and regulations laid down by officials and publicly criticizing and denouncing officials of the Indian Service." Most dramatically, Susie McDougall was accused of destroying reports regarding tribal land sales, something she vehemently denied but which nonetheless indicates officials' doubts about Native employees' dedication to the federal government.[96]

When white administrators chastised Native employees, they used words that ascribed racial politics to their statements and actions. Key phrases that white supervisors repeated in the efficiency reports of Indian employees included "trouble maker," "too political," and forming part of an "Indian clique." For instance, when Lucy Jobin's superintendent described her as a "trouble maker," he claimed that "she causes factions in school. . . . She was apparently forming a clique of Indian employees to work against the principal and white employees."[97] An earlier administrator described Jobin as "very independent, as many Indian employees are" and commented that this "sometimes interferes with her efficiency."[98] In another instance, when Chippewa Sophie Picard disagreed with her superintendent at the Crow School in Montana, he charged "she has fallen back in the race" and had become "a member of the 'Indian clique.'" It is quite possible that Picard had found common cause with the people at Crow or with her fellow Native employees, but the letters in her file also indicate that she was angry because she had been demoted to assistant matron while a new white employee was given her position as matron at the school. She found this, as she wrote to the commissioner, "very disagreeable."[99] Her superintendent's accusations displaced the real reasons for her complaint onto racist stereotypes about rabble-rousing Indian employees. These stereotypes appear to have been codified into the official Indian Office rules of 1929, which stated: "An attitude on the part of any employee of continuous fault-finding or grumbling . . . or a disposition to become a trouble-maker will be deemed sufficient cause for separating the employee from the service."[100]

As these incidents suggest, the experiences of Native employees reflected the interaction between the Indian Office's desire to assimilate Native people and its simultaneous marking of them as different, as well as the racial preconceptions prevalent among most white employees. The clearest example of this tension occurred when Native women were hired as matrons to implement the maternalist goals of teaching Indian girls gender norms—this despite the fact that policy makers had characterized Native women as unfit mothers in order to justify the removal of their children to federal boarding schools.[101] The result was that supervisors repeatedly insisted that Native women in the post of matron were insufficiently "motherly" to succeed in that position. Native matrons' efficiency reports were studded with criticism that reinforced the racial stereotypes used to demonize Indian women. They "flitted" and were "dirty" and "clannish." They failed to keep the dormitory rooms clean, allowed children to run wild, were disheveled in appearance, and neglected the children's clothing. Such accusations were often followed by a request to transfer the Native woman to a menial position, especially that of cook or laundress, and to hire a white woman in her place. When filling out the efficiency report for boys' matron Emma Ledger (Concow), the superintendent at the Round Valley Reservation in Northern California did precisely this. The matron, he wrote, was a good employee who "serves as well as any Indian woman on this reservation would . . . but a good White Matron with a proper conception of cleanliness would have a great and beneficent influence on the Indian boys."[102] The superintendent at the Keshena School in Wisconsin likewise evaluated Julia Wheelock Metoxyn (Oneida): "Has no motherly instinct and is not fitted by nature to have charge of the small boys. She might succeed as a cook, but is really not qualified for the position she holds." Another administrator suggested that Metoxyn be transferred to the position of laundress and "a white woman sent here to take her place."[103] The Indian Office tended to support the explicit bias of these reports. In Emma Ledger's case, the office noted that no funds were available to offer the larger salary necessary to hire a white matron, so the school would have to make do with a Native woman. In Julia Metoxyn's case, the office patronizingly responded that they were leaving her in the position and were "particularly interested in assisting her to make a success of her work" because she was an Indian.[104]

It is probably no coincidence that whites responded to Native matrons in such a conflicted way because that position was especially associated with the surrogate motherhood federal employees were meant to provide to Native students. Likewise, the very few Native men who were promoted to the position of school superintendent—the corresponding fictive father figure—also had their status contested. Superintendent was the highest rank obtainable at an individual agency or school and carried with it substantial decision-making authority, including over white employees. In keeping with the patriarchal household model, superintendents were almost always male. Only one Native woman seems to have attained the rank of superintendent, while several Native men reached that position.[105] Despite the rhetoric of assimilation, whites seemed uncomfortable with the idea of Indian men in positions of such authority, most likely because they disliked the idea of serving under an Indian or coveted the positions themselves.

The Native men who achieved a superintendent's position fit policy makers' ideal of "civilized" men. They were well educated and behaved according to middle-class standards of comportment. Joseph Estes (Yankton Sioux), one of the first Native men appointed superintendent, had attended the Hampton Institute in Virginia, worked for the Riggs Institute (the Episcopal missionary station in South Dakota), and married a white woman.[106] After several years of requesting promotion to a high-ranking position, Estes finally received an appointment as the superintendent of the Santee Agency Boarding School in 1901 through his connections to the state Republican Party. Almost immediately, the Indian agent presented charges against Estes that focused on his treatment of white women (especially his wife) and accusations of alcoholism. He also stated that white employees chafed under the supervision of a Native man, snidely commenting: "I do not believe that he is a person under whom a white employee who wished to retain his self-respect could or would work long."[107] Accusations of sexual misconduct, especially with white women, periodically surfaced as a way to attack Indian men who gained higher positions in the service, as we will see in the next chapter. But what may be more central to the agent's actions is that as a resident of the reservation who also spoke the Dakota language, Estes presented a special threat. Estes himself believed that this was the case. He claimed that the agent's antagonism sprang from his public accusation that the agent was involved in shady land deals on the reservation. Similarly, Charles Hoffman (Dakota) became superintendent of the Fort Berthold Training School around 1912. He, too, was immediately accused of corruption. The Indian Office responded to both Estes's and Hoffman's situations in the same way: it removed them from their superintendent positions and reassigned them to day schools, a far less prestigious position and one where they were isolated from other employees.[108]

These outcomes were contingent rather than predetermined. Other Native superintendents appear to have suffered somewhat less prejudicial treatment. The brothers Leo and Raymond Bonnin (Yankton Sioux) both attended White's Institute in Wabash, Indiana, and the Haskell Institute in Lawrence, Kansas. Between 1910 and 1932, Leo served as the superintendent of the Kickapoo School in Kansas, the Fond du Lac School in Minnesota, and the Cheyenne and Arapaho School in Oklahoma and ultimately as the superintendent of the entire Cheyenne and Arapaho Agency. Leo's race rarely appears as an issue of concern in his personnel file. Raymond also became a superintendent when he was promoted from clerk at the Standing Rock Reservation to superintendent of the Uintah Boarding School in Utah in 1908. But after leaving the Indian Service, his repeated requests for reinstatement as a superintendent in North Dakota were denied. His supervisor had endorsed the request, adding that Raymond (and his wife, Gertrude, the writer also known as Zitkala-Sa) did not really act like Indians and thus could fill the position admirably: "In giving the official recognition which is undoubtedly due the few thoroughly competent members of his race, I think Mr. and Mrs. Bonnin should be considered in that class. In my opinion, they are both absolutely honest and dependable. . . . He is devoid of the eccentricities often found among the more competent of his race."[109] But despite the service's policy of special hiring and Bonnin's qualifications, officials did not see fit to give him the job. He and Gertrude ultimately moved to Washington, D.C., where he took a job in the Army Quartermaster's Office and she focused on her writing and activism. He continued to seek a superintendency in the Indian Service but never received one.[110]

Native peoples' career paths were often heavily influenced by the attitudes and dispositions of their superiors and their ability to mobilize allies on their behalf. When Lucy Jobin came into conflict with her superintendent, she wrote to the commissioner and asserted: "I am very much astounded to think that such ungrounded charges should be made against me. I emphatically deny that I have been disloyal to Mr. Garber. I have performed my duties in a loyal and faithful manner despite the fact that Mr. Garber has shown prejudice towards me since the time of his arrival here. He is also prejudice[d] against all Indian employees, and has shown and expressed himself openly in the matter."[111] Jobin was supported by a local Catholic priest, who noted: "Of late, it seems, if I write in favor of any employee, it is for some Indian. . . . An unfair treatment, not intentional, of course, on the part of the Indian Office towards Indian employees seems more likely to happen than towards others who have no prejudices from other employees to overcome."[112] His somewhat weak recognition of prejudice nonetheless hints at the difficulties Native employees confronted from the very people who were supposed to be working for their benefit. Likewise, when the superintendent of the Albuquerque Indian School accused Annie Abner of "talking poorly about the school" at her home in Laguna Pueblo, Abner noted: "Being a full blood Indian means a hard struggle, not only in obtaining work; [but] to keep straight in all things in the eyes of those who are ever watching and are ready to put a stumbling block of some sort in the weak places."[113]

Indian employees who encountered inequitable treatment also used their knowledge of Indian Office rules and bureaucratic tactics to defend their claims. When Mrs. Salena Kane felt that she was unjustly passed over by the superintendent at the Shawnee Indian School for several positions that were given to white women, she wrote a forceful letter to the commissioner. She asserted that she was a Pottawatomie and her husband was employed as an engineer and blacksmith at the school. As the positions of laundress, seamstress, and matron opened up, she had asked the superintendent for appointments to each. Although Kane had passed a noncompetitive exam for the seamstress position, the superintendent denied her requests and gave the positions to white women (one of whom had young children, which was contrary to the regulations of the service). Asking the commissioner for his "protection," she described her frustrating discussions with Superintendent Buntin:

> I went to Superintendent's office and talked to him about it and talked reason with him and told him I thought an Indian had ought to be given a position in preference to the whites and he answered yes, and yet he employed the white instead of the Indian. . . . So I said he was mistreating me all the way through which I do not deserve. . . . [I]t offended him so he would not talk about it and insulted me in the office and also told me to go home. . . . [H]e would notify my husband to quit work but has not yet. . . . [A]s I am Indian and I said he had ought to protect me instead of turning me down. . . . I said he was going contrary to the Government rules and he knew it and he had mistreated me enough for me to report it to you.

She added, perhaps in anticipation of retaliation: "I have said nothing un-just. . . . [He] can not say we are trouble makers, for it is not so."[114] She had reason to be concerned. Indeed, as we have seen, superintendents often sup-ported their accusations by painting Indian employees as troublemakers.

Like Kane, many Native employees used bureaucratic procedure to pro-test what they perceived as unjust treatment. Julia Wheelock Metoxyn, for example, refused a transfer from assistant matron to cook. She "dismissed the offer of transfer lightly," her superintendent wrote, "with the remark that she did not like to cook." Yet she remained stuck in her assistant matron position despite correspondence expressing her wish to be a teacher.[115] Alice Cornelius's (Oneida) fight had a more successful outcome. When the Oneida School in Wisconsin was closed in 1919, she was offered a transfer to the Keshena School in the same state, but with her salary reduced from $720 per year to $660 per year (possibly from a "white" to an "Indian" rate). She declined the transfer, and the superintendent bemoaned the Indian Office's position as one that "would deprive the service of an excellent employee." He also sympathetically pointed out that Cornelius resented the apparent "lack of appreciation of her long and faithful service." In light of his advocacy and the support of Alice's nationally famous sister, Laura Cornelius, the Indian Office relented and offered Alice the position at her former salary.[116]

Not all struggles were between Native employees and whites. Indian Service employment could also accentuate fault lines within Native com-munities. Among members of the same tribe, tensions often existed between "mixed bloods" and "full bloods"—categories that were, as Melissa Meyer has demonstrated in her excellent study of the White Earth Reservation, based on "basic cultural or ethnic differences—not solely genetic ones." Mixed bloods were those who "identified themselves as 'Indians'" but whose ideas about "the accumulation of wealth" placed them at odds with full bloods, or the more conservative faction.[117] Examples on other reservations reveal simi-lar tensions within Indigenous communities over the identity of Indians in the Indian Service. As at White Earth, the differences often coalesced around heritage, education, or behavior. For example, in 1912 the business commit-tee (a term that the Indian Office often used instead of tribal government[118]) of Standing Rock petitioned to have Agnes Reedy removed from her field matron position. Reedy, a woman of "Minnesota Sioux" and Anglo heritage who claimed "knowledge of the language," was married to an Irish man work-ing as an Indian Service farmer. The petition, with eight signatures and seven thumbprints, reveals the political alliances at Standing Rock that fell along lines of "blood." The committee charged that Reedy did not visit the older full-blood women who needed her help but only mixed-blood women who "are capable of entertaining her in a royal manner." They called on the Indian Service to terminate the field matron position and reallocate the funds to clerical work at the agency office that they described as "of great importance to every Indian on the reservation, instead of a select few of mixed-blood." Reedy's white superintendent defended her, writing: "Her duties have been performed in a satisfactory manner." He stated that she "makes her headquarters at the Agency, and visits Indians in this immediate vicinity" but was unable to go further afield, suggesting that reservation residential patterns may have mirrored (or contributed to) the divide that the business committee described.[119] Similarly, Essie Horne pointed out that working on one's own reservation could be difficult. She turned down a transfer to her home at Wind River and later wrote: "I said it wouldn't be fair to the students *there* because many were related to me in one way or another. It would be difficult for me to be impartial—parents and kids alike would have expected special treatment."[120] These kinds of political lines existed in various configurations on all reservations, and as we saw in the case of Joseph Estes in the previous chapter, they also arose between people of different tribes.

CONCLUSION

The goal of federal assimilation policy was to destroy the tribal (and thus political) identities of Indigenous people and incorporate them into the citizenry of the United States. The Indian Office attempted to use labor in the federal Indian Service as one weapon in its efforts to assimilate Indians. But despite the government's ideas about the civilizing power of work, Native people had their own reasons for taking jobs in the service. Many sought employment as an economic survival strategy. In particular, many Native people entered the colonial bureaucracy in an attempt to remain in their communities. Some Indian employees even reached high positions of authority in the service. We know the stories of some of these people—Charles Eastman, Carlos Montezuma, Susan LaFlesche Picotte, and Angel DeCora, for example[121]—through biographical studies. But that methodology tends to imply that they were anomalous when in fact they were part of a larger cohort who often tried to use their positions to steer or at least mitigate the course of Indian Office policy. They were also part of a key generation who helped mediate the imposition of federal authority in the everyday lives of Native people.

This influx of skilled Indian employees created a great deal of discomfort among white administrators, who were concerned about having contingents of educated Native people serving on their own reservations. In response, these administrators attempted to scatter local Native employees across the reservation and school systems while inventing excuses not to promote them. This effort to create an interchangeable set of Indian employees unmoored from tribal and thus political affiliation had the ironic effect of strengthening a sense of a shared intertribal identity among many Indigenous people.

Sociability in the Indian Service

Commissioner of Indian Affairs Francis Leupp clearly enjoyed holding forth in his annual reports to the secretary of the interior. In somewhat bombastic prose, he energetically described the Indian Office's work for the year, punctuating the paragraphs with confident assertions of his many opinions on the matters at hand. But even he found it difficult to enliven the statistical discussion of educational programs in the 1906 report. After slogging through almost twenty pages enumerating the kinds of Indian schools under his supervision—their capacity, enrollment, and average attendance; the funds appropriated for each; and the employees who were appointed or had declined their appointments—he couldn't help but conclude with a droll comment: "A not uninteresting feature of these dry statistics is the report that 132 employees were married during their service in the schools."[1]

Commissioner Leupp's attempt at humor actually revealed an important aspect of everyday life in the Indian Service. The distinctive labor needs of the service brought men and women together on the reservations and in the schools, where they not only worked and socialized together but also sometimes courted and married each other. On one hand, the development of workplace friendships and romances was a very modern phenomenon, one experienced at the same time by the men and women who worked in the new skyscrapers of the banking and insurance industries in America's cities.[2] On the other hand, the Indian Service's goals and its diverse workforce meant that when its personnel struck up workplace relationships, they were navigating more treacherous ideological waters. The racially integrated nature of the service was initially quite forward-looking, but a close look at the interactions among employees also reveals the limits of white America's acceptance of its own terms of assimilation.

Examining employees' pursuit of leisure, friendship, and intimacy illustrates the social world of the Indian Service and offers a clear and striking example of how intimate colonialism operated in the field. The federal government's policy of encouraging teachers to love their students as they would their own children and urging adult Indians to admire and emulate their white neighbors was an effort to harness personal relations in the service of the state. Administrators assumed that influence in these relationships would flow in one direction only: from Indian Service employees to their Indian "wards." But administrators placed too much reliance on personal influence and underestimated how bringing whites and Indians together would change all the people involved.

SEEKING OUT A SOCIAL LIFE

In building its bureaucracy, the Indian Service constituted a group of people who were young, often single, and invariably social (Illustration 6.1). Yet socializing in the Indian Service could be difficult. The 1892 *School Service Rules* warned that personnel had "little opportunity for recreation or social pleasure."[3] Employees were exhorted to devote all of their time to their work, and female employees in particular were expected to go beyond their regular duties to help in other departments. For example, Allie Busby's superintendent evaluated her classroom work as "good" but added that she has "shown an unwillingness to take hold and help out when it has been necessary for the lady employees to perform duties other than their regular work. Being without a dining room girl at present in the employees' mess, all of the lady employees, excepting Miss Busby, are taking their turn doing this work."[4] Jobs in the service were often physically and emotionally draining, as employees labored to feed, clothe, and supervise large numbers of children; fought epidemics; endured the extremes of hot and cold weather; and dealt with the often frustrating bureaucracy of Indian Office administration. Even without exacerbating circumstances, employees found themselves exhausted at the end of the workday. One teacher remembered that "social life here [at Yuma] was a decided improvement" from her previous post, "although the extreme heat added to the hard work, prevented my taking much part in it until the winter months came." "There were few opportunities for congenial companionship," another recalled. "Weary at the end of the day, employees returned to their rooms to comfort or muddy their thoughts."[5] Janette Woodruff remembered: "Our duties kept us so busily employed that we found ourselves fairly well separated from each other during the day, and sometimes far into the night."[6]

ILLUSTRATION 6.1. School faculty and staff, Albuquerque Indian School, New Mexico. This photograph illustrates the racial and sexual diversity, as well as the youthful character, of Indian Service employees. This helps explain why the service produced so many relationships, especially those that were interracial and intertribal. (Courtesy of the National Archives and Records Administration, Rocky Mountain Region, Denver)

Moreover, with the exception of the large off-reservation boarding schools, Indian Service posts tended to be isolated from white settlements, meaning that most regular employees turned to their coworkers for entertainment. Special Inspector L. A. Dorrington observed in 1916 that due to the remoteness of the Hoopa Valley Reservation in Northern California, the "means of social entertainment and diversion rests entirely with the employees themselves," but he concluded that they "seem to be equal to the occasion and manage to create considerable social enjoyment among themselves."[7] This was true at some places even as late as 1929. Frank Kyselka wrote of the Colville Agency in Washington: "The absence of picture shows, theaters, lecture or Chautauqua courses, lodges or fraternities (excepting the Grange, to which most of us belong), throws the residents into greater intimacy than at most places."[8] This isolation was much worse at the day schools, which were typically located far from white settlements and staffed by only two employees. On the Pine Ridge Reservation, for instance, Day School No. 29 was almost fifty miles to the northeast of the agency.[9]

As with many aspects of the Indian Service, employees' experiences depended in large part upon the tone set by their superiors. For example, teacher Gertrude Golden remembered that at a posting in Oregon, a conservative superintendent employed "antiquated regulations" when it came to socializing, including a ban on playing cards or visiting by men. Golden concluded, however, that this "was not a sample of the management in Indian schools in general." The superintendent at the Rapid City Indian School in South Dakota frowned on card playing, gambling, and smoking but allowed them if employees kept these activities confined to their private rooms. Most workplaces seemed to have been integrated despite the underlying prejudice of many of the white employees, but again, this depended upon the leadership at the school or agency. Upon transferring to a school in Arizona, Golden was "surprised to learn that segregation of the races was practiced here. The Indian employees, that is—the Tyndalls and Joe Escalanti—had a table to themselves, and I was not long in finding out that there was not the best feeling between them and the teachers of the school."[10] Even if a school or agency was not explicitly segregated, the prejudice of white employees could make for uncomfortable situations for Native personnel. Minnie C. King (Cherokee/m), for example, described the white employees at the Leech Lake School in Minnesota as hostile and mean: "With the exception of one or two, who are friendly, [they] treat us with scorn and contempt, and those that are friendly receive the censure of laughter from others." Indeed, leisure activities and the discussions around them often reveal the tensions of working in a hierarchical, heterosocial, and mixed-race environment.[11] Other employees experienced only mild discord. Janette Woodruff described the atmosphere at her first post as a matron at the Crow Boarding School, noting: "We lived together as one large family, usually in harmony, but with occasional ripples of disagreement. . . . On the whole, though, we were a congenial family."[12]

Despite the many barriers to relaxation, employees did find ways to socialize and occasionally even engaged in outright merriment. One common site for everyday interaction was around the table at mealtimes. At most schools, regular employees did not share board with the students but instead contributed to an employee club that hired a separate cook. Although initiated by the employees, by 1928 this practice was required by the Indian Office.[13] Memoirists especially remembered the excitement of meeting new employees at meals. Gertrude Golden described the anticipation that the arrival of a new male employee created among the single women at her school: "At noon, before going down to lunch where we would meet this interesting gentleman face to face, we took extra care with our toilets in the hope of making a favorable impression upon him."[14] Eventually, employees came to use the clubs for other purposes, from reading groups to wedding receptions and regularly scheduled parties. At Hoopa Valley, for example, the employee club hosted the Hoopa Social Club, a group "composed principally of the employees of the Indian School [that met] every two weeks."[15] Essie Horne remembered that on Sundays, when the employee mess was closed, the Native personnel at Wahpeton gathered together to share their cultural traditions: "For Sunday evening get-togethers, we all took our turns providing a main dish for our evening meal. Occasionally, we would cook our Native American specialties: Irving Shepard, a member of the Tlingit tribe, would make clam chowder; I would cook fried pheasant, and others would cook frybread. It tasted so good."[16]

In keeping with staff members' full schedules, much employee entertainment revolved around the work of the schools and agencies. Indian Service–sponsored reservation fairs, outings with pupils, and end-of-the-year exercises all offered employees the opportunity for a good time. In 1893 teacher William Howard described the changing nature of student entertainment at the Dawes Institute, later renamed the Santa Fe Indian School.

> The socials or receptions are very interesting. They have since I came here been changed from a sort of military affair to the plan of civilized social gatherings. . . . We don't talk much but get them [the students] playing as soon as possible. Drop the handkerchief, The Miller, Blind Mans B[l]uff, Bean-bags, Old Maid, Checkers, Word and Picture Building, and the Sixteen Puzzle have met with the most success for entertainment. . . . These Saturday receptions are really interesting to us employees as well as to the pupils. I have not missed one since my advent into this institute.[17]

Janette Woodruff remembered that at the Crow Boarding School, "all the employees assisted with Christian Endeavor" and Wednesday night singing. "It was good to be like this, and to have the employees joining so wholeheartedly in the song fest," she wrote.[18] A special inspector at Hoopa Valley in 1916 reported that "considerable attention is given to social gatherings and other meetings leading towards the culture and refinement of the pupils."[19] The school regulations made such evenings mandatory, part of the homelike atmosphere of the school: "The 'evening hour' in boarding schools should not be devoted to perfunctory and spiritless so-called study in a poorly lighted and ventilated schoolroom, but should be a true home hour."[20] Although employees often enjoyed these extracurricular activities, they also added to their workload by requiring them to work late into the evenings and often on weekends.[21]

Holidays, in particular, brought the employees and the people of the reservation together for festivities.[22] Government policy emphasized the celebration of holidays as a colonial tool, a way to replace Native cultural traditions with Christian and patriotic fare, but these also created opportunities for shared enjoyment. The school rules of 1892 stated: "New Year's Day, Franchise Day (February 8), Washington's Birthday (February 22), Arbor Day, Decoration Day (May 30), Fourth of July, Thanksgiving Day, and Christmas, are to be appropriately observed as holidays." Christmas was particularly important. Superintendent Kyselka at Hoopa Valley described his school's celebration to the commissioner in his annual report for 1902: "The Christmas cantata deserv[es] special mention. Through the generosity of employees and friends, gifts were provided for the pupils. School closed with an enthusiastic reproduction of Ernest Seton-Thompson's animal play, in costume, the afternoon being devoted to athletic and aquatic contests. Music, recitations, and drills in costume comprised part of the evening's programme."[23] As Kyselka's report indicated, the government did not supply the school with gifts or decorations; those were the result of employee generosity and organization. In their memoirs, many former non-Native employees remembered the difficulty of organizing presents but also the pleasure in giving them. Flora Gregg Iliff recounted how they avoided disaster at the Truxton Canyon (later Valentine) School in Arizona when the employee in charge quit right before Christmas. Her resignation, Iliff wrote, "brought the problem of Christmas to the fore. Miss Calfee had been Christmas—she and the Massachusetts Indian Association [a branch of the Women's National Indian Association]. Who would inherit the task of providing the program and gifts for the children?" The remaining staff ultimately decided to ask the mail-order houses for "unmarketable merchandise," and the "replies were prompt and generous. They would be happy to contribute to the Indian children's Christmas, and since this was their gift, they reserved the right to pay the freight."[24] Living among the Karuk in Northern California in 1909, field matrons Mary Arnold and Mabel Reed used their own resources to ensure that each of their friends received a gift. They wrote of that year's planning: "The number of presents stands at forty fancy bags, thirty plain bags, twenty dress pieces, fourteen shirtwaist lengths, and a large number of toys. But we have only twenty-six articles that, in a pinch, can be given to the men, and we have reckoned about fifty Indian men among our rather close personal friends."[25]

When schools sponsored Christmas programs, one of the male employees or older boys would often play Santa Claus. Joe Iliff, Flora's future husband, had the role one year at the Supai School in Arizona, and his performance convinced the Native children and parents that he was a "quigete," or ghost, until they realized he was Mr. Iliff, their industrial teacher. Despite such cultural misunderstandings, white employees fondly remembered these celebrations as moments when the community came together as one.[26]

Other holidays also served as moments of revelry for the staff and local Native people. The employees threw Halloween parties and put on St. Patrick's Day dances. Fourth of July celebrations seem to have been primarily organized by the Native residents of the reservation, perhaps because they took place during summer vacation. Many employees attended Independence Day celebrations that ranged in form from powwows with Native dances to a "sham battle commemorating the Custer Massacre" at Pine Ridge. At the Hoopa Valley Reservation in 1907, a local paper touted the celebration of an "old-time fourth of July" that was sponsored by the Hoopa Businessmen's Association. The events included an "Indian Brush dance, boxing, rodeo, logging show, field events, a public dance, barbecue, an all-Indian pageant and parade, plus the now famous 60-mile Klamath-Hoopa boat race."[27]

Other entertainments were less elaborate and focused on outdoor activities in the vast western landscape. Employees went on picnics and took hikes during their leisure time. Flora Gregg Iliff noted that there was no church service at Supai, Arizona, so she "went out for a leisurely view of my surroundings" instead. At other times, she "slipped on an old dress in lieu of the bathing suit I did not have, and took a plunge in the wide pool only a few yards from our cottage." Essie Horne (Shoshone/m) enjoyed taking outings with her students at Wahpeton: "In the summer, we made frequent visits to the nearby Minnesota lakes, and I particularly remember Sunset Beach on Otter Tail Lake as a favorite of the kids. We transported the children to the lake, and the kitchen personnel prepared a great picnic lunch for us to take. Activities for the outing included softball, sack races, three-legged races, and fifty-yard dash, and other competitions. We'd also rent boats and swim and have a great time."[28] William Howard combined hiking with the employees' other entertainment staple: gossip. "Mr. Roberts and I took a five or six mile walk last Sunday morning," Howard wrote to his fiancée, "and we gossiped all the way—he did most of the talking and told me many things not to be observed on the surface" about the quarrels and tensions at school.[29]

Calling upon and visiting with fellow employees, missionaries, white settlers, or Indians provided one of the primary means of social interaction for personnel. Day-school teachers were particularly dependent on such visits.[30]

Despite the distance between schools, employees traveled to see each other, providing important information, moral support, and entertainment. Albert Kneale, who taught at Pine Ridge, fondly remembered: "Day-school teachers helped each other. Although separated by long miles, we made warm friends among them. The third day after our arrival, we had a white visitor in the person of Dr. Charles Wood, a physician, the teacher at No. 12 Day School—which No. 12 was fourteen miles below us on the Wounded Knee. This made him our nearest white neighbor. During his visit we received a great deal of much-needed advice."[31] Indeed, the Kneales often spent their weekends on horseback, riding out to call upon neighbors who lived as far as forty miles away.[32] Corabelle Fellows, a day-school teacher, recalled that she regularly rode "the seven miles to the nearest camp school which had just been established under the direction of George and Belle Douglas." Later, when she taught at Day School No. 4 on the Cheyenne River Reservation, she and her fiancé took longer trips: "When cold weather set in we drove a bobsled on the frozen river to Chargus' Camp or White Horse Camp to see William and Rebecca Holmes, a couple who served the Episcopal Church thirty miles up the river."[33]

Nellie McGraw Hedgpeth, a Presbyterian missionary at Hoopa who served briefly as a temporary employee, recorded in her diary the whirl of sociability among the missionaries, school employees, and reservation inhabitants in 1901.[34] She and Mrs. Jane Spinks, the school cook, were close friends and often visited at each other's homes. Many of the other agency employees also came to call on Hedgpeth and Miss Chase, her fellow missionary. One evening in June, for instance, Miss Engle, a teacher, and Mr. Tyler, the principal teacher, visited, and the group "talked and had arguments till after 10."[35] A few days later, teachers Mrs. Manning and Miss Engle and kindergarten teacher Mrs. Hillis called on the missionaries. The following weekend, Mrs. Spinks and Mrs. Hillis called again, and that evening, Hedgpeth went to visit with Mrs. Freer, the superintendent's mother, and Mr. Snyder, the agency clerk.[36] Hedgpeth and Perry Tsamanwa (Laguna Pueblo), the agency blacksmith, both owned cameras and were often called upon to take pictures. Hedgpeth recorded that she photographed the seamstress's "Indian [basket] collection" and took pictures of the temporary seamstress with her pupils. But Hedgpeth's diary also reveals a very tragic component of socialization on the reservation: her attendance at numerous funerals. Many of them were held during the winter months and were primarily for Native people, both young and old.[37]

Sometimes, employee revelry attracted criticism from superiors. Dances were often lightning rods for disapproval (Illustration 6.2).[38] Essie Horne

ILLUSTRATION 6.2. Omaha dance at Pine Ridge Agency, South Dakota, 1891. Service employees often learned a great deal about the cultures of the Native peoples among whom they worked. Albert Kneale, a white day-school teacher at Pine Ridge, attended Omaha dances like the one held here at the boarding school. For Native employees, such experiences helped solidify intertribal or tribal ties. (Courtesy of the Denver Public Library, Western History Collection, creator Clarence Grant Morledge, call no. X-31524)

secretly attended local dances at her first posting in Eufaula, Oklahoma: "My supervisors would also have been dismayed if they had learned that one of my most enjoyable off-campus activities was Creek Stomp Dancing with former Haskell acquaintances. . . . Although I'm Shoshone and they were Creek, I felt a really strong kinship with them." Such friendships and shared experiences strengthened the intertribal identity of many Native employees and, as we will see, also led to intertribal marriages.[39] But dances also brought white and Native employees together. In 1921 Maggie Goulette Keith, a Yankton Sioux woman serving as housekeeper with her white husband at Day School No. 7 on the Pine Ridge Reservation, was reported to have held a dance at the school. The superintendent insisted that orders had been issued "that no dances were to be held at any of the school buildings, either the cottages or school-rooms, his reason being that it was a bad example for the Indians and that it detracted from the efficiency of the employees." Although Mrs. Keith, a former Hampton student, denied holding the dance (at least on the date specified), the superintendent was adamant that she had done so in "violation of this rule" and "that several employees of this office were present." He went on to add that dismissing her without also dismissing her husband would be useless, because "Mrs. Keith is without question, the head of the Keith family and her husband will do almost anything that she directs." It is unclear from her file whether or not she was fired. What is clear is that although she was Yankton Sioux, she seems to have had strong connections to the Pine Ridge community, both through her years of working on the reservation and through her son-in-law. The dance most likely included her relatives, local Native people, and Indian Service employees.[40]

Even more worrisome in the eyes of administrators were the dances held by white employees, who were perceived as setting bad examples for the Indians. In June 1921, a worried Commissioner Burke contacted the superintendent at the Klamath School in Oregon. "It is further reported," he wrote, "that the school and agency employees hold social dances about once a month to which the general public is invited, and that after serving supper in the school dining hall about midnight, dancing is resumed until 2 or 3 o'clock in the morning." Given the importance of employees serving as object lessons for their Indian wards, he admonished, "a dance prolonged beyond 12 P.M., particularly on a Saturday night, is a questionable example to the Indians, especially if offered by our Service." He then went on to explain that many Native people had indeed noticed this disjuncture between ideal examples and employee behavior. "Probably the reply oftenest made to [the legal restrictions on Indian dances] is a reference to the character and freedom of some styles of white dances," he noted crossly.[41]

FRIENDSHIP AND INFLUENCE

But perhaps administrators should have worried less about the example employees set for their Indian wards and more about the example those wards offered employees. Assimilation theory assumed that all Native cultures were inferior to that of "civilized" Anglo-Americans and were inevitably disappearing. Policy makers had assumed that the power of object-lesson pedagogy meant that one white family serving as "practical missionaries of the gospel of cleanliness" in the "heart of barbarism" of the Indian camps could change an entire community.[42] Various commissioners glowingly described the day schools, staffed primarily by husbands and wives, as "centers from which radiate some measure of better living, better morals, and better habits generally."[43] What sometimes happened instead was that living in Indigenous communities altered the convictions of the white employees who were ostensibly teaching the benefits of their own "civilization" but who were in fact greatly influenced by the culture of their wards (Illustration 6.3). In the

ILLUSTRATION 6.3. *Miss Chase [right], Miss McGraw [left] on Their Way to Captain John's.* These Presbyterian missionaries served as federal field matrons for part of their time at the Hoopa Valley Reservation. Like many white employees, they often displayed ambivalence about their work, teaching that Native cultures were destined to disappear while simultaneously demonstrating great curiosity about those cultures. Here, the women are using Hupa baskets—a baby carrier and a burden basket—to carry their supplies. They also helped Hupa basket makers reach a national market. (Courtesy of the Phoebe A. Hearst Museum of Anthropology and the regents of the University of California; photograph by Nellie T. McGraw Hedgpeth [catalogue no. 15-20902])

process, some of the non-Native Indian Service personnel came to question the totality of assimilation ideology.

A sense of isolation from white communities and a proximity to Native cultures sometimes led white employees into personal relationships with individual Indians. This was especially the case at day schools. As one service employee noted: "The [day-school] teachers were judged largely by their success in raising the standard of daily living . . . and their capacity to live and thrive in isolation. They made the long drive to the Agency once every 3 months to receive their salary that was paid quarterly and to stock their larders for the next 3 months."[44] Under these conditions, everyday contact could lead to acquaintance and even familiarity with Indians. Albert

Kneale recalled his friendship with Old Foam, a Native man who lived near their day school on Pine Ridge: "There were many ways he showed his friendship and many a meal he had at our home," Kneale wrote.[45] The close quarters of boarding schools also nurtured companionship, and many employees left behind close friends when they transferred or quit. In 1901 Nellie McGraw Hedgpeth attended a going-away party for three employees, Perry Tsamanwa and Mr. and Mrs. Snyder, at the superintendent's house at Hoopa Valley. She noted: "25 present, served turkey, sandwiches and cake. Got home at 12."[46] And years later, Gertrude Golden still remembered the pain of leaving her good friend Esther Southern, who was of Sioux and white heritage: "How I hated to say good-by to her! The farewell was made a little easier, however, by our twin resolves not to be separated for more than this year."[47]

At times, the course of instruction between white employees and Native people was reversed. Flora Gregg Iliff recalled how she and a white coworker bought some donkeys from people in the village at Supai, Arizona, thinking it would be fun to ride them "off to one of the ranches farther up the canyon for a refreshing chat with people who were as isolated socially as we." She remembered that their attempts to purchase and then ride the stubborn donkeys caused great amusement among the Hualapai people. She also realized that it changed the dynamic between them: "Being donkey riders brought us to their level. Daisy and I took advantage of this pleasant relationship to learn as much as we could of the things the Indians believed but spoke of only among themselves."[48]

Indeed, as Iliff's experiences imply, despite their mandate as agents of assimilation, many white employees found American Indian cultures fascinating and took the opportunity to explore them. Native ceremonies and dances often created occasions to do so. Indigenous people regularly allowed very curious school employees to attend ceremonies and dances that were closed to others outside the tribe. For example, teacher Gertrude Golden cheerfully attended a Fourth of July powwow with the school farmer and several of the other female employees. Golden claimed that although the Indians did not mind visitors during the day, "the dance held every night in the big lodge was not for white people to witness. However Esther Southern, Mr. Betz and I, wrapped in Indian blankets that covered us to the eyes, would often go to the dimly-lighted tent, sit down on the grass with the natives and view with delight all the ceremonies of the evening." Their curiosity about and presence at such events sent a mixed message about the government's agenda of destroying Native cultures. "Some of the Indians recognized us as the teachers of their children," Golden noted, "but allowed us to remain while excluding other whites."[49] Similarly, Julia Tuell, who served for six years as housekeeper at a day school on the Northern Cheyenne Reservation with her husband, P. V. Tuell, was one of only two whites allowed to witness the 1911 Cheyenne Massaum, or animal dance. (The other white witness was anthropologist George Bird Grinnell.)[50] The Cheyenne permitted Tuell to attend and take photographs of the ceremony because of the close relationship of amity and trust she had formed with the tribe over her years of teaching on the reservation, especially her friendship with Chief American Horse. Tuell had learned to speak the Cheyenne language from American Horse, whom she believed knew no English. Years later, he revealed that he was fluent in English but knew she would have no incentive to learn Cheyenne if he spoke her language.[51] Other employees also learned to speak Native languages, though this was harder to do if they did not remain on the same reservation for long. Albert Kneale reported that when he and Edith arrived at Pine Ridge, they eagerly began to learn "to speak Indian," but upon their transfer to the Crow Reservation, they were dismayed to learn that there was more than one "Indian" language. "We had thought we were studying Indian only to learn that we were studying Sioux; that in addition to the Sioux language there was the Crow language, the Cheyenne, the Arapaho, the Shoshone, the Navajo—these and about two hundred more."[52]

Local Native employees sometimes served as "cultural brokers" by explaining their way of life and traditions to their coworkers. When Gertrude Golden attended a traditional Yuma (Quechan) funeral, which included a cremation and the burning of the deceased's possessions, she recalled that "a Yuma employee of the school who stood near us explained that in this sermon the Crier recounted a sort of history of the woman's life, stressing her good deeds." In other cases, employees learned about the tribe from their own observations or other reservation residents. Julia Tuell, for instance, carefully listened to what the Cheyenne told her about their culture and traditions and wrote up detailed captions for her photographs.[53]

These experiences point to the complex relationships between white employees and Native people and suggest that many Indians deliberately allowed whites to learn about their cultures, perhaps in the interest of using non-Native curiosity to validate rather than discourage Native ceremonies and traditions. Some white service employees thus learned that the people they encountered on the reservations were not blank slates waiting for enlightenment; they were thoughtful human beings with their own understandings of the world and a dedication to preserving their cultural identities.

It is unclear how many white workers were influenced in this way. Several former employees later published memoirs of their work in the Indian Service, framing their recollections as narratives in which they had become enlightened after living in Indian country. Certainly, white concern about the problem Native cultures posed to America had subsided by the time their books were published in the 1950s,[54] and cultural relativism had flourished in the previous few decades. Their opinions may simply have reflected larger cultural changes. It is nonetheless clear that all of them were decidedly influenced by their work in Native communities. They had come to know Indian people as individuals, sometimes as close friends, and they had learned to understand and in some cases appreciate Native cultures and Indians' experience of conquest. Flora Gregg Iliff, for instance, opened *People of the Blue Water* (1954) with a reminiscence about moving from Kansas to Oklahoma as a child and seeing scalps on the prairie. "Even then," she wrote, "I knew that the Indians' side of the conflict was not told in the history books." She concluded the memoir by stating that her "years with the Indians . . . were more than adventure, they were an education." She added that Americans could all learn from their first peoples.[55] Estelle Aubrey Brown dedicated her memoir *Stubborn Fool* (1952) to John Collier, the commissioner of Indian affairs (1933–42) who ended many of the culturally destructive policies of assimilation. In her introduction, she confessed: "The story . . . is an American story, yet it is known to few Americans. Because it should be known to all, the story is here told by a woman who lived it, who found much of it infamous, and who freely confesses her own shabby part in it."[56]

Other memoirists reinterpreted the Indians they had worked with through a decidedly antimodernist lens.[57] In *Red Moon Called Me* (1950), Gertrude Golden portrayed Indians as primitive and doomed to disappear, but also as purer and more authentic than Americans in industrial society. For example, she mused: "To those who have never heard Indians sing, it is impossible to convey the spiritual quality which seems to well from the very soul of the singer. To me the music of their songs was enchanting. . . . Savage, primitive, unrestrained? Yes, but awakening in one a feeling of affinity with these first Americans struggling against an unfriendly environment, against the encroaching white man and, finally, against disease and death."[58] Despite her sentimentality and her experiences, she remained uncritical of federal policy, concluding: "The Indian Bureau disapproved of these Indian encampments . . . and discouraged them as much as possible. The government officials had very good reasons for doing so . . . [and] the government policy was to discourage undesirable practices while gradually educating the youth to their folly and evil." Instead, Golden placed the blame for problems on indifferent administrators and teachers, whose attitude toward their work was "anything is good enough for a lousy Indian."[59]

Taking a slightly more self-critical approach, Albert Kneale poked fun at his own naïveté about American Indians throughout his memoir, *Indian Agent* (1954). He structured his experience to highlight how much he learned over the course of his thirty-six-year career. Describing himself as having been totally ignorant, Kneale wrote that his initial knowledge of Indians was completely based on James Fennimore Cooper's novels. Early in the book, Kneale admitted that he and his wife, Edith, harbored doubts about the Dakota peoples they were going to teach at Pine Ridge. He described one evening early in their first year of teaching when, startled by the face of an Indian in the window, he "seized the gun . . . and rushed to the door . . . [and] fired two shots aimed well over his head." It was only later that Kneale learned that looking in before knocking was standard practice at Pine Ridge. He must have been, he wrote, "just a little jittery anyhow."[60] Toward the end of the book, Kneale related another incident from his time as the superintendent on the Uintah and Ouray Reservation in Utah, one that sat in sharp contrast with his violent overreaction at the beginning of his career. In this anecdote, he made abundantly clear how much his opinions about Native peoples had changed. Kneale and Etta, his second wife, went on an overnight visit to one of the outlying camps on the reservation. They spent the night under the stars in the middle of the village, and the next morning Etta awoke to a peculiar predicament.

> Etta was dismayed. Here she was in the midst of an Indian village, garbed in a mere nightgown. . . . Had it been any other place in the world, with conditions similar, I should have shared her apprehensions, but not on an Indian reservation, nor among Indians. . . . I knew that she could stand erect in that bed and don her clothing. . . . I knew there was not an Indian in this village that would see her and, not only would he fail to see her, but in some subtle manner would make her aware of the fact that he did not see her. It took some persuasion . . . [but] after that experience, she never again expressed hesitancy about dressing in the midst of a group of Indians. She had gained a new conception of the meaning of the term "gentleman."[61]

This was rather incredible, given the gender norms that white women were supposed to represent for the Indians. The sight of Etta in her nightgown in front of Natives would have horrified policy makers, who expected employees to serve as examples of "better living, better morals, and better habits."[62] Moreover, in describing the Indian men of the camp as gentlemen the likes of which would not be found in "any other place in the world," Kneale implied that perhaps they did not need to be "civilized." Elsewhere in his memoir, Kneale more explicitly described how his own experiences undercut the tenets of official policy. When he began teaching, he wrote, the Indian Office "always went on the assumption that any Indian custom was, per se, objectionable, whereas the customs of whites were the ways of civilization." But over the course of his career, he found that "every tribe with which I have associated is imbued with the idea that it is superior to all other peoples. Its members are thoroughly convinced of their superiority not alone over members of all other tribes but over the whites as well."[63] As these examples demonstrate, some of the employees who entered their posts believing in the project of education and assimilation came away changed after living in Indian communities and interacting with Native people. They became less rigid in their expectations about cultural change, more appreciative of aspects of Native culture, and better able to see Indians as distinct human beings rather than a "race" to be assimilated.

LOVE AND MARRIAGE

The government's insistence on assimilation and its strategy of using personal interaction to foster it ultimately encouraged some service employees to move beyond racial and tribal identities through that most intimate of relations: marriage. As personnel worked and played together, it was not unusual for friendship to blossom into love.[64] They often shared occupational concerns, social lives, and similar education levels and class expectations, and they might bond over shared ideas about their work, mutual dislike of their superiors, or simply the time they spent in each other's company. Some of these relationships were seen as unremarkable, while others created great controversy and became the subjects of national newspaper coverage.

Like Commissioner Leupp, other employees noticed and joked about the propensity of service personnel to marry their own. In 1893 William Howard addressed the marriage of the Santa Fe school's disciplinarian to one of its teachers, humorously attributing it to the romantic environment of the school: "It was a quiet but pleasant affair. . . . It is said that the atmosphere of the school room is infected with the most contagious form of matrimony. Never in the history of the school, has one of its teachers left the institute unmarried."[65] Similarly, local newspapers announced a number of weddings among the personnel at Hoopa Valley in the first years of the twentieth century. For example, L. M. Lady and Miss Annie Meyers were wed at the superintendent's cottage on Christmas Day 1916. One witness described the event: "The bride was beautifully attired in white messaline. Invitations were extended to all employees of the school and after the hearty congratulations from their many friends, the bridal party marched to the banquet given in the

ILLUSTRATION 6.4. Annie Kouni (Laguna Pueblo) and Joseph Abner (Oneida). This couple met while employed at the Albuquerque Indian School. Like many Native employees who married coworkers, the Abners had an intertribal relationship, and they lived at the United Pueblo Agency after their wedding. (Courtesy of the National Personnel Records Center, St. Louis, Missouri)

employee's club room. A dance was given in the evening for the happy couple in which there was quite the display of pretty fashioned gowns."[66] In 1900 Frederick Snyder, the "desperately popular" white clerk at the agency, married Miss Charlotte Brehaut, a white woman serving as the school matron. In 1910 employment on the reservation brought another white couple together: Cyrus Mills, onetime blacksmith at the agency, and the seamstress Gifford Spinks. Miss Alice Hansen was working as secretary and stenographer when she met C. S. Anderson, the agency doctor; in 1916 they tied the knot.[67]

Marriages in the Indian Service were not limited to non-Native couples. Local tribal members who were employed in the service also wed, although they probably did not need the workplace to bring them together.[68] But the movement of Indians throughout the service also resulted in a kind of union historians rarely discuss: intertribal marriages. Many of these couples likely met while students in the boarding schools before going on to work for the government. For example, Bob Horne (Hupa) met his wife, Esther Burnett (Shoshone/m), at the Haskell Institute; they married and remained in the service together.[69] In 1906 Sam Oitema (Hopi) entered his first service position as the shoe-and-harness maker at the Hoopa Valley School. He had met his wife, Clara Carpenter, a Hupa woman, at the Phoenix Indian School and may have requested a position at her home reservation.[70] Similar couples appear throughout the Indian Service. Annie Kouni from Laguna Pueblo worked as a seamstress at the Albuquerque Indian School, where she met Joseph Abner, an Oneida man from New York who worked as the engineer at the school. After they married, Joseph lived at United Pueblo Agency with Annie (Illustration 6.4).[71]

These intertribal couples and their children had the opportunity to learn the ways of both sides of their families. As Paula Gunn Allen has written, "the descendents of such matches were often twice-blessed: They got two sets of languages, customs, traditions, and styles of cooking, dressing, and singing. Of course, they also got two sets of responsibilities."[72] While many continued to identify primarily with one tribe, they often came to appreciate and sometimes incorporate aspects of both. Essie Horne remembered that when she went with her husband, Bob, to visit his family at Hoopa Valley, Bob's grandmother showed her how to make acorn soup, a traditional Hupa meal. She also tried to teach Essie the art of basket weaving, but Essie later wrote regretfully, "I didn't have the time or patience to learn."[73] Jack Norton Sr. and his future wife, Emma, met at the Haskell Institute in Kansas before joining the Indian Service in the 1930s. Their son, Jack Norton Jr., recalls that while he and his siblings "were raised Hupa," his mother reminded them of her tribal heritage, keeping Cherokee newspapers around the house and taking the children to visit her relatives in Oklahoma.[74]

Intertribal marriages could also reconnect people to other tribal communities after the colonial process had disrupted their ties to their own tribes. For example, in a certain light, Katie Brewer appears unmoored from tribal affiliation. An Alaskan woman who was enrolled in the Chemawa Indian School at a young age, Brewer continued to work at the school for over fifty years after her graduation. She never seems to have returned to her home in Alaska. That does not mean she became an Indian without a tribe, however; she married a fellow student and employee, David Brewer, a member of the Puyallup band. She and her children were ultimately listed on the Puyallup tribal census, and Brewer also moved to Puyallup in Washington State when she retired from the Indian Service.[75] Service employment may also have given intertribal couples an alternative to choosing between their heritages or avoiding family disapproval. For example, in the 1930s, novelist N. Scott Momaday's parents, Al (Kiowa) and Natachee (Cherokee/m), joined the Indian Service to get away from Al's family, who considered Natachee an outsider and treated her with contempt.[76]

The same demographic characteristics of the Indian Service that led to intertribal weddings also resulted in relationships between Natives and whites. As Thomas Biolsi has astutely noted, "the middle ground has commonly been a 'marrying ground.'"[77] Marriages between Native women and white men do not seem to have caused any particular concern among officials. While the negative title of "squawman" was often applied to white men who married Native women, lived on the reservations, and were seen as having "gone native," this epithet was apparently not affixed to most white husbands in the Indian Service.[78] Indeed, the service employed many white men who were married to Native women. We might once again take the employees of the

Hoopa Valley Reservation as an example of the service more broadly. July 1901 saw the marriage of disciplinarian J. P. Cochran, a white man, and Lottie Horne, a Hupa woman who worked as an assistant seamstress and assistant matron. The previous year, Albert Simpson, a white man, arrived at the Hoopa School to take up the carpenter's position. There he met assistant cook Martha Owl, a Cherokee woman from North Carolina, and they married the same year.[79] Frank Kyselka, who served as the superintendent at Hoopa, had met his future wife, Harriet Holliday, while employed at the Fort Lewis School in Colorado. They may have bonded over their shared Michigan roots—he was from Traverse City and she from the Chippewa community at L'Anse— finding such commonality more important than their racial differences. The fact that the Indian Office appointed a number of white men married to Native women to the position of superintendent implies that these men did not suffer opprobrium as a result of their relationships. It is possible, however, that officials still felt free to meddle in these marriages. Superiors often commented on the Kyselkas' relationship, for example. In one instance, during a period of marital turmoil in which the couple had requested to be assigned to different reservations, administrators debated ways to help strengthen the marriage.[80] This effort to shore up a mixed-race marriage contrasted sharply with the attacks on unions between white women and Native men, as we will see below. This difference in official reaction was likely due to the fact that white husband–Native wife pairings did not disrupt white notions of power and race. Many of these women were of mixed heritage, and they were often well educated. It is also possible that non-Native men saw marrying well-educated Native women as a way to gain class status, something Jacki Rand has discussed for a later period. Their boarding school–educated wives could teach them proper middle-class manners, while their own whiteness solidified the racial status of the marriages.[81]

White women and Native men also met, found common ground, and fell in love in the Indian Service.[82] While they assumed that their marriages would arouse no more interest than those of their coworkers, in point of fact these pairings were often thrust into public controversies. Popular and official attention, as well as the couples' responses, demonstrate how people involved in the debate mobilized the language of assimilation and interrogated the assumptions of intimate colonialism.

The rhetoric of kinship and family that permeated Indian policy led some white female employees to believe that marrying Indian men stemmed naturally from the assimilation process. If they were supposed to create individual relationships with Indians in order to convert them to civilization, and if white women were supposed to be like mothers and matrons to Indians, then why could they not be wives? If one kinship type was applicable, why not another? Indeed, their thinking followed the same logic as that of leading figures like Samuel Chapman Armstrong and Richard Henry Pratt, two of the most influential voices in the field of Indian education.[83] Both openly encouraged interracial relationships as the best solution to the "Indian problem." In 1885 *Harper's Magazine* reported: "General Armstrong thinks that the pure-blooded Indian will soon die out and the whole Indian problem will at last be solved by intermingling." Pratt's biographer, Elaine Goodale Eastman, a former employee under Pratt and herself married to a Native man, recalled: "He consistently advocated amalgamation by marriage as a necessary and desirable part of the assimilation process."[84] Historian David Smits has demonstrated that while there was never unified opinion on intermarriage, army officers, reformers, and federal agents did raise their voices in official discussions in support of the "desirable mixture of the races, the inferior being elevated and finally absorbed and lost in the superior."[85]

It is difficult to determine what drives people in matters of the heart, even more so when the historical record is limited. In a few cases, however, we have considerable detail about interracial marriages between Indian Service employees. Looking closely at the marriages of Edith and Wellington Salt (Chippewa/m), Minnie Dickson and Richard Smith (Cherokee/m), Corabelle Fellows and Samuel Campbell (Dakota, Santee/m), Charlotte and Charles Hoffman (Dakota), Anna Johnson and Joseph Estes (Yankton Sioux), and Elaine Goodale and Charles Eastman (Dakota, Santee) — couples who worked in the Indian Service between the 1880s and the 1910s — helps bring into focus the complicated ways in which assimilation and intimacy were intertwined.[86]

These were middle-class marriages between well-educated men and women.[87] By the standards of white America, these Native husbands were true gentlemen: they had sought out a good education, showed ambition at work, involved themselves in Christian missionary endeavors, and chosen respectable women as their partners. According to the tenets of assimilation theory, these behaviors made them ideal partners for the middle-class women who married them. Indeed, the women themselves believed this to be true.

All six of the men had been well educated, especially by nineteenth-century standards. Along with missionary school, several of them went on to institutions of higher learning.[88] Joseph Estes spent three years at the Hampton Institute in Virginia, while Samuel Campbell had attended the Lincoln Institution in Philadelphia.[89] Wellington Salt attended public elementary and high schools in Collingwood, Ontario, went on to commercial courses at the Toronto Business College, and finally took teachers' courses at Dundas College, Ontario. Richard Smith had an equally impressive résumé: he attended Trinity College in North Carolina, the Indiana State Normal School, and the North Carolina Business College. Charles Eastman excelled in his studies at a missionary school in Minnesota and went on to Beloit and Knox Colleges, graduated from Dartmouth College in 1887, and earned a medical degree from Boston College in 1890.[90] At a time when less than 10 percent of Americans graduated from high school each year and even fewer went to college, these men stood out as the cream of the crop.[91]

Several of the men also had close connections with Christian missionary associations as students, assistants, or ministers.[92] In 1885 Charles Hoffman translated hymns from English into the Yankton dialect of Dakota for the Protestant Episcopal Church's hymnal, *Okodakiciye wakan tadowan kin*.[93] When he returned from the Hampton Institute, Estes served as a printer for the Dakota-language newspaper *Iapi Oaye*, which was published out of the Riggs Institute, an Episcopal missionary station. Moreover, his school file described him as a "church-worker" after he left the Indian Service in 1912.[94] Charles Eastman served as the YMCA's Indian secretary of the International Committee in between positions in the Indian Service.[95] Wellington Salt taught at an Episcopal mission school in the decade before he entered the Indian Service, and after he was employed by the government, he continued to serve as an Episcopal minister to the Native community at Dunseith on the Turtle Mountain Reservation.[96] While Christian missionaries and the federal government did not always agree on the means of assimilation, they absolutely agreed on the ends. During this period, they cooperated closely to ensure the acculturation of Indians and their incorporation into the nation as Christian citizens.[97]

The women in these relationships also shared certain characteristics, though not as consistently as the men. All of them seem to have been from the middle and upper middle classes and were fairly well educated, some more formally than others. Like their husbands, they all held positions in the Indian Service. Three of them—Dickson, Fellows, and Goodale—were American-born women who grew up in the East (New York, Washington, D.C., and Massachusetts, respectively). Salt, Johnson, and Hoffman all hailed from the West and, while of northern European ancestry, were either immigrants or the children of immigrants. Edith Salt relocated from Ontario, Canada, to Rolla, North Dakota, with her parents in 1888, but she listed her "race" as "Scotch" in her job applications.[98] At age seventeen, Anna Johnson emigrated from Norway and became a naturalized citizen in 1883, nine years before she married Joseph.[99] Charlotte Hoffman's father was English Canadian, but she was born in Michigan.[100] Several of the women had taken courses beyond the high school level. Fellows, Dickson, and Salt had attended seminary or public high school, and Dickson and Salt went on to take normal-school and teachers' courses.[101] Fellows studied the Dakota language at the Riggs Institute before beginning her work among the Indians. Goodale had the least amount of formal education, having been schooled at home by her mother.[102] In sum, their race, their education, and, as we will see, their standards of conduct marked these women as respectably middle class.

Courtships often began in the Indian Service. We can be certain that four of the six couples — Corabelle Fellows and Samuel Campbell, Elaine Goodale and Charles Eastman, Minnie Dickson and Richard Smith, and Anna Johnson and Joseph Estes — met while working in the service.[103] (It is unclear whether or not the Hoffmans and Salts met while working together in the Indian Service, but they all went on to work in the service for a number of years after their marriages). Fellows had gone to the Dakotas as a missionary but was soon appointed as a federal day-school teacher on the Cheyenne River Reservation.[104] One day in 1888, on her way to the post office near Fort Bennett, she met Campbell. She remembered her first impression of her future husband in her memoir. He was, she wrote, "a handsome young man. He was sunburned, and his face bore traces of Indian ancestry, but his clothing and mien were that of an English gentleman. . . . He was the son of a trader and a Sioux Indian woman. His mother had died when he was young, and he had been reared by the Episcopal clergyman of the little church at Fort Bennett. . . . We rode and talked together, and fell in love."[105]

Their courting looked much like that of any other young couple; they spent their time riding, sledding, and visiting. During that time, Campbell inscribed a message in Dakota in Fellows's autograph book, the translation of which read: "I wait at home, my friend, to write this to you. If, sometimes, I ask you to remember me, if sometimes I ask you to think of me, if only once you will remember me, this I beg, that you meet me on the hill and talk to me."[106] In the spring, Fellows wrote, Mr. Campbell, who "had been adding to his herd of cattle . . . came telling me that he thought himself wealthy enough to marry."[107]

Three years later, Charles Eastman and Elaine Goodale also met as Indian Service employees. Eastman, also known as Ohiyesa, had been born in 1858 into a Santee Sioux band and was raised by his grandmother in the Dakota cultural tradition in Canada. Upon graduating from medical school, Eastman received his first Indian Service position as the doctor at the Pine Ridge Agency in South Dakota.[108] Like both Fellows and Dickson, Goodale had been raised in a middle-class family and learned the ideology of female moral authority and true womanhood from her mother. Like Fellows, she became fluent in the Dakota language and culture through her position as the supervisor of Indian Schools of the Dakota Territory, which required that she travel through the reservations visiting the schools.[109] During that time, she met Eastman at the Pine Ridge Agency. She later wrote: "I had read of his college career in a chance newspaper clipping, had several times met his brother, the Reverend John Eastman, and had looked forward with more than common interest to our meeting. After that first evening, an invitation affair, he came often to the rectory, and I helped carry food and other little comforts to his patients."[110] He knew of her also through her writings, poems, and articles on Indian affairs. Expecting her to be dignified and reserved, he remembered being deeply impressed by her earnest personality when he met her in person at a birthday tea party, and he began to woo her after agency events like the employee reading circle. Like Fellows, Eastman remembered being struck by Goodale's physical attractiveness. He would be a "callous man," he later wrote, if he did not admit that she was "the prettiest of the school teachers."[111] Charles and Elaine announced their engagement in December 1890, just days before the Wounded Knee Massacre. They spent the next week working among the dead and injured victims of the tragedy.

Richard Smith and Minnie Dickson had a courting experience similar to the other couples while employed at the Eastern Cherokee Agency in North Carolina. Smith was a well-educated young Cherokee man, the son of Nimrod Smith (or Tsaladihi), a former principal chief of the Eastern Band of Cherokee, and a white woman. He had worked for the Indian School at the Cherokee Agency and was also very active in its politics. Dickson had grown up in Chautauqua County, New York, where her father farmed and sometimes served as a preacher.[112] After completing normal school, Dickson taught several terms in New York public schools, where she received glowing recommendations.[113] In 1892 she joined the Indian Service and received a teaching position at the Eastern Cherokee School, where she met Smith.[114] One witness described their romance as "long walks with him, long talks at the gates, visits during the evenings on the porch, meetings every afternoon at the [post office]."[115]

While all of these courtships clearly arose from mutual attraction, the government's rhetoric of assimilation found its way into the women's descriptions of the romances. Notably, they claimed that their initial interest arose from the men's "civilized" behavior, which made their race irrelevant. Fellows, for example, emphasized Campbell's "clothing and mien" as more important than the "traces of Indian ancestry" seen in his face. In certain cases, the women explicitly linked their pairings with the government's civilizing mission to the Indians. When Fellows reapplied for a position in the Indian

Service after her marriage, she explained: "I have married a gentleman of Indian blood, and since my home will be among the tribe, I should like to live the[re] to elevate and instruct."[116] In her memoir, Goodale wrote that she left the Indian Service for the bigger (and not so different) job of being a wife and mother: "I gave myself wholly in that hour to the traditional duties of wife and mother . . . [and] embraced with a new and deeper zeal the conception of life-long service to my husband's people."[117] While we might question the sentiments expressed while applying for a job or writing a memoir years after the fact, for some Indian Service employees the rhetoric of assimilation and female moral authority clearly influenced their feelings. For instance, in her memoir of her work as an Indian Service teacher, Estelle Aubrey Brown told the story of a coworker at Yuma, Arizona. In 1910 Miss Rachel, the school clerk, fell in love with Joseph Escalanti, a Yuma (Quechan) man who was employed as the school disciplinarian. Miss Rachel's confidences to Brown revealed that she saw herself as the embodiment of assimilation's ideal. "You think it strange that I can love an Indian, a full blood—that I want to marry him," she said, but then insisted, "I could help him." Miss Rachel had internalized the civilizing mission. In claiming that she could "help" Escalanti by marrying him, she demonstrated that she saw the object of her affections also as the object of her influence.[118]

There is less evidence that the men thought about their relationships in terms of assimilation theory, although by choosing spouses whose backgrounds equipped them with the manners and respectability appropriate for a middle-class man's wife, they were behaving like the assimilated men that policy makers hoped to form. Richard Smith, for example, praised Minnie Dickson's work with Cherokee children, describing her as "an excellent teacher, [and] a most refined and cultured lady."[119] But the men may also have been attracted to women who could be described as "cultural brokers" who were seemingly comfortable moving between Native and white worlds.[120] (This would certainly have coincided with some of the men's family histories, which included interracial relationships among their parents and grandparents.[121]) All of the women had been willing to leave their homes and families for jobs on Indian reservations and in Indian schools. Moreover, both Fellows and Goodale spoke the Dakota language and had spent considerable time living on a reservation. The women's willingness to be in these places and their interest in Native culture seems to have made them attractive to their husbands. As Charles Eastman later wrote, he was charmed by this woman whose "sincerity was convincing and whose ideals seemed very like my own. Her childhood had been spent almost as much out of doors as mine. . . . She spoke the Sioux language fluently and went among the people with ut-

ILLUSTRATION 6.5. Corabelle Fellows and Samuel Campbell. One of the first marriages between Indian Service employees that involved a white female and a Native male, the Fellows-Campbell pairing was relentlessly ridiculed in white newspapers nationwide. (Courtesy of the Special Collections and University Archives, Wichita State University Libraries)

most freedom and confidence. Her methods of work were very simple and direct."[122]

When they described their courtships, these couples only occasionally drew direct links between their relationships and assimilation theory. That would change dramatically in the years that followed their weddings, when the rhetoric of assimilation became the central feature in discussions of their marriages. In several of the cases examined here, the marriages came under attack, forcing the spouses to defend themselves in considerable detail that reveals how their understanding of their relationships was influenced by the ideology of assimilation.

Of all the women examined here, Corabelle Fellows suffered the most public criticism for marrying a Native man (Illustration 6.5). She was also one of the first to do so during the assimilation period, marrying in 1888, three years before her contemporary Elaine Goodale. Fellows faced an assault on her character in the national press, with newspapers exaggerating the racial and class differences between her and Campbell. Editors seized on the titillating sensationalism of the symbolic disparity between the highest level of civilization, represented by a native-born white woman, and savagery, represented by a Native man. Unfortunately for Fellows and Campbell, members of the press turned their full and intense gaze onto the relationship, catching them in the maelstrom of that fascination. Under blazing headlines like "A Social Sensation: A Former Washington Girl to Wed a Sioux Indian" and "To Be Married To-day: Miss Fellows' Love for Her Indian Lover Will Prevail," the articles emphasized the contrasts between the couple. Newspapers always referred to Campbell by the "Indian name" Chaska.[123] One article stated that "a lady from Washington was betrothed to a full-blood Indian chief." The *New York Times* salaciously reported that Fellows, "the pretty, infatuated, and determined school teacher," was to be married to "Chaska, the big buck Sioux Indian, in whom ordinary white people can see no traits that would call for admission beyond the outermost bars of intimacy." Fellows's family read about the engagement in the *Washington Post* and were horrified. Her Auntie May wrote in a letter: "It is too *dreadful* and an *insult* to you, to believe for a moment, but that such a thing should be published has nearly killed your mother, and made the whole family all too wretched to describe. Your mother fell over *dead* as it were this morning at the breakfast table."[124]

Stories about the Campbells' marriage appeared in newspapers across the nation and into Canada. Splashed across the front page or in the gossip sections, the articles served as warnings to other white women who might consider marrying Indians that they, too, would be subject to public ridicule. In 1891, under the column heading "Whispers about Women," the *Lincoln Evening News* in Nebraska noted ominously: "Mrs. Cora Belle Fellows Chaska applied for a divorce from her Indian husband in the same week that witnessed the Eastman-Goodale marriage."[125] A few years later, the *Middletown Daily Argus* in New York, reprinting a story from Boston, reported that "the two New England girls who attracted notice a few years ago by wedding Indians, one Nora Belle [sic] Fellows, the former schoolteacher, has found life unbearable with the Sioux Chaska and has left her husband. The other, Elaine Goodale, the poet, found life on an Indian reservation unbearable and has come east with her husband. The result in both cases seems to show the nonsuccess attendant on attempted affiliation of Indian savagery and white civilization."[126]

The press had attributed the origins of these relationships to the influence of assimilation theory and the romantic notions of the young women, and when the relationships failed, journalists could gloat that Native men could never achieve the full standard of bourgeois manhood. The *Lorain County Reporter* of Elyria, Ohio, admonished: "The Cora Belle Fellows fiasco is a lesson to white girls that it is unwise to marry Indians with the idea of reforming them."[127] In Ogden, Utah, the *Standard* concluded: "Lo [the poor Indian] fills a high mission as a creature of imagination; but when romantic young ladies test the unsophisticated original in the crucible of matrimony they naturally find that civilization means something more than paint and feathers."[128] Perhaps most cruel was the wag from Ohio's *Newark Daily Advocate*, who penned these lines under the headline "Cora and Chaska: A Romance Set Forth in Something Worse Than Blank Verse":

> A moral this tale bears to girls who,
> through folly or strange love of romance,
> imagine it jolly to cast their sad lot with the sons of the wildwood
> and seek a divorce from the trends of their childhood.
> This romance is short, as in this case related[,]
> for Cora now knows she was sadly mismated
> and has, with the rest, the unhappy reflection
> of duty to half-breeds that need her protection.
> The question of Indian civilization
> involves not the horrors of mixed procreation. . . .
> And [I] think that the law should receive a few patches
> to shut off these semi-barbarian matches.[129]

By mocking these women's marriages, the press offered a critique of assimilation policy as a whole. The notion that young, idealistic white women could purge Native men of their savagery was laughable, the articles implied.

The press also attacked the idea that Indian men could become civilized when they derided Samuel Campbell's efforts to live up to assimilation theory's manly ideal by providing for his family. Try as he might, he could not escape public emphasis on his race despite his "civilized" behavior. Immediately after he and Fellows married, they began to receive "offers of all kinds" from entrepreneurs hoping to capitalize on the public's fascination with Indian-white intermarriage.[130] They ultimately took a job touring with "a stereopticon bureau . . . speaking on Indians and explaining [the] pictures."[131] Despite the couple's efforts to portray this as respectable work, however, the press refused to let their behavior determine their public identity. Journalists insisted on ridiculing them and reinforcing a stereotypical portrayal of Campbell. One newspaper reported: "Mr. and Mrs. Samuel Campbell will pose as museum freaks. . . . [They] have gained notoriety as Chaska and bride. . . . [I]t is announced that Chief Chaska will receive the crowds in war paint and feathers and wield the tomahawk he doesn't know how to use, while Cora will wear her bridal dress."[132] The press continued to hound them as they sought to use their earnings to purchase various goods essential for a normal middle-class household. To the press, an Indian buying these things was striving for a respectability that he could never achieve. One headline blared: "Chaska and His Bride Wasting the Money Earned in Museum."[133] Another reporter mocked their efforts to outfit a farm in Dakota: "The small fortune they accumulated in their five weeks of exhibition is almost gone, and they have nothing to show for it save an abundance of wearing apparel, horses and carriages, and farming implements. Chaska has not learned how to use the latter, and is not likely to until starvation compels him."[134] In these reports, the press interpreted Campbell's behavior through a racialized lens that denied that Native men could legitimately make good economic decisions or that Campbell could support his wife in a manly fashion. Significantly, this tactic echoed the racist assumptions that African Americans who dressed and behaved in a middle-class manner were merely aping their white betters or being "uppity," both of which implied that respectability and blackness were incompatible.[135]

Corabelle Fellows and other white brides were initially surprised by the negative reactions because they apparently believed that the promises of assimilation — that behavior rather than race made a man — would place their marriages beyond reproach. Indeed, in the titles of their memoirs years later, Fellows and Goodale both described themselves as surrogate kin to Indians, employing the official language of assimilation policy: Fellows used her adopted Dakota name, Blue Star, and Eastman entitled her memoir *Sister to the Sioux*. Moreover, they both remarked that before their marriages, they had been aware of similar relationships that existed free from public comment. Fellows remembered that a fellow teacher, Rebecca Holmes, had hosted her wedding reception. She described Holmes as "like myself . . . a schoolteacher who had married a man with Indian blood."[136] Goodale maintained: "Though I had not consciously considered marriage with a Dakota, I had closely observed several such marriages which appeared successful. The idea certainly did not repel me in any way."[137] Indeed, as we will see, other couples, such as the Hoffmans and the Salts, do not appear to have faced censure over their marriage choices.[138]

At the time, Corabelle Fellows countered newspapers' public criticism of her choice of marriage partner by insisting that her husband did indeed meet the standards of assimilation and stood as an example of proper husbandly behavior. She repeatedly emphasized the respectability of their relationship, though this seemed to have little impact on press coverage. After their wedding, for example, Fellows and Campbell took a honeymoon to the fashionable seaside resort of Old Point Comfort, Virginia, an act that emphasized their solidly middle-class standing.[139] In a later interview, Fellows underscored Campbell's responsible behavior, stating: "I received a letter from Sam Chaska this morning, and he said the house was ready for us. You know we sold our original home-stead, and Sam has been busy building a house on our new claim, west of Forest City. We still love each other, and I am proud of the father of my babies."[140] By emphasizing Campbell's ability to provide a home for his family, Fellows highlighted his fulfillment of his husbandly duties. While Elaine Goodale Eastman's name appeared several times in conjunction with articles about the Campbells, no other couple appears to have received so much scrutiny from the press.[141] This placed enormous pressure on the Campbells' marriage, perhaps more than it could support, as their story ended tragically. After years of rumors of marital trouble—also widely reported—Samuel Campbell and Corabelle Fellows divorced sometime around 1894. Reports in 1898 stated that Sam Campbell had been arrested and jailed in Lincoln, Nebraska, where he attempted suicide.[142]

The abuse that these couples suffered was unfortunately not limited to the public realm. Many of these relationships also became fodder for wider internecine struggles in the workplace. Once again, the rhetoric of assimilation was central to these conflicts and was used both to discredit and defend the relationships. The Indian Office did not have an official policy against interracial marriages, but individual agents could and often did fire women for their involvement in such relationships. As single working women, they were especially vulnerable to attacks on their propriety. Indeed, supervisors often used charges of improper relations with the opposite sex as a pretext for disciplinary action. White women who consorted with Native men were even more vulnerable to these charges.[143] Indian Service teacher Gertrude Golden described how flirtations could be used against employees by their supervisors. In a section of her memoir entitled "What Chance for Romance?," she wrote: "After I had been at the school but a short time, the lady employees warned me that I must be very careful not to show the slightest interest in the older boys. . . . They pointed out that [the superintendent] and her favorite would grossly misconstrue any such interest shown. They had been known to talk scandalously about some entirely innocent young woman who had been indiscreet enough to speak to an Indian boy and to be 'alone with a man.'"[144]

Indeed, scattered throughout Indian Office records are incidents in which white women lost their positions or were reprimanded for "inappropriate relations" with Indian men or adolescents.[145] For example, Minnie Dickson's superintendent requested her dismissal, writing that her behavior was "in every way . . . a detriment to the best workings of the school. An unfortunate personal attachment to one of the Indians also sets a bad example for the girls."[146] The agent's emphasis on her relationship with Richard Smith seems to have been intended to impugn her reputation and add weight to his list of her other transgressions, most of which involved her refusal to cheerfully do extra duties she considered outside of her job description as a teacher.[147] In the investigation that followed, she initially did not address her relationship, trying to rise above the implication that no respectable white woman would socialize with an Indian. But later, she decried "[the agent's] efforts to slander me in all his reports" and protested "*it was most certainly* his purpose . . . to injure my reputation . . . [with] *malicious*, lying gossip over the country, especially among the more vulgar classes concerning my dismissal."[148] Like Fellows, Dickson defended her relationship by pointing out how her fiancé's behavior conformed to the middle-class standards of assimilation policy: "Mr. Smith is an educated man, gentlemanly, refined, intelligent, of good principles and an excellent reputation of home," she insisted in a letter to the commissioner of Indian affairs.[149]

Dickson's fiancé also wrote to the commissioner to protest her firing, particularly the fact that the agent had cited their relationship as a primary reason for her dismissal. In Dickson's defense, Smith highlighted the apparent hypocrisy within the promise of assimilation and also emphasized his own adherence to "civilized" behavior. He made his case in two frank letters to the Indian Office.[150] Focusing on his superior's implication that his race barred him from consorting with a white woman despite his impeccable behavior, an irritated Smith observed: "I hope I may be a gentleman enough to know how to act before ladies so as not to disqualify them from teaching 'Indian children.'"[151] He condemned the inconsistency within the promises of assimilation rhetoric: "I suppose the objection is because of my being a Cherokee, I must say it is to be hoped that the new Administration just going into power . . . will not be guilty of the contemptibly low, narrow-mindedness . . . and of such an ignominious failure in its Indian policy as to still try to teach the Indian that it is a mere matter of sacrifice on the part of the Great Government to give him a few glimpses of civilization, but that he must not aspire to the attainment of that *too high* a thing of equal rights and privileges of independent American citizenship."[152] For three months, Smith continued to write to the Indian Office, attempting to get his fiancé reinstated and to secure a position for himself as well. When these requests were repeatedly denied, Smith's frustration boiled over, and he lambasted the racism of the government for persisting in viewing him as an Indian rather than a "true man."

I wish to say I did not know that it was considered a crime to be an Indian [or] to associate with one; at least I notice there are always people and White men who like to hold "Indian Offices." But if you had never thought of it, I being three fourths White and one fourth Indian you might call me "White Man" "three fourths" of the time, for a change. But however much Indian I am maybe as to Race lineage, I mean to be a *whole* White man, or a *true man* in my life and actions. . . . Really, if there is any truth in the proposition that the mixing of the Races makes them better as I have heard it said, I being ¼ Irish, ¼ D[u]tch, ¼ White, and ¼ Indian I think *I* ought to be *better* than a White man. But that's a joke if you wish; still I think I have a reasonable right to have or expect the same respect accorded me by your Department that I receive from other respectable people.[153]

Although Smith used humor to make his point, his deep-seated frustration with the Indian Office's unwillingness to look beyond race and see him as an individual is obvious.[154] For Smith, his behavior should have afforded him the privileges of manhood and citizenship, including the right to fraternize with respectable white women. His race should have been irrelevant; after all, this is what assimilation policy had promised him.[155]

Joseph Estes's alleged poor treatment of his white wife was similarly used to attack him when he received an appointment as the superintendent of the Santee Agency boarding school. His superior bluntly charged: "He is married to a white woman whom he frequently beats; he became involved in a row at the hotel here in which he made display of a revolver against girls and women."[156] Estes protested that he was being attacked as revenge for accusing the agent of graft, proclaiming that "there is no truth in what he alleges, except the single statement that I am married to a white woman."[157]

Like the other white women whose marriages were attacked in the press or on the job, Anna Estes sought to defend her husband by emphasizing the machinations of the agent and contrasting her family's adherence to the standards of middle-class respectability with the vulgarity of their accusers. Writing to the commissioner of Indian affairs in response to the agent's charges against her husband, Anna insisted that the agent's depiction was completely false. Instead, she described Joseph Estes as a good husband and a gentleman, highlighting the traits that policy makers would have recognized as the ideals of assimilation. "Mr. Estes is a kind, affectionate husband and father, and devoted to his family," she wrote. Portraying their marriage as one of companionship and balance, she also emphasized that he properly provided for his family. "He has been teaching most of the time, and I have been with him as his companion almost constantly. . . . My husband has not only treated me kindly and provided for me properly ever since our marriage, but in 1896 he had his life insured for my benefit in the New York Life Insurance Company."[158]

Having defended the character of their relationship, she offered her version of what happened in the Greenwood Hotel. Instead of a crazed man with a gun, she presented the respectable behavior of a husband and father's righteous defense of his family's honor. "The servant girl at the hotel," she wrote, "was somewhat rude and sometimes used harsh and unladylike language towards us and about our children but my husband seldom spoke to her. . . . [T]he servant finally became so rude that we withdrew from the dining room and left the hotel." Like Dickson, Anna linked the behavior of her family's accusers to their class status, describing the "unladylike" "servant" who rudely attacked her family, possibly by slurring the children's mixed-race heritage. But she maintained that the Estes family had behaved in the civilized manner of the middle class by controlling themselves, withdrawing from the dining room and leaving the hotel.[159]

While many interracial relationships became caught up in agency politics, not all of them did. For example, Dakota Charles Hoffman was one of the first Native men to hold a supervisory position when he was appointed superintendent of the Fort Berthold Training School sometime around 1912. While he quickly became mired in accusations of corruption and was removed from the position and reassigned to a day school with his wife, the fact that he was married to a white woman does not appear in the correspondence.[160]

Wellington Salt's personnel file offers a telling exception to the litany of scandals and troubles that plagued many other intermarried employees. Salt's record in the Indian Office was impeccable. He was a beloved employee who served faithfully for years in day-school positions with his wife, Edith. As his supervisor wrote in a 1913 efficiency report, "Mr. Salt . . . is very dependable and causes me no trouble or anxiety of any kind. He has very little condemnatory criticism to make about anything or any body and this is a blessed quality which apparently is more a gift than any thing else, as it appears to be entirely impossible for some people to cultivate this desirable trait of character."[161] It is probable that Salt's amiability, the isolation of his day-school position, and the fact that, as another supervisor pointed out, "he has a very slight amount of Indian blood, not enough so he would ever be recognized as an Indian" worked in his favor.[162]

The experience of these couples suggests that while not all marriages between Indigenous men and white women were attacked, such interracial pairs were especially vulnerable to criticism when they laid claim to middle-class social status and earning power. A similar pattern appeared involving a number of interracial couples who were caught up in bureaucratic infighting in the Indian Service. In these cases, the attacks on the marriages often served the immediate purpose of blocking Native men from positions of power and high pay or removing them as allegedly undesirable employees.[163] It was often when ambitious Indian men were challenging their superiors, applying for promotions, or assuming higher-paid posts that white superiors tried to use their marriages to white women against them. The couples discovered that their positions as respectable families could be questioned at any time by accusers who played upon white stereotypes and prejudices about the behavior of nonwhite men.

CONCLUSION

While Commissioner Leupp thought that employee marriages were merely a colorful anecdote that would enliven his report, exploring the social life of Indian Service employees exposes the currents and shoals—the assumptions, affections, and animosities—of the strategy of intimate colonialism that underlay federal assimilation policy. In hiring Native and white employees for work on the reservations, the government created scores of interracial communities that, while not always harmonious, were comparatively more forward-looking than most other sites of American race relations. Native and white employees shared a culture of work, living and laboring side by side while the Indian Office exhorted them to encourage, influence, inspire, and even love the people among whom they worked.

These configurations often led to friendships among white and Native employees as well as reservation residents. In this context, Indians and whites could grow to like and learn from each other. Just as some white service employees found that their interactions with individual Native people led them to question assimilation's fundamental tenet—that Indian cultures lacked value and needed to be replaced—other white Americans were beginning to express ideas of cultural relativism and to assert the worth of Native cultures. For Native employees, the friendships that they made in the Indian Service helped them navigate the difficulties and frustrations of their jobs; and those they created with people of other tribes contributed to an emerging modern intertribal identity.

It was when these friendships developed into love and then marriage that the implications and limitations of intimate colonialism became especially apparent. The government's use of familial rhetoric and its decision to post thousands of Native and white employees in Indian country brought into being a particularly fertile "marrying ground."[164] The marriages it produced were part of a large population of interracial and intertribal couples that often slip through our scholarly categories into obscurity. The resulting pairings — especially those between white women and Native men — were not limited to one or two well-known cases or restricted to individual schools; instead, such couples were scattered throughout the Indian Service. By looking closely at how government policies contributed to these matches and how white Americans responded to them, we can see how ideas about race were challenged, contested, and maintained.[165] But despite the very real egalitarian aspirations of this aspect of federal Indian policy, it also contained a kind of equality that the American public and policy makers themselves were not quite sure they could countenance. When white women married Indian men, they often encountered severe condemnation, and their families were denied middle-class respectability. The reactions to these marriages reveal that the public and most administrators were unwilling to live up to the radical promises of assimilation theory.

7

The Hoopa Valley Reservation

The Office of Indian Affairs administered scores of reservations across the country, attempting to force them along a single path toward assimilation, but each of these local places had its own history, context, and culture(s) that complicated the Indian Service's efforts. Understanding the ways many Native people used Indian Service employment in order to navigate larger economic transformations requires a close look at the local context of individual reservations. The last few chapters have offered a bird's-eye view of the system of agencies and schools that were tied together by the Indian Office bureaucracy and the movement of employees through the system. This chapter focuses on one reservation—Hoopa Valley in Northern California—in order to demonstrate how federal employment played out at the local level and within specific regional circumstances.

We might begin this inquiry by citing a remarkable statistic from Hoopa Valley: in 1888 more than a quarter of Hupa men over the age of eighteen were working for the Indian Service.[1] This reveals the local meaning of a striking fact about Native labor in the Indian Service: temporary workers massively outnumbered permanent, regular employees. In 1912, for example, the commissioner of Indian affairs reported that the service employed 2,516 Indians in regular positions; but it had also hired an astonishing 12,420 Indians as temporary employees.[2] While Native people employed in regular positions had greater opportunity to modify or attenuate the impact of federal policy, most Indian people experienced work in the service as temporary laborers on their own reservations. Looking at Hoopa Valley shows how Hupa people devised labor strategies that allowed them to sustain themselves economically while simultaneously fighting to safeguard their culture.

Given the ideological importance of work in assimilation policy and the high participation in the labor force by Hupa people, policy makers surely expected to see the quick acculturation of the Hupa tribe. To the frustration of Indian Service superintendents, however, Hupa people, even those employed by the Indian Service, retained many of their distinctive cultural practices and found ways to pass them on to future generations. Employees resisted the totalizing efforts of assimilation in a variety of ways, from continuing to participate in sacred dance ceremonies to shooting the reservation superintendent.

THE CENTER OF THE HUPA WORLD

At the heart of Hupa territory is *Natinook*, "the place where trails return," which whites renamed Hoopa Valley (Map 2). The Trinity River flows through the middle of the valley, and in the nineteenth century, the Hupa villages, divided into northern and southern districts, were strung like shell beads along the river. Most of the villages were nestled on the eastern bank to catch the sun that warmed the smooth cedar plank roofs and walls of the *xontas*, the main dwelling structures of Hupa families and the sleeping places of the women and children, and the roofs of the subterranean *taikyuw*, or sweathouses, used exclusively by the men. The Trinity River empties into the Klamath River at the Yurok village of Weitchpec.[3] The Yurok tribe lived downstream along the Klamath River, while the Karuk tribe lived upstream from Weitchpec, at the place where the Salmon River entered the Klamath. The Hupa shared (and continue to share) with these neighbors a culture based on these rivers and the salmon that inhabited them. Although they spoke different languages, the tribes interacted through extensive trade, intermarriage, and a shared religion centered on world renewal ceremonies.[4]

When white fur traders arrived in the area in the 1820s and 1830s, they first learned of the people who lived in the valley from the Yurok, who referred to their neighbors as Hoopah.[5] This name stuck, even though the Hupa call themselves *Natinook-wā*, the people of *Natinook*. The Hupa called these white men *yimandil* ("across they go around") because of their peripatetic ways or *kiwamil* ("creatures with fur") for their trading enterprises. These white traders began to work the areas surrounding *Natinook*, setting in motion a wrenching transformation of the Native world. Little direct violence reached Hoopa Valley itself, however, until the 1849 Gold Rush.[6]

After John Sutter's famous discovery near Sacramento, outsiders flooded the state looking for gold, and by the spring of 1850, the Trinity River was crawling with 3,000 miners. The Hupa called these newcomers *misah kititlut* ("mouths that flap"), a derisive term indicating the miners' rude manners. They were primarily single men, both white and Chinese, and their presence

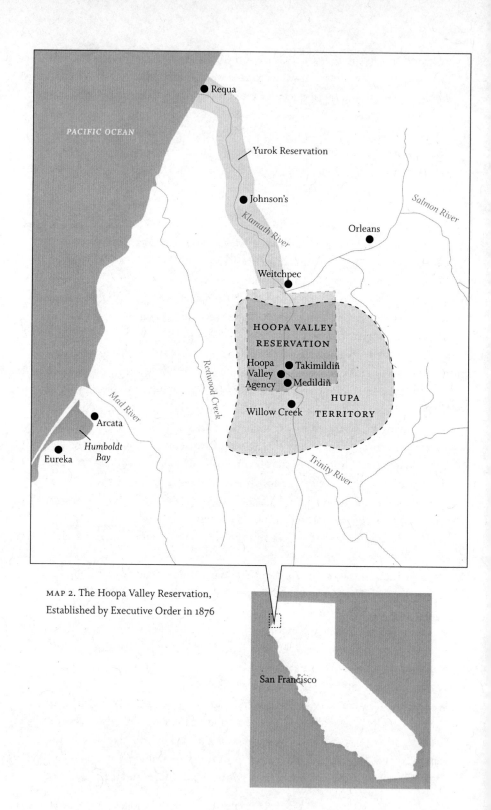

PACIFIC OCEAN

Requa

Yurok Reservation

Johnson's

Orleans

Salmon River

Klamath River

Weitchpec

HOOPA VALLEY

RESERVATION

Hoopa
Valley
Agency

Takimildiñ

Medildiñ

HUPA

TERRITORY

Willow Creek

Redwood Creek

Mad River

Arcata

Humboldt
Bay

Eureka

Trinity River

MAP 2. The Hoopa Valley Reservation,
Established by Executive Order in 1876

San Francisco

signaled disaster for the Native people in the mountains. The miners brought disease, machinery, and violence. Historian Jack Norton, himself of Hupa descent and a member of the Yurok tribe, writes: "Upon our ancestors' beautiful world there fell a pillaging horde that raped and plundered the land and the people."[7] Cholera, smallpox, tuberculosis, measles, and venereal disease spread by the gold seekers devastated the local Indigenous populations. The miners also brought their destructive methods of extracting minerals. Giant hydraulic cannons violently spewed forth torrents of water that crumbled mountainsides, choking streams and rivers with silt and huge piles of rock and destroying the shallow gravel beds where salmon lay their eggs. Special Indian Agent E. A. Stevenson described the devastation in 1853: "The miners have turned the streams from their beds and conveyed the water to the dry diggings and after being used until it is so thick with mud that it will scarcely run."[8] The miners who flooded into the area also hunted game in the mountains and chopped down trees for building materials. Worse still, miners and the American soldiers sent in to "protect" them placed scant value on Native lives. Numerous accounts of the rape and abduction of Native women and children appeared in local newspaper articles and in the reports of military and Indian Office officials. The miners drove Native people from their villages, and the memories of these violent actions remain on the landscape even now; the hamlet bearing the name of Burnt Ranch in Trinity County, for example, testifies to the massacre and burning of a South Fork Hupa village upriver from Hoopa Valley by white miners in 1850.[9] Environmental destruction and the disruption of the Hupa people's seasonal gathering by violence resulted in want and starvation in previously prosperous communities.

During the 1850s, the tribes living around Hoopa Valley, including the Yurok, Whilkuts, and Redwood tribes, retaliated with force against similar attacks on their people and livelihoods. White settlers who had provoked these responses through massacres, kidnappings, and environmental destruction then called for the "extermination or removal" of the Indians in the area.[10] The U.S. Army—first from Fort Humboldt on the coast and, after 1858, from Fort Gaston, which was established in the middle of Hoopa Valley—waged bloody campaigns against the tribes. Initially, the Hupa worked to keep the violence outside of their territory by using a mix of diplomacy and subterfuge. They declared neutrality while simultaneously helping their neighbors by providing food, weapons, and information. While whites doubted their neutrality, they had no strong proof until 1863, when three men involved in attacks at New River were caught at the Hupa village of *Medildiñ* ("the place of the boats"). When the army demanded that the village turn the men over, a group of Hupa warriors fled to the mountains and initiated open war. The conflict was complicated by an intervillage feud based primarily on a specific incident but also closely corresponding to differences in opinion about whether peace or resistance was the best way to respond to the army. The local U.S. military commander did nothing to stop the feud in hopes that the villagers would eradicate each other. For over a year, Hupa warriors fought the U.S. Army and local militias. By 1864, however, the population in the valley was less able to support those fighting in the mountains, and the warriors returned to the valley and sued for peace.[11]

The federal government negotiated a treaty with the Hupa, South Fork, Redwood, and Grouse Creek Indian tribes. The treaty created a reservation of twelve square miles primarily encompassing Hoopa Valley, as well as a "sufficient area of the mountains on each side of the Trinity River as shall be necessary for hunting grounds, gathering berries, seeds, etc.," which is now often called "the square." Although the reservation included their villages and sacred religious centers, especially *Takimildiñ* ("place of the acorn feast"), the Hupa lost almost 80 percent of their territory. In return, the treaty pardoned "all Indians who have taken part in the war." The U.S. government agreed to provide clothing and blankets, instruction to women in sewing and "household affairs" and to the men in "farming and harvesting," and the services of a doctor. The tribes agreed to obey the agent, remain on the reservation, and give up their guns. The treaty was never officially ratified, however, because, as the commissioner of Indian affairs wrote, "it was not the policy of the United States to enter into formal treaties with California Indians." The Hupa, however, considered it binding and fulfilled their obligations. Despite the lack of ratification, the Hoopa Valley Reservation received its first agent in October 1864, and the reservation was officially established by executive order in 1876.[12] In 1891 another executive order added the Lower Klamath "extension" to the square. The addition, a strip of land one mile wide along each side of the Klamath River from Hoopa Valley to the Pacific Ocean, had been created for the Yurok tribe by executive order in 1855.[13]

The violent changes that whites brought to Hupa territory happened almost within a single lifetime. Many Hupa, like sixty-seven-year-old John Matilton, who served as a member of the Indian police in 1889, had been young men and women when whites arrived in the valley.[14] They witnessed their community's population fall from almost 1,000 to roughly 430 as a result of that contact.[15]

The Hoopa Valley Reservation was (and remains) the largest in California, but initially it was far removed from white settlements. The reservation was supplied from the town of Arcata (formerly Union), a port on Humboldt Bay about forty miles to the southwest. Mule trains brought in supplies over the mountainous trails between Hoopa Valley and Arcata.[16] The only other way to reach Hoopa Valley from the coast was to take a canoe up the rivers, but few if any whites did so. Employees heading to the reservation followed the same route as the mules. Superintendent Kyselka described the trip in 1902. From San Francisco, he wrote, one traveled "230 miles on the Pacific, 18 miles by rail, 16 miles by carriage, and 16 miles on horseback over the trail."[17] When field matrons Mary Arnold and Mabel Reed accepted jobs at Hoopa Valley in 1909, the trip was an uncomfortable adventure for the newly self-taught horseback riders. "At first," one of them wrote, "I was too much alarmed by the character of the trail to notice anything else. I clung to my horse and prayed. My prayer was that he knew what he was about for I certainly did not."[18]

LABOR PATTERNS AT HOOPA

In the late 1880s, Reverend Berler, a visitor to Hoopa Valley, described the view that met weary travelers upon reaching their destination: "Hoopa Valley is to the eye, after the tedious trip, as an oasis in the desert. On descending the mountain the traveler looks upon a fertile valley several miles long profusely dotted with grain fields, vegetable gardens, clusters of trees and horses. . . . A portion of [the Trinity River] connects with a mill, another supplies the fish hatchery, reservation fountain and grounds. From a distance the whole valley looks very much like a cultivated park."[19] His description emphasized the "improved" nature of the area, its resources, and its economic possibilities. This was in keeping with federal policy makers' plans for the valley: the Indian Office hoped to convert the reservation into another market-oriented farming community. Administrators intended to use Indian employment to accelerate that conversion. They believed that free labor— both as an economic theory and an everyday practice—would destroy tribal identity and achieve assimilation.

Beyond the rhetoric, hiring Indians was essential to the Indian Service's mission because the service needed enormous amounts of labor to construct, operate, and maintain its infrastructure and programs. This reliance is made clear by an examination of the day-to-day details of work at Hoopa Valley. A close look at this reservation is possible because Indian Service clerks kept a quarterly record of employees between 1884 and 1911, scrupulously inscribing entries on vital statistics as well as positions and pay on page after page of a large, leather-bound ledger book.[20] The ledger details the daily, monthly, and yearly labor of individuals whose work was essential for running assimilation programs.[21] In addition, the agents at Hoopa emphasized their dependence on Indian labor time and again in their annual reports. In

1887, for example, the agent wrote that "[a]ll manual labor performed on the reservation to maintain the Government establishment is performed by Indians."[22] A quarter century later in 1911, they still relied on Hupa labor. "We need considerable Indian help," the superintendent reported, "and cannot get along without as many laborers as we are now carrying."[23]

Although white administrators believed that Indians lived in a primitive state and needed to be taught the tenets of capitalism, the idea of paying for labor or goods was by no means foreign to the Hupa. Nor was the concept of money. Traditionally, the Hupa and their neighbors used dentalium shells from the coast of Vancouver Island as specie. Hupa historian Byron Nelson has described this monetary system: "Only shells longer than 1-⅞ inches could be used as money. The shells were sorted, measured, wrapped in fish-skin or snake-skin, tipped with red feathers and strung according to size. Men had tattoos on their forearms which were used to measure the individual shells and the 25-inch strings. Each string of money had shells of a single size or unit of value; the most valuable were those made of the rare 2½-inch shells. The people carried this money wrapped in mink or moleskin, or in special elk-horn cases decorated with geometric designs." In trade, one could pay for items with dentalium shells or barter with other desired items, such as redheaded woodpecker scalps, deerskins, redwood canoes, or tools.[24]

In point of fact, concepts of money, payment, and wealth permeated Hupa society. Different families held rights to specific gathering and hunting areas in the valley and surrounding mountains. Men who did not have their own hunting territories worked for relatives who did in return for a share of the kill. Feuds arising from insult, injury, death, or property damage required payment or revenge for the aggrieved parties. Ceremonial dances such as the White Deerskin Dance and the Jump Dance were sponsored by certain families in the principal spiritual villages of *Takimildiñ* and *Medildiñ*. Those families were responsible for maintaining the dance grounds, preparing and preserving the regalia, providing food for the feasts, and making payment to any families who had experienced a death during the year. Moreover, they had to ensure that all feuds were settled before the dances could begin.[25]

In recognizing that the Hupa were not completely ignorant about exchange values, we must also be careful, as Jack Norton has pointed out, to distinguish their social systems from capitalism. Norton faults early anthropologists such as Alfred L. Kroeber, Edward Curtis, and E. W. Gifford for failing to describe Northern California Indigenous societies as "unique communities," pointing out that they "used the standards of European institutions in their analyses." They failed, Norton argues, "to understand that each person's special ability and inherent integrity formed a reciprocal responsibility" to the community and that Native society was permeated by "an atmosphere of communal respect" rather than by the individualistic ethos of capitalism.[26]

Along with a traditional culture in which wealth had contributed to status and social power, the Hupa had not remained isolated from the market system before the establishment of the reservation. When white traders, miners, and settlers arrived in Hoopa Valley, they brought Western ideas of wealth and payment as well as greed. Hupa people incorporated some of these ideas into their traditional systems. Indeed, a number of whites had settled in Hoopa Valley before the 1864 treaty (which required them to leave) and had lived side by side with tribal members. Thus when white officials began to hire Hupa men and women to work for the government, they confronted a people who had their own system of exchange, had lived near whites for many years, and knew the value of their labor.

At Hoopa, as on other reservations, the Indian Service's initial efforts during the 1880s focused on employing local men in temporary, unskilled positions, especially freighting. This was an essential job because the railroad ended at the foot of the mountains, and all supplies had to be packed and transported over almost forty miles of winding trails from the railhead. In such steep terrain, freighting was a very perilous task. In 1889 a local paper, the *Acorn*, reported an accident involving a Hupa freighter coming into Redwood, a halfway point.

> It is a rather dangerous drive as the hill down which the road runs is very steep. It is usually the custom for teamsters to tie trees behind their wagons to serve as a sort of rough lock to assist in holding the wagons from going ahead too rapidly. It was while preparing one of these rough locks that the accident happened. . . . One teamster, an Indian, whose name is George Simus, but better known as Little George, was standing ahead of the wagon. . . . [H]e was unable to get out of the way and was knocked down and two of the wheels passed over his right leg, mangling it most horribly. He also sustained two broken ribs.[27]

Hupa men did most of this hard, dangerous work. Without freight, the Indian agent could not provide rations to the Indians or outfit the soldiers at Fort Gaston, the local military installation.

Despite the government's goals of teaching equal exchange and market participation, and notwithstanding its reliance on Native labor, federal agents' ambivalence about a freely functioning market contradicted the stated ideals of Indian policy. Indeed, the Hupa seemed more willing to abide by the rules of the capitalist marketplace than their white agents. Worried that Indians would use their wages to buy ostensibly superfluous items or liquor, not all agents were willing to pay the Indians cash for their labor. During Captain Charles Porter's three years as agent at Hoopa Valley, for example, his annual reports to the commissioner of Indian affairs revealed both the Hupa people's understanding of the labor market and Porter's hesitancy to allow it to function. In 1883 Agent Porter grumbled that the Indians "refuse to work for the reservation unless paid regular wages in money."[28] Two years later, he again complained that the Hupa were making economic arguments about their labor: "It is, however, becoming every successive year more and more difficult to get able-bodied male Indians to work for the reservation. They think they ought to be paid for all such work at the rates prevailing for similar work in the surrounding country, and they contend that the amounts of rations and clothing issued to them are but a very inadequate compensation for such labor as they do from time to time perform for the reservation." Porter paradoxically blamed the Indians' disinclination to work on the influence of "evil-disposed parties" who have "told Indians that they are entitled to be paid," although he agreed in principle that "at the present stage in [the] civilization of these Indians," they should be paid "a direct equivalent for their labor." Porter also believed that they wasted their wages: "I have observed that whatever money a majority of these Indians earn by labor is too often wasted in dissipation or useless extravagances, and that in place of being a service it is too often the source of unmitigated evil."[29] Native people were often sent mixed messages about wage labor. Porter's reluctance to pay Native laborers the going market rate in exchange for their work was not unusual; many administrators had similar qualms.

But the next agent at Hoopa Valley, Captain William Dougherty, completely disagreed with Captain Porter. He urged Congress to "honestly compensate Indians whom the Government engages to do its part of the work, as is done for the Sioux and other tribes not as peaceably disposed as the Hoopas."[30] Agent Porter's and Agent Dougherty's differing views on work had a major impact on the patterns of Native labor at Hoopa Valley. Porter, who served between 1882 and 1885, was quite pessimistic about the potential of Native labor; as a result, during his tenure, only one or two Native men were hired each year in regular positions, usually as an interpreter or freighter. When Dougherty replaced Porter, however, he put many more Hupa on the employment rolls in a wide variety of jobs. In keeping with the idea that men should be the productive heads of their households, most of the Hupa hired were indeed male. During Dougherty's term (1886–90), Hupa men filled the positions of farmer and industrial teacher as well as interpreter, Indian policeman, and general laborer.

Yet even as Dougherty expanded the number of jobs available to Indians, these positions often paid less than the regular positions available to whites. During the first quarter of 1888, for example, white men filled five of the ten regular posts: doctor ($1,000 per year), carpenter and miller ($720), blacksmith ($720), clerk ($600), and messenger ($60). Native men served in five regular positions: industrial teacher ($720 per year),[31] farmer ($360), interpreter ($240), and two police privates ($8 per month). One white woman was employed in a regular position as the day-school teacher ($720). The irregular laborers also consisted of both white and Indian men. The agent temporarily hired four white men as sawyer, carpenter, blacksmith, and miller and paid them one to two dollars per day. The clerk listed six Native men as employed temporarily in the category of laborers earning only fifty cents per day. For those Native men, the length of employment varied. For example, Francis Rennett and William Major both worked for thirty-nine days, but Charles Saxon only worked for four. All of the Native men were born in Hoopa Valley, while the white employees hailed from eastern states and even from overseas.[32]

The Indian Service's reliance on temporary labor became even clearer in the second quarter of 1888, when hiring ballooned to accommodate a spate of construction projects. Again, the service engaged white men living in Hoopa Valley and nearby Arcata for the specific positions of carpenter, painter, and mason and paid them between one and four dollars per day. It also employed thirty-three Native men from Hoopa Valley as irregular laborers, most receiving fifty cents per day.[33] A majority of the Hupa men worked from 2 April to 10 April, but a few worked for the entire month of May. In some ways, 1888 was an unusual year, one in which the men were engaged in building and repairing agency facilities, but it nonetheless demonstrates that Hupa men took advantage of the increased federal employment. In his annual report, Agent Dougherty described the work:

> During the year one agency employé's [sic] dwelling was constructed; a water-tank was set up and 2,500 feet of inch pipe laid to conduct water to the school-house, stable, blacksmith's shop, and physician's quarters. Extensive clearing, fencing, etc., was done above and below the agency; a ferry-boat, 39 by 16, was built and put in place on the Trinity River, and general repairs were made on the grist and saw mills, now very old and dilapidated. All this work was performed by Indian labor directed and assisted by two white employés, beside much other necessary work on roads, bridges, dams, and flumes.[34]

Dougherty rightly emphasized the role of Native labor in facilitating this work; as noted earlier, he hired just over 25 percent of the adult men on the

Hupa rolls to do the work,[35] and some of these men, like Bigmouth Tom and Matilton Captain, were reservation leaders.[36]

Dougherty's encouragement of Indian employment, a cornerstone in assimilation theory, dovetailed with a second program also designed to encourage Indian people's participation in the market: road building. Indian Service officials believed that there were three compelling reasons for hiring Native men to build the roads: it inculcated a work ethic, it supplied cheap labor, and it advanced economic connections between local communities and the reservations. Those connections would, administrators hoped, stimulate the reservation economies by providing links to markets. They would also facilitate the movement of people—whites in and Indians out—through the reservations, further blending assimilated Indian peoples into the national population, eroding their connection to place, and dispossessing them of their land. The commissioner of Indian affairs charted this progress in three columns in his *Annual Report*: "roads repaired (miles)," "roads made (miles)," and "days labor by Indians."[37]

At Hoopa, the road-building programs received substantial support from all parties because they offered benefits to multiple constituencies, from the Hupa tribe and Indian Service administrators to local whites and members of Congress. In 1887 the Hupa tribe petitioned Congress for funds to "construct a wagon road from the valley to the western line of the reservation to connect with the public road from Humboldt Bay to the interior, and thus open a route to a market for the surplus product of the valley." Captain Dougherty reported that they were "anxious" for a good road to replace the "mule trail" and give them access to local markets for their produce and fruit.[38] Along with a better trade connection to white communities, the Hupa would also benefit from the money that road-building work injected into the local economy. The process of road building seems to have been divided between some required number of unpaid days (generally three) and paid work, and many Hupa men worked more than the required three days. The ledger is thick with lists of irregular laborers assigned to road-building work and receiving from fifty cents to a dollar per day. For comparison, one dollar in 1892 would be worth approximately twenty-four dollars in 2009.[39] For some of the Native workers, this translated into a small infusion of cash. For example, in 1892 the service hired Berryman Lack (Hupa) as the road-building superintendent and John Sherman (Hupa) as the superintendent of labor. Each received $1.50 per day and worked twenty-four and forty-five days, respectively. Sherman also served for twenty-three days at seventy-five cents per day. He made $84.75 during the two months. Berryman Lack's wife, Susie Lack (Hupa), also worked as a cook for the road crew for twenty-three days at seventy-five cents per day. Together, the couple made $53.25 for the month. The men laboring under them on the road gang made less. At seventy-five cents per day, their stints on the crew ranged from Frank Gardner's thirty-four and a half days to Sambo's sixty-eight days, which netted them $28.50 and $51.00, respectively. Notably, in his annual report, the Hoopa Valley agent stated that "the last year has no doubt been the best ever known for them financially," adding that they had had good crops, sold wood to the fort, and "earned quite a large amount . . . in finishing the Hoopa Valley wagon road."[40]

Indian Service officials viewed road building as an important lever for "improving" Indians. Dougherty and other policy makers were pleased by the Hupa people's willingness to work on the roads, believing it signaled compliance with the government's plans for assimilation. Dougherty considered the reservation an excellent prospect for success, noting that it was agriculturally fertile and that the Hupa people were ambitious. To encourage congressional appropriations for a wagon road, he noted that the thirteen orchards in the valley had produced "a surplus of about $2,500 worth of fruit that went to waste on the ground" because the Indians lacked the infrastructure to sell their products in the coastal towns. "Without a road to a market, where the Indians may enjoy the advantages of competition in selling and buying," he warned, "it will not be possible to give effect to the policy of the Interior Department to make the Indians self-sustaining and independent of the Government."[41] The lack of an easy route to market continued to bedevil administrators at Hoopa, in part because roads often washed out during the winter and had to be repaired annually.[42] Without good roads, the only market for Hupa produce was either the federal government or the single reservation trader licensed by the Indian Office. In 1903 another agent requested funds to build a shorter wagon route over the mountains. He gave a number of reasons why the project was important, including the agency's increased access to timber and the fact that "the actual distance to the railroad station will be shortened from 44 miles to 32. The grade will be so much better that about twice as large a load can be hauled. The better market will stimulate the Indians to greater efforts in the raising of produce."[43] Two years later, he sounded a note of alarm, reporting that progress toward "civilization" might be endangered by this problem: "Largely because of the limited market, fruit orchards have been much neglected."[44]

Despite some agents' concerns over the condition of roads, local newspapers often reported on road building, applauding the new links between Hoopa Valley and white communities. In 1891, for example, one paper informed its readers about the road between the reservation and the town of

Willow Creek, about eleven miles to the south. It cited California state senator Frank McGowan, who "tells us that the road from Hoopa to Willow Creek
is nearly completed, only about ½ mile being required to make the connection. The Hoopa Valley, he represents as to [sic] fine a spot to be so far out of
the world. It is well cropped by the Indians."[45] In 1908 another article enthusiastically reported on the "appropriation of $10,000 by the U.S. government
for building a wagon road through the Indian Reservation at Hoopa Valley,
connecting with the Humboldt County line."[46] For these whites, regional
economic development was one important purpose of the roads; but their accounts also reveal that they supported road building because it heralded the
transfer of Indian land into white ownership. The road, a paper reported, was
part of the agency superintendent's plan for "great improvements at Hoopa
which will greatly benefit both Indians and white people when the reservation is open to settlement."[47]

A NEW SCHOOL AND NEW NATIONAL LINKS

In 1893 the Indian Service opened a boarding school in Hoopa Valley, an
event that dramatically altered employment patterns in the valley. The
school replaced Fort Gaston as a market for local agricultural products and
also created new employment opportunities. In particular, the school began
to hire substantial numbers of women who previously had few prospects in
the Indian Service at Hoopa. Few women held positions before the boarding
school was built. The year before it opened, the Indian Service workforce at
Hoopa comprised five white men, one white female teacher, and eight Native
men in regular positions and thirty-three in irregular positions, mostly on the
road crew. Only three Native women were employed, serving as temporary
cooks for the road-building gang.[48]

   In 1896, three years after the school opened, the numbers looked quite
different. That year, the school employed two white men in the highest positions of school superintendent and principal teacher. The nine white women
working at the school also served in teaching positions as well as the support
positions of matron, seamstress, laundress, and cook. The school also employed four Native women to assist in these support positions, while three
Native men served as industrial teachers, one was a baker, and one was an
assistant. The agency employed five white men and twelve Native men in
regular positions (including the four members of the Indian police force),
as well as three white men and one white woman, one Native man, and one
Native woman serving as irregular laborers. Along with all of these positions,
the construction of a wagon road also created work, and the agent hired

Berryman Lack to serve as foreman of the nineteen other Hupa men making a dollar a day on the road gang.

In 1896 the school enrolled 138 pupils and even boasted a kindergarten. Like other boarding schools, part of the children's education consisted of working for the school and performing tasks meant to train them to participate in the agricultural economy that policy makers envisioned for the valley. Under the supervision of male employees, the schoolboys planted and cultivated the school garden and corn and potato fields and spent time splitting firewood. The girls worked in the sewing room, expending "a great amount of labor, in both making and mending clothing," and also did laundry and kitchen work under the supervision of the seamstress, laundress, and cook. The superintendent lauded the members of his staff, stating that they "have been efficient, conscientious, and untiring in their labors, into which they have infused that love for human souls without which the work of the teacher is devoid of lasting influence for good."[49]

The Hoopa Valley Reservation was distant from other settlements, and most of its Native employees remained local, but it, too, was touched by the larger currents in the Indian Service. The experiences of three teenage girls signaled the first inkling of a new labor regime, one that was split between local and national. In 1895 Laura Ammon,[50] Lottie Horne,[51] and Jessie Beaver[52] were appointed at Hoopa Valley as assistant seamstress (Ammon) and assistant matrons (Horne and Beaver). All three of the girls had returned to the area after attending Carlisle Indian School in Pennsylvania. Their employment represented a new departure in which a rising number of former off-reservation boarding-school students joined the workforce of the Indian Service. By 1897 the employee ledger for Hoopa Valley began to include the names of Native employees who had been born in Oregon, Washington, New Mexico, Arizona, Montana, Wisconsin, New York, Michigan, and North Carolina.[53] Many of them had attended off-reservation boarding schools, including Carlisle, Chemawa in Oregon, and the Phoenix Indian School in Arizona. These nonlocal Native personnel were always employed in permanent regular positions as opposed to temporary or irregular positions.[54] Their jobs ranged from skilled vocational positions such as baker, shoe-and-harness maker, seamstress, and farmer to white-collar appointments such as teacher, clerk, and nurse. They often brought their off-reservation boarding-school training to bear at these smaller reservation schools. For example, shoe-and-harness maker Perry Tsamanwa (Laguna Pueblo) was probably the person local papers were referring to when they wrote in 1902: "The Indians have had a Carlisle man coaching them and should be in fine fettle."[55] Sam Oitema, a Hopi man who had attended Phoenix Indian School, also served as shoe-

ILLUSTRATION 7.1. From left: Wilson Pratt, Sam "Hopi Sam" Oitema, and Frank Davis. At the Hoopa Valley Reservation, the establishment of an on-reservation boarding school in 1893 ushered in new labor patterns in which many non-Hupa Native employees came to work on the reservation. For example, Sam Oitema (Hopi), the school's shoe-and-harness maker, hailed from Arizona. (Courtesy of the Phoebe A. Hearst Museum of Anthropology and the regents of the University of California; photograph by Alfred L. Kroeber [catalogue no. 15-3659])

and-harness maker at Hoopa, where he was given the nickname of "Hopi Sam" (Illustration 7.1). Oitema reorganized the school's brass band, providing "a source of pleasure to parents, pupils, and employees." At the same time, some Hupa left home and worked elsewhere in the reservation system. Bob Horne, for instance, attended the Haskell Institute in Lawrence, Kansas, and went on to work at the Wahpeton School in South Dakota.[56] The experiences of these employees illustrate the wider links between local reservations and an expansive national Indian Service system. As we learned in the previous chapter, such movement facilitated the development of intertribal ties and exchanges.

Just as regular Indian Service employees often moved from post to post across the country, local agencies also experienced the rapid shifting of employees, especially temporary ones, through different positions. In 1916, for example, an inspector reported that there were thirty-two such changes at the Hoopa Valley School alone.[57] A glimpse at a week and a half in 1919 from the agency diary at Hoopa demonstrates the fluidity of employment on local reservations, as personnel at Hoopa Valley moved from position to position and in and out of the service.[58] Moreover, it highlights the agency's reliance on temporary laborers and its connection to local communities. The entry also illustrates the multiracial and gendered composition of agency and school workforces.

Saturday, May 24: Daisy Hill [Hupa] called to get permission to take the Hanson girls home [from the on-reservation boarding school] for the remainder of the year. Permission not granted. The Hoopa Hospital was closed indefinitely by Superintendent Mortsolf, Mrs. Melott, temporary nurse having resigned. Imogene Marshall [Hupa] went with Julius [Hupa/Yurok] to move Mrs. White from the hospital off duty half day without permission charge to annual leave.

Sunday, May 25: Superintendent Mortsolf, P. L. Young, and A. A. Freeman returned from Eureka and Arcata. Mahlon Marshall [Hupa, working as axeman on road survey] returned to Johnson's [a downriver town] in company with Miss LaVerne Preston [a white teacher].

Monday, May 26: Hattie Steve [Hupa] dropped from position of school clerk at close of business today. Miss Candina Tonini entered on duty today as teacher, temporarily. Dr. Rosenkrang and family drove to Willow Creek [an upriver town] in afternoon. Doctor being called for professional business.

Tuesday, May 27: Superintendent Mortsolf in company with P. L. Young drove to Trinity road camp on business. Paid Minnie Johnie [Hupa] $6.95 for five days work as laundress in absence of Mrs. Ida Abe [Yurok]. Daisy Hill came to the office to get permission to take the Hanson children home.

Wednesday, May 28: William Jarnaghan, Jasper Hostler, and George Nixon [all Hupa] left for Korbel after Government supplies. Dr. Rosenkrang went to Weitchpec on professional business and returned.

Thursday, May 29: Work began on Weitchpec-Hoopa road, John Carpenter [Hupa] Foreman of the gang at this end. Daly Brothers,

Eureka Merchants, called at the office for a few moments. Peter Sock-tish [Hupa] paid $7.00 for a thresher. Harry Campwell, Henry Frank, and Anderson Mesket [all Hupa] came in with freight.

Friday, May 30: [Indian policeman] Willie Dowd [Hupa] came in from Weitchpec.

Saturday, May 31: Issue day to all Departments and flour to old Indians. Monthly pay checks drawn. Dr. Rosenkrang called to Trinity Road camp to treat man who fell from cliff. Dr. came home late in the evening. John Carpenter [Hupa] dropped from rolls as Indian Judge. Now employed as Foreman on Hoopa-Weitchpec road.

Sunday, June 1: Superintendent Mortsolf left in Agency Ford for Arcata and Requa.

Monday, June 2: [Farmer] Ed Marshall [Hupa] and details of boys picking cherries. Jasper Hostler, William Jarnaghan, and George Nixon [all Hupa] left for Korbel for Government supplies. Julius Marshall [Hupa] left afternoon for supplies. Bob Pratt [Hupa] called at the office and paid $34.21 on his wagon.

Tuesday, June 3: Mr. Hemsted [temporary carpenter] made a coffin for body of Meta Matilton. Canning cherries at school kitchen, Mrs. Melott [the former nurse] and Mrs. Moses. Dr. Rosenkrang went to Weitchpec having been called to set a broken leg. Dr. returned late in afternoon.

Wednesday, June 4: Oscar McCardie [Hupa and an Indian police-man], Louis Matilton [Hupa], Mason Steve [Hupa] and Mr. Padilla [white disciplinarian] piled flour in Store houses. Canning cherries in kitchen, Mrs. Melott. Mrs. Moses reported for duty but help not needed. James Montgomery [Hupa] came to office and complained about Oberly Atone [Hupa] threatening him while having a revolver in his possession.[59]

Supplementing the glimpse of reservation life revealed in these entries with information from other sources illuminates the character of employment on the reservation. Employees were treated as if they were in some respects interchangeable, especially people in support positions.

This seemed particularly true for the Native women in the service. During this week in May, Minnie Johnie filled in as temporary laundress for the widowed Ida Abe,[60] while Hattie Steve, who had been serving as school clerk, was dropped for summer vacation. Steve, whose husband, Mason, was also working at the agency as a laborer, appeared on the employee rolls throughout the year in a variety of functions, including cleaning the hospital and being temporarily in charge of the kitchen during vacation. She also worked as an assistant matron of the boys' building, and when she was dropped from that position, she was taken up again as a temporary cook.[61] Imogene (née Masten) Marshall, who was docked half a day's vacation because she and her husband were moving an invalid from the hospital, also filled a number of positions. She first appears on the employee rolls in 1908, when she served as temporary assistant matron. She resigned upon the arrival of the permanent appointee and later did office work, served as a laundress, and appears to have filled in for the vacationing cook during the summer.[62] The experiences of these women seem consistent with the way in which Hupa people used service employment as ad hoc work in conjunction with their other economic options.

The diary also emphasizes that the Indian Service depended heavily on the labor of Indian men to fulfill the daily operations of the reservation; indeed, more Indian men appear than any other group of employees. As we are reminded in the above excerpt, Indian men consistently worked in road building, freighting, and law enforcement. Moreover, as the actions of John Carpenter moving from judge to foreman of the road-building gang demonstrate, men often served in more than one of these positions, perhaps in an attempt to maximize their income or take advantage of better working conditions.

White women also supplied a great deal of temporary labor on the reservation. For example, Miss Candina Tonini, normally the day-school teacher downriver at Weitchpec, had been hired as temporary teacher at the boarding school. Mrs. Melott had resigned from the hospital in response to "charges of mismanagement" issued by Ada Masten (Hupa), who had "called at the [agency] office to get Mrs. Melott fired as she called it." But Mrs. Melott was quickly reemployed canning cherries and serving as temporary cook for the school (Illustration 7.2).[63] Mrs. Moses, who assisted Mrs. Melott with the canning, had previously worked for the service at the Warm Springs Reservation in Oregon before moving to Hoopa Valley. Her husband began working as financial clerk at Hoopa in 1916, and she began to hold a series of temporary posts in the bakery and the hospital and was hired as the seamstress in 1922. The couple remained employed in various positions at the agency until 1927, when Mrs. Moses died of influenza while working as matron of the girls' dormitory.[64]

The white employees mentioned in the diary often moved back and forth between reservation employment and off-reservation jobs. The carpenter, Frances (sic) Hempstead, who was making a coffin in the first week of June 1919, had initially been employed by the Indian Service at Hoopa in 1885. By

ILLUSTRATION 7.2. Three women gathering peaches. Native and white women often did similar work in the Indian Service, but Native women tended to receive less pay and to be employed as temporary laborers, a status that barred them from the benefits of regular employees. (Courtesy of the Phoebe A. Hearst Museum of Anthropology and the regents of the University of California; photograph by Nellie T. McGraw Hedgpeth [catalogue no. 15-20906])

1894 he had become the agency's miller and sawyer in charge of the flour and lumber mills. He had left the employee rolls around 1900 and apparently was living in Willow Creek, a town a few miles upriver from the reservation. He came back in 1919 to fill in temporarily as the carpenter after a labor dispute between the superintendent and the previous carpenter, Sherman Norton (Hupa), led to Norton's resignation (an episode that will be explored in detail below). Hempstead was seventy-one years old in 1919, but the wartime economy made carpenters scarce.[65] During that year, he also worked temporarily as a disciplinarian and a laborer. Richard Padilla had also previously worked for the agency and returned to serve as a disciplinarian in 1919.[66] Similarly, many service employees used their federal employment as a jumping-off point for careers outside the service. This is illustrated in the case of the white day-school teachers Candina Tonini and LaVerne Preston. Both were twenty years old in 1919 and hailed from the local towns of Arcata and Hydesville. They each continued their work in education after being employed by the Indian Service. Preston moved to the public schools of Eureka, California, while Tonini, the daughter of Swiss immigrants, went on to teach grammar school in Honolulu, Hawaii, the following year.[67]

Finally, the diary reveals a number of other insights into life at Hoopa Valley. In particular, we are reminded of the coercive nature of the agency and the constant presence of sickness and death. Daisy Hill appears and reappears, requesting that the Hansen children be allowed to come home for the summer.[68] The agency doctor's very busy schedule and the building of a coffin hint at frequent illness and death among the Hupa people during this period.

INDIAN SERVICE LABOR AND NATIVE ECONOMIC STRATEGIES

The Hupa people used the federal government as an important part of their larger survival strategies after the incursion of whites into Hoopa Valley had destroyed or drastically disrupted many of their traditional forms of economic subsistence. The mining industry and the canneries at the mouth of the Klamath River had substantially reduced the supply of salmon, previously an abundant food source. Soldiers at Fort Gaston had chopped down many of the oak trees in the valley, decimating the other major Hupa food source: the acorn crop.[69] With their traditional subsistence economies in shambles, the Hupa were forced to look for other options to earn a living.

Although there were limited economic possibilities in Hoopa Valley, few tribal members were willing to leave their homes and community.[70] This was clearly exemplified in 1914, when the school superintendent received a memo from the Indian Office in Washington, D.C., indicating that too many former students were looking to the Indian Service for employment. The memo requested that superintendents indicate what other sources of work, including domestic service for Indian girls, were available outside of their reservations. Superintendent Asbury responded that there were few job opportunities at or near Hoopa Valley, but more important, that the former Hupa students did not want to leave the reservation: "A few boys go out to work in the neighboring lumber camps and this is about the only opportunity afforded them for work on the outside. However, nearly all of them prefer to stay at home and help their parents work their ranches. . . . They can usually find for themselves what little outside work is available in the vicinity. They do not want to go to the towns for employment." These towns were far away on the coast, and working there would have made it difficult for Hupa people to return on a regular basis to the center of the Hupa world.[71]

This determination to remain in the valley led the Hupa to develop multifaceted family-survival strategies that often combined many small economic niches. Their cash-producing options were limited to government jobs, sales of their produce and crafts, and a few other less-reliable opportunities. Incorporating all of these, they fought to remain in their tribal home, where they could participate in the everyday routines of Hupa daily life as well as the annual ceremonial events that were inseparable from local places.[72] While some Hupa continued to use traditional hunting and gathering methods to augment their food supply, these means could no longer provide all of their needs and had to be supplemented with other options.[73] For example, George Nelson and his wife continued to "dry fruit, jerk venison, gather acorns, dry corn and salt salmon for winter use." But he also raised cattle, hogs, hay, and grain, and his wife canned fruit and vegetables for the family. Nelson also periodically hauled freight for the Indian Office.[74]

Wage work for the Indian Service was a key part of many Hupa families' everyday means of getting by. Indeed, Superintendent Asbury noted in his response to the memo regarding job opportunities that "a good many of the graduates are given employment from time to time in the school and agency work here."[75] Many Hupa used Indian Service employment as a flexible economic option, shifting between regular and irregular positions and moving in and out of employment as it suited their needs. This can be seen by following individuals over the course of decades. Robinson Shoemaker, for example, worked for the Indian Service for at least a part of every year except two between 1890 and 1903, hiring on as an irregular laborer, irregular carpenter, shoe-and-harness maker, farmer, additional farmer, and school laborer. Frank Gardner worked as an irregular laborer for the service throughout the 1890s.

In 1891 he briefly served in the regular position of industrial teacher and again as additional farmer in 1901. In 1893 the twenty-two-year-old Gardner was living with his mother and stepfather, Chicken Hawk. Hawk also periodically worked as an irregular laborer at the agency during the early 1890s, and in 1894 he took a regular position as industrial teacher, a post he held for two years.[76] The benefits of this flexibility are illustrated by the reasons people gave for their periodic resignations, including "to do his own work," "to attend private business," "her own wish," and on "account of illness of wife." These statements indicate that they left service work to engage in a wide variety of other commitments, both economic and familial.[77]

Native families supplemented work for the Indian Office by selling their produce to the federal government, another important source of cash. When the government decided to close Fort Gaston in 1892, over 100 Hupa signed a petition requesting that the government keep the soldiers in the valley because their leaving endangered the tribal members' livelihoods.[78] The agent supported the petition, warning that the abandonment of the military fort meant that "many of the Indians will miss a large portion of their incomes" from sales of produce.[79] Cyrus H. Mills, a local white man who later served as the agency blacksmith, also concurred, noting in an interview with the *Blue Lake Advocate*: "Number of whites in Valley 16 to 18 aboriginal population exceeds 400. Everybody would be glad to see the troops back. They made business lively and scattered lots of money about."[80]

The founding of the Hoopa Valley Boarding School in 1893 helped make up for the closing of Fort Gaston by providing another market for Hupa produce. In 1897–98, for example, the federal government purchased $5,000 worth of hay and grain from the Hupa. The products were then sent to the school to augment its supplies. In the agent's reports, the amount purchased by the school remained fairly stable, while the amount purchased by "others" fluctuated, suggesting that government purchases could be especially important during economic downturns when sales to private parties may have fallen.[81] Freighting for the government and others also brought in money. In 1901, for example, Superintendent Freer reported that out of $20,123.96 in total Indian earnings, Hupa men earned $1,280.40 hauling freight for the government and $1,470.00 hauling for "others."[82] The following year, Superintendent Kyselka reported that Indian men "haul[ed] all the freight for agency, school and employees" and chopped and sold firewood.[83]

It is worth noting the contrast between these figures and the economic options of the Yurok. Yurok men rarely worked for the Indian Service, in part because their residence in "the extension" was far from the agency. But they also appear to have had more opportunities for wage labor, as well as fewer agricultural options, on their heavily timbered territory. In 1916 the agent reported that the Yurok "will continue to have their homes here" in the reservation strip along the Klamath River "but must of necessity work a large part of the time away from home in the lumber camps, mines, and fisheries." Their ability to work away from the reservation allowed the Yurok more leeway in ignoring Indian Office demands. The Hupa living in Hoopa Valley were more dependent on the government for their economic survival. One agent recognized the power that this economic reliance gave the government. He lamented that he could only get "a portion" of the Indians on the reservation to do their share of the required road-building work. According to the employee ledger, the men who worked on the road appear to have been drawn almost exclusively from men listed on the Hupa census, and thus they were most likely living in the Hoopa Valley. Their proximity to the agency and their reliance on the Indian Service for employment and as a purchaser of their produce seemed to have made them more willing to put in the required days. As the agent noted, he had few options to compel the men to work "except to deprive the Indian who does not do his share of an opportunity to sell supplies to the school or to haul freight."[84] The agent's threats may have been somewhat of a bluff; the federal government depended on Hupa laborers to temporarily fill the regular positions left open by employee movement and to perform the irregular work necessary to operate its programs, especially construction, freighting, and road work. This dependence is made plain by the large number of Native employees in the ledger and by the superintendents' willingness to rehire employees who had been dismissed from the service for infractions ranging from drunkenness to "improper relations with pupil."[85]

Native women in Hoopa Valley also contributed to their families' cash flow through the sale of butter, eggs, canned vegetables, and especially "curios," primarily the baskets for which they were renowned. Basket sales, in fact, brought in a great deal of money. Initially, Indian Service administrators overlooked or downplayed the economic importance of Hupa basket making, perhaps because Native craftswomen did not fit into assimilation theory's emphasis on male productivity. By the turn of the century, however, officials were paying more attention to these products. In 1903 the agent at Hoopa Valley reported: "This industry has been encouraged and greatly revived during the past two years, and the demand for fine baskets now far exceeds the supply."[86] He reported that 11 percent of the income earned by the Hupa came from such sales.[87]

This newfound enthusiasm was most likely a response to the suggestion by Estelle Reel, the superintendent of Indian schools, that such skills be incorporated into the Indian school curriculum. Reel had even called on agents and superintendents to recommend Native people who could teach their crafts.[88] She worked closely with the members of the Women's National Indian Association (WNIA) to encourage women's artistic production; this was visible at Hoopa Valley, where the female employees and missionaries encouraged basket sales, serving as brokers between Native basket makers and white women across the country (see Illustration 6.3). For example, Cornelia Taber, corresponding secretary of the Northern California Women's Indian Association, a branch of the WNIA, received many letters from women stationed as employees and missionaries throughout California. Miss Chase, a Presbyterian missionary at Hoopa Valley, wrote: "A large package of baskets has just been started on its way to your home. . . . I feel sure you will sell everything and order more."[89] In response to several requests for baskets from Taber in the fall of 1907, Marie Johnson, the field matron stationed among the Yurok at Requa on the Klamath River, replied that she was unable to gather enough to be worth the shipment because the women were busy with their subsistence strategies. "The huckleberries and acorns have been so plentiful this fall that none of the women have had time to make baskets. They all tell me, 'Dis is the time, we commence now.'" These letters suggest that women's participation in basket weaving and the "curio" trade were important sources of income for families, especially when other options failed. They demonstrate that female missionaries and employees understood the baskets as a source of economic contributions to the women's families, similar to the "egg and butter" money of many white farm women. They also reveal that Native women were willing to tailor their work to the market; writers noted that they could ask for baskets of different colors, and one author recalled that two of the artists were amused by her request that they create miniature versions of their baskets.[90]

Other Hupa adopted more distinctive strategies. John Brett took advantage of the federal postal service, working as a mail carrier for the Brizard Company, which held the mail contract for the reservation. Brizard's also employed Pedro Freddie as a horseshoer for their pack trains; Freddie had previously worked as a blacksmith for the government. Charles Beaver made "considerable money from bounties on mountain lions, coyotes, etc, and trapping for furs," while his wife, a former Carlisle student, served as postmistress. The Beavers apparently did quite well economically, as they owned an eight-room home and an automobile. By 1922 Thomas Marshall, who had taken irregular jobs in the Indian Service during the 1890s, had trachoma and could not farm, but he was hired on as a day laborer in a tan oak-bark camp a few miles outside of the reservation. George Latham, who had worked for the service for almost fifteen years, was running "a hotel for Indians."[91]

Over the years, these survival strategies made it possible for the Hupa to at least stabilize their damaged local economy. The medium-term results could be seen in 1922, when the federal government took detailed surveys of many Hupa households as part of a larger national survey of Native homes (see Illustration 9.1). Almost all of the families surveyed had a member who had worked for the Indian Service at some point in the previous three decades. There are two possible explanations of how this employment helped these families survive. One possibility is that the male heads of household in these surveys—many of whom were prosperous farmers by 1920—used the cash from government labor to help them outfit farms when they were younger. The other possibility is that before the allotment process at Hoopa was finalized in 1918, land ownership was unresolved and men were unable to fully invest their efforts in improving farmsteads that might not be theirs. Either way, it is clear that wage labor for the government filled an important economic niche for Hupa people. It offered jobs on the reservation for young people and supplemented family incomes, thus helping the Hupa to remain in their community.

The surveys also reveal that Hupa economic strategies involved whole families, both nuclear and extended.[92] For example, the survey described household head Francis Colegrove as "one of the most intelligent and prosperous Indians on the reservation. He has a large family and in addition to his own family he partly supports his wife's people, who are also numerous."[93] The story of the Marshalls illustrates how one Hupa family used the Indian Service within wider economic strategies. James Marshall (Hupa) was described as "one of the most prosperous men on the reservation." He and his wife, Mary (Yurok), lived in a large, six-room frame house "about three miles from the agency across the Trinity River." His property included "seven horses, two mules, sixty head of cattle, [and he] raises chickens. Has twenty-five acres of oats, fifteen acres of wheat, six acres of alfalfa and clover, has a fine garden, and a nice young orchard." Like many of the women in Hoopa Valley, Mary Marshall used these resources to make butter and can fruit and vegetables for her family. James Marshall also rented land from other Hupa and paid them partially in cash and partially through improvements to their land. This arrangement may have harkened back to traditional Hupa economic patterns in which men without hunting territories worked for others. The surveyor noted that the family's home was clean and healthy, as were the homes of their married children, an indication of "progress" to the Indian Office. The reproduction of "civilized" traits in the next generation would also have been an encouraging sign. Moreover, Marshall had a bank account and owned Liberty Bonds.[94]

James Sr.'s prosperity in 1922 may have been partially founded on his ability to use Indian Service labor earlier in his life. He repeatedly appears in the employee ledger between 1888 and 1895, first as the industrial teacher at the day school and later as an additional farmer, assistant farmer, irregular laborer, wagon-road laborer, and assistant foreman on the wagon road. In 1895 he became the beef contractor for the agency.[95] A number of Marshall's children and at least three of his daughters-in-law also worked for the Indian Office.[96] Indeed, employment for the government often seems to have been multigenerational, both at Hoopa Valley and elsewhere. In a 1941 interview, for example, Isaiah Reed, an Oneida man from Wisconsin, stated: "When I came back from school [my father] was police for the Oneida Boarding School. . . . Well, it was through his recommendation that I got my work at the Oneida Boarding School." Perhaps James put in a good word for his sons, or maybe he encouraged them to apply for service work.[97]

James Sr.'s oldest son, Julius, appeared similarly prosperous and "progressive" when his household was surveyed in 1922.[98] Julius first appeared on the employee rolls as a temporary baker in 1899, when he was fourteen. By 1900 he was the agency butcher (perhaps in conjunction with his father's beef contract), but he was involved in a hunting accident that year that apparently resulted in the loss of his left arm. This limited his ability to farm and most likely forced him out of the butcher position, but he periodically took up work in the service in later years. In 1919, for example, both Julius and his wife, Imogene, worked for the service as a temporary farmer and freighter and a laundress, respectively.[99] In 1922 Julius, now thirty-seven, and Imogen lived on their new allotment in the Bald Hills. This land was further from the agency and better suited to grazing than to farming, and the couple owned cattle, horses, and pigs. They had also put in "a fine garden," and Imogene canned vegetables and made butter. The agent also noted that "she is a fine needle worker, making all kinds of fancy work, which she sells to any one who wishes to purchase."[100] Three years later, the Marshalls were again working for the service, Julius as a temporary baker and Imogene as a cook.[101] While the couple had no children of their own, the surveyor noted that they had adopted two orphan boys of the Eel River tribe.[102]

Edward Marshall, James Sr.'s second son, lived near his parents with his wife, Matilda, their daughter, and their three sons. Edward had attended the Hoopa School, and his wife had gone to the Haskell Institute in Lawrence, Kansas. Both Matilda and Edward had worked for the Indian School. Edward was employed as a farmer and shoemaker at the Hoopa school in 1917 and worked as a temporary farmer, laborer, and disciplinarian in 1919. By 1922 he owned a small sawmill and was raising hay, which he sold to the government

ILLUSTRATION 7.3. Hupa traditional stick game players, ca. 1912. Front row (from left) are John Matilton, Jerry Horne, and Amos Holmes; back row (from left) are George Nixon Sr., Anderson Meskit, and Ed Marshall Sr. Several of these men also played on the Hupa baseball and football teams and had worked in the Indian Service. This shows how Hupa people incorporated many aspects of white culture into their lives while simultaneously continuing to practice some of their Hupa cultural traditions. (Courtesy of the Roberts Photograph Collection, Humboldt State University Library)

school. His wife canned produce for the family. The agent wrote that Edward was "a very intelligent Indian, subscribes to a number of papers and reads them. He is a very good worker, and is never idle."[103]

Despite the praise they received from the agent and their apparent embrace of wage labor and farming, the Marshalls and other Hupa employees had not rejected their Hupa culture and remained closely connected to their tribal community. Members of the Marshall family were very involved in tribal politics. In 1910, for example, Edward Marshall wrote several letters to the editor of a local paper defending his tribe's reputation.[104] Julius was on the Hoopa baseball and football squads, while Edward played baseball and the Hupa stick game (Illustration 7.3).[105] When the Hoopa tribal council was established in the 1930s, Edward and Gilbert represented two of the tribal districts, while James and Julius were subcouncil members. Although historians often describe these councils as mouthpieces for the federal government, the Hoopa Council was in fact seen as a source of trouble for agency officials.[106] Gilbert and Julius continued to serve throughout the 1930s, while Mahlon Marshall, James Jr., and Earnest Jr. (James Sr.'s grandson) served during the 1940s.[107] Indeed, many of the names from the employee ledger match those on the tribal council list from the 1930s forward.[108]

RESISTANCE TO CULTURAL ASSIMILATION

In 1902 Kyselka dejectedly reported that the "tenacity with which the majority of Indians" at Hoopa Valley continued to follow their traditional beliefs was "very discouraging." The Indian Office had established a boarding school, started the process of allotting the reservation, and employed scores of Hupa people during the previous decades. Its theories of assimilation suggested that the Hupa should have melted quickly into the citizenry. Instead, as Kyselka reported, they refused to give up their cultural identity, even as they took advantage of the economic possibilities occasioned by the federal presence in Hoopa Valley.[109] While many of the Hupa employees incorporated aspects of American culture—working for the government, farming their allotments, living in nuclear families in frame houses rather than in the sex-specific *xontas* and *takyuw*, and playing on the valley's football and baseball teams—they also, as their agents lamented, continued to attend tribal ceremonies and live many aspects of their culture. Three examples clearly demonstrate how many Hupa managed to maintain key aspects of their culture for future generations: the Native men who worked as Indian policeman and Indian judges, the Indian Service employees who served as anthropological informants for Pliny Earl Goddard, and the career and family legacy of agency carpenter Sherman Norton.[110]

The conflict between federal and tribal authority was perfectly illustrated in 1883, when Agent Charles Porter reported that his effort to set up a tribal police force had been "abandoned" because Hupa men continued to be influenced by the "internal quarrels and dissensions" of the tribe and could therefore not be objective. "The results," he wrote, "would have been a mere aggravation of disorder and existing animosities." Porter also despaired of finding anyone he thought qualified to serve as an Indian judge. He refused to appoint the men who the Hupa themselves would have found credible. "The older men and medicine men already mentioned; as to *their* utter unfitness for judicial duties nothing additional can be added," he dismissively wrote. Porter indicated that an Indian police force would be rendered impotent because tribal members would continue to use their traditional means of settling feuds—asking tribal leaders to mediate their disputes and agreeing to make payments according to their judgment.[111]

Even when an official police force was finally established in 1887, it still did not completely fulfill the Indian Service's hopes of undermining and displacing tribal authority.[112] Certainly, the police force often upheld the government's efforts to destroy Hupa culture, such as when Superintendent Kyselka ordered policemen Arthur Saxon and Charles Finch to halt the building of the traditional fish dam — an annual communal construction project that made possible the mass gathering of salmon during their seasonal run upriver — by threatening the Hupa with imprisonment if they completed it. On another occasion, the tribal police dragged Emma Henry to jail when her son failed to come to school.[113] These actions led to bad feelings toward the police by their fellow tribal members. In 1902, when Superintendent Kyselka left the reservation to attend a football game in Eureka, violence erupted between the agency police force and other tribal members. The event prompted a local white newspaper to employ the headline: "Fierce Fracas up at Hoopa: Bad Indian Braves Fight Police and Terror Reigns."[114] Later, several policemen were also threatened with personal violence, possibly in response to their positions. In 1919 Willie Masten, the policeman at the downriver town of Johnson's, was shot and killed in the mountains by an unknown assailant. George Latham, a former police chief, was shot at "by Indian Frank an employee on the reservation," although no reason was given.[115]

By the 1920s, however, even some of the men who had served on the Indian police force in previous decades had begun to rebel against their federal employers, earning reputations among white administrators as troublemakers. The men's refusal to remain silent and their resistance to cultural attack despite their embrace of wage labor and market capitalism created great frustration for the superintendent.[116] Filling out the industrial surveys for Indian households in 1922, Superintendent Mortsolf described a number of former policemen in negative terms that indicated their resistance to assimilation efforts. Of George Latham, former chief of police, Mortsolf wrote: he is "the source of probably half the trouble between the Indians and the [Indian] office, being very talkative, and officious."[117] He described Jacob Hostler, who served as a police private for two quarters in 1899, as "an Indian of little importance on the reservation," adding that he was "childish, and rather quarrelsome" and worked "very little." Mortsolf revealingly added that the Hostler family was refusing to follow a course of full assimilation; Hostler's son had "married [a] widowed relative in old Hupa custom," and they refused to send their son to the school after their daughter had died there.[118] The complexity of using an Indian police force to uphold federal authority was most dramatically illustrated when Richard Hayden — whom Mortsolf described as "one of the Indians we are not proud of. He is illiterate, quarrelsome and nonprogressive" — shot and wounded the unpopular Kyselka in 1906. This likely was the reason for Hayden's subsequent discharge from the police force.[119]

The men serving as Indian judges also had multiple loyalties; their authority on the reservation derived from both their status within the tribe and their federally created judicial positions. In 1900 the Indian Office established a Court of Indian Offenses at Hoopa, and Agent Freer stated that he had appointed "three of the best and most influential Indians" to the position of judge.[120] The Indian judges helped settle a variety of disputes and infractions. Some offenses, like drunkenness and divorce, reflected the goals of assimilation policy, but others were local tribal matters. In 1903 Kyselka reported that the judges had ruled on the "possession of a sacred dance rock" (probably one of the ceremonial flints used in the White Deerskin Dance), which "ended in general hand shaking and settlement of an old factional feud."[121] Several of the men serving on the court that year had worked for the Indian Service before becoming judges, including Berryman Lack, Willis Matilton, Robert Hostler, and John Socktish. The men appear to have been tribal community leaders as well. In 1911 the tribe elected Berryman Lack and Robert Hostler to the newly created tribal business council.[122] Two of the other judges, James Jackson and Francis Colegrove, also seem to have been influential men on the reservation. Both were prosperous—an essential characteristic for leadership among the Hupa since only wealthy families could sponsor the ceremonial dances and were resonsible for settling any outstanding feuds before the dances began. Colegrove, who was described as supporting his extended family, was also active in Hupa ceremonial life. He owned the sacred regalia used in the Jump Dance, Brush Dance, and White Deerskin Dance and later became an honored elder of the tribe.[123] The judges may have been able to bring this influence to their positions on the Court of Indian Offenses. The exercise of this influence may have led Kyselka to describe the judges as being of "great assistance in helping to settle minor differences and disputes among the Indians."[124]

Further evidence of how many Hupa employees maintained their cultural traditions while incorporating new economic strategies can be seen in their willingness to share their tribal language and family stories with anthropologist Pliny Earl Goddard. Goddard had come to Hoopa Valley as a missionary for the WNIA in 1897 and returned in 1901 to gather linguistic data for an anthropology degree at the University of California, Berkeley. His resulting work, *Hupa Texts*, demonstrates that many of the men who held employment in the Indian Service also remained closely connected to their Hupa culture. In June 1901 employee Robinson Shoemaker shared a number of his family's ceremonial stories with Goddard, including "Origins of the KinaLdûñ Dance," "Formula for the Salmon Medicine," and "Formula of a Deer Medicine." Goddard noted that in Shoemaker's family, "the celebration of this medicine is an hereditary trust" and that the salmon medicine was an important part of Hupa culture and ceremonies.[125] James and Mary Marshall, whom Superintendent Morstolf had praised as some of the most "progressive" Indians at Hoopa, received a special acknowledgement as important collaborators in Goddard's introduction. Thanks were due, he wrote, to "James Marshall [who] assisted with many of the texts, especially those recorded from his wife, Mary Marshall." Several other Hupa men who had worked extensively for the Indian Service also maintained their cultural knowledge and related it to Goddard. He specifically thanked Julius Marshall, who "in many cases suggested correct renderings for the Indian words." He also expressed gratitude to Oscar and Samuel Brown and James Jackson. "To these Hupa thanks are due for their patience and interest in this most difficult task of preserving the language and lore of their people," Goddard wrote.[126]

Their work with Goddard reveals that, although they were often living lives that white officials deemed "progressive" and had been employed by the Indian Service, many Hupa men and women had by no means lost their cultural connections to their tribe, nor were they people of low status who had turned to the federal government to augment their positions in the valley. Instead, we see that they were thoroughly conversant in both Hupa and white worlds. As Goddard observed, they were actively participating in an effort to preserve their tribal heritage for future generations.[127]

The experiences of Sherman Norton, a Hupa man who worked as the agency's carpenter between 1912 and 1918, illustrate in great detail how tribal members tried to use Indian Service employment within their own cultural survival strategies; they also show some of the difficulties encountered. The subsequent experiences of Norton's son and grandson illustrate that these struggles often resulted in success, especially if we take a generational perspective. Norton was the son of a white man and a Hupa woman. After being educated at the Chemawa Indian School in Oregon, he married a white woman and continued to live off the reservation for some time. In 1912 they moved back to the Hoopa Valley Reservation with their three children. Norton's wife died soon thereafter, and he married Ella Jarnaghan, a Hupa woman. He entered the Indian Service in September of that year when he was hired as a temporary school carpenter at a rate of $60 per month, the same rate the previous white carpenter had received. When Norton was officially appointed two months later, however, the Indian Office adjusted his salary to the "Indian" rate of $45 per month.[128]

Norton, outraged, spent the next six years demanding a raise. He wrote to the commissioner of Indian affairs requesting the resumption of his former salary, pointing out that he was well educated and was performing a substantial amount of work beyond that required of the carpenter position since he served unofficially as both plumber and electrician for the school, while also maintaining the laundry machinery and forty-four miles of telephone line. "Now as I am a man with three children in this school all quite young yet," continued Norton, "I should like to stay here at my former salary." If his former salary could not be restored, he suggested an alternative solution: he should be transferred to "one of the better paying positions but on the same reservation."[129]

Norton's first superintendent, Edward Holden, was generally sympathetic and endorsed his request for a raise, indicating that Norton was a skilled worker who could have earned more off the reservation. He added that market conditions in the area were such that they would not be able to "secure a very good man" even at the original carpenter's salary of $720 per year.[130] When Superintendent Jesse Mortsolf replaced Superintendent Holden, Norton continued to agitate for adequate compensation for his labor, but by 1918 he was exasperated and submitted his resignation. After six years, he still had not received the salary that the white carpenter had been paid. He wrote in his resignation letter: "I cannot afford to work for the salary I am receiving." Seven years later, in 1925 — the same year that Superintendent Mortsolf left the reservation — Norton reappeared on the agency employee rolls along with his wife. Norton was employed as chief policeman at the agency for $720 per year, while Ella received $760 per year as the laundress.[131]

Norton's return to Hoopa Valley and his refusal to leave again offer the key to understanding his actions during this period. He was unmistakably committed to his family and tribal community rather than to the Indian Service, and he tried to use his employment in the service to protect the people most important to him. Although Norton recognized the value of his work and knew that he could be better paid off the reservation, he deliberately chose to remain. For him, the ability to earn a living while remaining within his tribal community was precisely the benefit of an Indian Service job.

Norton opposed a transfer to another reservation for a number of compelling personal, political, and social reasons. One of these involved his children, who were enrolled in the Hoopa Valley Boarding School. Mortsolf's reports to the commissioner of Indian affairs portrayed Norton as a man who held strong opinions about a wide range of reservation issues, especially the treatment of his children at the school. Norton, wrote Mortsolf, had "interfered at times with the discipline in the school" and "complain[ed] considerably" about the treatment of his children. Moreover, he was "quite a talker, very critical of the management of the school." Mortsolf's reports reveal Norton's strategies of resistance. Working at the school permitted Norton to keep an eye on his children and allowed him to complain and confront other staff members when he disagreed with them or when he thought they were mistreating his children. Norton also clearly had his own ideas about what his children's education should entail. He wanted them to attend the agency boarding school but also participate in Hupa cultural and religious events; notably, the superintendent also complained that Norton had made requests "to take his oldest child, a girl about sixteen years of age, out [of school] to attend dances," most likely the Hupa ceremonial dances.[132]

Norton's involvement in tribal affairs at Hoopa encompassed a range of activities. In 1912 he was among the "fifty of the prominent families in the valley" who drew up a petition for reallotment.[133] He also served three terms on the tribal council and played on the Hupa baseball team.[134] Mortsolf reported that Norton had a "tendency to mix in reservation affairs" and later described him as "a kind of lawyer and advisor among the Indians" who maintained great influence. This suggests that as an employee of the Indian Service, Norton was able to offer advice to his fellow tribal members about dealing with the agency bureaucracy. (Nor was Norton the only Hupa man to earn Mortsolf's ire for trying to advise his fellow tribal members. The superintendent characterized John Carpenter in similar terms: "He is a very intelligent Indian . . . and aspires to be a leader. He is something of an agitator, and I have found him not altogether to be trusted, although he is a good worker. . . . He was formerly a citizen living outside the reservation . . . and then moved into the reservation, adopting the habits and customs of the reservation Indians."[135]) Like other superintendents who dealt with "local agitators," Mortsolf suggested transferring Norton to a different reservation where he had no personal—or, more important, tribal—stake in governance. As we saw in chapter 5, superintendents' constant calls for the transfer of local Indian employees demonstrates the level of resistance they met, even from Indians who were working within the colonial apparatus of the federal Indian Service.

Norton also resisted while on the job itself. Mortsolf claimed that Norton "has been generally dissatisfied, and his work has not been satisfactory for some time. He is not good at planning his work ahead, and lets the various small matters accumulate, and then sits down and complains of being overworked."[136] Mortsolf attributed this to laziness and irresponsibility, but a more plausible explanation is that Norton was participating in a one-man work slowdown. In 1914 Norton had explicitly informed Superintendent Holden that he was quite willing to do the work mandatory to his position as carpenter but would no longer perform the mechanical work for which he was not being compensated.[137] He may have carried out this plan in response to Mortsolf's unsympathetic stance. In that same letter, Mortsolf indicated that Norton was not the only resistant Native employee at Hoopa. He elaborated in that letter on the recalcitrant behavior of other Indian employees, accusing them of favoritism and theft. "In all reservations, Indians have their friends and enemies . . . [and] they permit their prejudices to interfere with their work," he alleged, implying that white employees did not behave in this way. He also claimed that "much if not practically all of the property shortages at Hoopa are due to having local Indians employed." He complained that they thought that the farm implements were theirs to keep, going on to say that "it is very hard for a local Indian to keep from taking Government property home with him, or giving it to his friends." He especially accused the female employees of stealing food and clothing to give to their friends.[138] One wonders whether, like Norton, others felt they were underpaid and compensated by taking things from work or whether Mortsolf was particularly prejudiced against Indian employees.

Norton clearly used his Indian Service work strategically, moving in and out of employment as it suited his needs and fit his options. When he left his service position, as he did between 1918 and 1925, he made other arrangements. It is quite possible that he was able to quit in this instance because the new allocation of allotments at Hoopa in 1918 gave him an alternative economic option: farming on his allotment. This allowed him to remain on the reservation and support his family, both important objectives for Norton. As Superintendent Mortsolf wrote: "Mr. Norton wants to be allotted at Hoopa, and is afraid if he goes away he will lose his rights." He added that Norton's wife, Ella, refused to leave her home in the valley. After he resigned, Norton may have found some bitter satisfaction in the fact that no one would fill the position for the salary he had been paid.[139] In fact, there was an overall shortage of men listed as eligible carpenters on the civil service rolls due to the wartime economy, and many agencies had vacancies.[140]

The subsequent history of Norton's family also confounded the ideals of assimilation policy that posited that educated Indians would impart the lessons of "civilization" to the next generation. Like many Hupa children, Sherman Norton's son, Jack Norton Sr., left Hoopa Valley in 1915 at the age of twelve to attend the Phoenix Indian School. In 1918 he transferred to the Haskell Indian School in Lawrence, Kansas. There he met his future wife, Emma, a Cherokee woman. As his son, Jack Norton Jr., writes, "Both my parents had lost their mothers when they were young and their fathers had hoped that they would become educated in a rapidly changing world."[141] Jack Sr. took his father's wishes to heart and went on to Northeastern State University in Tahlequah, Oklahoma, and in 1929 became the first Hupa tribal member to graduate from college. Like his father, Jack Sr. joined the Indian Service, working first in Oklahoma near Emma's family and then moving to the Navajo Reservation. There he became superintendent of schools for Kinlichee, Klagetah, Tohatchi, and several day schools during the "tumultuous years of the New Deal and the Indian Reorganization Act," as his son remembers. In 1942 the Nortons returned to Hoopa Valley, where Jack Sr. took up farming and later returned to teaching. Jack Jr. began attending elementary school in the old boarding-school buildings where his grandfather had served as carpenter. The family's connection to the Indian Service remained alive at Hoopa Valley. Jack Jr. recalls: "I met my cousins, aunts and uncles as classmates or employees in the Indian Service."[142]

After graduating from college, Jack Jr. spent time in Hoopa watching the nation—with his father serving as tribal chairman—battle against federal efforts to terminate the tribe. Impressed by the tribal council's refusal to bow to federal pressure, he witnessed the Hupa nation escape the fate of almost forty other California reservations and rancherias that were terminated by the Rancheria Act of 1958. Jack Jr. also became an educator. In 1976 he published his first book, *Genocide in Northwestern California*, as a Native response to the unreflective patriotism of the U.S. bicentennial celebration. He also played a pivotal role in helping to establish the Native American Studies Department at Humboldt State University, and in 1997 he became the first Native Californian appointed to the Rupert Costo Chair in American Indian History at the University of California at Riverside.[143]

The men of the Norton family have embodied the Hupa name for Hoopa Valley, *Natinook*—"the place where trails return." While leaving Hoopa for educational or occupational opportunities, including those within the Indian Service, the Nortons have repeatedly returned to Hoopa Valley to nurture their cultural identity and fight for tribal political sovereignty. Thus, Sherman Norton's resistance to cultural assimilation encouraged two more generations to join the struggle. Jack Jr. continues to share his grandparents' sense of the importance of place. As he recently wrote: "Most Indian communities share an idea of place; a homeland that carries the racial memories and energy of a people; where cultural and social mores along with spiritual beliefs are demonstrated." Norton himself participates in this place making as a singer and dancer of the Five High Dance tribes in Northern California. He returns to the Trinity River several times a year to take part in the religious rituals of the Jump or Mountain Dance and the White Deerskin Dance, ceremonies designed to "fix or renew the world." For him, this continued connection to his tribal homeland is as important as his work as an educator. He writes hopefully: "As an educator and a singer and dancer in the ceremonies of the

Five High Dance tribes, I believe that someday there will be a gracious acceptance of views whereby all life will be enhanced, not lessened."[144]

CONCLUSION

By the 1920s, the Indian Service had established a boarding school at Hoopa, allotted the reservation, and employed scores of Hupa people. If at that time somebody had informed the Indian agents at Hoopa Valley that almost 100 years later, the Hupa tribe would not only still exist but also continue to hold their sacred dance ceremonies, fish for salmon, and manage several business enterprises and a museum, and that many members would continue to live along the banks of the Trinity River, they might have been shocked. After all, the Indian Office's theory of assimilation posited that educating and employing so many of the Hupa people meant that they would long since have been absorbed into the citizenry, leaving the valley a community of white landholders—some, perhaps, with a small measure of Indian ancestry.

The continued existence of the Hupa tribe attests to the resourcefulness and perseverance of its people. The environmental disruption of their traditional sources of food and raw materials, as well as the political legacy of conquest, constrained their choices. Within these constraints, however, the Hupa people fought to protect their territory, their cultural knowledge, and their sovereignty. One significant way they did so was by refusing to leave their homeland; it is no accident that one of their published tribal histories is entitled *Our Home Forever*. Staying in *Natinook* meant finding new ways to sustain themselves. They pieced together multiple tactics, including the use of Indian Service employment to supplement other means of subsistence. Indeed, at Hoopa Valley, tribal members often used their work for the Indian Service to undermine the very goals the service was established to achieve. Many of the same employees who filled positions within the colonial administration—some of whom earned high praise from their administrators— were the very people who strongly resisted the destruction of their tribal identity and passed their values on to the next generation.

Further studies of local reservation economies and the place of federal employment within them will illuminate the multiple and creative means by which Native people persisted and challenged the vision of assimilation. Many Hupa people experienced Indian Service employment as temporary laborers. It is likely that this was the case for most tribal communities throughout the nation, since the systemwide reports from the Indian Office indicate that it relied heavily on local Native labor to keep the reservations and schools running. That said, other Native communities may not have used service work in quite the same way. Even on the Hoopa Valley Reservation, there were differences between the Hupa and Yurok tribes' participation in federal employment. In his study of the Round Valley Reservation, located roughly 200 miles south of Hoopa Valley, William J. Bauer has shown that while some Native people used federal employment like the Hupa did, migratory agricultural labor played a much more important role in the community and cultural maintenance of Round Valley tribes as the reservation became a "hub" in a wider Native landscape beyond its boundaries. The likely reason for this different pattern lies in the historical context of the two reservations. Unlike Hoopa Valley, which was the center of the world for the Hupa tribe, many of the people at Round Valley had been removed there from other parts of Northern California; migratory labor thus helped them revisit their homelands and any tribal members who lived off the reservation. Moreover, the migratory worksites became places where Native people could participate in cultural and community building away from the oversight of federal agents.[145]

Despite its location in the rugged mountains of the Coastal Range, in many ways, Hoopa Valley was not at all isolated. It was connected through federal policy to a larger system: far-flung reservations, off-reservation boarding schools, and Washington, D.C. It is to the shifting currents of national policy that we now return.

A Nineteenth-Century Agency

in a Twentieth-Century Age

At the turn of the century, policy makers and others concerned with Indian affairs took stock of their progress. The tensions we saw in the last several chapters—the reality of Indian Service personnel who worked at a distance from, at cross purposes with, or even in opposition to the policies formulated in Washington, D.C.—were increasingly drawing notice at the national level. This, combined with widespread Indigenous resistance to cultural assimilation, led to a period of "great confusion in Indian Affairs."[1]

Some observers of Indian policy believed that it offered a successful model for the nation's other dependent populations. After the Spanish-American War, for instance, the Board of Indian Commissioners (BIC) recommended that the Indian Service could serve as an example for the administration of the Philippines and Cuba. A few years later in 1904, the Lake Mohonk Conference changed its name to the "Lake Mohonk Conference for the Friends of the Indian and other Dependent Peoples" and expanded its discussions to include the Philippines, Puerto Rico, and other U.S. dependencies. The Philippine Service did resemble the Indian Service in some ways.[2] Consisting of a large teaching force, it was composed of both women and men, many of whom were married couples. Some of the personnel had in fact transferred to it from the Indian Service. For example, after serving for four years as the superintendent of the Hoopa Valley Indian School, William B. Freer transferred to the Philippines as the assistant superintendent of public instruction; former field matron May Faurote also transferred there.[3] In her memoir, Indian Service teacher Minnie Braithwaite described both her own desire to transfer to the Philippine Service and instances in which fellow employees made the move.[4]

In his 1907 autobiography, General O. O. Howard described what he saw as the logical progression of social provision for federal wards. General Howard was well positioned to make such a judgment, having served as the former head of the Freedmen's Bureau before becoming a military commander during President Grant's Peace Policy.

> This sort of legislation in 1865 [the establishment of the Freedmen's Bureau] was quite new to our Government. It was the exercise of benevolent functions hitherto always contended against by our leading statesmen, even when providing for the Indian Bureau. The Nation, as something to love and cherish and to give forth sympathy and aid to the destitute, began then to be more pronounced than ever before. Our attitude toward the Indians in General Grant's peace policy and in giving them land in severalty; our intervention in Cuba and our subsequent neighborly action toward the people of that island; our national efforts to lift up the people of Porto Rico [sic], and our sending instructors in large numbers to set in motion the work of education in the Philippine Islands: these and other benevolences suggested by this reference make the people of today feel that at last we have a Nation which cares for its children.[5]

In Howard's estimation, these new policies stemmed from the same source: a post–Civil War sense of national benevolence and a new legislative agenda that created extensive federal social programs. He noted that antebellum Indian policy had been much less elaborate, and that it was only after the war that a flood of new initiatives was unleashed by the national government. These programs shared the characteristic of being "aid to the destitute," benevolence aimed at the nation's "children."

By contrast, other commentators argued that the government had been a poor parent to the Indians because it had failed to make them self-sufficient. Assessing the previous three decades of federal policy, Commissioner William Jones concluded in 1901:

> For about a generation the Government has been taking a very active interest in the welfare of the Indian. In that time he has been located on reservations and fed and clothed; he has been supplied lavishly with utensils and means to earn his living, with materials for his dwelling and articles to furnish it; his children have been educated and money has been paid him; farmers and mechanics have been supplied him, and he has received aid in a multitude of different ways. In the last thirty-three years over $240,000,000 have been spent upon an Indian

population not exceeding 180,000. . . . What is his condition to-day? He is still on his reservation; he is still being fed; his children are still being educated and money is still being paid him; he is still dependent upon the Government for existence; mechanics wait on him and farmers still aid him; he is little, if any, nearer the goal of independence than he was thirty years ago, and if the present policy is continued he will get little, if any, nearer in thirty years to come.[6]

While General Howard and many of the Lake Mohonk participants drew upon older social theories, Jones and other policy makers were influenced by new Progressive ideas about efficiency and professionalization, as well as about race. Policy makers had not totally given up on assimilation, but they sought to modify its terms and extend its timeline further into the future.[7] The service had been developed in the nineteenth century using a model that emphasized the individual influence of each employee; under this older plan, employees were not interchangeable and their jobs were deeply personal. The rising Progressive ideas about professionalism and rationalization contrasted starkly with the older model of the Indian Service.[8] As a result, Office of Indian Affairs employees and administrators began to reconsider their options and experimented with different kinds of programs, marking significant rethinking of the methods and goals of assimilation policy.

These changes had a substantial effect on all employees in the Indian Service, but it was Native employees who experienced the largest disruptions. Many service workers, especially teachers, found professionalization, particularly participation in specialized associations, a useful way to develop their skills, facilitate their jobs in the service, and become part of a larger community of specialists. In some cases, their enthusiasm influenced administrators who began to place greater emphasis on employee training and development. But Indian Office officials were also responding to outside charges of disorganization and inefficient administration in the Indian Service. They attempted to rationalize service work by focusing on employee training and policing employee job performance.

These shifts had a much darker side as well. Even as officials were calling for greater efficiency in the agency that served the nation's wards, they began to argue that these wards were incapable of full citizenship. The Indian Office shifted its emphasis to manual labor and began to downgrade educational expectations for Native students. In making these arguments, officials willfully ignored the presence of a vibrant Native middle class that organized into a national association — the Society of American Indians — that endorsed professionalism while simultaneously embracing Native cultural identity.

CHANGE FROM THE BOTTOM UP

Some of the emphasis on professionalization and efficiency proceeded from the bottom up as part of a movement for employee development. In this area, it was the personnel themselves who led the drive for change. Although many of them had educational training and experience,[9] the challenge of teaching in Indian Schools was unlike anything most of them had ever undertaken. They were expected to transmit both academic and cultural knowledge to students who often had little or no understanding of English and whose cultural norms were usually strange and unfamiliar to their teachers. Even when students were not openly resistant, service employees found themselves frustrated, exhausted, and drained of creative ideas. Moreover, many employees, especially day-school teachers, were isolated from colleagues or professionals who might be able to offer advice. Motivated by a desire for self-improvement, some employees searched for practical knowledge that would help them with their students. In addition, they sought the emotional support of coworkers who could understand the challenges they faced. Many also hoped that better training might lead to opportunities for promotion.

Many service employees turned to teaching institutes for professional development opportunities and networks of friendship and support. The first teaching institute on record was held in 1884 in Puyallup, Washington. While this gathering did not arouse much interest, a few years later the movement took off. Elaine Goodale Eastman established an early teaching institute while employed by the Indian Service as the superintendent of Sioux education in the Dakotas. In 1890, after her round of inspections, she decided to hold an institute to help prepare the teachers. She planned it with the "active aid of the superintendent of the Oglala boarding school, who happened to be a trained man." At the three-day meeting, Eastman remembered, "his best teachers gave demonstrations; the agency doctor and the missionary favored us with talks; and there was open discussion at every point. Here the primitive log day schools were scattered over a radius of seventy-five miles, but every man and woman was in attendance, eager for help."[10] The event was so well received that the Indian Office in Washington authorized permission for her to hold similar institutes on the rest of the reservations in the Dakotas in subsequent years. That success, as Eastman noticed, was premised on the desire of the school employees for help and instruction. They sought to learn new methods and pedagogical techniques. She also encouraged the teachers to begin taking a professional teaching journal, and several accompanied her to the annual meeting of the National Education Association (NEA) in St. Paul that summer.[11]

That same year, other Indian Service employees enthusiastically embraced the idea and organized two other teaching institutes — one in Marietta, California, and a second in Puyallup, Washington. The next year, the commissioner of Indian affairs noted the good effect of these institutes. Three years later, following the lead of the employees, the secretary of the interior issued directions to hold summer institutes at several of the larger boarding schools. Personnel flocked to the events, eager to take advantage of the opportunities they offered. During the summer of 1893, 132 service workers arrived at Chilocco, Oklahoma; over 90 came to Fort Shaw, Montana; between 200 and 250 traveled to St. Paul, Minnesota; attendance at Chemawa, Oregon, exceeded 100; and despite a railroad strike, more than 50 employees made their way to the institute at Santa Fe, New Mexico. This employee enthusiasm helped to make the institutes a "most gratifying success" in the eyes of the commissioner of Indian affairs.[12]

The Indian Office continued to hold its own teaching institutes into the twentieth century. In the summer of 1900, it held three other regional institutes at Chemawa, Puyallup, and Pine Ridge.[13] A few years later, Commissioner Leupp praised the local institutes as offering the opportunity to employees to discuss the challenges specific to working among particular tribes and cultures. In 1906 he enthused: "The purpose of holding several institutes each year is to bring the system of Indian education to a higher standard of efficiency. In different localities are found different types of Indians and varying conditions, and by comparison of methods and interchange of ideas each teacher present and each school represented receives the benefit of the experience of the others. Thus the local institutes are as valuable in their way as the general institutes, and are attended by many who would otherwise be deprived of any institute opportunities."[14]

For employees, the institutes provided an important support network. Gertrude Golden, a boarding-school teacher, remembered going to a convention at Newport on Yaquina Bay, Oregon, in 1901 during her first year in the Indian Service. It was, Golden wrote, "one of the happiest occasions in my life. Truly it furnished a scrapbook of memories never to be forgotten: the many pleasant people met at the convention, the inspiring talks and good music . . . [and] the fellowship with the Indian young people attending the convention."[15] While teaching in Arizona, Minnie Braithwaite attended an "absorbingly interesting" local summer institute at the Keam's Canyon School on the Hopi Agency, and she remained friends with several fellow employees she met there.[16]

Employee enthusiasm for professionalization rapidly spread beyond the Indian Service itself. In 1899 a number of Indian Service teachers petitioned the NEA to create a Department of Indian Education, which it did. The NEA was a professional organization for educators that had previously shown interest in the problem of Indian education, but it was the growing pressure from Indian Service teachers that forced it into the spotlight. Teachers who endorsed the petition saw this professional association as an important source of support and information.[17] Commissioner of Indian Affairs William Jones endorsed the idea of service employees meeting with the NEA at its national conference. He praised it as an opportunity at which "notes may be compared upon the best means of effecting the civilization for the Indian." After the convention, he reported that "employees were thus given an ample opportunity to participate in this great gathering of educators from all sections of the country and to hear the best exponents of pedagogy."[18] For the employees who could not attend the national conference, the NEA also sponsored teaching institutes around the country—what one historian has labeled "normal schools on wheels."[19] By 1914 the Indian Office was encouraging individual employees to attend the conference. Superintendent John Brown, for example, received a letter suggesting that he go to a meeting of the NEA's Department of Superintendence.[20]

Meeting with the NEA meant that Indian Service employees could take advantage of larger discussions in the field of education while also participating in the concurrent special sessions on the specifics of Indian education. The Department of Indian Education was one of several separate departments within the NEA that focused on specialized teaching fields; others included the Department of Science Instruction and the Department for Deaf, Blind and Feeble-Minded.[21] Every year the commissioner of education addressed the assembled Indian Service workers, as did a series of invited speakers. The bulk of the Department of Indian Education's time, however, was made up of roundtable discussions and papers given by employees themselves.[22] Superintendents often presented these papers at the national meetings, but regular employees sometimes did as well. The latter group was especially represented in the Indian Service regional conferences. The papers addressed practical pedagogical questions as well as criticisms of the Indian Service. In 1902, for example, some of the paper topics at regional meetings included "How to supplement the work of the pupils," by Mrs. Nellie F. Hunt, a housekeeper at Pine Ridge Day School No. 18; "Helps in Securing attendance in day schools," by Miss Fannie J. Dennis, a teacher at Paraje Day School in New Mexico; and "A suggestion toward making life in the Indian school service more agreeable," by Charles H. Koontz, the superintendent of the Menominee School in Wisconsin.[23] Here, at both regional and national institutes, employees received encouragement from their coworkers based on their common experiences and their shared belief in the work of the Indian Service.

The meetings were attended by both Native and white employees. In 1903, for example, Commissioner Jones singled out the former when reporting on the national NEA conference held in Boston: "A number of Indians (teachers and students from various schools) were in attendance, and their interest in the features of the institute and practical suggestions in discussion demonstrated the earnest manner in which they are taking advantage of the educational opportunities offered them and their desire to assist in the uplifting of their race."[24] Native employees also made presentations. For instance, Carlisle art teacher Angel DeCora (Winnebago/French) lectured on "Native Indian Art" at the 1907 meeting in Los Angeles,[25] and teacher Minnie Jenkins remembered that at an institute in Pasadena, California, "Miss Anderson, an Indian educated at Carlisle, Pennsylvania, who was now a teacher at one of the reservation day schools, discussed the paper that was read on this subject. She was very clever and handled the subject in a masterly manner."[26]

Beyond the teaching institutes, Native and white employees also began to take advantage of another opportunity for professional development: enrollment in summer courses offered by local or regional colleges. Again, this seems initially to have been driven by the desire of individual employees, but it was later heartily supported by the Indian Office. By 1912 employee access to these professional development opportunities had been codified in law. Employees were allowed educational leave of no less than thirty days in addition to their annual leave "for attendance at educational gatherings, conventions, institutions, or training schools, if the interest of the service require, and under such regulations as the Secretary of the Interior may prescribe, and no additional salary or expense on account of the leave of absence shall be incurred."[27] The Indian Office encouraged its employees to participate by recommending universities and courses, and by 1922 it apparently drew up a designated list of schools that offered courses for service workers.[28] By 1928–29 it had gone even further by requiring employees in teaching positions to attend summer-school courses every other year and granting them educational leave to do so. Indian Office regulations stipulated that employees had to "take at least six credit hours of serious work having direct bearing on their duties."[29] The office also created another version of the efficiency report around 1931 that included a section in which employees could list their summer school, extension courses, or other professional training experiences.[30]

Employees who took summer courses often enjoyed themselves. Lavinia Cornelius (Oneida), a nurse at the Tomah School in Wisconsin, wrote to Elinor Gregg, supervisor of nurses for the Indian Service: "My experience at that University was *wonderful* and profitable. My regular subjects were 'principles of public health nursing' and 'health supervision of [the] school child.'

I listened in on some other subjects of preventive medicine. It was a busy time but enjoyed it all immensely. My education was so limited I felt handicapped among all the girls and women who I know have had better chances. . . . Now I feel like I must go to summer school again."[31] Employees who could not attend summer school or who wanted to extend their learning enrolled in correspondence courses. Homer Bibb, a clerk at Seger, Oklahoma, and Clarence Birch, the principal teacher at Chilocco, both took correspondence courses from Sprague's Correspondence School of Law in Chicago.[32]

The experiences of one teacher, Mary Baird, offer an illustration of how employees sought to use education to their advantage and how the Indian Office understood staff professional development efforts. Baird participated in several of the professionalization opportunities available to service employees, and her superiors praised her efforts. In 1912 her superintendent enthused that she was "successful because of the hard work she does and because she 'keeps up' professionally. Miss Baird attends Teacher's Institutes and association meetings and reads professional literature. Teaching with [her] is a profession, not merely a way to earn a little money or a stepping stone to some other occupation."[33] But as with many employees, Baird had multiple reasons for participating in these opportunities, and advancement was one of them. In 1919 she requested a transfer to a clerical position. "There is," she wrote, "more opportunity for advance in salary in clerical work than in that of teacher." She added that "for the last two years I have tried, at every opportunity, to fit myself for clerical work. . . . [A]t the business department of the Wichita University, I took twelve weeks work in bookkeeping . . . [and] I have taken twelve weeks in short hand, and am continuing the study at home." Unfortunately for Baird, her supervisor believed that since she was "one of the best teachers in the Indian service . . . it would be a distinct loss for her to quit teaching," and he denied her request (though he did recommend an increase in salary).[34] Baird continued to actively update her résumé, and by 1931, the year before she retired, her file indicated that she had taken summer-school and extension courses on teaching English in high school, Shakespeare, and ideals in character building at both Greeley State Teachers College and Iowa State University.[35] Employees and the Indian Office thus saw professional development as important, albeit not always for the same reasons.

Contemporary critics of the Indian Service tended to paint all employees as unqualified or corrupt, something subsequent historical evaluations have often echoed. And some of them certainly were. But many of them did have experience and training similar to public school teachers and were simply unprepared for the full demands of their jobs in the Indian Service. Some clearly worked hard to improve their ability to accomplish their educational mission—which, it must be remembered, was an effort to destroy Native culture by targeting children by either removing them from their families or, at the very least, denigrating everything about their parents and communities. The gulf between teaching white children in local schools and teaching Native children in schools with a colonial curriculum was vast. While many service employees turned to the professional resources offered to them by experts in the field of education, those resources were still premised on the righteousness of the Indian Service's mission and the superiority of Anglo cultural norms.

CHANGE FROM THE TOP DOWN

In his autobiography, president Theodore Roosevelt recalled that the Indian Service had provided the "actual case" of bureaucratic inefficiency that led him in 1905 to establish the Committee on Department Methods, also called the Keep Commission. Its task was to "find out what changes [were] needed to place the conduct of the executive business of the Government . . . on the most economical and effective basis in the light of the best modern business practice." Recalling the case, Roosevelt wrote:

> An officer in charge of an Indian agency made a requisition in the autumn for a stove costing seven dollars, certifying at the same time that it was needed to keep the infirmary warm during the winter, because the old stove was worn out. Thereupon the customary papers went through the customary routine, without unusual delay at any point. The transaction moved like a glacier with dignity to its appointed end, and the stove reached the infirmary in good order in time for the Indian agent to acknowledge its arrival in these words: "The stove is here. So is spring."[36]

President Roosevelt's example was indicative of bureaucratic concerns that led to changes in the Indian Service in the decades before World War I. Under the guidance of Roosevelt appointee Francis Leupp, who the president once called a "capital" commissioner of Indian affairs, the Indian Office began to reflect wider national changes that characterized the Progressive Era. Leupp's administration oversaw a revolution in record keeping and an increased emphasis on efficiency and professionalization in the service. Together, these initiatives encapsulated the contradictory trends of announcing the impending end of the Indian Service while simultaneously illustrating the need to strengthen its bureaucracy. Commissioner Leupp acknowledged this seemingly incongruous state of affairs but argued that "improved organization is almost more important in a diminishing than in a growing bureau."[37]

As President Roosevelt asserted, there was good reason for reform in the administration of Indian affairs. The growth of the Indian Office, as well as the other federal departments, had reached a critical point by the end of the nineteenth century. No one had anticipated the increased volume of paperwork that had been stimulated by the growth of the federal bureaucracy. The methods of record keeping had become unwieldy given the size of the offices' employee rolls and the scope of their administrative functions. This led to several pressing reforms, including some involving storage space and record keeping. As early as the 1870s, office buildings in Washington, D.C., were running out of space for documents. Piles of records in the Department of the Interior, the Treasury Department, and the Post Office Department were reported to have spilled out into the hallways. Compounding the problem was the fact that Congress had not provided any system for the evaluation and disposal of records; everything had to be retained even though there was no central record-keeping facility to house or maintain the documents.

In a parallel development, the letter-book system of record keeping, the method used by the Indian Office, had been severely outpaced by the volume of correspondence. The letter-book system was composed of "a voluminous series of indexes and registers of letters received and copies and indexes of letters sent. A part of the system, too, was the time-consuming method of folding, briefing, and annotating letters received."[38] For example, in August 1893, Mrs. Emily Tunison of Somerville, New Jersey, sent a letter to the secretary of the interior requesting a teaching position in the Indian Service. Tunison's letter was forwarded to the Indian Office, where a clerk received it, read it, folded it into thirds, and numbered it 29267, which signified that it was the 29,267th letter received by the commissioner of Indian affairs for the year 1893. The clerk then wrote the name of the sender, the date, and the place from which it was sent, as well as a summary of its contents, under the number on the front of the letter; in this case, the clerk summarized the letter's purpose as: "wants place as teacher in an Indian school." He or she then recorded that information in two different indexes — first, a subject index in which the clerk recorded the number under its appropriate subjects (most likely the name of the sender, Emily Tunison); and second, a numerically ordered register in which the clerk wrote the number and summary. Later, the clerk also noted the action taken on the front of the letter ("Ansd [Answered] Aug. 9/93"), as well as any further directives ("File"). Finally, Mrs. Tunison's letter was filed behind letter number 29266.[39] This was a cumbersome system, especially for an office with a high volume of correspondence.

It was made more difficult by the fact that not only were the offices in the Department of the Interior the last to use handwritten letter books, but they also had few typewriters, so all clerical work was done by hand. Given the Indian Office's reputation for protracted and slow correspondence, it is no wonder that President Roosevelt used it as his example of federal bureaucratic inefficiency.[40]

The Keep Commission was one of six executive commissions that Roosevelt assembled. Gifford Pinchot—chief of the Forest Service in the Department of Agriculture—and James R. Garfield—commissioner of the Bureau of Corporations, son of the former president, and soon-to-be secretary of the interior—developed a plan for the new commission on the basis of reforms enacted within their own agencies. In June 1905 Roosevelt appointed employees and administrators from across the executive departments to the committee and its subcommittees.[41] After considering the problems, they offered proposals to encourage greater interbureau and interdepartmental exchanges, to investigate personnel administration, and to probe federal publication policies and programs.[42] Wary of any limitation of its prerogatives, Congress never officially passed legislation making these recommendations into law, and many department heads ignored the suggestions.

In the Department of the Interior, however, under the guidance of the newly appointed Secretary Garfield, the recommendations of the Keep Commission resulted in an organizational revolution. Garfield encouraged the bureau heads beneath him—including the commissioner of Indian affairs—to execute the Keep Commission's proposals.[43] Leupp zealously complied. In his annual report for 1907, he informed Garfield that he had worked to reorganize the administration of the Indian Office "to put an end to all duplication of labor, to bring all closely allied subjects under one head, and to provide a system of checks on the one hand and of automatic cooperation on the other, designed at once to guard against errors, lighten the present expenditure of energy, increase the capacity for output, and result progressively in substantial economies."[44] One goal in improving efficiency was to make employees interchangeable. Previously, long-term employees served as the institutional memory of the departments, as we saw in the case of Robert Burns in chapter 5. By 1907 Leupp happily reported that "the end of the 'indispensable man' is an administrative blessing."[45]

Responding to Garfield's call for increased efficiency, Leupp also tackled the notoriously outdated letter-book system.[46] He detailed the changes in his 1907 annual report to Garfield: "The old folded filing and the cumbersome letter books have been abolished. The mastery of any one case used to mean consulting perhaps seven or eight letter books for letters sent out and going to a distant part of the office where incoming letters had been filed; now, all the papers in a case are filed together, and the clerk who has to write a new letter concerning it is able to keep the whole case clearly in mind." He also noted that "as one example of many reforms in paper, the abolition of the old form of report of employees . . . saves the service in time and clerical hire at least $3,000 a year." (That shift also resulted in a completely different set of sources for historians.)[47]

Roosevelt's successor, President William Howard Taft, built on the Keep Commission by creating a Committee on Economy and Efficiency.[48] Both Leupp and his successor Robert Valentine served under President Taft and continued this effort in the Indian Office as well. Valentine, for example, surveyed the ten years of administration between 1902 and 1912, focusing on the amount of correspondence received by the Indian Office.[49] His survey revealed the immense amount of paper flowing into the Indian Office. The commissioner reported: "In 1902, 77,000 letters were received by the Indian Office, which to conduct its correspondence had 132 employees; in 1911, 209,000 letters were received and there were 227" people employed as clerks. He also noted that much of this increased correspondence was the result of an increased push for assimilation: "In the last 10 years Indian office affairs have taken on a magnitude, a breadth, and a detail which are significant of a real attempt to master the "Indian problem" by preparing the Indians to leave their status of wardship, at last to lose their anomalous character as a people set apart and to join their white neighbors in the body of American citizenship."[50]

Many of the changes instituted in Washington, D.C., made their way to the Indian Service schools and agencies and affected the everyday lives of employees. A multitude of new administrative forms began to appear in their personnel files. Some forms were merely reconfigured to correspond with typewriter technology that the clerks would now be using. Others solicited new information. Many of these new forms reveal the Indian Office's attempts to better measure the efficiency of employees. For example, in 1912 the Indian Office began using a new efficiency report document that required employees to list the books and periodicals that they had read during the previous year. The office eventually required efficiency reports twice a year—on 1 May and 1 November. All this was an effort to encourage employees to improve their job performance as part of a larger push for professionalization.[51] The majority of the readings that employees listed were fairly mundane and included local newspapers and national periodicals such as *Good Housekeeping*, *Ladies' Home Journal*, and the *Delineator*.[52] Native employees more often listed publications specific to their experiences, such as alumni newsletters from boarding schools and national journals like the *Native American* and *Indian Leader*.[53] Some employees demonstrated a clear desire for self-improvement, having read various pedagogical works. Agnes Fredette from Standing Rock, for example, consistently listed books such as *Common Sense Didactics*, *School Management*, *A Brief Course in Teaching*, *The School as a Social Institution*, and *The Personality of the Teacher*.[54] Another teacher, Minnie Braithwaite, stated that she found a similar pedagogical book "invaluable in [her] teaching."[55] Other employees listed young-adult books such as *Laddie* and *Little Sir Galahad*, which they may have read to their students.[56] More generally, however, the lists indicate a wide range of reading tastes. Popular literature dominated among service employees. This more-popular fare—what one supervisor dismissed as "of miscellaneous character (light)"[57]—may not have been what the Indian Office expected, but it was what the employees were enjoying. Historical novels and western fiction, such as B. M. Bower's *The Lure of the Dim Trail* and especially the works of Zane Gray, had a large audience among both Native and white employees.[58] Adventure stories like *Tarzan* and the works of Jack London appeared along with popular novels like *Brewster's Millions* and *Main Street*.[59]

By 1915, in an apparent effort to guide reading choices more aggressively, the office began to require teachers to fill out "vocational reading report" forms as well. The forms asked employees to record books read from "the reading and study course for the present school year as suggested by the Office of Indian Affairs." The form also asked for a list of "other books and journals on my vocation" and, finally, miscellaneous matter. The suggested reading list included works such as *School and Home Gardens*, *What Children Should Study and Why*, and *A Brief Course in Teaching Process*.[60] Around the same time, another new document—the "report on supervision of individual instructors"—appeared. It required the superintendent to observe a teacher's classroom performance and report the subject matter, materials, and methods used during the lesson.[61]

Officials also sought to rationalize the work of Indian Service personnel by sending out printed copies of the rules and regulations, as well as circulars informing employees of the official policies of the service. The BIC noted, however, that many employees complained that these new attempts at efficiency actually backfired. "The men in the Indian field service are hampered in their efforts by the delays caused by multiplicity of laws and cumbersome rules and regulations in the Indian Office in Washington," they reported. "Too many circulars are received from the Washington office modifying regulations or calling for various reports or giving instructions on this, that, and the other thing. The exact number of circulars issued from the Washington office from

July 7, 1913, to July 8, 1914, is 122, or a little more than one circular every third day. The field employees complain, with apparent ground, that while they are instructed from the office in Washington to spend most of their time in the field among the Indians, compliance with the numerous circulars makes it impossible for them to do so."[62] Employees felt overwhelmed by the pages of guidelines streaming out of Washington, and they also often found the information contradictory and confusing, leading, as the Board of Commissioners pointed out, to less efficiency rather than more.

A shift toward more professional bureaucracy can be seen in one more area: the recruiting of Indian Service employees. The ways in which prospective employees learned about positions in the service had gone through three rough stages: first, the patronage system, which required having connections; second, the civil service system, which demanded access to information about and proximity to the exams; and third, active recruiting, in which the Indian Office sought out certain kinds of skilled personnel, especially for medical positions. The rising cachet of professional expertise in the twentieth century, especially in the field of health care, led to active recruiting in the Indian Service. The atrocious health conditions in the boarding schools, especially the high rates of tuberculosis and the eye disease trachoma, along with new understandings of disease, led the Indian Office to prioritize Indian health as a major concern.[63] In 1908, for example, the Indian Office and the Smithsonian Institution collaborated on a tuberculosis survey that demonstrated exceedingly high rates of the disease in the Indian Schools. The findings of the report spurred the Indian Office to try to improve Indian health. It sought to correct sanitary problems, built several hospitals and sanitariums, and stressed educational measures designed to prevent disease, as exemplified by the "Save the Babies" campaign. Related to the national "Better Baby" movement supported by the Children's Bureau, the service's version also sought to reduce infant mortality by enlisting Native mothers in the fight to raise clean, healthy, and assimilated children, especially by sponsoring competitive baby shows.[64] It also increased the hiring of medical professionals. Professional nurses began to replace field matrons, for example.[65]

In order to obtain skilled employees, the government began to actively recruit trained personnel. The Civil Service Commission published directions for applying for jobs in numerous publications, often indicating which positions offered the applicant the best chance of appointment. In 1911 it put out a call in the *American Journal of Nursing* noting the need for nurses in the Indian, Isthmian Canal (Panama), and Philippine services. A similar call appeared in *Nursing World* the following year.[66] In 1924 Elinor D. Gregg was appointed as the supervisor of public-health nursing in the Medical Division of the Indian Bureau. Her primary task was to recruit qualified nurses for the Indian Service. She did so by working with the "Nursing Leaders" in Washington, going to national nursing conventions, speaking to "nurses—students and graduates," and writing articles for the *American Journal of Nursing*.[67] This increased emphasis on employee training soon had, as we will see, a major impact on the composition of the Indian Service.

PROGRESSIVISM AND PERSONNEL

Progressive Era thinking also had a darker side, from which flowed lowered expectations of Indian people's capacity. National shifts in racial ideology, combined with population movements and changing labor markets, resulted in important changes to the Indian Service's educational system and hiring policies. Looking first at these wider changes is essential to understanding what transpired in the Indian Office.

After the end of Reconstruction, popular thinking shifted away from free-labor ideology and its optimistic assumption that all men could become independent, self-supporting citizens. Instead, a growing number of people embraced a class-conflict model that accepted the notion that some Americans would inevitably be relegated to a permanent working class. Under the terms of free-labor ideology, it had been theoretically possible for anyone who followed the tenets of hard work and proper behavior to gain admission into the respectable classes regardless of their race. New ideologies heavy with scientific racism increasingly suggested that people of color were largely incapable of substantial improvement and were suited only to serve as a laboring class. This undermined the belief in a quick and temporary transition period after which Indians would join the nation as full citizens, instead suggesting a long-term subordination more suitable to their race.[68]

Another key influence on the changes in Indian policy was Americans' changing understanding of the West. By the turn of the century, the region was no longer seen as a vast, empty space threatening another conflict over the nation's soul. Instead, it had been rapidly settled by white Americans and become a territory safely incorporated through statehood. As Commissioner Jones observed in 1903: "It is true . . . that with the influx of population in the Indian country, the construction of railroads, and the building of cities, the line of demarcation between the older reservation and non reservation institutions is rapidly disappearing."[69] For Jones, the growth of respectable white populations in the West made off-reservation schools in which Indian children could be isolated and surrounded by proper object lessons unnecessary, as the reservations had themselves been surrounded by good examples.

As that demarcation between frontier and states dissipated, so did the fear of wicked white westerners, whom policy makers had spoken of during the 1870s and 1880s as a "fringe of scum" on the "wave" of civilization.[70]

Not only did these new western states have mature structures of social institutions, but, as Fred Hoxie has deftly argued, their political influence on national Indian policy also had increased along with their growing populations. By 1900 all of the western states except Arizona and New Mexico had gained statehood and thus wielded votes in Congress that gave them the political power necessary to influence Indian policy. Moreover, these states had a voracious appetite for agricultural, domestic, and industrial labor.[71] When they looked at Indian reservations, whites saw an untapped supply of workers in their midst. These circumstances left Indians vulnerable to white westerners' desire to fully dispossess them by ending federal oversight and thus converting them into a permanent laboring class.[72]

Beginning with Commissioner Jones (1897–1905) and gathering strength under his successor, Commissioner Leupp, policy makers began to move the Indian Office away from its goal of rapid and full assimilation and toward a racialized vision of a people destined by heredity for permanent manual labor. This change was most striking in the way it realigned the Indian School system, moving it away from comprehensive education and toward vocational instruction.[73] Along with changing the curriculum, Jones and Leupp—and Commissioners Valentine and Sells, who followed them—redirected the focus of the Indian School system away from the off-reservation boarding schools and toward the day schools.

Administrators had also begun to argue that the curriculum of the off-reservation boarding schools was too extravagant and did not prepare Native students for life on and around the reservations.[74] Superintendent of Schools Estelle Reel, a westerner herself and the sister of the governor of Wyoming, asserted that "higher education has no place in the Indian schools." The day schools, with their less academically rigorous curriculum,[75] became the alternative to boarding schools. Commissioner Jones had concluded that "day schools should be established at convenient places where [Indians] may learn enough to transact the ordinary business of life. Beyond this in the way of schools it is not necessary to go."[76] This was also a step in the direction of dismantling the Indian School Service because the basic assumption behind federal policy was that once Indians became assimilated citizens, they would enroll their children at local public schools. "The Government cannot indefinitely provide separate schools for Indians," Jones admonished. "The earlier and more conscientiously the States and Territories undertake their political duty to the children of their red citizens the easier will the transfer be accomplished. As stated, the ultimate object of Indian schools is to prepare these children for an easy entrance into the public-school system."[77]

Over the next few years, policy makers began to put these changes into effect. The number of day schools grew dramatically, and by 1911 Congress began to dismantle the off-reservation boarding-school system.[78] That year, Congress granted the Ouray School in Utah and the Fort Lewis and Grand Junction Schools in Colorado to the governors of those states, with the stipulation that they continue to offer admission to Indian students.[79] Several years later, in 1914, Commissioner Sells argued that moving Indian children to public schools offered "a splendid example of the elimination of the Indian as a distinct problem for the Federal or the State governments."[80] What these policy makers ignored was the fact that Indian children rarely attended public schools because of the racism they faced from students and teachers in the classrooms. For example, local whites often argued that Indian children were too dirty to attend school with white children. The 1918 closing of the Carlisle Indian School, the gem of the off-reservation institutions that had "symbolized the commitment of the transformation of Indian children into civilized citizens," drove home this new vision of Indian education.[81]

This new agenda fit handily into whites' desire for a large pool of Native laborers in the West. President Roosevelt, who was sympathetic to western interests, appointed Francis Leupp as his commissioner in 1905. Commissioner Leupp argued that a much longer period of social evolution would be necessary for assimilation, and that even then, Indians would remain a second-class citizenry destined for manual labor. He proposed that the goal of Indian policy be "improvement, rather than transformation," and that such improvement should consist of "realistically" training Native people for jobs available in their regions. Drawing a comparison with the racially ordered working class of color that had emerged in the South, Leupp concluded: "Our first duty to the Indian is to teach him to work. . . . Even the little papoose can be taught to weed the rows just as the pickaninny in the South can be used as a cotton picker."[82] As the quote indicates, the example of African American labor that policy makers were following was no longer the heady optimism of Reconstruction but the racial separation represented by Booker T. Washington. Indeed, under the tenure of Commissioner Leupp, Superintendent of Indian Schools Estelle Reel directed superintendents to pattern Indian School graduation ceremonies "after the one at Tuskegee Institute where in the place of academic robes and speeches, students donned rough clothes and demonstrated manual skills."[83]

To further this vision, Leupp set up a Bureau of Indian Labor within the Indian Service to assign gangs of Native men to seasonal labor across the

West. These Indians worked on railroads, for beet and cotton farmers, and in mining camps under the supervision of white men.[84] While he did not dispute that independent farming would continue to be a major goal of assimilation policy, Leupp hoped to move more and more Native people into the region's labor force. In his 1905 annual report, he projected that "at least three-fourths will settle down in that part of the West which we still style the frontier. Most of these will try to draw a living out of the soil; a less—though, let us hope, an ever increasing—part will enter the general labor market as lumbermen, ditchers, miners, railroad hands, or what not." Leupp perceived the program as having several benefits for assimilation. "The advantages gained," he wrote, are "pecuniary profits . . . understanding of the need of regularity and method . . . [and] bringing him [the Indian] bodily into the atmosphere of competitive activity developed in a white community."[85]

Leupp's ideas ran up against the older vision of assimilation that sought to create stable family farms and communities. The BIC was scathingly critical of the commissioner's new work policy. Their points of criticism were abundantly visible in the title of their 1905 report: "Effect on Family Life of the Breaking up of Indian Homes by Organizing 'Gangs of Indians' for Work at Distant Points."[86] In fact, this disagreement was an example of the fading prominence of the reformers who had previously exerted enormous influence on Indian Office officials. Although he had once been among these reformers, Francis Leupp now wanted to run his office his own way.[87]

Leupp generally had a low opinion of Indians holding high positions in the Indian Service. To oversee his new labor bureau, however, Leupp appointed an Indian, Charles Dagenett (Peoria), as the supervisor of Indian employment, making Dagenett the highest-ranking Native employee in the service.[88] Notwithstanding this choice, Leupp explicitly argued that Indians were racially inferior to whites and could not competently fill the same positions in the service. He continued to believe that Indian Service work was an important tool for teaching Indians about market participation, but he held that it should be labor appropriate for people at a lower stage of civilization. Leupp rejected the vision that policy makers had developed during the 1880s and 1890s in his revealingly titled book, *The Indian and His Problem*, which was published in 1910, the year after he left office. "The policy of all the administrations since Commissioner Morgan took office [in 1892]," he wrote, "has been to give educated Indians every practicable chance to serve their people; but the experiment of putting them into the places of highest responsibility has, except in rare instances, not worked so successfully as has been hoped." As justification for this position, he argued that Indians were unable to remain in a job for long and that such transience was problematic for the service.[89]

> The traditional freedom of the Indians from those forms of artificial obligation which are second nature to people of our Caucasian heritage, makes them impatient of the restraints of office when continued for any great length of time. They get tired, and are liable for no other cause to throw up their positions and go home for an interval of leisure. . . . [T]hey cannot be depended on to stick to one job for a long term, as white persons will. If such whimsical changefulness is inconvenient in private business, it may be positively ruinous in public employ in the Indian West.[90]

At another point, he asserted that paying Indian laborers on a monthly basis had the "effect of disheartening the Indian, who is not trained to look far ahead like the white man, and who is only too disposed to yield to the temptations of an idle life if he can see no speedy return from his labor."[91] In his denigration of Native personnel, Leupp disingenuously implied that white employees did not exhibit such whimsical changefulness, when in fact, as we have seen, they constantly contributed to the problem of transfers, rejected promotions, and resignations that plagued the service. Leupp continued to advocate that the service employ Indians, but he emphasized temporary laborer and reservation law enforcement positions as more suited to what he perceived as a racially inferior people.

When Leupp and other Indian Office administrators emphasized manual labor and began to dismantle the off-reservation school system, they in effect barred most Indian people from skilled positions in the Indian Service. As a result of their policies, the proportion of Indians in nonmanual positions in the service decreased. As we saw in chapter 5, the highly placed Native employees in the service were often products of the off-reservation boarding-school system, which had provided them the proficiency to fill such positions. But the cutting of funding for these schools and the shift toward rudimentary education in the day schools, as well as the lowering of educational standards overall, meant a shrinking number of qualified Native men and women available for higher-status and higher-paying positions. Even when Natives were qualified, administrators hesitated to promote them because of assumptions about their racial capacity.[92] Lisa Emmerich has identified this trend in her study of Native women serving as field matrons, noting that their numbers grew between 1895 and 1905 and that during that period, "they played an active and occasionally prominent role in civilization work." Their participation peaked in 1899, when they constituted 33 percent of the field-matron corps. Not surprisingly, almost half of the women who served in these positions had attended the Indian School Service's off-reservation boarding schools. After 1905, the year Francis Leupp took office, their participation declined drastically: between 1905 and 1927, the highest percentage of participation was in 1910, when Native women constituted 12 percent of the total corps.[93] Field matron was an especially symbolic position in assimilation policy because the employees who held it were meant to stand as examples of civilized womanhood. Policy makers' shift toward thinking of Indian people as racially inferior left little room for Native women to act in that capacity.

There were similar trends throughout the Indian Service. At the end of Leupp's administration in 1909, Native employees staffed 40 percent of all regular positions. Indian people also filled 20 percent of the service's white-collar jobs. Nonetheless, Leupp had raised concerns about their abilities and contributed to the reshaping of the Indian School Service to reflect those racial assumptions. As a result, the number of regular Indian employees began to decline; two decades later, in 1927, their presence in the service had fallen in both percentage (from 40 to 30 percent) and real numbers (from 1,920 to 1,700).[94]

But the BIC's vision of families happily farming on their allotments was being disrupted by other changes in Indian policy as well. For instance, Congress was revising the Dawes Act itself to fix a number of issues that had surfaced. Some reservations had still not been allotted, and a number of other problems had arisen where allotment had occurred. In some cases, the surveys were contested; in others, there was the complicated question of inheritance of land from allottees who had died. Particularly confusing was the citizenship status of allotted Indians. The Dawes Act had stipulated that Indians taking up allotments became citizens, but their land was to be held under a twenty-five-year trust, thus negating the freedoms of citizenship. At the same time, administrators argued that some allottees whose trusts were drawing to a close were still not "competent" for citizenship, and their trust periods needed to be extended. In 1906 Congress passed the Burke Act in an effort to address some of these concerns. The act declared that Indians whose allotments were still under trust were not citizens (a stipulation meant to facilitate the policing of liquor sales on reservations). It also created a mechanism by which the secretary of the interior had the power to determine competency. As a result, the secretary could either extend the trust period or end it early at his discretion. As it was practiced, such decisions were often based on the racial identity of the allottee, and officials determined Native people of mixed heritage to be "competent" more often than those who were "full-blooded." The provisions of the Burke Act would thus simultaneously reduce the number of Indian wards for whom the government was responsible and extend the length of wardship for others, therefore prolonging the need for the Indian Office.[95]

THE SOCIETY OF AMERICAN INDIANS

A few years after administrators in the Indian Office began arguing that Indian people inherently lacked the abilities to reach the same level of "civilization" as whites, a group of well-educated Indians formed a *"race organization,"* the Society of American Indians (SAI), for "the purpose of the protection and the advancement of [the] race." Founded in 1911, the SAI was not the first intertribal organization, but it was the most successful.[96] Eventually encompassing both elite and local reservation leaders, it sought to promote a positive image of Indianness to white Americans and to address a variety of concerns shared by Native people, especially federal Indian policy. The SAI members' professional standing and political activism gave the lie to white arguments about the racial limitations of Indians.

The society's Native founders had a variety of experiences and ideas in common. Many of them had attended the Carlisle Indian School and admired the philosophy of its founder, Richard Henry Pratt. As well-educated professionals, they celebrated and advocated individualism, education, and intertribal unity as the solution to the "Indian problem." Like other middle-class Progressive reformers, they turned to associationalism — complete with conferences, an organizational hierarchy, and a journal — as a way to confront problems they hoped to address. The SAI, which became a national voice for Native people between 1911 and 1923, was "a crucial forum — a meeting ground — at the headwaters of a century-long (and ongoing) process among Indian peoples . . . to reclaim control from whites to represent themselves culturally and politically."[97]

One characteristic that many of the members had in common was past or current employment in the Indian Service. Many of the SAI's most well-known members had worked in the service, including Gertrude Bonnin (Yankton Sioux),[98] Charles Eastman (Santee Sioux), the Reverend Sherman Coolidge (Arapaho), Carlos Montezuma (Yavapai Apache), Charles Dagenett (Peoria), Chauncey Yellow Robe (Dakota), Angel DeCora-Deitz (Winnebago), Rose LaFlesche (French-Chippewa), and white organizer Fayette McKenzie. Many members who are less familiar, such as Dennison Wheelock (Oneida), Gabe Parker (Choctaw), Emma Johnson Goulette (Potawatomi), Marie Baldwin (Chippewa), Martin Archiquette (Oneida), Benjamin Caswell (Anishinaabe), and Henry Kohpay (Osage), also were service veterans.[99]

Their employment experiences gave them firsthand knowledge about the Indian Office and reinforced their recognition of the shared concerns of Native people. And indeed, almost all members of the SAI believed that the Indian Office needed to be reformed or abandoned, though they disagreed on the details.[100]

However, the SAI was also split over the issue of Indians working for the government, and intense debates wracked its meetings over the "loyalty" of government employees to their "race." In both of these cases—criticism of the Indian Office and responses to charges of disloyalty—Indian Service employees often responded with the language of intertribal, rather than tribal, identity.[101]

Members of the SAI who were also Indian Service employees used the society's meetings and the pages of its journal to criticize federal policy toward Indigenous people and the workings of the service itself. For example, during a discussion about reservation administration, Emma D. Johnson (Pottawatomie), an Indian Service teacher, testified: "My experience of twelve years has been that it is not the Indian pupil that has been first, but it is the beautiful grounds and the beautiful buildings and the feather in the cap for the officials, the money has gone for that. The child has come secondary."[102] Simon Redbird (Ottawa), a carpenter at the Genoa School in Nebraska who gave an address entitled "Responsibility of the Indian School employee" at the 1915 conference, stressed that personnel must respect Indian children and "have no prejudice against them because of their race, as so many of the white employees do."[103] Marie Baldwin, a lawyer of Chippewa-French ancestry, was the society's treasurer and worked as an accountant in the Education Division of the Indian Office in Washington, D.C. She was quite critical of federal policy: "I am one of those Government clerks that my brothers have been speaking of today. . . . *I am sure that very many times I have told Indians that I feel and I want the Indian Bureau to be abolished, but I do not believe that it ought to be abolished on the instant.*"[104]

Some SAI members posited that the solution was for the Indian Service to hire more Native personnel. At the second conference in 1912, the membership passed a platform plank that urged the employment of more Indians in the Indian Service, especially calling for their employment in better positions. The platform recognized the role the service played as an important source of employment for Indians and stated that this position was "entirely in accord with the general policy of the Indian department to put the Indian on his feet."[105] Others argued that Indian employees were essential for mitigating the problems of the service. Gertrude Bonnin (Yankton Sioux), a former Indian Service employee, the secretary of the SAI, and the editor of its journal, *American Indian Magazine*, argued that Native personnel offered an important check on the Indian Office and urged them to remain on their jobs "from a sense of duty" rather than the inadequate compensation. Their presence, she argued, provided the "kind of help that money could never buy."[106] (Bonnin's fictional depictions of the Indian Office, written under the name Zitkala-Sa, were more critical; she portrayed the Indian Office as motivated by self-perpetuation rather than the goal of eliminating poverty.[107]) Member Joe Mack Ignatius, chief of the Prairie Band of Pottawatomie of Kansas, agreed. He argued that white superintendents did not help the tribes, urging: "I think [the] Indian ought to do for himself. His welfare will be better." Unlike most of the membership, he did not believe the Indian Office oversight was near an end. "Of course we will be under the government forever," he noted. "We ought to have our own Indian employees, Indian teachers, Indian blacksmiths, Indian wagonmakers, Indian clerks, Indian superintendents and Indian inspectors. We don't have to have [a] high, well-educated man to be Superintendent, just so he is honest and has a good head. These smart men they know how to do wrong and they know how to get out of it."[108] Carlos Montezuma also agreed that Indians could work for the service. He wrote: "It is not a question of their qualifications. We claim that an Indian can fill any position in the Indian Service, and, having the special interest of his race at heart, he can do better work than one who is not an Indian."[109] The difference was, Montezuma did not think that Indians *should* involve themselves in the work of the Indian Service.

Montezuma was part of a group of SAI members called "the radicals" who questioned the participation of Indian Service employees in the society.[110] This became an intense debate that strained the society's meetings. The SAI's founders, for example, had discussed whether or not service personnel should hold "principal offices." The role of Charles Dagenett (Peoria) became a lightning rod for this question. He was nominated for leadership positions several times but withdrew his name after it became contested. During a debate over Dagenett's position in 1912, for example, the conference held a vote on the question of whether employees of the Indian Office should be officers in the SAI. The results—30 votes for and 31 against—demonstrated a deep division in the membership.[111]

Dagenett was responding to the arguments of other SAI members, especially Carlos Montezuma, whom some called "the fiery Apache."[112] Montezuma agreed with the individualist philosophy of Richard Henry Pratt and ardently believed that the solution to the "Indian question" was to abolish the Indian Office and let Indians make their own way in the world.[113] Moreover, he believed that Indians who worked in the Indian Service were traitors to

Edited by Wassaja (Dr. Montezuma's Indian name, meaning "Signaling") an Apache Indian.

Vol. 3, No. 3   ISSUED MONTHLY   June, 1918

ILLUSTRATION 8.1. *Wassaja* masthead. Many Native employees or former employees of the Indian Service helped found the Society of American Indians (SAI) in 1911. The society was highly critical of the Office of Indian Affairs but was split on whether or not Indians should continue to work for the government. Dr. Carlos Montezuma (Yavapai Apache), a former service employee and SAI member, adamantly argued against the Indian Office and its Native employees in the pages of this newspaper, which he founded and edited. (Courtesy of the Newberry Library, Chicago; call no. Ayer1.W27)

their people. His voice was the most vehement at the SAI meetings, and the issue often exploded whenever he attended. At the 1915 conference in Lawrence, Kansas, for example, he launched "a highly polemical attack" urging the immediate abolition of the Indian Office in an address he titled "Let My People Go." The next year, he started a newspaper, *Wassaja*, expressly to critique the federal Indian Service (Illustration 8.1). The paper's "sole purpose," he wrote in the first edition, "is Freedom for the Indians through the abolishment of the Indian Bureau."[114] The paper launched a vitriolic attack on all things connected to the Indian Office—the white employees, the policies, the SAI's lack of criticism, and especially Indian employees of the Indian Service.[115] In one piece, he parodied the SAI's membership as not only weak and ineffectual but also as being a mere imitation of white reform organizations and pawns of the government: "Clear Cut Attitude of Procedure of the Society of American Indians at the Lawrence Conference as seen by Wassaja. The sky is clear and we meet only to discuss. There is nothing wrong. We meet only to discuss. It is so nice to meet and discuss. We can meet and discuss as well as the Mohonk Conference, the Indian Rights Association, Indian Service Teachers' Association and the missionaries. We will show them we can meet and discuss. . . . Sh-! Sh-! Don't whisper about the Indian Bureau. We are to meet and discuss."[116]

Montezuma's comments on Indian employees in the Indian Service, however, were often his most polemical. In the paper, he (and his editorial persona, Wassaja) adamantly insisted that Indian people could not serve both the government and their communities. "Choose ye this day! Whom will you serve?" rang out the headline of one article. "Real Indians cannot work for the Indian Bureau and, at the same time, for the interest of their people," he argued. "We have come to the conclusion that we must make a clean cut demarcation, whether we are for the Indian Bureau or for the Indians."[117]

While Montezuma understood that many Indians worked in the service as a result of economic necessity, he urged them to see the big picture in which they were agents of colonialism. He disparaged them as helping to keep their people trapped.[118] Montezuma admitted that his own years in the Indian Service as a doctor had already helped him make his choice: "About 22 years ago WASSAJA stirred the country by saying that by encouraging Indians to enter the Indian Service the Indian Office was using the Indians to hold their race in bondage. . . . WASSAJA was in the Indian Service for over seven years. It was by reason of experience and study that we said, 'You encourage Indians to enter the Indian Service—you encourage them to hold their people in bondage.'"[119] He urged all Indians to immediately leave the service on the principle that no Indian could serve both the government and Indian people. He argued from an ideological standpoint that called for immediate action:

> Again, we say, that Indians who are working in the Indian Service, are working against the best interest of the Indian race. By their saying that, "the Indians are not ready for freedom and citizenship" is not to their credit. If that is the judgment of their race, they are in the same boat, ARE THEY NOT OF THE SAME BLOOD AND FLESH AS THOSE WHOM THEY MISJUDGE? It is plain to see that they are in the Indian Service for a selfish purpose and not to help to elevate their race. Their judgment goes no further than their bread and butter at the expense of having their people held as slaves and outcasts.[120]

For Montezuma, Indian employees could only be enemies to their own people.

In defending themselves against the accusations of the radicals, many members of the SAI likewise used the language of race loyalty, which presupposed an intertribal identity. For example, Charles Dagenett argued: "I was an Indian before I entered the service of the Indian Bureau . . . and I shall be an Indian, and loyal to my race, long after I leave that service." The Reverend Sherman Coolidge made a similar point, stating: "I don't think I was disloyal to the Government when I was in the Government employ . . . neither do I believe that I was disloyal to my race."[121] Dagenett defended the employees more broadly by pointing out that these attacks damaged the unity that the SAI sought among Native people: "If the Society declares itself against Indians in the Indian Service, it is going to drive a good many Indians from the Society and cause them to lose interest. There are hundreds of progressive honest men and women in that service who are loyal to their race first of all."[122]

The politics stirred up by this debate was one of the reasons that the SAI ultimately collapsed. But while it lasted, it offered an important site of intertribal political activism. It revealed the ways in which Native people had come to think of themselves as Indians as well as members of specific tribes, and their work in the Indian Service was one focus of that identity. But their discussions also raised important issues about what the government was and should be doing in Indian country. As David Anthony Tyeeme Clark has argued, the society and its members shifted national conversations about the Indian problem to the problem of Indian administration. Certainly, their voices at their annual meetings and in testimony before Congress reached the ears of many of the "friends of the Indian." Indeed, many of the Indian Rights Association, BIC, and Lake Mohonk Conference attendees were associate members of the SAI, and many Native SAI members attended Mohonk, so there was a great deal of information sharing. And some members also participated in several of the investigatory studies of the Indian Office in the 1920s, bringing their perspective to those important reports.

CONCLUSION

Progressive ideas had major ramifications for the Indian Service. When policy makers formulated assimilation programs in the 1870s and 1880s, they exhorted employees to be more than mere federal agents; they described work in the Indian Service as fundamentally personal and requiring a measure of dedication and self-sacrifice different from other positions. The influence of Progressivism, however, led both personnel and administrators to rethink their expectations for what made a good employee; the result was an increased focus on professionalization, rationalization, and efficiency. But Progressivism also had negative aspects, ushering in hardening ideas about race that also affected the service. The first decades of the twentieth century saw policy makers pull back from a vision of full citizenship for Indians that included landholding and political participation; instead, they turned to a new goal of making Indians into a racially marked working class. The previous generation's educational ideals likewise dissipated in the early twentieth century and were replaced by new policies—prioritizing local day schools, closing several off-reservation boarding schools (including Carlisle), and emphasizing vocational training.

As a result, an important avenue for Native advancement into the middle class was closed off. At precisely the same time that the Indian Office was refusing to offer Indian students greater opportunities for advanced education, credentials were becoming a more important qualification for employment.[123] While many Native people had certainly resisted the federal government's attempts to destroy their cultures and their communities, they had not rejected all aspects of American culture. Some had even elected to embrace the middle-class ideals of white society while also retaining their Indigenous identity. Many of that group became politically active, either on behalf of their own tribes or on the larger national scene in intertribal organizations like the SAI. Consequently, when Indian Office administrators declared Indians racially unfit for full assimilation, they had to deliberately overlook or exclude from consideration this cohort of Native people, many of whom were Indian Service employees. This new direction in the Indian Office ultimately destroyed an important avenue to economic security for Indian people, creating dire long-term effects on their families and communities.

9

An Old and Faithful Employee

THE FEDERAL EMPLOYEE RETIREMENT ACT

AND THE INDIAN SERVICE

The increased emphasis on professionalization and expertise by the Office of Indian Affairs in the early twentieth century created new expectations for employee qualifications. Administrators' definition of what prepared someone to be a good Indian Service employee had changed. The new Progressive faith in training, expertise, and education clashed with the values of loyalty, mission, and self-sacrifice upon which the Indian Service had been built. This also reflected the shift between the personalized approach of the Gilded Age and the professionalized ethic of the Progressive Era. The split often occurred along generational lines and affected older employees, who were viewed as "nonprogressive" because they were not expertly trained or were physically less capable than they had been.

There were two main lines of thought about this new problem of "superannuated" personnel. On the one hand, administrators argued that these aging employees lacked the training, skills, and energy to do the important work of the Indian Service. On the other, their superiors recognized that longtime employees had faithfully served the government, sometimes for decades, and that this dedication to their jobs made them deserving of support from the Indian Office. While this problem mirrored similar concerns throughout the federal bureaucracy as the first generation of civil servants grew older, the language of loyalty and sacrifice held deeper sway in the Indian Office because it had been so central to the ideology of the Indian Service. Administrators tried to address this problem in two ways: first, through ad hoc bureaucratic shuffling, typically at the local level; and second, by lobbying for a national law guaranteeing pensions to federal employees.

EFFICIENCY VERSUS LOYALTY

The Indian Service's aging workforce presented a problem for superintendents, inspectors, and fellow employees who saw older workers as "unprogressive" and inefficient. A 1909 report, for example, described Anna Bowman, who had been in the service for seventeen years as a teacher and a matron, as one of "the old class of Indian employees." The writer commented: "I do not know how long this woman has been in the service, but a very long time." His criticism arose in part from tensions between the older vision of assimilation and the administration's efforts to shrink the Indian Office's role in Indian affairs: "She is quite elderly and her methods are decidedly ancient. She is non progressive and is one of the strongest opponents to the practice of placing Indian children in public schools." The efficiency report of Anna Bowdler, another teacher, stated that she was "probably beyond the age where she will be able to study and prepare herself to do successful teaching." Bowdler was thirty-six years old. Nora Buzzard's superintendent mused on the problem of age in the service in 1912, writing disparagingly that "often the younger blood in the Service is superior to that which has been drifting or remaining stationary in the Service for many years."[1] Madeline Jacker's (Chippewa/German) superiors did not deny that she had the necessary skills to serve as a seamstress, but they argued that the clothes she produced were woefully out of style, noting that the schoolgirls "ought to look like little dolls. Instead they are running around campus dressed like little old ladies."[2]

The most vehement accusations against old employees were aimed at women. A few of the male employees' files contain similar concerns about their lack of professional training, but these were usually articulated without additional comments on the age or attitude of the employees. Nonetheless, the Indian Office did emphasize a need for its male employees to be trained professionals as well. For instance, in 1909 Lewis L. Brink had difficulty obtaining a promotion to the position of expert farmer because he did not hold a college degree in agriculture. The Indian Office also denied Victor E. Brown a promotion to demonstration farmer in 1910—in spite of his "twenty five years practical experience, and 5½ years [as] Indian Service Farmer"—because administrators hoped instead to obtain "scientifically trained men."[3]

Although older employees may not have had college degrees, they were not ignorant of the tasks that their positions required them to perform. Indeed, at the very least, their years of experience were evidence of familiarity with their subjects. Some of the more senior teachers tried to counter the perception of themselves as unprogressive and unprepared. Often they pointed to long experience as qualifying them for their positions. For example, Allie B. Busby, a teacher who wrote to the commissioner of Indian affairs in 1921 in hope of a promotion, asserted: "I have been twenty-five years in the Indian School Service, both non-reservation and reservation boarding schools, as a teacher. I am in touch with the progressive education movement of the present time and its great possibilities."[4]

The ramifications of the changing requirements for service personnel are particularly visible in the administrators' discussions about what to do with the growing problem of older "loyal" employees. Employees who had remained in the service despite superior economic opportunities in outside employment won high praise as "loyal" and "faithful," but many of them were growing old and creating new problems for their superiors. By the 1910s, employees who had entered under the civil service provisions of the 1890s were reaching their second and even third decades in the service. They were becoming increasingly visible as members of an aging bureaucratic cohort, one that portended an impending crisis in the civil service. Administrators had endowed Indian Service work with patriotic and emotional weight. They had conceived of Indian Service employees as participating in a national mission and increasingly used such rhetoric to justify low salaries. After making these demands, administrators found it difficult to fire employees who had become too old to work effectively.

Superintendents and agents called on the Indian Office to address the problems of what to do with old but faithful employees.[5] In their discussions, administrators struggled between the need for efficiency and their sense that the government owed long-term employees something for their service. For example, at the beginning of the summer of 1916, a flurry of correspondence passed back and forth between the commissioner of Indian affairs and Superintendent Scott of the Cheyenne and Arapaho Indian School in Oklahoma. They were writing in regard to the school's laundress, Mrs. Jennie Brown, who had entered the federal Indian Service on 1 October 1899 at the age of fifty-three or fifty-four. While this was beyond the civil service's preferred age limit of forty-five for the position, Brown had still qualified.[6] By all reports, she enjoyed her job and was good at it. She received a raise in 1911, but her superintendent noted that her age was affecting the quality of her work. He pointed to the new sanitation policy that required each child to use his or her hand towel only once before it needed to be laundered, which meant that Brown's duties included the "washing of 900 small hand towels each day."

Nonetheless, she remained in her position for the next four years, until she turned seventy. During the winter of 1915, she became ill, and although she recovered, she was left weak and suffered from impaired eyesight. At that point, Superintendent Scott initiated a revealing discussion with the commissioner that explored Brown's retirement options.

Brown had worked for the service for nineteen years, and her superiors believed that she deserved something for her years as a "faithful employee." Scott made several suggestions, including transferring Brown to a school that would require less work, but those requests were denied. The commissioner instead asked what sort of support she had in her old age from outside sources: "You failed to say whether Mrs. Brown has children or relatives who are willing to support her, and also to say whether there is available a home for soldiers' widows, or a Masonic home, to either of which you report she would be eligible for admittance." The commissioner was also willing to consider another suggestion that Scott made "in justice to an old employee." He agreed that the Indian Service would continue to provide Brown with a home and a small amount of money rather than turn her out without support. "The Office will consider your recommendation that her salary be reduced to $300 a year. This will give Mrs. Brown a home and she will no doubt be able to render services which will entitle her to that salary," he wrote. Brown, who had told her superintendent that it would "break her heart" to leave the service, apparently chose this latter option, and her 1918 efficiency report noted that "Mrs. Brown is an old and faithful employee."[7]

In another case, Otis F. Badger, a miller at the Green Bay Agency in Wisconsin, was hoping for a retirement pension. He waited throughout the 1910s as Congress debated retirement act legislation, but his age was becoming an issue on the job. In 1918 his efficiency report had stated: "Mr. Badger, even at his advanced age, fits the position at present. However, when the war is over . . . it will be necessary to have a younger man in the position." Two years later, Badger's superintendent, a visiting inspector, and the commissioner all discussed the possibility of using some administrative reshuffling to lower Mr. Badger's salary without reducing his family's income. A letter from the superintendent noted that "while Mr. Badger was rather liberally paid for the actual work he performs, his daughter who is a clerk in this office is very much underpaid for her service. . . . Mr. Coleman [the inspector] was advised that any amount taken off of Mr. Badger's salary should be added to that of his daughter which process would [i]nvolve no consequence other than the humiliation of the father[,] for the family exchequer, as I understand it, is not divided."[8] Given the Indian Office's previous emphasis on patriarchal households, their solution was rather surprising, but it demonstrates the creative efforts of Indian Office bureaucrats to treat their older employees fairly while also balancing the needs of the service.[9]

In lieu of actual pension legislation, federal administrators recognized and acted on their belief that faithful employees deserved some sort of entitlement for their years of service. Indeed, one commissioner praised older Indian Service personnel, saying that "these men and women are with little exception faithful, capable, loyal, and often self-sacrificing workers, whose average annual salary of but little over $800 strongly suggests an interest in their work not measured by money alone."[10]

THE FEDERAL EMPLOYEE RETIREMENT ACT

The Indian Service was not the only federal bureau to experience problems with elderly personnel. Pension legislation for federal civil servants was introduced in every session of Congress between 1900 and 1920.[11] In 1916 government workers formed the Federal Employees Union as a member union of the American Federation of Labor and made the passage of a retirement law one of their primary goals. Because most Indian Service personnel were scattered across the reservations and schools, they were not as involved in union efforts as were other federal employees, especially those in Washington, D.C., and other urban areas with a large constituency of federal workers. But some service employees were members of the union and received its newsletter, the *Federal Employee*, at their posts.[12] And those who worked in the Indian Office in Washington, D.C., were very involved in union affairs. Miss Florence Etheridge, a probate examiner for the Indian Office, served as the union's first treasurer and later its fourth vice president, and she was also a frequent contributor to its newsletter. Other employees from the Washington Indian Office were nominated to be or served as union representatives.[13]

The congressional debates over what became the 1920 Federal Employee Retirement Act (FERA) demonstrate that the problem of aging civil servants was the logical result of the merit system.[14] As one astute congressman noted, the need for a federal employee pension system was "a concomitant of the nonpartisan method of appointment." Unlike patronage politics, in which employees were removed from office by partisan opponents when their own party fell from power, the merit system offered lifelong employment that ended when the employee chose to retire or was forced out by administrators. As is clear from the concerns over superannuated employees, elderly workers were not choosing to retire, in part because many could not afford to do so. Other departments also struggled with elderly civil servants who had had lifetime careers in government and were now imploring Congress to pass the pension legislation. Legislators pointed to the substantial number of "inefficient" and "superannuated" employees on the federal payroll who had also been "faithful" public servants but were now costing the government millions of dollars because they were unable to keep up with the work for which they were being paid.

Some congressmen recognized that some supervisors, such as the commissioner of Indian affairs, often thought with their hearts rather than their heads when they allowed older employees to remain even after they stopped being effective at work.[15] Representative William N. Vaile, a Republican from Colorado, described the consequences of that sympathy, observing that "we have, in effect, been pensioning many old civil-service employees for some time, merely because the simplest dictates of humanity forbade throwing out upon the street or into the poorhouse old people who had faithfully served the Government for years, even though they were no longer able to earn their pay." The retirement act, he asserted, would "substitute . . . a scientific system" for "this haphazard, unofficial, and inequitable, although well-intentioned pensioning."[16]

Pensions for federal employees also corresponded to nineteenth-century models of social provision that were premised on selective groups of beneficiaries. Unlike the social programs for Indians that administrators justified as meeting the federal government's obligations to its wards, federal retirement pensions fit the pattern of rewarding a group for its service to the nation. As scholars such as Theda Skocpol and Linda Gordon have demonstrated, such programs, especially those created for veterans, laid the foundations of a distinctly American welfare system based on entitlement.[17] Indeed, FERA proponents argued that civil servants were "analogous to soldiers in the army."[18] They asserted that civil service, like military service, enhanced national well-being by protecting the public good. New Jersey representative Frederick R. Lehlbach, a Republican and the bill's sponsor in the House, stated that "every employee of the Government . . . in any capacity is there for the purpose of protecting the public interest."[19] Senator Charles S. Thomas, a Democrat from Colorado, described a hierarchy of deserving pensioners that began with "those who give their lives to their country . . . and their dependents" and extended to "those who serve the country in a civil capacity. The men and women devoting their lives to such service, giving the country the best that is in them, should . . . be also the subject of our generous consideration."[20] Like soldiers, civil servants who dedicated their lives to government service had made sacrifices for their country. Civil servants "owe[d] their supreme and entire allegiance" to the federal government.[21]

Those who became lifetime federal employees not only had "devoted the greater part of their lives" to the country but also had sacrificed their own careers to do the work of the nation.[22] In choosing to serve, supporters argued, these individuals gave up many of the opportunities of the private sector, including the possibility of advancement and "the hope of ever becoming [their] own 'boss.'" Supporters also claimed that government salaries were not high enough to supply all the needs of employees, let alone allow them to save for retirement.[23] The government owed the employees pensions, they maintained, as part of a quid pro quo arrangement in which it benefited from employees' long-term sacrifices. The bill "rests upon the proposition that the Government requires a class of permanent employees," Democratic senator William H. King of Utah declared, adding that "persons who . . . are expected to give their lives to their duties and therefore should feel assured that in their declining years they will not be turned adrift without means of support."[24] At stake was not only efficiency but also the honor of the nation. "It is said that 'republics are ungrateful,'" remarked Representative Vaile. "I do not believe the statement is true, broadly speaking, but the way to disprove it is for the Republic to be just to those who serve it."[25]

The bill did not have unanimous approval. Indeed, throughout the previous decade, Congress had refused to pass similar bills. Most congressional supporters of the bill seemed to come from the West and the urban North; southerners resisted it.[26] The bill's opponents drew upon stereotypes of government employees as lazy, imprudent, and apathetic. Pension legislation, they argued, created a "special class" who benefited at the taxpayers' expense. "What right have we," asked one, "to take the people's money year in and year out and pay it for civil pensions?" Federal pensions, they warned, would create a group of improvident dependents who lacked ambition and who refused to save for the future. Representative John Moon, a Democrat from Tennessee, characterized a federal employee under the pension system in this way: "He has not been provident. He has saved no money." The ironic result of this legislation would be to turn federal employees into "the ward[s] of a nation."[27] Federal "paternalism" would only limit people's ambitions, asserted Democratic representative Carlos Bee of Texas. It would make them into "absolute dependent[s]," agreed Ohio representative James Begg, a Republican.[28] Strikingly similar to concerns about the creation of social programs for Indians that had taken place four decades earlier, the debates over the passage of pension legislation for civil servants highlighted the ongoing use of the language of obligation and fears of dependency in considerations of federal social provision.

Despite its detractors, the Federal Civil Service Retirement Act became law on 22 May 1920. The bill covered "all members in the classified civil service of the United States," ranking them into "six classes of membership" determined by their "years of service and time of retirement." The retirement age was placed at seventy and retirement was made compulsory, although exceptions could be made for short continuances. The act required that all employees make a monthly contribution of 2.5 percent of their salary to the Civil Service Retirement and Disability Fund, from which pensions would be drawn.[29]

EFFECTS OF WORLD WAR I

As Congress debated FERA, the Indian Office faced a challenge that was even greater than its aging employees: World War I. The conflict radically disrupted the work of the Indian Office and decimated the Indian Service, as many of its personnel left to join the army or to take jobs in the war industries.[30] In 1918 the Board of Indian Commissioners (BIC) lamented the impact that the war already had on the workforce: "The Indian Service has not escaped the disturbing influences of the war, for the bureau has lost many good men and women, some of whom were particularly well qualified for their work. A number entered the military service of the Government and others resigned to take up more lucrative employment in civil life. The Washington office and every school and agency are short-handed with little prospect of any betterment in the condition until after the close of the war."[31]

The health division was particularly hard hit when medical personnel were called into service overseas. The BIC reported that the Indian Service was "seriously handicapped by reason of the loss of nearly one-third of its staff of surgeons and physicians. Almost all the men who left enlisted in the Medical Department of the Army." According to a report that the Indian Office provided to the House Committee on Indian Affairs, almost 40 percent of the regular physician positions stood vacant in 1918. The number of regular doctors authorized for the service in 1917 was 128, but in November 1918, only 79 were actually employed. Medical support staff also suffered attrition. Congress had authorized 99 nursing positions, but only 55 were filled. During these years, contract doctors held many of the medical positions on reservations; they were local physicians who were hired primarily on an emergency basis.[32]

Despite their hope that the service would recover after the war, the BIC was still reporting problems in 1920. "The inspection activities of the board," they wrote, "brought to light the fact that there is much discontentment prevalent throughout the Indian field service." There were a number of reasons for that discontentment, especially low pay. The BIC added several other causes, including "long work days, isolation, and in many cases, unattractive living conditions, indefinite hopes of a future worthwhile within the service." These problems were not entirely new, but they had been exacerbated by the war and the failure of Congress to raise appropriations for the Indian Office after the armistice. The BIC concluded: "While the world war is accountable for much dissatisfaction prevailing in field personnel . . . the conditions responsible . . . are long-standing."[33] In the postwar period, the Indian Office attempted to restore the equilibrium and smooth operation of its programs, but it confronted a new set of concerns that led it further away from the Reconstruction-era redefinition of its mission.

COMMISSIONER CHARLES BURKE
AND THE SCIENTIFIC SURVEYS

Historians have described the Indian Office after the war as having lost sight of the forest for the trees, as being a "honeycomb[ed]" assortment of programs focusing on education, health, irrigation, and other issues without a larger vision to propel the agency.[34] Charles Burke, the man who tried to steer the Indian Office through these problems, became the commissioner of Indian affairs in 1921 and held the position for the next eight years. In that time, he used Progressive ideas about information gathering to take stock of the Indian Office's work and assess the distance left to go in the assimilation of Native people. Burke had a long history with Indian policy. He had served as a U.S. congressman from South Dakota from 1899 to 1906 and 1909 to 1915. In 1906 he had authored the Burke Act, which attempted to clarify the citizenship terms in the Dawes Act by freeing some Indians (and their land) from bureaucratic oversight while simultaneously extending the wardship status of others whose land the government held in trust.

While in office, Burke followed his predecessors in supporting some of the basic commitments of the older vision of assimilation while also discarding many of its ideological underpinnings. He believed that Indians had to be taught to labor or they would remain paupers on the government dole, and he praised the Native employees in the service as examples of hardworking Indians. He also remained committed to education and pushed Congress to appropriate funds to repurpose old military forts as Indian schools. At the same time, his vision of education was more aligned with Commissioner Leupp's emphasis on day schools. While Native parents and students pushed for higher educational options in the off-reservation boarding schools—programs that would have helped more Indian people qualify for better positions in the Indian Service and other jobs—Burke denied their entreaties, instead insisting that before the office could provide high school facilities, all Native children not yet in school needed to be enrolled in the lower grades. He also sought to shut down the Indian Office, just as policy makers claimed they would from the beginning of the assimilation period. In 1922 he described his efforts to shrink the Indian Service over the past year: "We have in every instance where we could see our way clear to discontinue employees in the service dropped them from the rolls." Pointing specifically to Oklahoma, Burke noted that since his terms in Congress, he had been hearing that the work of the service would soon be completed; but when he returned to Washington as the commissioner, he "found that the force and the appropriation for the administration of that work were very much the same as they were 20 years before."[35] Although some of this language was meant to impress the congressional committee with his administration's efficiency, it also reiterated the belief that the Indian Office was a temporary bureau.

One way that Commissioner Burke sought to hasten the end of the Indian Office was by instituting a major industrial survey program in 1921 that would describe every home on every reservation in order to assess how much assimilative work the service still had left to do. This ambitious effort reflected a colonial drive to make conquered subjects legible. More specifically to the United States, it reflected the Progressive faith that to quantify was to know and that compiling information would result in a clear picture of how to solve problems. Each survey (Illustration 9.1) was meant to offer a snapshot (literally as well as figuratively) of where individual Indian families stood on the scale of civilization.[36] Thus for Burke, the houses on Indian reservations served as barometers of civilization—the concrete evidence of the progress of Indian families—just as they had for the policy makers who had formulated the Dawes Act thirty-five years earlier. Burke instructed superintendents that after completing the surveys, they must construct a five-year plan for each family that would ultimately make the Indian Office obsolete: "The purpose of the survey is to formulate for each reservation a definite program or policy which may be followed for such term of years as will place the Indians on a self-supporting basis."[37] In this way, Burke attempted to use the Progressive technologies of information gathering to advance the older vision of assimilation based on individual family farms.

But Burke also departed in some cases from that earlier vision of assimilation. This is especially illustrated by his attack on the service's policy of spousal hiring. Just as individual superintendents had been finding "fixes" for keeping older employees in the service before the passage of FERA, some had used the spousal hiring policy to address other personnel issues, especially the decline in the real salaries of service employees. As one commissioner

Lac du Flambeau Agency, Wisconsin.

Ba gwan e gi jig (John Whitefish)

Photo

Allotment No.	Age	Degree	Status	Family
616	51	Full	Comp.	Wife, Son, and Stepdaughter.

Flambeau Lake...Good painted 4 room house with cellar..10 windows, 3 doors.
Log barn 20'x14', shed, chicken house, outhouse, summer tepee.
8 acres cleared - large garden.

1871	Husband	Laborer. Hunts, traps, fishes.
1887	Wife	Makes moccasins, bead and birch bark work.
1900	Son	Paul Whitefish is employed at Lac du Flambeau School.
1911	Stp.dau.	Emily Corn excused from school. Is Tubercular, now improving in health.

A comfortable, well kept home given to the wife by her father, Big
George Skye.

Reimbursable Funds....

Date of Survey........May 10, 1922.

ILLUSTRATION 9.1. House of Ba gwan e gi jig (John Whitefish), from Survey of Indian Industry, Lac du Flambeau, Wisconsin, 1922. Surveys conducted by the Indian Office for over 100 reservations captured the myriad economic survival strategies used by Native families in this period. Note the employment information listed for each member of the household; note also the persistence of Ojibwa culture as indicated by the mention of a "summer tepee," his wife's craftwork, and what may be an Ojibwa spirit pole erected in front of the frame house. (Courtesy of the National Archives and Records Administration, Great Lakes Region, Chicago) noted: "The fact is the practice [of hiring wives] must be regarded largely as a means of paying the Farmers more."[38] Discussing the practicality of giving Frank Kyselka a raise, his superior offered a similar solution: "It has occurred to me that as a man and wife occupy these positions we might meet the demands of justice to some extent by increasing her salary." Indeed, in another case in which an employee had no relatives on the payroll, one administrator indicated that he was at a disadvantage: "Mr. Buntin has no member of his family on his payroll so must rely wholly on his own salary."[39] Certainly, officials had increasingly turned to spousal hiring to ameliorate the personnel disruptions caused by World War I and postwar congressional decisions not to adjust appropriations for inflation.

If reservation administrators viewed the practice as merely utilitarian, Commissioner Burke saw it as an embarrassing policy with implications of nepotism, petty corruption, and fraud. His assistant commissioner, E. B. Merritt, was similarly disdainful and repeated the trope (discussed in chapter 4) that a married woman "usually presumes on the fact that she is the wife of the superintendent, and occasionally gives instructions to other employees, which those employees resent." Merritt understood that many positions filled by wives were too low paying to be filled by other employees but countered: "[W]e are discouraging superintendents employing their wives in the service. We have found that it results in abuses." Several congressmen on the appropriations committee agreed with him.[40]

Burke moved to put his vision of the role of married employees in the service into effect by issuing circular number 2148 to agents and superintendents in 1925. The circular called for them to rein in the practice of hiring the wives of employees: "The main purpose of the paragraph of the circular referred to was to terminate the practice of employing temporarily the members of the family of an employee when such employment was not in the interest of the service. . . . This practice . . . has caused a great deal of criticism both of the superintendent and the Office, and such employment must be restricted."[41] That same year, Burke laid out his opinion on the hiring of superintendents' wives in a response to an employee's request that his spouse be appointed seamstress at the Phoenix Indian School. The commissioner stated that spousal hiring had arisen "under [the] exceptional circumstances" of the personnel shortages during World War I. He intended to "discontinue this practice" since the war had ended and "prospects are now much more favorable" for hiring qualified employees. Burke also articulated a gendered construction of labor in which men should be given available positions and married women should rely on their husbands' salaries, positing that he "doubt[ed] the wisdom of giving preference to dependents of those now employed at good salaries." Overall, he concluded, the policy's "elimination, I am convinced, will remove various embarrassing conditions and strengthen the Service."[42]

In pushing to end spousal hiring, Indian Office officials seem to have completely forgotten the original ideological underpinnings of the policy: to present Native people with ideal families and incorporate the moral authority of women into the bureaucracy as part of an effort to purge the service of corruption. Instead of emphasizing the importance of couples as object lessons for Indians to emulate, Burke's lens of Progressive efficiency and concern with bureaucratic malfeasance made spousal hiring appear as "embarrassing" nepotism that needed to be stopped. His positions demonstrate that the Indian Office was moving away from a policy that it had endorsed for over four decades and that had contributed to the unique makeup of the Indian Office's bureaucracy.

Burke's efforts to purge the Indian Service of "unnecessary" employees and his battle against spousal hiring did not solve the Indian Office's problems. In response to the growing criticisms of the agency—especially from a vocal group of reformers led by John Collier who protested the program of assimilation, in particular the repression of Native religions[43]—Interior Secretary Hubert Work approached the Institute for Government Research in 1926 and requested that it undertake a study of the Indian Office. He asked that the report be made "in thoroughly impartial and scientific spirit with the object of making the result of its work a constructive contribution in this difficult field of government administration." A cadre of ten professional and academic researchers using the latest social-scientific methods conducted the study, which came to be known as the Meriam Report for its lead author, Lewis Meriam.[44] Of the ten members of the research team, two were former Indian Service employees who were active in the Society of American Indians (SAI). Henry Roe Cloud (Winnebago), president of the American Indian Institute in Wichita, Kansas, served as the "Indian adviser"; and Fayette A. McKenzie, a sociologist, white organizer of the SAI, and former Indian Service teacher, was appointed as an expert in "materials relating to Indians."[45]

The Meriam Report, officially titled "The Problem of Indian Administration," was released in 1928. The conclusions of the report may have been more than the secretary of the interior had bargained for when he requested the study. The experts concluded that the Indian Office was in need of a number of changes. In 847 pages, the report detailed the problems of federal Indian policy and administration, pointing to a variety of concerns ranging from failing infrastructure to employees with low pay, low morale, and low retention rates. It revealed massive health problems and poverty among Native people and a failing educational system. On the other hand, it also supported what other critics and even administrators had been saying for years: appropriations were far too low for the successful operation of all the programs expected of the Indian Office.

The Meriam Report did not question the validity of the project of assimilation but rather focused on the problem of how to make the administration and personnel of the Indian Service more efficient.[46] One condition the researchers commented on extensively was the presence of untrained or unprogressive employees.[47] As an older bureau within the federal system, the Indian Office was rooted in a different tradition than many of the Progressive Era departments. A major suggestion of the report was the need for professionally trained personnel. In the chapter on education, for example, one subhead indicated the "need for knowledge of modern methods." The report further described the service as a bureaucracy whose employees were "as a rule not possessed of the qualifications requisite for the efficient performance of their duties" and as "notably weak in personnel trained and experienced."[48]

PROBLEMS WITH FERA

The Meriam Report also made clear that older employees remained a problem for the service. Looking back from their vantage point of eight years after the passage of FERA, the authors of the report could see more clearly that the retirement law, while a step in the right direction, had left a number of issues specific to the Indian Service unaddressed. They urged further adjustment of the legislation: "The Indian field service is no place for an employee of advanced age. Only the exceptional person in the late sixties is physically fitted for the rigors of outside work in the Indian country." They recommended lowering the retirement age to sixty, or sixty-five in unusual cases. They also suggested an increase in the retirement allowance "so that the more highly paid employees will have less incentive to remain in service after their physical capacity for the work has begun to wane."[49]

The seventy years required by the act was indeed quite an advanced retirement age, especially considering that the conditions of work in the Indian Service were often difficult and unhealthy. After the passage of FERA, many employees struggled with old age and poor health in order to make it to their seventieth birthday in the service and qualify for a pension. Employment in the boarding schools was especially difficult; the environment there, which was often deadly for Indian children, also adversely affected the health of personnel. Many employees recalled outbreaks of illness, during which they themselves became sick from the environment and overwork. Estelle Aubrey Brown described the horrible task of emptying the pupils' slop buckets during a measles outbreak at the Crow Creek School. Another teacher, Miss Allie Busby, claimed disability on the basis of the rigors of her work, describing her "gradual loss of health with entire disability." She experienced a "severe break down causing complications, extending from June 20, 1920 to present time, Sept 3, 1921 . . . frequent colds, and bronchitis generally caused by insufficient heating of class rooms during severe weather of South Dakota (U.S. Indian School) probably association with diseased children. Care of 19 girls in Flu epidemic of 1919 at Girls Quarters of U.S. Indian School, Lower Brule, S.D., with no assistant so that I suffered a collapse from over work — virtually no rest or sleep and unsanitary conditions of Quarters from which unhealthful conditions resulted to myself."[50] In such a work environment, the health of many employees began to deteriorate well before they reached retirement age. Congress amended FERA in 1926 to lower the number of years of employment required for pension eligibility, but it still placed the age of retirement at seventy regardless of the number of years of service.

The difficulties faced by elderly employees are illustrated by the case of sixty-three-year-old Robert Burns, the Cheyenne man discussed in chapter 5. In 1926 Burns had been in the service for over thirty years and had become too old and deaf to work efficiently in his position as agency clerk. His superintendent, Leo Bonnin (Yankton Sioux), urged the commissioner to use the service to support Burns for seven more years until he reached the age of retirement. Bonnin certainly wanted an efficient clerk, but he argued that Burns's years of service deserved a better conclusion. Because pensions were determined as a percentage of one's salary for the last ten years of work, Bonnin pointed out, any reduction in salary would be unfair to Burns because it would endanger his ability to support his family. "I hesitate to recommend that this old, faithful employee who has served more than thirty years in the Service be now reduced to the position of laborer at a much smaller salary," he wrote. Trying to find a way around the requirements of FERA, Bonnin suggested disability retirement. "If he absolutely can not be retired under the Retirement Act, would the change from the position of clerk to laborer debar him from participating in the Retirement Act should he live to the required age of seventy years?" he asked, acknowledging that this was not an ideal solution because "it would certainly reduce his pension."[51]

As an Indian employee, Robert Burns was exceptional in that he qualified for a pension at all; a majority of Indians served in temporary positions and were not eligible for retirement, regardless of their age. Moreover, with a few exceptions, FERA's language excluded regular Native employees because

ILLUSTRATION 9.2. Civil Service photograph of Katie Brewer. Native Alaskan Katie Brewer (right) worked for over fifty years at the Chemawa School in Oregon and earned the title of "The Mother of Chemawa," but she nonetheless had to fight for ten years to receive her retirement pension because Native employees were excluded from the program until 1929. (Courtesy of the National Personnel Records Center, St. Louis, Missouri)

of the Indian Office's special hiring policy. In its effort to employ Indigenous people, the Indian Office had exempted many of them from competitive classified status; this meant that they did not have to take Civil Service exams in order to obtain their positions. But because only classified employees qualified for FERA, these Native personnel were shut out from its benefits. A few, like Burns, had taken competitive exams (probably at the urging of sympathetic superintendents) in order to access the pension benefits, but most had not or could not do so.

Commissioner Burke had cavalierly suggested in 1921 that the retirement act as passed the previous year would be an "inducement" to the "intelligent and progressive Indians who are now filling exempted positions" to take a competitive exam to become classified, but in fact it was not always as easy as he suggested.[52] Although an earlier case, the experience of Nellie Santeo (Papago) is illustrative of the difficulties that often arose. Santeo, a former Carlisle student and employee for eleven years at the Phoenix Indian School, failed to pass her exam for the matron position by less than two points out of 100. Despite the fact that she had been filling the position temporarily for several months, had an established record of work at the school, and had received a strong endorsement from the school's superintendent, the Indian Office denied her the position. Thereafter, her employment file abruptly ends.[53]

Katie Brewer's story also exemplifies how Indian Service hiring rules ultimately left Native employees at a financial disadvantage as compared to their white colleagues (Illustration 9.2). Brewer was a Native woman of mixed heritage who was born in 1865 in Sitka, Alaska. When the Forest Grove (later

Chemawa) Indian School in Oregon opened in 1880, she was one of the first students to attend, making it as far as the sixth grade. At the school, she met and married David Brewer, a Native man from the Puyallup Nation in Washington. After graduating, they stayed on as employees of the school, Katie serving first as a laundress and later as a cook, baker, and matron and David working as the school's disciplinarian until his death in 1906.[54] Together, they raised a family of seven children while employed at the school. White officials praised the couple for having "helped establish the school"[55] and went on to describe Katie as "the mother of Chemawa" who had been there "ever since the school was first opened."[56] Katie Brewer's superiors universally acknowledged her as an excellent and loyal employee.[57]

Despite all of this praise, however, Brewer encountered massive bureaucratic impediments in her attempt to receive a retirement pension. Her ten-year struggle to qualify for a pension began a year after the passage of FERA. Her superintendent wrote to the commissioner, noting that Brewer "desires to be included with the employees who will eventually take advantage of the Retirement Act."[58] Because Brewer had entered the service in 1883 — over a decade before the positions came under civil service oversight — and because she was an Indian employee, she had never taken an exam to become classified. Initially, the Indian Office responded to her request by saying that she was too old to take the exam. The story might have ended there, but Brewer subsequently received the support of Oregon's Senator Charles McNary, who personally wrote to the commissioner on her behalf. The commissioner responded by proposing that Congress fix FERA by "broadening the provisions of this act in a way that will, at least, entitle those Indians to share in the benefits of the act who are now without classified competitive status, or unable, as in the case of Mrs. Brewer, to attain one under the present restrictions."[59] Katie Brewer and her supportive superintendent kept up the pressure for six years until 1927, when an Indian Office clerk wrote that despite her age, Brewer would be allowed to take a civil service exam and try to qualify.[60] Brewer passed the exam (if she had failed, she would not have been eligible despite her years in the service), but Indian Office rules stipulated that employee lists could only be submitted twice a year, forcing her to wait several more months. During that time, President Calvin Coolidge issued Executive Order No. 325, which declared that "all efficient Indians now serving under a noncompetitive status will be given a classified status effective April 1, 1929"; the commissioner noted that "Mrs. Brewer's case will be taken care of at that time."[61] President Coolidge's executive order was a double-edged sword. While it conferred classified civil service status upon all Indians currently holding regular positions, it also stipulated that after 1 April 1929,

JOURNAL SHEET AND LINE	NATURE OF ACTION	POSITION AND GRADE	SALARY (PAY LESS ALLOWANCES / AGGREGATE PAY)	EFFECTIVE DATE	DEPARTMENT OR ESTABLISHMENT OFFICIAL STATION	TOTAL SERVICE (MOS. DAYS YRS.)
	Apptd.	Field Matron	600	Aug. 30/98	Interior-Indian-Ft.Berthold	
	Term.			Aug. 31/3?		
	Apptd.	Assistant Matron	450	June 7/30	Jicarilla	
	A. Trans.			July 1/01	Albuquerque	
	Term.			Aug. 25/01		
	Apptd.	Assistant Matron	400	Sept. 9/31	Rosebud	
	Term.			Jan. 31/03		
	Apptd.	Seamstress	420	Feb. 10/03	Winnebago	
	Res.			Apr. 9/03		
	Apptd.	Seamstress	360	Aug. 24/04	Kickapoo	
	Pro.	Seamstress	500	Aug. 1/05	Klamath	
	Res.			Apr. 10/08		
	Matron X	Assistant Matron	500	Aug. 4/08	Pierre School	
	Trans.		300	Jan. 18/09	Kickapoo	
	Res.			Feb. 28/09		
	Reins.	Seamstress	500	Apr. 29/10	Vermillion Leke	
	Pro.		540	July 1/11		
	Res.			Aug. 8/11		
	Reins.	Seamstress	540	Dec. 11/11	Rapid City School	
	Pro.	Assistant Matron	540	Feb. 4/12		
	Res.			May 14/12		
	Exc.	Cook	300	Aug. 1/12	Wittenburg School	
	Res.			Dec. 14/12		
	Reins.	Seamstress	540	Dec. 10/13	Tohatchi-Navajo	
	Trans.	Seamstress	540	Apr. 11/16	Crow Creek School	
	Res.			Sept.30/16		
	Exc.	Assistant	480	Oct. 5/18	Winnebago Hospital	
	Res.			Feb. 16/19		
	PTV	Matron	600	Sept.19/19	-do-	
	Rlvd.			Apr. 15/20		
	PTV	Matron	600	Dec. 6/20	-do-	
	Rlvd.			Mar.11/22		

ILLUSTRATION 9.3. Retirement card of Julia DeCora Lukecart (Winnebago/French). One of the few Native employees to receive a pension, Lukecart served from 1892 to 1932 in six different positions and at fifteen different locations. Her retirement card, an example of one of the new forms created as part of the professionalization of the Indian Service, tracked her employment to the day in determining her eligibility. (Courtesy of the National Personnel Records Center, St. Louis, Missouri)

"Indians entering the service, except in certain minor positions, are required to qualify in open competitive examination."[62] In other words, it undid the special hiring policy that had been in effect for almost four decades.

Katie Brewer was lucky. Her superintendent was on her side, as was a U.S. senator. Moreover, she was able to remain in the service for ten additional years while continuing to fight for her pension. All told, she served for over fifty years at Chemawa. But of the thousands of Native women who worked in the Indian Service, few received pensions. In a sample of fifty-five Native female service personnel who were working as regular employees in 1905, only seven of the women, or 12.7 percent, eventually received retirement pensions (Illustration 9.3). Even when eligible Indian employees did receive pensions, severe structural disparities remained. Special hiring policies that allowed for the employment of Indians in the service in "at large" positions such as laundress, cook, and baker without any formal civil service entry exam facilitated job opportunities for Native people, but they also encouraged them to accept lower-paying positions—as did the unofficial practice of channeling Native employees, especially women, into menial jobs. Because the amount of a pension was estimated through a percentage of an employee's salary, these wage disparities between Native and white employees affected the amount of pension benefits given to each group. These differences, along with the fact that the majority of Indian employees were never eligible for pensions in the first place, contributed to ongoing economic inequalities between Native and white Americans in government service.

The economically precarious position of Native employees—especially women—in government service is clear from their files. Despite their hard work, Indians were often economically marginalized. And while many white female employees faced similar financial difficulties, the overall economic strain experienced within Native communities structurally disadvantaged Native women to an exceptional degree. These women had a very small safety net or none at all, and they necessarily sought federal government aid. One strategy undertaken by several women (often those who had been widowed or divorced) was to request reinstatement or financial assistance in their old age. Harriet Chapman (Maidu), for example, who had left the service in 1918, wrote in 1929 to inquire whether she was entitled to a pension due to her employment of more than twenty-one years. As the primary caregiver for her two grandchildren, who had been orphaned when their parents died in an automobile accident, she had been unable to return to work and hoped the pension would offer support. Chapman received an encouraging response from the superintendent of the Sacramento Agency, but to no avail: the government denied her request because she had been hired as a cook in the service without an exam (she insisted that she had passed an exam, but the Civil Service Office was unable to locate it). Regardless of the exam, her application was rejected primarily because her career had ended before FERA had been passed. She continued to seek assistance from the federal government—both the Indian Service and other agencies—over the next several years. All of her requests were denied. Her correspondence illustrates the economic hardships common to many older Native women.[63] Along with serving as caregiver for her grandchildren, Chapman mentioned that although she owned a house, her property was in desperate need of repair, and when she was seventy-six years old, she described being "reduced to beggary." Like other elderly Native women who unsuccessfully sought relief from the federal government, Chapman pointedly referred to her years of hard work in the Indian Service, her shouldering of family obligations, and her efforts toward achieving self-sufficiency. She hoped that this evidence of her productivity might be rewarded, but it was not.[64] Even those who had careers in the service and who were able to receive pensions often lived on the brink of poverty. When Dollie Johnson (Chinook) died in 1932 after thirty years in the service, her heirs, who were described as "destitute," received the money deducted from her salary for her pension. It amounted to $47.15. Dollie Johnson had nothing else.[65]

CONCLUSION

The problem of aging civil servants was not limited to the Indian Office; it was widespread throughout the federal government. The distinctive characteristics of Indian Service employment, however, meant that FERA had unique ramifications for its workers. Assimilation policy had originally been founded on the idea that employees had a special mission that required intense dedication. Indian Service personnel held positions that were unlike those of most federal workers, who were primarily white-collar employees. The intense physical nature of so many Indian Service positions, as well as the rudimentary conditions at most posts, weighed heavily on older workers, making it difficult for them to remain healthy until the retirement age of seventy. So when Indian Office administrators used the language of faithfulness and loyalty to describe their elderly personnel, they harkened back to that earlier idea of service employment and used it to argue that the government had a special obligation to such self-sacrificing employees.

But the biggest difference between the Indian Service and other federal workforces was the presence of Native employees who had been hired through special policies. Because assimilation policy had stressed the transformative power of work, and because the reality of the service was that it relied heavily on Native labor, the Indian Office had facilitated the incorporation of thousands of Indians into its ranks by waiving the requirements of competitive civil service exams. This made the Indian Service an unusually diverse bureau for its time, but it also placed Native employees outside the qualifications for federal pensions.

Policy makers had premised assimilation policy upon the idea that Indians fit into the category of people who were eligible for social programs on the basis of their status as wards, dependents to whom the federal government owed a debt for past wrongdoing. In administering these programs, however, the government created a large number of new federal employees, who were eventually recognized as another category of beneficiaries: retired civil servants. The decision to pension federal employees, however, was based on the contributory model of welfare in return for loyal service to the state. Ironically, then, when policy makers developed social programs to move Indian wards off the federal budget, they set in motion events that helped create a new set of federal dependents. As a result, just as social programs for Indians were languishing for lack of funding, new federal pension legislation was established that overwhelmingly benefited white employees.

Conclusion

Essie Horne, a Shoshone teacher in the Indian Service, remembered the coming of the Indian New Deal with great enthusiasm. "Those days were so exciting!" she wrote. "Finally, we no longer had to hide the fact that we were incorporating our cultural values into the curriculum and student life." It is essential to note that what had changed for Horne was not her methods but the willingness of officials at the Office of Indian Affairs to accommodate and even celebrate Native traditions. Indeed, during the 1930s, the Indian Office commended Horne for her pedagogy and appointed her to be a "Demonstration Teacher in Elementary Education and Indian Lore" at summer teaching institutes.[1] Horne's account reminds us that personnel played a key role in the implementation of federal policy, often according to their own agendas. Her story also suggests how the Indian Office's employment of thousands of Native people compels us to reinterpret the changes of the Indian New Deal as part of a much longer and less visible period of resistance by Native workers in the Indian Service. This should encourage us, in turn, to interpret federal policy more broadly by paying close attention to the people who actually carried it out "on the ground."

Our knowledge of the Indian New Deal generally focuses on John Collier, the commissioner of Indian affairs who set much of the legislative agenda into motion.[2] Collier's administration did enact major changes to federal Indian policy by introducing an emphasis on cultural relativism and a willingness to celebrate "traditional" Native ways of life. But there were also continuities with earlier policies, particularly the Indian Office's tendency toward paternalism and essentialist thinking about Indigenous cultures.[3] The centerpiece of the Indian New Deal was the passage of the Indian Reorganization Act (also known as the Wheeler-Howard Act) in 1934. The act had three substantive components. The first repealed allotment, restored surplus reservation lands to tribal ownership, and set aside limited funds with which tribes could buy back land. This represented a dramatic shift in policy because it reversed the changes brought on by the Dawes Act of 1887, which had resulted in the loss of more than 90 million acres of land previously held by Indian people. This part of the Indian Reorganization Act accorded with Collier's desire to protect the communal nature of Native life by ensuring that tribal lands would be held collectively rather than individually. The act's second main component provided for the establishment of tribal councils that would be recognized by the federal government. This provision also followed Collier's views on communitarianism, but it imposed United States–style constitutional governance on the tribes rather than respecting any "traditional" division of power within Native societies. And while the act gave tribal councils primary jurisdiction over affairs on the reservation, it perpetuated Indian Office oversight of dealings with people from outside because the white men who drafted the legislation were ambivalent about the tribes' capacity for self-governance.[4]

It is the third aspect of the Indian Reorganization Act—the stipulation in section 12 that Indians could be appointed to the Indian Service "without regard to civil-service laws" and would "have the preference to appointment to vacancies in any such positions"—that brings us back to the topic of this study and the role of colonial agents in Indigenous affairs.[5] Scholars have cited this clause as the origin of the preferential hiring of Indians in the Indian Office.[6] As this book has demonstrated, however, this was not a new policy at all; it had been in place in some form for almost half a century and had only been discontinued five years before the Indian Reorganization Act was passed. Thinking about the policies in section 12 as part of a longer history obliges us to reassess what happened after 1934. We know next to nothing about whom the Indian Office employed in its bureaucracy during the New Deal and in the decades thereafter. We are learning more about workers in the New Deal emergency relief programs on Indian reservations; we know that federal employment remained an important source of income for Native people and that relief programs were structured around the idea of a male breadwinner.[7] Unlike in the assimilation period, administrators stressed the local nature of work in keeping communities together. But these positions were temporary emergency relief measures that ended in 1941. The Indian Service continued (and continues) to exist.

Federal Fathers and Mothers has shown that bureaucracies are made up of individual employees who meaningfully influence the success or failure of the agendas of policy makers. It has focused directly on Indian Service personnel at all levels and argued that the shape and evolution of the agency they served must be reinterpreted through the inclusion of their stories. After all, policy makers themselves emphatically asserted that assimilation could only work if the service employed the right kind of people, and throughout this book we have witnessed how the identities and actions of employees affected federal policy. Moreover, after the advent of civil service reform, employees remained in place even as Democratic and Republican administrations came and went, making personnel a source of continuity.

The most striking thing about the Indian Service was the fact that it employed unusually large numbers of women, Native people, and married couples. From the beginning of the assimilation era, the gender and race of Indian Service workers were inseparable from the larger goals of the Indian Office. Policy makers developed complex theories in which the presence of particular kinds of employees was an essential component of the transformation of Indigenous people. By envisioning Indian Service personnel as federal fathers and mothers to the nation's wards, they committed themselves to hiring actual women and spouses; and by emphasizing the importance of personal object lessons, they were compelled to employ Indians. This brought people who were generally excluded from governance into the bureaucracy. When their stories are taken into account, we can see how their agendas and actions made the bureau particularly contingent and discordant, messy and divided.

Women were central to all aspects of assimilation policy. Female policy makers helped devise programs in which women would try to make Native girls into "respectable" mothers who would in turn raise "civilized" children, thus reshaping Native households into engines of social reproduction. In the field, these assimilation programs were staffed by thousands of female employees. The Indian Service therefore embodied an early version of the "domestication of politics" and stands as an example of how the federal government incorporated aspects of the maternalist welfare state. But bringing women into the agency raised a number of unexpected issues. In particular, policy makers' assumptions about white women's household knowledge overlooked their day-to-day realities. Officials failed to acknowledge that married couples' family responsibilities limited the work they were able to do and the places they were willing to do it. Moreover, having so many white employees spend so much time among Native people resulted in a much wider variety of relationships than policy makers initially anticipated. Faced with the determined resistance of Indigenous people and communities, white women often abandoned the ideas of moral suasion that had brought them into the service and instead adopted the tools of state power, thus revealing the coercive force behind the familial metaphors. In addition, friendships, romances, and marriages between whites and Indians undermined central tenets of government policy, especially the belief that Native people were pliable and Native cultures inferior.

Even more important, the incorporation of thousands of American Indians into federal employment had major ramifications for Native communities and the policies that were aimed at them. For many Indigenous people, work in the Indian Service became an important economic survival strategy and an opportunity they eagerly embraced and often fought hard to keep. Service jobs were some of the only employment possibilities on reservations, and for Native people who wanted to remain in their communities, the limited options made these jobs desirable. Unskilled laborers were able to take advantage of the service's reliance on temporary labor by combining periodic work for the government with a range of other economic strategies to support themselves and their families. For more skilled workers, especially those in white-collar positions, the Indian Service offered an opportunity for employment that they rarely found in white society. Moreover, the benefits of civil service work—vacations, a lifetime career path, reinstatement, and, for a few, pensions—were benefits rarely available even to white employees at this time. Indeed, the Indian Service was the primary employer of the first generation of white-collar and professional Native workers. Their shared experiences in the Indian Service provide a unifying context for understanding the careers of Native individuals who, despite often being presented as exceptional, were part of a much larger cohort.

Despite their desire for employment and their recognition of the benefits that the Indian Service could provide, Native personnel were not blind to the limitations and impediments of service work for themselves and their communities. Most of them did indeed manifest considerable ambivalence about working for the government, and virtually all rejected the assumptions about total assimilation that lay at the heart of federal policy. Instead, they tried to use service work to their advantage while maneuvering within a system of constraints not of their own making. The fact that they insisted on their right to hold positions in the service demonstrates the value they placed on these positions; and the way they attempted to subvert the service using their detailed knowledge of how to navigate a complex and often hostile bureaucracy reveals that in addition to the "weapons of the weak,"[8] they quickly learned the weapons of the white collar.

This book has engaged in several ongoing discussions in Native history. In the field of education, it adds to our knowledge of the lives of former Indian students after they left school. Scholars have emphasized that the federal Indian education system was constructed to train a colonized labor force, and that was certainly one of its goals: in point of fact, the federal government was absolutely dependent on Indian employees to staff positions, both regular and temporary, throughout the service. But when we look at the experiences of former students who went on to work in the service, we see that although they rejected policy makers' assumptions about full assimilation, they also saw federal employment as a rare opportunity to earn a living while remaining in Indian country. Their efforts to stay in their communities, or at least among other Native people, was in and of itself an important form of resistance to assimilation, and it worked to foil the government's agenda of breaking up tribal relations. The stories of Native service employees also complicate narratives that often put white officials on one side and tribal members on the other, when in fact the reality was less dichotomous. On a related note, the incorporation of Indian employees into the Indian Service extends our understanding of how a modern intertribal identity emerged and solidified. The fact that the service was a national bureaucracy in which Indian employees moved through multiple reservations and schools further exposed them to different tribal cultures; equally important, it allowed some Native employees to work on behalf of other Indian nations.

Scholars of Native labor have illuminated how Indigenous people engaged with the capitalist marketplace as an economic survival strategy that allowed them to maintain key aspects of their cultures. But Native people were not participating only in private markets; they also found work in the public sector. Researchers have overlooked this important component of their economic strategies. As we have seen, a large proportion of Native people found work of one kind or another in the Indian Service; in particular, an enormous number of Indians worked in temporary positions. The service was also probably the single most important source of jobs for the first generation of white-collar Native laborers. While previous scholars have fruitfully explored Indian participation in manual and domestic labor, artistic production, and work in tourist markets in this era, white-collar employment has been virtually unexplored. In addition, many of these Indian Service employees, or in some cases their children, left an important legacy by playing key roles in their nations' struggles for survival and sovereignty.

To acknowledge the benefits of Indian Service employment for some people, however, is not at all to deny what scholars of the Native experience have demonstrated: when Indian people confronted the federal government, they faced a powerful system intent on crushing their resistance and their cultures. While many people who worked in the Indian Service were able to resist the government's efforts, they were mightily constrained by its structure. Indeed, we have seen how many of them ran up against the limits of assimilation's promises in their efforts to gain positions with more authority or better pay. Moreover, the very structures of the service emphasized race, and even Native employees who fulfilled every qualification were still classified as undifferentiated "Indians" and often denied the same opportunities as white employees.

Turning now to the question of the state, we can see that federal policy as it was applied to Native Americans was part of a broader history of administrative development. *Federal Fathers and Mothers* has shown that numerous individuals who had been administrators in the Freedmen's Bureau and other federal programs during Reconstruction became the architects of assimilation policy. They brought with them their experience in running government programs and their ideas about incorporating a noncitizen population into the nation. But it was not until these policies were applied to the American West that they could be fully developed into a large, durable bureaucracy.[9] While the Freedmen's Bureau lasted only two years and employed a relatively limited number of people, the Indian Service grew rapidly over decades and employed thousands of people, ultimately becoming a permanent part of the federal government. This development also revealed the results of the extension of civil service reform into federal agencies. The Indian Service provides a good example of the unanticipated challenges that arose from the creation of a permanent bureaucracy, including the question of efficiency in a rapidly expanding agency and the problem of an aging workforce.

Historiographically, I have sought to demonstrate the importance of federal action on the national periphery for our understanding of state development. This responds to recent calls for historians to consider how the story of the American West fits into broader narratives of the development of federal capacity. Indian policy was the largest and longest component of administering wardship, a major category of federal action that spanned nearly three-quarters of a century and reached from the American South through the trans-Mississippi West and across the Pacific Ocean to Asia. What these three efforts had in common was their attempt to incorporate federal wards into the national system and the fact that they took place under direct federal jurisdiction. In this case, the American West may not have been the "kindergarten of the state," but it certainly was the "middle school of the state" since it was there that theories first conceived during Reconstruction were extended, elaborated, and experimented with on a far larger, more complex, more intrusive, and longer-term basis before being applied overseas.[10]

This study of federal Indian policy also adds to our understanding of what scholars have identified as the maternalist welfare state—government policies that focus on the role of mothers and children and are enacted by women, often on the basis of their female identities and ostensibly for the good of other women. When the federal government developed a new kind of social provision based on repaying national obligation by incorporating federal wards into the citizenry, it was characterized by a series of social programs, particularly education programs. These programs sought to transform the households of wards into respectable units modeled on white, middleclass, nuclear families. The newly transformed homes would then perpetuate this new way of life through the social reproduction of children and families, ending the need for federal intervention. This plan depended on the role of women, both newly trained mothers and the female employees who would train them.

Despite the importance of women and children in the federal government's Indian policy, scholars of the welfare state have overlooked it as an example of federal social provision in general and maternalist social provision in particular. Almost all students of the U.S. maternalist welfare state have concentrated their analyses on mothers' pensions and the work of the Women's and Children's Bureaus. Assimilation policy has not been a part of these conversations, even though it offers one of the earliest instances in which the federal government incorporated maternalist assumptions. The Indian Service, and the Indian School Service in particular, was an early example of a feminized federal agency. Moreover, compared to other federal bureaus with similar agendas, the Indian Service employed a much larger number of women.

Assimilation policy was not just an example of maternalist social provision; it was also a colonial project that used many of the same methods of intimate colonialism that were present in other essentially imperial ventures. Indeed, the categories of social provision and intimate colonialism arguably differed mainly in that they were aimed at women with very different status. Maternalist social provision by and large operated upon white women who were seen as vulnerable but who were nonetheless citizens with at least indirect political representation and the ability to call upon local authorities to help them. Intimate colonialism was aimed at women of color who were by and large not citizens and whose access to power in the colonizing state was limited or nonexistent. The similarities between the two, however, were considerable. Both maternalist welfare policies and intimate colonialism focused on the importance of reproduction in the physical and social senses of the word. Both occurred at the level of individual relationships, whether through attempting to transform those relationships through personal influence (for example, by performing social work among the poor or substituting white employees for Native parents) or attempting to prohibit them (as with bans on intermarriage between the colonizers and the colonized). And in both cases, the role of women—real and symbolic—often became the focal point of public discussions. What I think this suggests is that these two categories of government policy are similar enough to justify side-by-side comparison as part of an exploration of the development of modern states and empires.

But the example of the Indian Service also differs from studies of intimate colonialism elsewhere in the world. In the United States, intimacy played two important roles in federal theories of assimilation. First, assimilation's success hinged on transforming intimate relations between Native people. Second, policy makers believed that this transformation would be achieved by the creation of close personal relations between Indian Service employees and the government's Indian "wards." The goals and methods of the U.S. Indian Office constituted a remarkable and perhaps unique colonial effort. Most colonial administrations carefully policed the lines between white women and subaltern men, drawing and defending stark demarcations between colonizers and colonized and using white women as the measure of the purity and superiority of their dominant culture. By contrast, the United States actually encouraged the blurring of these boundaries and the absorption of Native Americans into the nation through education and, in some cases, intermarriage. In the United States, intermarriage fit comfortably into broader strategies of intimate colonialism, whereas in Dutch Java and elsewhere, it was stigmatized and prohibited.[11] In the United States, white women were recruited as an active part of the colonial administration through their labor as teachers or matrons to Native children as well as employers of Indigenous people. What is particularly remarkable about this is that the Indian Office did not see Native men as a sexual threat to white women, and the government consistently endorsed sending white women out to reservations. This was a startling shift from just a few decades earlier, when Indigenous men were described as a savage threat to white women.[12] These relationships are also surprising in light of the anxiety that white Americans exhibited during this period over real or imagined liaisons between white women and men from China and the Philippines. More powerfully, they also stand in striking contrast to the countless contemporaneous racial murders perpetrated against black men in the American South over the smallest hint that they had crossed the sexual color line.[13]

In the end, after more than a half century of intensive efforts backed by the expenditure of billions of dollars and the machinations of the entire policy-making arm of the Indian Office in Washington, the U.S. government failed to assimilate the nation's Native peoples by annihilating their cultures. The era of assimilation was not the last time the federal government attacked Native nations or sought to destroy tribal identities. In the 1950s, Congress attempted once again to terminate tribal sovereignty, this time by ending the government-to-government relations established by the Indian Reorganization Act and relocating Native people from their reservations to urban areas. But this revival of the federal war on Indigenous America soon ran up against the resurgent American Indian activism of the 1960s and 1970s. After that, the era in which policy makers could speak in serious tones about Indians disappearing had come and gone.[14]

Today, the Bureau of Indian Affairs, as the Indian Office is now known, continues to oversee the federal government's trust responsibilities to Native nations. But it is in many respects very different from its nineteenth- and twentieth-century predecessor and operates under changed conditions. There have been a number of economic and demographic shifts in Indian country. Most Native people now live in urban and suburban areas. Tribes have developed a number of enterprises on their lands—the most visible example being gaming operations—that bring employment and capital into the community. Many reservations, however, remain isolated and suffer from some of the highest rates of poverty in the nation. Their natural resources have been exploited with little of the profits actually going to the tribes, and mineral extraction has left massive environmental damage in its wake. Under such conditions, government jobs, both federal and tribal, remain an important resource within those communities. Indigenous people, who fought to gain employment in the Indian Service at the turn of the century, now hold 78 percent of the positions in the agency, and several directors have been Native.[15] Overall, the Bureau of Indian Affairs, inclusive of the Indian Health Service, is the nation's largest employer of Native people.[16] It is telling that the next largest is Walmart.[17]

The Native presence in the Bureau of Indian Affairs has not been enough to prevent the federal government's frequent failure to protect Indian property, however. The persistently strange career of Indian policy is in many ways epitomized by *Cobell v. Salazar*, a lawsuit against the Department of the Interior for monies derived from the sale and lease of Indian land, some of which date all the way back to the Dawes Act of 1887. The federal government was responsible for the funds in some 300,000 personal accounts for individual Native people, but over a century later, it could not even give an accounting of the amounts in them nor would it distribute the money to its rightful owners. In 1996, after generations of delays and excuses, Elouise Cobell (Blackfeet) brought a class-action suit against the government for mismanagement of the funds. The case has exposed extraordinary negligence, fraud, and incompetence; to give just one example, the Department of the Interior could find records for only about 17,000 of the 300,000 accounts. Moreover, the Native plaintiffs litigating the case have had to fight four very reluctant presidential administrations, both Republican and Democratic. In addition, during the litigation, the U.S. secretary of the interior was held in contempt of court for the handling of the case.[18] *Cobell v. Salazar* was settled by the Obama administration in December 2009 for $3.4 billion and Congress approved the settlement in December 2010. Where federal Indian policy goes next will do much to determine whether relations between Native people and the U.S. government revert back to outright mistrust, achieve some sort of détente, or continue to be characterized by their customary ambivalence.[19]

Notes

ABBREVIATIONS

ARBIC   Board of Indian Commissioners, *Annual Report*, 1869–1927
            (Washington, D.C.: Government Printing Office)

ARCIA   Commissioner of Indian Affairs, *Annual Report*, 1869–1927
            (Washington, D.C.: Government Printing Office)

CIA   Commissioner of Indian Affairs

CTC   Cornelia Taber Collection, California Historical Society,
            San Francisco, Calif.

HVA   Records of the Hoopa Valley Agency, Record Group 75,
            National Archives and Records Administration, San Bruno, Calif.

HVAD   Hoopa Valley Agency Diary, vol. 1 (1 January 1919 to 30 June 1919),
            Records of the Hoopa Valley Agency, Record Group 75, National
            Archives and Records Administration, San Bruno, Calif.

HVEL   Hoopa Valley Employee Ledger, 1883–1911, Records of the Hoopa
            Valley Agency, Record Group 75, National Archives and Records
            Administration, San Bruno, Calif.

IIS   Reports of Indian Industry Surveys, 1922–29, Record Group 75,
            Entry 762, National Archives Building, Washington, D.C.

LMC   *Proceedings of the Annual Meeting of the Lake Mohonk Conference of
            Friends of the Indian, 1883–1916* (N.p.: The Lake Mohonk Conference)

LR   General Records, Letters Received, 1824–1907, General Records of the
            Bureau of Indian Affairs, Record Group 75, National Archives Building,
            Washington, D.C.

NARA GLR   National Archives and Record Administration, Great Lakes Region,
            Chicago, Ill.

NARA SB   National Archives and Record Administration, San Bruno, Calif.

NMHP   Nellie McGraw Hedgpeth Papers, Graduate Theological Union,
            San Anselmo, Calif.

PF NPRC   Personnel Folder, National Personnel Records Center, St. Louis, Mo.

SBFP   Susie Baker Fountain Papers, vol. 34, Hoopa/Goddard/Indians,
           Humboldt County Library, Eureka, Calif.

WNIA   Women's National Indian Association

INTRODUCTION

1 Vine Deloria Jr., *Custer Died for Your Sins*, 125; McCarthy, "The Bureau of Indian
   Affairs and the Federal Trust Obligation," 6.

2 I use the terms "Indian," "Native," "Native American," and "Indigenous" inter-
   changeably for the sake of variation; however, when describing the identity of
   specific people, I have tried to use the terms the employees themselves indicated in their correspondence with the Indian Office. As a result, some of the
   tribal designations are historical names that are no longer in use. But I feel this
   better reflects the identities as recognized by these historic figures themselves.
   However, their self-identification was not always consistent, and employees often
   described themselves in different ways at different times. Many employees were
   of mixed Native and non-Native heritage, and I have indicated that by including
   "/m" in their tribal affiliation. But while they may have emphasized their mixed
   heritage in correspondence with the Indian Office, I hesitate to place too much
   emphasis on it as it may have been a strategy in their correspondence with white
   officials who placed a premium on "white blood." Because the Indian Office was
   not interested in tribal affiliation (employees were given the choice of White,
   Indian, or Negro on forms), many people only identified as Indian. In other
   cases, their white superiors noted a possible tribal affiliation, and in some cases,
   I have used the designation that appeared in the federal census records while
   recognizing that the latter two sources may be problematic.

3 Deloria suggested a restructuring of the agency in *Custer Died for Your Sins*, 140–
   45. Between 1966 and 1967, tribal governments blocked the transfer of education
   functions from the BIA to the Department of Education. Officer, "The Bureau
   of Indian Affairs since 1945," 67. Even the American Indian Movement (AIM)
   understood that the government has to have an agency that addresses tribal issues. The group made Point 14 in their "Trail of Broken Treaties 20-Point Position
   Paper" a demand for the abolition of the Indian Bureau by the symbolic date of 4
   July 1976; but in Point 15, AIM requested that a new agency, an "Office of Federal
   Indian Relations and Community Reconstruction," replace the BIA in order to
   continue to serve Native communities. ⟨http://www.aimovement.org/archives/
   index.html⟩ (accessed 6 January 2009). The National Congress of American
   Indians has also often defended the BIA from abolition. See McCarthy, "The Bureau of Indian Affairs and the Federal Trust Obligation," 8 n. 29. See Westerman's
   album, *Custer Died for Your Sins* (1970). Thanks to Kent Blansett for pointing me
   toward Westerman's song.

4 Prucha, *The Great Father*, 823; and ARCIA 1914, 7.

5 ARCIA 1912, 164–65, 307. See also *Report of the Executive Council*, 27.

6 Adams, *Education for Extinction*, 26–27; *Reports of the Department of the Interior
   1913*, 3.

7 Two recent exceptions are Cox-Richardson, *West from Appomattox*; and Rockwell, *Indian Affairs and the Administrative State*.

8 William J. Novak, "The Myth of the 'Weak' American State," 776.

9 Stoler, *Carnal Knowledge and Imperial Power*, 19, 7. See also Stoler, "Empires and Intimacies"; Stoler, *Haunted by Empire*; Summers, "Intimate Colonialism"; the special issue "Domestic Frontiers: The Home and Colonization," *Frontiers* 28 (2007); Jacobs, *White Mother to a Dark Race* (2009); and Rand, *Kiowa Humanity*, 5–10.

10 William J. Novak, "The Myth of the 'Weak' American State," 765. See also Edney, *Mapping an Empire*, 77–120.

11 There were many women in clerical positions in Washington, D.C., but they were not engaged in maternalist work. See Aron, *Ladies and Gentlemen*.

12 Gordon, *Women, the State, and Welfare*; Gordon, *Pitied but Not Entitled*; Skocpol, *Protecting Soldiers and Mothers*; Koven and Michel, *Mothers of a New World*. One exception is Jacobs, *White Mother to a Dark Race*. For additional sources on the maternalist welfare state, see Gordon, *Pitied but Not Entitled*, 55 n. 78.

13 I use the term "intertribal" to mean the recognition of a larger ethnic Indian identity that does not necessarily supersede or replace individual tribal (and thus political) identities. Intertribal identity can also be mobilized as a political tool. While scholars have often used the term "pan-Indian," Native people generally prefer intertribal. See Hertzberg, *The Search for American Indian Identity*; Ellis, Lassiter, and Dunham, *Powwow*, xiii; and Walter Johnson, "On Agency."

14 Rockwell, "Building the Old American State," 91–128. In contrast, Britain declared the continent of Australia to be "terra nulis" and denied land rights to Aboriginal peoples. Jacobs, *White Mother to a Dark Race*, 16–21; and Ellinghaus, *Taking Assimilation to Heart*, xxvi.

15 In 1819 the government established a "civilization fund" of $10,000 that it distributed to benevolent societies that had schools among the Indians. Overall, however, the educational efforts were "feeble and sporadic" and the bureaucracy small until the post–Civil War era. Prucha, *The Great Father* (abridged), 48; Prucha, *The Great Father*, 139–41.

16 Prucha, *The Great Father* (abridged), 32.

17 Utley and Mackintosh, *The Department of Everything Else*.

18 Danziger, *Indians and Bureaucrats*, 1–2, 13–14, 16–17; Rockwell, "Building the Old American State," 91–128; and Prucha, *The Great Father*, 412–13, 461.

19 Richard White, "The Winning of the West."

20 Namias, *White Captives*, 204–61; Danziger, *Indians and Bureaucrats*, 1–2, 13–14, 16–17; Prucha, *The Great Father*, 437–47.

21 ARCIA 1871, 544.

22 Walker also included a similar map for each census before 1870, thus visually representing change over time. Each subsequent census contained a similar image depicting the "filling in of the West," which Frederick Jackson Turner used to formulate his frontier thesis. Meinig, *The Shaping of America*, 32–33; and Monmonier, "The Rise of the National Atlas."

23 West, "Reconstructing Race." For earlier concerns regarding new states, see Onuf, *Statehood and Union*.

24 Please see note 2 in this chapter.

CHAPTER ONE

1 *Congressional Globe*, 1500.

2 Ibid., 1500.

3 Ibid., 1502.

4 Ibid., 1500–1501.

5 Ibid., 1501.

6 Ibid., 1502.

7 Ibid., 1501–2.

8 Ibid., 1501.

9 Ibid., 1502.

10 The Fourteenth Amendment, ratified in 1868, granted citizenship to freed slaves, but Americans continued to debate their place in the nation. See Welke, "When All the Women Were White."

11 Prucha, *The Great Father*, 527–33.

12 Skocpol, *Protecting Soldiers and Mothers*, 424–79; Patrick Kelly, *Creating a National Home*, 27–28; Jensen, *Patriots, Settlers*, 3, 9, 12; Sterett, *Public Pensions*; Baker, "The Domestication of Politics"; and Koven and Michel, *Mothers of a New World*.

13 White, "The Winning of the West"; Utley, *Frontier Regulars*, 93–343.

14 Milner, "With Good Intentions," 31; McLaughlin, *My Friend the Indian*, 1.

15 Milner, "With Good Intentions," 31–33; Simpson, "Ulysses S. Grant and the Freedmen's Bureau"; Genetin-Pilawa, "Confining Indians."

16 Although the denominations eagerly leapt at the chance, this aspect of Grant's policy barely outlasted his presidency, but cooperation between the churches and the federal government continued into the last decade of the century in the form of contract schools. Robert H. Keller Jr., *American Protestantism*; Prucha, *The Churches and the Indian Schools*.

17 Milner, *With Good Intentions*, 1–4; Prucha, *The Great Father*, 527–33.

18 *Congressional Globe*, 1484; for further examples, see *Congressional Globe*, 1487 and 1499.

19 Ibid., 1500–1501. Native peoples who were ignored generally preferred that treaty stipulations be honored as written, with tribes being treated as nations possessing sovereignty and entitled to agreed-upon payments. The question of treaty rights still bedevils Indian policy. Wilkins and Lomawaima, *Uneven Ground*, 64–97. Not all reservations were established through treaty negotiations. Some were created by executive order.

20 *Congressional Globe*, 736.

21 The massacre of a peaceful Cheyenne encampment by cavalry volunteers at Sand Creek in Colorado in 1864 continued to serve as a potent symbol of the failures of U.S. Indian policy for eastern reformers. Prucha, *The Great Father*, 458–61.

22 Moulton, *Chief Joseph*, 169–70; Josephy, *Nez Perce Country*, 128–37.

23 Mathes and Lowitt, *The Standing Bear Controversy*, 47–58; Prucha, *The Great Father*, 567–76.

24 For the conclusions to their stories, see Prucha, *The Great Father*, 570–71, 575–76.

25 Literature on the Civil War as a conversion experience or atonement includes James B. Stewart, *Holy Warriors*; and Ginzberg, *Women and the Work of Benevolence*.

26 Wanken, "Women's Sphere," 4–5, 17; Mathes and Lowitt, *The Standing Bear Controversy*, 69, 178; Adams, *Education for Extinction*, 1–3.

27 Mathes, *Helen Hunt Jackson*.

28 Jackson, *A Century of Dishonor*, xix, 29.

29 Hershberger, "Mobilizing Women, Anticipating Abolition"; and Zaeske, *Signatures of Citizenship*, 47–71.

30 On novels and sympathy as political strategy, see Elizabeth B. Clark, "'The Sacred Rights of the Weak'"; Mattingly, *Well-Tempered Women*, 143–62; Dorsey, *Reforming Men and Women*, 90–135; Yellin, *Women and Sisters*; Yellin and Van Horne, *The Abolitionist Sisterhood*; and Gordon, *The Mormon Question*, 29–37. Other authors who point to the role of women's novels in the debates they study include Franchot, *Roads to Rome*; and Carby, *Reconstructing Womanhood*.

31 Quoted in Mathes, *Helen Hunt Jackson*, 77.

32 Quoted in Kerber, "The Abolitionist Perception of the Indian," 287. See also Hershberger, "Mobilizing Women, Anticipating Abolition"; and Mathes, "Parallel Calls to Conscience."

33 See Hagan, *The Indian Rights Association*.

34 See Adams, *Education for Extinction*, 36–90; Richard Henry Pratt, *Battlefield and Classroom*, 109–22, 128–30, 154–64; Elaine Goodale Eastman, *Pratt*; Lindsey, *Indians at Hampton*, 18–43; Engs, *Educating the Disfranchised*, 115–29; and Adams, "Education in Hues."

35 Burgess, "The Lake Mohonk Conferences on the Indian." For more on hotels as sites of political activity, see Sandoval-Strausz, *Hotel*, chapter 8.

36 The following examples are drawn from the attendance list for the 1890 conference. *LMC 1890*, 151–56. They included the presidents of Marietta College (Ohio), Girard College (Pa.), Haverford College (Pa.), Amherst College (Mass.), College of New Jersey, Vassar College (N.Y.), and Cornell University (N.Y.).

37 State administrators included the Honorable Erastus Brooks of the New York State Board of Health and Philip Garret, the commissioner of public charities for Pennsylvania. Edward Pierce served on the Massachusetts State Board of Charities between 1869 and 1874. Federal politicians included U.S. senator Henry L. Dawes (R-Mass.) and U.S. representative Darwin R. James (R-N.Y.).

38 The Board of Home Missions of the Presbyterian Church; Episcopal Board of Missions; Woman's New York Synodical Committee of Home Missions; American Bible Society; Women's Executive Committee of the Presbyterian Church Home Missions; Presbyterian Board of Foreign Missions; and the American Missionary Association. Other reform associations included the Boston Indian Citizenship Committee and the National League.

39 Editors of the *Christian Union* (N.Y.); the *Christian Register* (Boston); the *Examiner* (N.Y.); the *Congregationalist* (Boston); the *Christian Intelligencer* (N.Y.); *Spy* (Worcester, Mass.); *Farm, Field, and Stockman* (Chicago); the *Courant* (Hartford, Conn.); *Southern Workman* (Hampton, Va.); *Education* (Boston); and the *Independent* (N.Y.) were also present.

40 The WNIA published a newsletter, *The Indian's Friend*, keeping its membership informed. *Annual Meeting and Report of the Women's National Indian Association* (1883), 1; Wanken, "Woman's Sphere," 42–54.

41 See the lists of attendees in the *LMC* from 1885 to 1890. From 1883 to 1885, the proceedings of the conference were published in the ARBIC, and the board held its official meetings at the Mohonk conference.

42 Jensen defines entitlements as "a particular *form* of public law or policy: one that grants public benefits to groups of 'like' individuals *programmatically*, on the basis of the statutory eligibility criteria of deliberately enacted legislation." Italics in original. Jensen, *Patriots, Settlers*, 3, 9, 12; Foner, *Reconstruction*, 68–69.

43 The primary female reformers drew their expertise from missionary, education, and temperance reform. However, Mary McHenry founded the Lincoln Institute in 1866 on Philadelphia's Chestnut Street as a home for orphans of Civil War soldiers. By 1884, she had transformed the home into a federal contract school, training some seventy Indian girls. McHenry had also been active in the Sanitary Fair. Scharf and Westcott, *History of Philadelphia*, 1698.

44 Most studies comparing postwar policies for blacks and Indians focus on the Hampton Institute in Virginia, but there are many examples of what colonial theorists call "circuits of exchange" of knowledge between the two movements. See Lindsey, *Indians at Hampton Institute*; Engs, *Educating the Disfranchised*; and Adams, "Education in Hues."

45 McPherson notes that Albert Smiley founded the Lake Mohonk Conference for the Friends of the Indian and hosted a similar conference on the "Negro Question" in 1890 and 1891, but he does not explore the connections between the two. McPherson, *The Abolitionist Legacy*, 137.

46 ARBIC 1883, 6; "Clinton B. Fisk," *Dictionary of American Biography*, 413–14; and Fisk, *Plain Counsels for Freedmen*, 7. Another BIC member, Eliphalet Whittlesey, was head of the Freedmen's Bureau in North Carolina. McFeely, *Yankee Stepfather*, 79–83.

47 ARBIC 1885, 126.

48 McPherson, *The Abolitionist Legacy*, 154.

49 Jones, *Soldiers of Light and Love*, 11. Strieby attended the Lake Mohonk Conference in 1883, 1884, 1885, 1886, 1889, 1890, 1893, 1894, 1895, and 1896.

50 Pierce attended the Lake Mohonk Conference in 1886, 1887, 1888, 1892, and 1894. "Edward Lillie Pierce," *Dictionary of American Biography*, 575–76; and Rose, *Rehearsal for Reconstruction*.

51 *LMC* 1886, 47. Italics added.

52 This list is the result of a comparison of Swint's compilation of the "Officers of the Leading Educational Associations" for the freedpeople and the Mohonk Conference attendees from 1886. See Swint, *The Northern Teacher*, 171–74.

53 Pierce also appeared. Strieby and Morgan are described as "very important to this study." McPherson, *Abolitionist Legacy*, appendix A.

54 *LMC* 1886, 42.

55 ARBIC 1885, 112.

56 ARBIC 1891, 13; ARCIA 1896, 356; Robert H. Keller, *American Protestantism*. Abolitionist rhetoric set a powerful template for subsequent nineteenth-century reform efforts. Elizabeth B. Clark, "'The Sacred Rights of the Weak.'"

57 *LMC* 1886, 42. He also likened Dawes to Lincoln and his bill to the Emancipation Proclamation.

58 Richardson, *The Death of Reconstruction*, 13; Stanley, "Beggars," 1273–76; and Stanley, *From Bondage to Contract*.

59 *LMC* 1886, 48.

60 Ibid., 7.

61 Ibid., 27. The Yearly Meeting of the Liberal Quakers in 1868 sent a memorial to Congress regarding Indian policy with the suggestion: "Invite the assistance of the philanthropic and Christian effort, which has been so valuable an aid in the elevation of the Freedmen." Quoted in Prucha, *The Great Father*, 500.

62 Jackson, *A Century of Dishonor* (1885), 24.

63 ARBIC 1885, 92.

64 ARBIC 1885, 85.

65 See Adams, *Education for Extinction*, 36–90. On Reconstruction, see Foner, *Reconstruction*; Rose, *Rehearsal for Reconstruction*; and Jones, *Soldiers of Light and Love*.

66 *LMC* 1886, 27–28.

67 Between 1848 and 1854, Dorothea Dix petitioned Congress to provide land to be sold for the relief and institutionalization of poor insane citizens. The bill passed Congress, but President Pierce vetoed it, arguing that it would be unconstitutional for government to become "the great almoner of public charity throughout the United States." Jensen, *Patriots, Settlers*, 12.

68 *LMC* 1886, 47.

69 See especially Hoxie, *A Final Promise*. Adams lays out three strands of thought in "Fundamental Considerations."

70 Western historians such as Richard White have emphasized the vast federal presence in Indian Affairs but do not engage in the debate over social provision. Policy historians have generally overlooked Indian policy. One very recent exception is Rockwell, *Indian Affairs*. See also Krainz, *Delivering Aid*; and Schackel, *Social Housekeepers*.

CHAPTER TWO

1 *LMC* 1890, 138–42. For conference history, see Burgess, "The Lake Mohonk Conferences."

2 Cott, *The Bonds of Womanhood*, 63–100; Douglas, *The Feminization of American Culture*, 44–56; Sklar, *Catharine Beecher*. Few Americans actually lived in families that matched this ideal, but it powerfully shaped their culture.

3 Jacobs, *Engendered Encounters*, 12.

4 ARCIA 1892, 342.

5 Dyk, "Preface," xii (with thanks to Margaret Jacobs); Jay Miller, "Families," in *Encyclopedia of North American Indians*, 192–97.

6 Rand, *Kiowa Humanity*, 27–30, 131–33.

7 This was true for the Kiowa, Crow, and Blackfeet, for example. On Kiowa women's tepee making, see Rand, *Kiowa Humanity*, 21–23.

8 For examples, see Carter, Chappell, and McCleary, "In the Lodge of the Chickadee"; and Nabokov and Easton, *Native American Architecture*, 123–25, 150–71.

9 Wissler, *Material Culture of the Blackfoot Indians*, 99–108; Oetelaar, "Stone Circles," 127–30.

10 A number of cultures, such as the Pueblos in the Southwest, had permanent villages and houses.

11 Densmore, *Chippewa Customs*, 119–23; Densmore, "Use of Plants by the Chippewa Indians."

12 ARBIC 1885, 27, 29.

13 Cook, "Frontier Savages, White and Red," 7–8.

14 The new communities of industrious Indian families would in turn serve as the basis of a Christian citizenry, "men and women capable of taking their places in the body politic of this Republic" who would stand in contrast to "the extravagant avarice of the land grabber and speculator." *LMC* 1886, 9; ARCIA 1900, 427. See also *National Education Association Annual Report* (1900), 683–84.

15 See Stanley, *From Bondage to Contract*; Edwards, *Gendered Strife and Confusion*, chap. 1; Hartog, *Man and Wife in America*; Cott, *Public Vows*; and Basch, *Framing American Divorce*.

16 *LMC* 1890, 138.

17 ARCIA 1900, 431–32.

18 ARBIC 1901, 8. See also Foucault, "Governmentality"; Scott, *Seeing Like a State*; and Torpey, *The Invention of the Passport*.

19 Quoted in Osburn, *Southern Ute Women*, 29–31. Administrators also required polygamous men to give up all but one wife or be punished. See Calloway, *Our Hearts Fell to the Ground*, 157–59.

20 Quoted in Jacobs, *White Mother to a Dark Race*, 155–62.

21 As a result of that legislation, the tribes lost millions of acres of treaty-guaranteed land. Not all of the support for these programs was of a humanitarian or even compensatory sentiment. Many saw assimilation programs as a way to open up the vast tribally held reservation lands to white settlement. See, for example, Dippie, *The Vanishing American*, 163; Hoxie, *A Final Promise*; and Wishart, *An Unspeakable Sadness*. See also Adams, "Fundamental Considerations."

22 "General Allotment Act," in Prucha, *Documents of United States Indian Policy*, 172. On Native responses, see Greenwald, *Reconfiguring the Reservation*.

23 *LMC* 1887, 85, 3–4; ibid., 104; ibid., 8; ibid., 13, 14, 30, 89.

24 *LMC* 1895, 50.

25 *LMC* 1877, 8, 110; *LMC* 1886, 45; *LMC* 1887, 6, 34, 85.

26 *LMC* 1887, 3.

27 Ibid., 25; ibid., 61.

28 *LMC* 1886, 45; *LMC* 1887, 6; ibid., 34.

29 The Indian Office's cooperation with religious organizations expanded dramatically in scope after the Civil War. See Prucha, *The Churches and the Indian Schools*; and Rockwell, "Building the Old American State," 137–38. On the Freedmen's Bureau, see Foner, *Reconstruction*; Jones, *Soldiers of Light and Love*; Rose, *Rehearsal for Reconstruction*; and Miller, "The Freedmen's Bureau and Reconstruction."

30 *LMC* 1886, 34.

31 *LMC* 1890, 55. Catholics received $118,343 out of $228,259 in 1886 and $347,689 out of $554,558 in 1889. *LMC* 1887, 49; Adams, *Education for Extinction*, 66; McAfee, *Religion, Race, and Reconstruction*, 175–202.

32 Commissioner Morgan also alienated contract-school sponsors when he at-

tempted to consolidate federal control by standardizing curriculum, instituting English-only education, and focusing on off-reservation boarding schools. Prucha, *The Churches and the Indian Schools*; Burton M. Smith, "Thomas Jefferson Morgan."

33 After 1896 the job of Indian agent became the focal point of the debate because it remained a position of appointment (with the power to appoint agency employees). Reformers worked to supplant the agent by placing reservation authority in the hands of the school superintendent. In 1893 Congress allowed the commissioner to abolish any unnecessary agent positions, and by 1908 they were all abolished. Adams, *Education for Extinction*, 66–68; Stuart, *The Indian Office*, 40–41; Hoogenboom, *Outlawing the Spoils*, 260–61.

34 One reformer said: "Whatever we may think about the post-office or any other material department when we come to deal with the bodies and souls of these Indians who are the wards of the nation, who were the original holders of the soil, we are responsible before God, and should give them an administration that will put their mental, moral, and spiritual interests above all." *LMC* 1891, 61–62.

35 ARBIC 1896, 7. See also ARCIA 1900, 433, 435.

36 ARCIA 1896, 231–32.

37 Jacobs, *White Mother to a Dark Race*, 424.

38 Some administrators urged the creation of a "good neighborhood." ARBIC 1885, 25; *LMC* 1903, 48.

39 David Rich Lewis, *Neither Wolf nor Dog*, 17–19.

40 ARCIA 1909, 6–7.

41 *LMC* 1887, 40.

42 See also Klibard, *Schooled to Work*, 5.

43 *LMC* 1887, 12 and Prucha, *Americanizing the American Indians*, 101–102.

44 Quoted in Adams, *Education for Extinction*, 23. Emphasis in original.

45 Cook, "Frontier Savages, White and Red," 9.

46 See also Simonsen, *Making Home Work*; and Buffalohead and Molin, "A Nucleus of Civilization."

47 Quoted in Emmerich, "'To Respect and Love,'" 8, 13–14, 45.

48 Arranging home space was a class-producing project. See Boydston, *Home and Work*, 85, 125, 137; Beecher and Stowe, *The American Woman's Home*; Sklar, *Catharine Beecher*; and Wright, *Moralism and the Model Home*.

49 ARCIA 1909, 6–7. See also ARCIA 1892, 45.

50 ARCIA 1892, 602.

51 *LMC* 1890, 22. See also *LMC* 1893, 29.

52 *LMC* 1890, 12.

53 See McClintock, *Imperial Leather*, 225.

54 *LMC* 1887, 54.

55 *LMC* 1893, 28.

56 *LMC* 1895, 29; ARCIA 1892, 510.

57 *LMC* 1887, 54.

58 As the Indian Office made it easier to lease allotments, the number of applicants for WNIA loans declined. Simonsen, *Making Home Work*, 84–85, 94.

59 *LMC* 1887, 54.

60 ARCIA 1896, 233.

61 *LMC* 1886, 2.

62 For examples, see Osburn, *Southern Ute Women*; Child, *Boarding School Seasons*, 9–25; and Bracken, *The Potlatch Papers*, 35–36.

63 *LMC* 1896, 75–76.

64 ARCIA 1892, 510.

65 ARCIA 1886; quoted in Nabokov, *Native American Testimony*, 458.

66 Quoted in David Rich Lewis, *Neither Wolf nor Dog*, 20. See also *LMC* 1886, 2; *LMC* 1896, 75–76; and ARCIA 1892, 510.

67 *LMC* 1886, 75–76.

68 ARBIC, in *Annual Report*, Department of Interior (1885), 778. On the strategy of using families to motivate workers to participate in the capitalist system, see Stanley, *From Bondage to Contract*, 138–74.

69 The Indian Office first compiled its directives, laws, and regulations in 1874. The School Service began issuing its own rules in 1890. Prucha, *The Great Father*, 718–20.

70 ARCIA 1909, 6–7.

71 *Regulations of the Indian Service*, 1904, 17–18.

72 Quoted in Steven J. Novak, "The Real Takeover of the BIA," 646. See also Ahern, "An Experiment Aborted," 263–304.

73 ARCIA 1881, xii. See also ARBIC 1885, 17–18; and *LMC* 1886, 29.

74 Ahern, "An Experiment Aborted," 269, 271.

75 ARCIA 1880–81, xviii. See also Hagan, *Indian Police and Judges*.

76 See the Appendix Employees of Indian Schools in the ARCIA from 1888 and 1895. The year 1888 is the first year that the numbers are broken down by race, and that was only for the employees in the School Service.

77 *Rules for Indian Schools*, 3.

78 *LMC* 1886, 45.

79 ARCIA 1885, 114.

80 ARCIA 1896, 348.

81 ARCIA 1898, 10. See also, ARCIA 1899, 4; ARCIA 1897, 11; and *LMC* 1895, 27. This matched missionary models. See Brumberg, *Mission for Life*, 41, 79–80; Hill, *The World Their Household*, 5, 12, 72–73.

82 ARCIA 1899, 29.

83 *LMC* 1895, 27.

84 ARCIA 1896, 348.

85 ARCIA 1899, 4. Institutional building did often overwhelm other goals. See Trennert, *The Phoenix Indian School*, 33, 54–56.

86 *Rules for the Indian School Service*, 15. While Protestant churches stopped taking government money in 1892, the Catholic Church resisted efforts to end the contract system until 1900. There were other exceptions, like the WNIA and the Hampton Institute. ARCIA 1899, 18–19; Adams, *Education for Extinction*, 66; and Prucha, *The Great Father*, 710–11.

87 *Rules for the Indian School Service*, 20; see also *Rules for Indian Schools*, 29; and *LMC* 1891, 88

88 *Rules for the Indian School Service*, 9.

89 *Regulations of the Indian Office*, 15.

90 *Rules for Indian Schools*, 16–17; *Regulations of the Indian Office, Indian Schools*, 19.

91 *Rules for Indian Schools*, 16–17; list from Schmeckebier, *The Office of Indian Affairs*, 335.

92 *Rules for Indian Schools*, 16.

93 Jean A. Keller, *Empty Beds*.

94 ARCIA 1908, 12.

95 Stoler, "Matters of Intimacy as Matters of State"; Stoler, *Haunted by Empire*; and Jacobs, *White Mother to a Dark Race*.

CHAPTER THREE

1 Jenkins, *Girl from Williamsburg*, 4–5. Home missions were often perceived as less dangerous than foreign missions. Hill, *The World Their Household*, 57–58.

2 Jenkins, *Girl from Williamsburg*, 4.

3 Of those twenty-eight, thirteen were employed on two reservations: the Michigan and the Pawnee Agencies. Cahill, "Only the Home," 375–76. See also *Register of Officers and Agents*, 166–78.

4 In 1898, 718 (43.8 percent) of the 1,636 women in the Indian School Service were Native. See Appendix of Employees, ARCIA 1898, 631–74.

5 In 1885 the School Service employed 468 white female employees, of which 307 were single. Of the 128 Native female employees in the School Service, 74 (57.8 percent) were single (their relationship to the Indian Office will be further discussed in chapters 5 and 7). There were only 556 actual positions in 1885, but due to high turnover rates, 977 employees were listed. In 1890 the federal census reported that the national average for single working women was 68 percent. Cahill, "Only the Home," 388–90.

6 See Varon, "Patriotism, Partisanship, and Prejudice," 113–38; and Aron, *Ladies and Gentlemen*, 5–6.

7 Fletcher worked on three special allotting projects: Nebraska, Omaha lands (1882–84); Nebraska, Winnebago reservation (1887–89); and Idaho, Nez Perce lands (1889–93). Hoxie, *A Final Promise*, 27.

8 Lomawaima, "Estelle Reel"; Stuart, *The Indian Office*, 145; Hoxie, *A Final Promise*, 26–27; Heizer, *Federal Concerns*, 83–84. The Indian Office also hired several female attorneys, including Florence Etheridge and Marie Baldwin (Chippewa); *Annual Report of the Secretary of the Interior for 1918*, vol. 2, 1919, 56; and Edmunds, *The New Warriors*, 43–44.

9 See, for example, Mink, *The Wages of Motherhood*, 4, 9–13. One source-based reason for this may be that in the Women's Bureau report "Status of Women in the Government Service, in 1925," the Indian Office is described as employing eighty-three women out of a total of 228 employees, omitting the employees in the field. The Veterans' Bureau, the Office of the Commissioner of Public Revenue, and the Public Debt Service all employed large numbers of women— 3,680, 3,428, and 1,572, respectively—but their missions were not the same, and it is most likely that the vast majority of those women were employed in clerical positions. See Nienburg, "Status of Women in the Government Service, in 1925," 44–45.

10 Gordon, *Pitied But Not Entitled*, 55–64; Skocpol, *Protecting Soldiers and Mothers*, especially part 3; Baker, "The Domestication of Politics"; Koven and Michel, *Mothers of a New World*; Jacobs, *White Mother to a Dark Race*, especially chapter 3.

11 On female moral authority, see Cott, *The Bonds of Womanhood*; Epstein, *The Politics of Domesticity*; Hewitt, *Women's Activism*; Ryan, *Cradle of the Middle Class*; Ginzberg, *Women and the Work of Benevolence*; and Pascoe, *Relations of Rescue*.

12 *LMC* 1887, 27.

13 *LMC* 1886, 27.

14 *Testimony of the Society of Friends*, 6. On the role of Quakers and the WNIA in encouraging the government to hire women, see Emmerich, "'To Respect and Love,'" 15–41.

15 Heizer, *Federal Concerns*, 83–84. See also *LMC* 1886, 44–45; and Ginzberg, "Pernicious Heresies."

16 Colleges with such agendas included: Denison and Yale (men's), Mount Holyoke and Rockford (female), and Oberlin and Grinnel (coed). See Cremin, *American Education*, 103–7. See also Brumburg, *Mission for Life*, 80–106; and Hill, *The World Their Household*, 40–44.

17 Duncan, *Blue Star*, 53.

18 See, for example, *The Indian's Friend* (May 1908), 6–7; and *The Indian's Friend* (March 1909), 2, 6.

19 Taber, *California and Her Indian Children*, 19, 13. See also Elaine Goodale Eastman, *Sister to the Sioux*, 17.

20 Miss Maggie Hogan of Donovan, Illinois to the Commissioner of Indian Affairs, 28 December 1884, LR #227.

21 Golden repeated this assertion twice. Golden, *Red Moon Called Me*, xi, 31, 57. See also Soulé, *The United States Blue Book*, 14; and Arnold and Reed, *In the Land of the Grasshopper Song*, 12.

22 See ARCIA 1899, 18–19.

23 Cleveland was the first Democrat elected after the Civil War, though by 1893 he was in his second term. Mrs. Jemima A. Davenport to the Commissioner of Indian Affairs, 1 May 1893, LR #16096. See also Miss Gussie Lee Whitacre to Mr. Cochran, n.d., 1889, LR #1597; Gifford, Wilson Co., Kansas, to the Commissioner of Indian Affairs, LR #23789; and Mrs. Mattie Carr to Major J. P. Woolsey, U.S. Indian Agent, Ponca O. T., June 1896, LR (number not recorded).

24 Elaine Goodale Eastman, *Sister to the Sioux*, 30–31. Miss Clara Faye Mason visited Mr. Albro, superintendent of Indian Schools in Washington, D.C. Miss Clara Faye Mason to Mr. Albro, Superintendent of Indian Schools, n.d., 1889, LR #1594.

25 The first Civil Service Act covering Indian Service personnel was passed in 1892. It applied to the positions of physician, superintendent of schools, assistant superintendent, teacher, and matron. In May 1896 the act was extended to include all employees except those employed as laborers or workmen or those who had been nominated by the Senate (the latter included Indian agents). See Prucha, *The Great Father*, 723–26, 731–736.

26 Isabella C. Simmons of Cedar Rapids, Iowa, to Dept. of Interior, Office of Indian Affairs, Washington, 31 July 1893, LR #28338.

27 Mrs. Mary Manning, Fall River Mills, CA, to CIA, June 1896, LR #24209.

28 Soulé, *The United States Blue Book*, 4, 9. See also the detailed appendix on appointments in E. E. White, *Experiences of a Special Indian Agent*, viii–ix, 3. Other women learned about positions through missionary societies, periodicals, or word of mouth. See Mrs. Emily Tunison of Somerville, N.J., to Hoke Smith, Secretary of the Interior, 5 August 1893, LR #29267; Miss Maggie Hogan to Commissioner of Indian Affairs, 28 December 1884, LR #227; E. E. Scribner to the Commissioner of Indian Affairs, 29 January 1889, LR #2861; and Corey, *Bachelor Bess*, 375–76.

29 *LMC* 1887, 33.

30 Duncan, *Blue Star*, 200.

31 The speaker, Francis Leupp, contrasted them to "mere men." *LMC* 1908, 14, 25, 30.

32 Estelle Aubrey Brown, *Stubborn Fool*, 13–19.

33 Brown states that Wounded Knee had taken place ten years before her appointment. Estelle Aubrey Brown, *Stubborn Fool*, 18, 21.

34 Ibid., 16.

35 Ibid., 20.

36 Ibid., 21.

37 Ibid., 28.

38 While women took oaths of abstinence and citizenship, few were taking oaths of office. See Bordin, *Woman and Temperance*; and Bredbenner, *A Nationality of Her Own*, 50.

39 Patrick Kelly, *Creating a National Home*, 1–5.

40 Elaine Goodale Eastman, *Sister to the Sioux*, 134.

41 Marie Johnson to Cornelia Taber, 2 October 1907, CTC.

42 Ibid.

43 Agent to Commissioner of Indian Affairs, 4 September 1911, 5, HVA.

44 On field matron duties, see ARCIA 1892, 101. Female employees' bodies were susceptible to critiques that were meant to discredit them. Brown was accused of having an abortion by an inspector after rejecting his amorous advances. Estelle Aubrey Brown, *Stubborn Fool*, 253.

45 Arnold and Reed, *Land of Grasshopper Song*, 36. See also Gay, *With the Nez Perces*, 10–11, 16–17.

46 Arnold and Reed, *Land of Grasshopper Song*, 41.

47 See Foucault, *Discipline and Punish*.

48 Duncan, *Blue Star*, 157.

49 Ibid., 166–67.

50 Ibid., 187.

51 Ibid., 188. Fellows's father held a high position the Pension Office, and the family had relatives in Congress. See ibid., 37–40; *New York Times*, 23 June 1891, 1; and *Washington Post*, 26 February 1888.

52 On the subject of "selective accommodation," see Connell-Szasz, *Between Indian and White Worlds*; and Fear-Segal, *White Man's Club*. On market participation, see Hosmer, *American Indians in the Marketplace*; and Littlefield and Knack, eds., *Native Americans and Wage Labor*.

53 Costo quoted in Philip, *Indian Self-Rule*, 48. See also McClintock, *Imperial Leather*.

54 Stewart's family was divided. Her maternal grandmother did not want her sent away to school, so her father asked the agent to send the policeman. Irene Stewart, *A Voice in Her Tribe*, 15–18, 33–35; and Jacobs, *White Mother to a Dark Race*, 164; see also 149–65. Many parents preferred on-reservation boarding schools or day schools where their children were not so far away. See Clyde Ellis, "'We Had a Lot of Fun,'" 69–72; and Coleman, *American Indian Children*, 72.

55 The Indian Office came under intense criticism for its forceful tactics, and in 1893 the commissioner of Indian affairs stated that children were not to be taken without voluntary consent of their parents. In 1894 Congress prohibited the removal of Indian children to out-of-state schools without the permission of their families, but many officials took advantage of this loophole by removing children for in-state schools without permission. Jacobs, *White Mother to a Dark Race*, 165–70; see also Adams, *Education for Extinction*, 210–22.

56 Quoted in Vuckovic, *Voices from Haskell*, 291; see also 211–46.

57 Irene Stewart, *A Voice in Her Tribe*, 17. See also Adams, *Education for Extinction*, 209–38.

58 For a student who saw her teacher as a mother figure, see Carney, *Eastern Band Cherokee Women*, 96–97. Brown remembered: "Miss Blanchard's girls loved and respected her. Never behind her back did they put brown, contemptuous thumbs to brown, contemptuous noses, as they did to many of us. Her girls seemed to know that she was there because she wanted to help them, just as they knew the rest of us were there to make a living." Estelle Aubrey Brown, *Stubborn Fool*, 47; see also 59.

59 Lomawaima, *They Called It Prairie Light*, 47–51. Italics in original.

60 ARCIA 1896, 348.

CHAPTER FOUR

1 Estelle Aubrey Brown, *Stubborn Fool*, 24–28; Golden, *Red Moon Called Me*, 4–7; Iliff, *People of the Blue Water*, 7–8; Jenkins, *Girl from Williamsburg*, 3–25; and Department of the Interior, *Routes to Indian Agencies*.

2 See Boydston, *Home and Work*, 85, 125, 137; Meyerowitz, *Women Adrift*, 1–20; Kwolek-Folland, *Engendering Business*; and Aron, *Ladies and Gentlemen*, 52–54. On firing married women, see Harris, *In Pursuit of Equity*, 46–48; and Clifford, "Man/Woman/Teacher," 293–343.

3 I am not denying that there was nepotism, but I am asserting that spouses were also hired for ideological reasons. See, for example, Adams, *Education for Extinction*, 66–67; Stamm, *People of the Wind River*, 77; and Houston, *Two Colorado Odysseys*, 49.

4 *Register of Officers and Agents* (1893), 755–74. The *Register of Officers and Agents* indicated the marital status of women through their titles (Miss or Mrs.) for only the years 1881 and 1893. I have assumed that women listed as Mrs. and bearing the same last name as the men employed at the school were their spouses.

5 ARCIA 1898, 13.

6 Seven couples staffed 13.72 percent of the fifty-one day schools. The following percentages were reached by dividing the number of day schools by the number

of couples employed in the schools that reported that year. ARCIA 1889, Appendix Employees of Indian Schools, 631–74.

7   In 1895 thirty-nine couples staffed 35 percent of the 110 day schools. For a listing of the total number of day schools, see ARCIA 1895, 9–10; and ARCIA 1895, Appendix Employees of Indian Schools, 511–62.

8   In 1900 eighty-two couples staffed 64 percent of the 128 day schools reporting (though there were 147 total schools). ARCIA 1900, 19; and ARCIA 1900, Appendix Employees of Indian Schools, 728–64.

9   In 1901 forty-six couples staffed 39.3 percent of the 117 day schools reporting. ARCIA 1901, Appendix Employees of Indian Schools, 728–64. In 1902 eighty-one couples staffed 61.36 percent of the 132 day schools that reported (out of 134). ARCIA 1902, Appendix Employees of Indian Schools, 36, 670–708. The year 1905 was the last year that the names of employees were included in the *Annual Report*. ARCIA 1905, Appendix Employees of Indian Schools, 541–73.

10 Cahill, "Only the Home Can Found a State," 388–90.

11 Application, Charles H. Groover, 1889, LR #216. See also VB to CIA, 10 February 1908, Victor Brown, PF NPRC.

12 Application, John S. McCain, 1889, LR #3714; ARCIA 1889, 359.

13 No one was employed as an assistant teacher at Siltez in 1889, but assistant teachers at two other schools received $360 that year. ARCIA 1889, 348, 361. In 1921 the commissioner was still complaining about the lack of uniform compensation both in the Indian Office and across federal positions. ARCIA 1921, 36.

14 Kneale, *Indian Agent*, 18.

15 Sedlak, "Let Us Go and Buy a School Master," 272–73.

16 Aron, *Ladies and Gentlemen*, 46, 5–52. See Ginzberg, *Women and the Work of Benevolence*, especially chapter 2; and Hewitt, *Women's Activism and Social Change*, 155–56.

17 Kneale, *Indian Agent*, 20.

18 Nock, "Teacher to the Mojaves," 145. Another white wife wrote: "Sometimes I think of our life at San Carlos and it is like a dream. It sends a shudder through me to think of the horrible Indians and the lonely place." Quoted in Douglas Firth Anderson, "Protestantism, Progress, and Prosperity," 329 n. 47.

19 Brumberg, *Mission for Life*, chapter 4.

20 ARCIA 1898, 12. See also *Rules for Indian Schools*, 26–27; LMC 1870, 30; LMC 1893, 108; LMC 1903, 48; and ARBIC 1894, 10.

21 By 1913 married women were barred from holding federal postmaster positions. Rai and Critzer, *Affirmative Action*, 22. It is unclear in the lists of Indian Office employees if widows were consistently listed as widowed or as married, but in those records, only 3 percent of white women in the Indian Service were described as widows as compared to 18 percent of women in the national population. Aron indicates that widows made up 13 to 28 percent of applicants for federal clerkships, while married women made up from 4 to 18 percent of applicants in those positions. Cahill, "Only the Home Can Found a State," 142; and Aron, *Ladies and Gentlemen*, 46, 50–52.

22 Kramer, *The Blood of Empire*. In 1904, for example, the Civil Service Commission

noted that their numbers had risen from 48 percent to 98 percent of the work-force. *31st Annual Report of the U.S. Civil Service Commission*, 1904, 14–15.

23 See U.S. Civil Service Commission, *Manual of Examinations* (1915) 130–31. See also *Annual Report of the War Department* (GPO, 1904) 767. The numbers of white women applying were fairly small. In January 1902, of the 277 exam takers, only forty were women; in March and April, the 217 total applicants included twenty women. There were also many fewer jobs for white women, as Filipinos were hired as regular teachers and whites (usually men) as English teachers. See *Annual Report of the Civil Service Commission* (1902), 16.

24 One official stated that having a matron who was related to the superintendent was preferable because they could more freely discuss delicate issues. H. B. Peairs to CIA, 28 October 1912, Lizzie Devine, PF NPRC.

25 Quoted in Welsh, *A Dangerous Assault*, 4–7.

26 *Regulations of the Indian Office*, 1904, 15; U.S. Civil Service Commission *Manual of Examinations for the Spring of 1915*, 95.

27 ARCIA 1911, 31.

28 Gregg, *The Indian and the Nurse*, 19. See also ARCIA 1893, 56.

29 ARCIA 1890, clxiii–clxv.

30 MP to CIA, 1 November, 1909, Maud Peacore, PF NPRC; Indian Application for Appointment, 18 September 1911, Mary Rockwood, PF NPRC; and Employee Record Blank, 2 January 1907, Sarah Wyman, PF NPRC.

31 Kneale, *Indian Agent*, 18; see also 26.

32 Ibid., 26; Estelle Aubrey Brown, *Stubborn Fool*, 92–94; Iliff, *People of the Blue Water*, 22–24.

33 Standing Bear, *My People, the Sioux*, 193. This is not the same Chief Standing Bear whose speaking tour inspired eastern reformers in 1879.

34 Kneale, *Indian Agent*, 305–6; CIA to JB, 28 February, 1914, Jennie L. Burton, PF NPRC. See also Jenkins, *Girl from Williamsburg*, 32, 40; Patricia A. Carter, "'Completely Discouraged,'" 53; Efficiency Report, 1 November 1914, Allie Busby, PF NPRC; and Andrew Spencer to CIA, 12 April 1893, LR #13592.

35 Jenkins, *Girl from Williamsburg*, 179.

36 *Rules for the Indian School Service*, 25.

37 Benson, *Counter Cultures*, 85; Deutsch, *Women and the City*, 95–98.

38 Indian Office officials did recognize the role of domestic servants in wider society. The outing programs set up in many schools were an effort to fill the servant needs of middle-class white households, especially in urban areas. See Trennert, *The Phoenix Indian School*, 70–73; and Jacobs, "Working on the Domestic Frontier." The Indian Service discouraged, but did not forbid employees from hiring students to work for them as long as they received "suitable remuneration." Patricia A. Carter, "'Completely Discouraged.'" *Rules for Indian School Service*, 25.

39 *United States Civil Service Commission Annual Report, 1901–1902* (1902), 301. No educational exam was required for the positions of baker, cook, and laundress, but applicants were evaluated based on physical ability (weighted at 40 percent) and training and experience (weighted at 60 percent). The age restrictions on matrons (twenty-four to forty-five) were waived for Indians and the wives of superintendents. *Manual of Examinations* (1915), 46–47, 95.

40 Riney, *The Rapid City Indian School*, 171–74.

41 *Indian School Service Rules*, 1892, 28.

42 *Regulations of the Indian Office*, 1904, 17. See also Riney, *The Rapid City Indian School*, 177–82; and the 1915 *Manual of Examinations*, 35.

43 For examples of employees who wanted their children with them on the reservations, see Application, Benjamin Wilson Tice, 1889, LR #1589; Application, Patrick Henry Hamlin, 1889, LR #1591; Application, Charles H. Groover, 1889, LR #216; and Application, Edward Narry Best, 1889, LR #1604. Widows also brought children with them; see Application, Ora Brunnette Hubbard, 1889, LR #4385.

44 Salena Kane to CIA, 11 February 1913, John Buntin, PF NPRC; CIA to RP, 4 April 1918, Ray Parrett, PF NPRC; RP to CIA, 20 April 1918, Ray Parrett, PF NPRC; memo, 3 May 1918, Ray Parrett, PF NPRC; and CIA to RP, 11 May 1918, Ray Parrett, PF NPRC.

45 I have assumed that the employees were nonwhite based on their appearance in the photographs. See ⟨http://hdl.loc.gov/loc.award/wauaipn.image.1853⟩; ⟨http://hdl.loc.pnp/cph.3c22837⟩; and ⟨http://hdl.loc.gov/loc.award/wauaipn.image.24⟩ (all accessed 14 June 2010).

46 Estelle Aubrey Brown, *Stubborn Fool*, 84–85.

47 Parents were also concerned about disease in the schools. Mrs. Lance Brown to Hon. G. M. Hitchcock, 2 November 1916, Jennie C. Brown, PF NPRC. Vaccination requirements in *Regulations of the Indian Office*, 22.

48 Iliff, *People of the Blue Water*, 264–65. See also Arnold and Reed, *In the Land of Grasshopper Song*, 38.

49 Thisba Hutson Morgan, "Reminiscences of My Days in the Land of the Ogallala Sioux," 46. Other employees hired a teacher for their children in a "private" school. *Indian Appropriation Bill: Hearings, 64th Congress, Second Session*, 480.

50 Wright, "Contributions: An Indian School," 83.

51 Schmeckebier, *The Office of Indian Affairs*, 482; *Rules for the Indian School Service, 1913*, 5; and *Regulations of the Indian Office, Indian Schools*, 8. While the acts do not specifically mention the children of employees, they undoubtedly benefited most from these new laws. See ARCIA 1909, 15–16; ARCIA 1907, 95–97; and ARBIC 1907, 5–6.

52 While these were real concerns, some employees may have used them as "safe" reasons to request transfers or submit resignations.

53 WB to CIA, 21 February 1916; WB to CIA, 17 January 1916; and WB to CIA, 11 July 1916, all in William Blish, PF NPRC. See also CB to CIA, 21 August 1909, Charles M. Buchanan, PF NPRC.

54 DJ to CIA, 5 August 1918, Dollie Johnson, PF NPRC. See also LB to CIA, 5 May 1927, Leo Bonnin, PF NPRC.

55 HK to CIA, 30 April 1918; HK to Supt. Asbury, 19 March 1923; and HK to CIA, 7 November 1917, all in Harriet Kyselka, PF NPRC.

56 *The Problem of Indian Administration*, 160–62.

57 Jenkins, *Girl from Williamsburg*, 61; JM to CIA, 15 December 1911, Jessie Morago, PF NPRC.

58 LJ to CIA, 14 June 1917, Lucy Jobin, PF NPRC; Rep. C. B. Miller to CIA, 18 September 1911, Julia DeCora Lukecart, PF NPRC. Emphasis in the original. See

also resignation JB to CIA, n.d., John H. Bailly (Sisseton-Wahpeton Dakota), PF NPRC.

59 Report of W. W. McConihe, 23 July 1909; Superintendent Evan Estep to CIA, 7 August 1909; and letter, 16 May 1911, in David U. Betts, PF NPRC; JB to CIA, n.d. (1908), John H. Bailly, PF NPRC.

60 *Regulations of the Indian Office, Indian Schools*, 5.

61 See Gay, *With the Nez Perces*, 7. In extreme cases, these tensions turned violent, as did one at Duck Lake, Nevada, in which whole families wielded guns. Adams, *Education for Extinction*, 70–82.

62 Efficiency Report, 1926, Leo Bonnin, PF NPRC. See also Special U.S. Indian Agent to CIA, 26 August 1909, Homer Bibb, PF NPRC.

63 Estelle Aubrey Brown, *Stubborn Fool*, 84–85; and Efficiency Report, 1 May 1916, Jennie C. Brown, PF NPRC.

64 Aadland, *Women and Warriors*, xviii, 2, 6, 30, 174.

65 See also Clemmons, "'Our Children Are in Danger'"; and West, *Growing up with the Country*, 131–32.

66 Nock, "Teacher to the Mojaves," 277; see also 19, 262, 149.

67 See, for example, Coleman, *American Indian Children*, 127–45; and Lomawaima, *They Called It Prairie Light*, 145–68.

68 See testimony of Dr. Gates, *Indian Appropriation Bill: Hearings, 64th Congress, Second Session*, 480.

69 Norton, *Centering in Two Worlds*, 14; see also 29–30.

70 "I grew up on Indian reservations which I think fortified my association with my Kiowa relatives who were extensively Indian and spoke Indian." Momaday, *Conversations with N. Scott Momaday*, 133–34, 186; see also 21, 32, 61–62, 100, 136, 141, 170, 179, 185–87, 193, 201, 221–22. See also Schubnell, *N. Scott Momaday*, 15–18.

71 Carney, *Eastern Band Cherokee*, 97, 96.

72 Report of House, Supervisor of Schools to CIA, 22 March 1904, Joseph Estes, PF NPRC.

73 Testimony of Stockbridge parents, 22 March 1904; and Testimony of Joseph Estes, 18 March 1904, both in Joseph Estes, PF NPRC.

74 Supervisor of Indian Schools to CIA, 23 March 1904; Report of House, Supervisor of Schools, to CIA, 22 March 1904; and JE to Special Inspector House, 18 March 1904, all in Joseph Estes, PF NPRC.

CHAPTER FIVE

1 Montezuma Papers, *Wassaja* 3 (March 1919): 1–2.

2 Montezuma Papers, *Wassaja* 1 (January 1917): 4.

3 Horne, *Essie's Story*, 57–58, 65.

4 Philip J. Deloria, *Indians in Unexpected Places*.

5 Stoler, "Matters of Intimacy," 895.

6 ARCIA 1903, 3. Jones also used employment to enforce "civilization" policy. In 1901 he ordered that Indian men in the Indian Service had to cut their hair or lose their jobs. Prucha, *The Great Father* (abridged), 264–65.

7 See also Steven J. Novak, "The Real Takeover of the BIA," 646; and Ahern, "An Experiment Aborted."

8 ARCIA 1888, xx–xxi (757 white and 137 Indian employees for a total of 894 regular employees); ARCIA 1895, 506 (1,981 white and 597 Indian employees for a total of 2,578 regular employees). In 1899 the ARCIA reported 2,562 employees in the school service, of which 1,160 were Indians, about half being "Indian assistants." ARCIA Appendix Employees of Indian Schools, 1899, 29. In 1906, 1,414 of School Service appointees were Indians, "of whom 1,266 resigned." ARCIA 1906, 64. For 1912, see *Report of the Executive Council*, 27.

9 ARCIA 1880–81, xii. In 1880 the government appropriated $73,647.88, or 1.575 percent of the total appropriation of $4,674,573.44, for this purpose. The following year, it appropriated $117,574.44, or 2.66 percent of the total appropriation of $4,418,320.76.

10 *Regulations of the Indian Office*, 14. The regulation quoted had been enacted in 1883. A similar clause was included in the 1894 Appropriation Act. Schemeckebier, *The Office of Indian Affairs*, 295.

11 ARCIA 1880–81, xii–xiii.

12 Ostler, *The Plains Sioux*, 141.

13 *Regulations of the Indian Office*, 45.

14 By 1878 one-third of the agencies had police forces, in 1880 two-thirds of the agencies were so staffed and by 1890 almost all agencies had them. Stuart, *The Indian Office*, 22. See also Hagan, *Indian Police and Judges*.

15 Mark R. Ellis, "Reservation Akicitas," 187.

16 ARCIA 1880–81, xvii–xviii.

17 *Congressional Record*, 6233. See also Howard M. Jenkins, "The Indians as Workers," *Christian Register* (Boston), 14 January 1892 (Indian Rights Association, Philadelphia).

18 Stuart, *The Indian Office*, 23.

19 Herbert Welsh, "Civilization among the Sioux Indians: Report of a Visit to Some of the Sioux Reservations of South Dakota and Nebraska" (Indian Rights Association, Philadelphia, 1893), 9.

20 Ingersoll, *To Intermix with Our White Brothers*, 247.

21 Mark R. Ellis, "Reservation Akicitas," 198–205, 208–10.

22 Both quotes in Ahern, "An Experiment Aborted," 269, 271.

23 Schmeckebier, *The Office of Indian Affairs*, 293–94; and Ryhner and Eder, *American Indian Education*, 138.

24 Quoted in Lomawamia, *They Called It Prairie Light*, 18–19 n. 24.

25 See Child, *Boarding School Seasons*, 43–54, 89.

26 Efficiency Report, 1 April 1933, Susie McDougall, PF NPRC; and Request for Reinstatement, 12 February 1910, Julia DeCora Lukecart, PF NPRC. The recent biography of Julia's sister, Angel DeCora, confirms this. See Waggoner, *Fire Light*.

27 Personnel Blank 17, April 1912, Violetta Nash, PF NPRC; Indian Application for Appointment, 14 March 1912, Nellie Santeo, PF NPRC; CIA, 25 April 1912, Nellie Santeo, PF NPRC; and Personnel Blank, 16 May 1911, Sophie Picard, PF NPRC.

28 ARCIA 1900, 517–18.

29 Employee Blank, 15 May 1911, Agnes Fredette, PF NPRC. This sample comes from fifty-five personnel files found from a list of all 265 female Native employees

reported as employed in the School Service in the 1905 ARCIA. Employees with longer careers had bigger files and were thus more likely to be found, which may have skewed the sample. Many of the white-collar employees had held manual positions at the beginning of their careers.

30 This list also includes assistant positions for those jobs.

31 Chilocco's school journal for 1906–7 listed sixteen graduates who obtained employment at other Indian schools. Of the sixty-one former students Lomawaima interviewed, ten (16.39 percent) had careers in the Educational Division of the Bureau of Indian Affairs. Lomawaima, *The Called It Prairie Light*, xv, 18 n. 24. A 1911 survey revealed "209 of Carlisle's 574 living graduates were employed by the government and 300 had nongovernmental jobs." Reyhner and Eder, *American Indian Education*, 147. See also Vuckovic, *Voices from Haskell*, 255–59.

32 Quoted in Steven J. Novak, "The Real Takeover of the BIA," 651–52.

33 See Littlefield, "Indian Education and the World of Work"; Bauer, "We Were All Migrant Workers Here," 43–63; Meeks, "The Tohono O'odham," 469–90; Ostler, *The Plains Sioux*, 144; and Jacobs, "Working on the Domestic Frontier," 167–70. The entertainment industry also provided some work; see Moses, *Wild West Shows*; and Philip J. Deloria, *Indians in Unexpected Places*, 52–108.

34 See, for example, Personal Record, 15 May 1911, Sarah A. Wyman, PF NPRC. Phyllis Palmer estimates that between 11 and 15 percent of employed Native women were in domestic service work between 1920 and 1930. Cited in Jacobs, "Working on the Domestic Frontier," 194 n. 25.

35 LO to CIA, 30 August 1916, Lillie Oshkosh, PF NPRC; Indian Application for Appointment, 23 November 1911; and Efficiency Report, 1 April 1912, in Addie Molzahn, PF NPRC; Personnel Blank, February 1912, and L. M. Compton to CIA, 4 October 1928, Lavinia Cornelius, PF NPRC.

36 Notably, the Indian Service employed a Harvard-educated African American doctor and several black nurses in this period. See files of Edward J. Davis, Eva Greenwood, and Lillian Henry, PF NPRC.

37 Application for Appointment, 28 April 1913, John F. Brown, PF NPRC.

38 Gregg, *The Indians and the Nurse*, 109.

39 Wyaco, *A Zuni Life*, 21–23. Laura Cornelius-Kellog suggested that some young people joined the Indian Service to earn money for college; quoted in D. Anthony Tyeeme Clark, "Representing Indians," 188.

40 Native employees Susie McDougall and Lucy Jobin both spent vacations in Europe. Superintendent and Special Disbursing Agent to CIA, 30 August 1907, Susie McDougall, PF NPRC; letter, 7 June 1930, from Principal Clerk in Charge, Lucy Jobin, PF NPRC. A 1916 law entitled employees injured on the job to employee compensation. *Regulations of the Indian Office, Indian Schools*, 5. See Kessler-Harris, *In Pursuit of Equity*, 46–47.

41 See ARCIA 1890, clv.

42 Most Native employees did not receive pensions until 1929.

43 LC to CIA, 11 October 1907; LC to C. F. Pierce, 21 April 1909; Efficiency Report, 1 November 1914; LC to CIA, 1 July 1925; all of which are in Lavinia Cornelius, PF NPRC.

44 Wyman was from Isabella, Michigan, and thus most likely was a member of

the Saginaw Chippewa Tribe. Superintendent L. F. Michael to CIA, 24 October 1912; and SW to CIA, 25 July 1914; all in Sarah Wyman, PF NPRC.

45 ND to CIA, 9 July 1909, PF NPRC; and Request for Reinstatement, 18 August 1915, Naomi Dawson, PF NPRC.

46 See also the 1922 Industrial Surveys for the Lac Du Flambeau Agency, NARA GLR.

47 Quoted in Philip, *Indian Self Rule*, 64–65.

48 Supt. L. M. Compton to CIA, 1 November 1909, Maude Peacore, PF NPRC.

49 Standing Bear went to the Carlisle Indian School in 1879. He returned in 1884 and received an assistant position in the Indian Service. In 1891 the agent, a former employee at Carlisle, offered Standing Bear the leadership of a day school at Pine Ridge. He took the position and simultaneously operated a small ranch. Standing Bear, *My People, the Sioux*, 190, 234; and Markowitz, "Luther Standing Bear," 608.

50 Request for reinstatement, 5 July 1911; request for transfer, 29 June 1915; and MJ to CIA, 10 November 1927, in Madeline Jacker, PF NPRC. Employees often requested to be stationed near their homes. See 19 October 1929, Nancy Palladeau, PF NPRC; and JM to Inspector Coleman, 5 November 1917, Jessie Morago, PF NPRC.

51 Johnson, 5 August 1918, Dollie Johnson, PF NPRC.

52 Schmeckebier, *The Office of Indian Affairs*, 482.

53 JM to Inspector Coleman, 5 November 1917, Jessie Morago, PF NPRC. See also Efficiency Report, 1 May 1926, Katie Brewer, PF NPRC; EM to CIA, 17 August 1917, Elizabeth Morrison, PF NPRC; Indian Application for Appointment, n.d., and Efficiency Report, 17 February 1922, Addie Molzahn, PF NPRC. Some had other family members in the Indian Service. See Request for Reinstatement, 18 August 1915, Naomi Dawson, PF NPRC; and LC to CIA, 3 July 1909, Lavinia Cornelius, PF NPRC.

54 Quoted in Carney, *Eastern Band Cherokee Women*, 97.

55 At the Round Valley Reservation in 1910, assistant matron Emma Ledger was reprimanded for eating with the students rather than at the employee mess, which she did most likely to be with her children (two of whom were enrolled in 1903). Superintendent to CIA, 2 August 1910, Emma Ledger, PF NPRC; CIA to Superintendent, 18 August 1910, Emma Ledger, PF NPRC; and letter to CIA, 31 May 1902, Record Group 75, NARA SB. Many thanks to Willie Bauer for sharing this information.

56 Indian Application for Appointment, 14 March 1912, Nellie Santeo, PF NPRC.

57 AA to CIA, 18 June 1915, Annie Abner, PF NPRC. On Carlisle, see Annie Kowuni [Tsa I Ka Weet Sa] from Laguna Pueblo at ⟨http://files.usgwarchives.net/pa/cumberland/education/knames.txt⟩ (accessed 9 May 2009).

58 *American Indian Magazine*, vol. 4, no. 3 (July-September, 1916), 255. See also *Report of the Executive Council*, 101.

59 Elaine Goodale Eastman, *Sister to the Sioux*, 82. See also Gregg, *The Indian and the Nurse*, 58.

60 The resolution was signed by the Resolution Committee made up of three important Cheyenne and Arapaho political leaders, two of whom had worked with Burns as tribal delegates in the past: Cleaver Warden, John Hutchen, and

Henry Rowlodge. Cheyenne and Arapaho Tribal Resolution, 12 December 1931, Robert Burns, PF NPRC; Fowler, *Tribal Sovereignty*, 39–40, 99–100 and Table 1, Cheyenne-Arapaho Business Committee Membership, 1938–41, 112; and Berthrong, "Jessie Rowlodge."

61 Personnel Blank, 16 June 1923, Robert Burns, PF NPRC.

62 After 1912 the reports began to criticize him for old age and political activity, but most emphasized his loyalty and faithfulness. See Efficiency Report, 1 October 1911; Efficiency Report, 1 November 1918; Efficiency Report, 26 May 1926; and Efficiency Report, 12 November 1926, all in Robert Burns, PF NPRC.

63 Report of Traveling Auditor, 1 June 1926, Robert Burns, PF NPRC.

64 Efficiency Report, 1 October 1911, Robert Burns, PF NPRC.

65 Efficiency Report, 1 October 1911, Robert Burns, PF NPRC.

66 In a similar case, Clarence Three Stars had worked as a teacher on the Pine Ridge Reservation for almost thirty years, but he was also a member of the Oglala Council and Sioux Black Hills Council. Working for the Oglala Council and as interpreter for Red Cloud, he testified before Congress in 1897. He became state attorney for Bennett County, South Dakota, for 1912 and 1913. D. Anthony Tyeeme Clark, "At the Headwaters," 75; and Andrews, "Turning the Tables on Assimilation."

67 Fowler, *Tribal Sovereignty*, 100.

68 On the composition of 1928 delegates, see Berthrong, "Jessie Rowlodge," 229–30.

69 Fowler, *Tribal Sovereignty*, 100, 101–2.

70 Efficiency Report, 1 October 1911; and 1911 Application, both in Robert Burns, PF NPRC.

71 Efficiency Report, 1 October 1911; Efficiency Report, 1 November 1917; and Efficiency Report, 1 November 1918, all in Robert Burns, PF NPRC.

72 AR to CIA, 16 July 1908, Ada Rice, PF NPRC; and Personnel Record Blank, 12 May 1911, Agnes B. Reedy, PF NPRC.

73 RB to CIA, 30 October 1913; RB to Chief Supervisor Holcombe, 8 February 1912; Supervisor Martin to CIA, 31 October 1913; and Personal Information Card, n.d., all in Raymond A. Bonnin, PF NPRC. CIA to Agent, 12 October 1907; and MP to CIA, 21 October 1907, both in Mary Paquette, PF NPRC. Ada Rice added: "[B]oth of my parents being dead and having been away from the Reservation for so many years, I am almost a stranger there." AR to CIA, 16 July 1908, Ada Rice, PF NPRC. Lizzie Devine wrote: "I am a Chippewa Indian, but not one of those knocking the Service." LD to CIA, 30 June 1919, Lizzie Devine, PF NPRC.

74 Petition of Menominee Delegation, head chiefs Nepil, Chickeney, and M. Oshkenaniew to Commissioner of Indian Affairs, 24 April 1885, LR #9447.

75 Petition, 16 September 1910; and Rev. C. H. Beaulieu, 20 September 1910, both in Susie McDougall, PF NPRC. On Beaulieu's position, see Densmore, "The Words of Indian Songs," 451. This incident also hints at the struggles over identity within communities. Several of the families who signed the petition—the Warrens, Beaupres, Fairbankses, and Beaulieus—share the surnames with the mixed-blood families who played a central role in the political upheaval at White Earth as described by Melissa Meyer. She argues that categories of "blood" were based on "basic cultural or ethnic differences—not solely genetic ones." Mixed bloods

"identified themselves as 'Indians,'" but their ideas about "the accumulation of wealth" placed them at odds with full bloods, or the more conservative faction. Meyer asserts that mixed bloods at White Earth were generally opposed to the Indian Service, perceiving its white employees as incompetent. Their support for McDougall suggests their desire for a Native-run Service or her ties to their politics. Meyer, *The White Earth Tragedy*, 178, 182, 200.

76 Indian Application for Appointment, 14 March 1912, Nellie Santeo, PF NPRC.

77 L. M. Compton to CIA, 29 August 1924, Lavinia Cornelius, PF NPRC. See also Susie McDougall to CIA, 30 December 1909, Susie McDougall, PF NPRC; Superintendent Creel to CIA, 23 September 1910, Ida Lowry, PF NPRC; and Angus Nicholson, Supt. to CIA, 20 January 1915, Julia Wheelock, PF NPRC.

78 Superintendent Mayer to CIA, 12 July 1918, Naomi Dawson, PF NPRC; U.S. Census 1930, "Ottawa, Ottawa, Oklahoma," roll 1923, 3-B, Enumeration District 22. Retrieved from Ancestry.com (accessed 29 June 2010). She is listed as Indian with a mixed mother and Wyandotte father. Indian census rolls list her as $\frac{1}{32}$ Indian.

79 The geographic designation is Hoopa Valley; the tribal designation is Hupa.

80 Supt. Mortsolf to CIA, 17 October 1915, Sherman Norton, PF NPRC.

81 McAnulty, "Angel DeCora" and Retirement Record Card, n.d., Julia DeCora Lukecart, PF NPRC.

82 Retirement Record Card, n.d., Dollie Johnson, PF NPRC.

83 The median number of positions was also four and the median number of locations was five. The number of locations varied from a low of one school to a high of fifteen over the course of a career. See Annie Abner, Katie Brewer, Lavinia Cornelius, Rose Dougherty, Madeline Jacker, Susie McDougall, Ada Rice, Dollie Johnson, and Julia DeCora Lukecart, PF NPRC.

84 While scholars have used the term "pan Indian," Native people tend to prefer "intertribal." I have therefore used intertribal, by which I mean to acknowledge that Native people came to recognize that they shared a larger ethnic identity as "Indian" but did not consequently abandon their individual tribal identities; instead, they used both, depending on the circumstance. See Hertzberg, *The Search for American Indian Identity*; and Ellis, Lassiter, and Dunham, *Powwow*, xiii.

85 Horne, *Essie's Story*, 41–44, 58, 65–67, 83, 86, 163. Other Native teachers also used alternative pedagogical methods, especially using Native languages. See Andrews, "Turning the Tables on Assimilation"; and Qoyawayma, *No Turning Back*, 125–31.

86 Jobin described herself as Indian but does not seem to have had a tribal affiliation (though some of her superiors called her Chippewa). She never requested to be stationed in a particular place, and her permanent address shifted as she changed jobs. Fr. Leopold, OFM to Mr. Endicott, 9 April 1920, Lucy Jobin, PF NPRC.

87 Dollie Johnson, 26 December 1921, Dollie Johnson, PF NPRC.

88 Petition, 8 December 1915, Ada Rice, PF NPRC. For some employees, intertribal identity gave them flexibility. Emma Johnson, a Pottawatomie teacher, stated: "It was a pleasure because I was a teacher and I could investigate and see their needs. . . . I live upon a reservation now. At my own home it is not a pleasure, but where I can investigate when I am not under the thumb of the government it is."

Report of the Executive Council on the Proceedings of the First Annual Conference of the Society of American Indians, 124.

89 Many regular Native employees had been trained in the federal school system and often subscribed to ideas of class based on Anglo standards, which differed from traditional tribal ways of assessing status. This often fell out along phenotypical lines, and many, though not all, Native employees were of mixed heritage. Nonetheless, the Indian Office regarded them all as "Indian" employees. See Mihesuah, *Indigenous American Women*, 62–80; and Mihesuah, *Cultivating the Rosebuds*. There were also a few employees listed in one of three other racial categories: African Americans (classified as "N" for negro), Mexicans ("M"), and Chinese ("C").

90 Federal Indian law has had a similar effect of structuring the discourse into the biracial terms of "Indian" and "white." See Biolsi, *Deadliest Enemies*.

91 Sometimes a white male employee would be described as "no good"; this often occurred when the man was married to a Native woman and had the stigma of "squawman," but this was rare.

92 Acting CIA to CH, #75144, 1912, Charles Hoffman, PF NPRC.

93 He added: "Mr. and Mrs. Bonnin are worthy Indians, capable and efficient and undoubtedly merit what ever recognition they may receive. They have one qualification of rare value in a worker—they BELIEVE in the ultimate outcome of even THESE Indians." Emphasis in original. Superintendent Martin to CIA, 12 December 1913; and Efficiency Report, 1 October 1913, both in Raymond A. Bonnin, PF NPRC.

94 See, for example, Efficiency Report, 1 April 1912, Susie McDougall, PF NPRC.

95 CIA to Earl Place, 21 February 1923, Lucy Jobin, PF NPRC.

96 J. H. Crickenberger, Fort Hall Senior Clerk, to Superintendent Janus, 31 December 1926, Harriet Kyselka, PF NPRC; Efficiency Report, 1 May 1917, Lucy Jobin, PF NPRC; Superintendent Howard to CIA, 14 February 1910, Susie McDougall, PF NPRC; and McDougall, 30 December 1909, Susie McDougall, PF NPRC.

97 Efficiency Report, 13 May 1918, Lucy Jobin, PF NPRC.

98 Efficiency Report, 1 November 1910, Lucy Jobin, PF NPRC.

99 Picard's superintendent added, "You will suffer no decrease in salary by reason of this change, nor is this assignment made because you are inefficient." Efficiency Report, 1 November 1915; SP to CIA, 17 November, 1915; and CIA to SP, 23 October 1915, all in Sophie Picard, PF NPRC.

100 *Regulations of the Indian Service*, 5.

101 Jacobs, *White Mother to a Dark Race*, 42–48.

102 Assistant CIA to VN, 8 December 1916, Violetta Nash, PF NPRC; Efficiency Report, 4 January 1914, Louisa Higheagle, PF NPRC; and Efficiency Report, n.d., Emma Ledger, PF NPRC. See also Superintendent C. W. Randall to CIA, 4 January 1911, Lucinda George, PF NPRC; and Efficiency Report, 11 January 1909, Mary Rockwood, PF NPRC.

103 Efficiency Report, 1 November 1913; and Superintendent Wilson to CIA, 1 November 1909; all in Julia Metoxyn, PF NPRC. See also Efficiency Report, 27 April 1913; Efficiency Report, 1 April 1915; and Efficiency Report, 1 May

1913, all in Julia Wheelock [Metoxyn], PF NPRC. See also Superintendent Norton to CIA, 28 July 1915, Dollie Johnson, PF NPRC.

104 Assistant CIA to Superintendent Wilson, 18 August 1910, Emma Ledger, PF NPRC; CIA to Superintendent Nicholson, 10 April 1914, Julia Metoxyn, PF NPRC.

105 Agnes Fredette (allotted Standing Rock) listed herself as superintendent of the Grand River Boarding School [Standing Rock] between 1893 and 1897 on her personnel blank, but her file gives no further information. This is corroborated by the ARCIA 1895 list of employees in the School Service that describes her as "H," or "halfblood." ARCIA 185, 539. One study suggests that "several" of Haskell's graduates served as superintendents, but the author does not break that down by sex. Vuckovic, *Voices from Haskell*, 263.

106 See Joseph Estes, PF NPRC; and Brudvig, *Hampton Normal and Agricultural Institutes American Indian Students, 1878–1923*. See also Joseph Estes, Hampton Institute Alumni student files. Many thanks to Bert Ahern for generously sharing his notes on Estes's time at Hampton with me.

107 John Harding, Agent to CIA, 6 February 1901, Joseph Estes, PF NPRC.

108 Acting CIA to CH, #75144, 1912, Charles Hoffman, PF NPRC.

109 See Leo Bonnin, PF NPRC; RB to Holcombe, 8 February 1912; RB to CIA, 30 October 1913; Personal Information Card, n.d.; Supervisor Martin to CIA, 31 October 1913, all in Raymond A. Bonnin, PF NPRC.

110 In 1936 a final letter appeared in Bonnin's file from the secretary of the interior to a congressman noting that if an agency were to be reestablished at Greenwood, South Dakota, consideration would be given to Bonnin for the position of superintendent. Admin. Asst. to Sect. of Interior to Hon. Fred Hildebrant, 16 May 1936, Raymond A. Bonnin, PF NPRC.

111 LJ to CIA, 14 June 1917, Lucy Jobin, PF NPRC.

112 Fr. Weber, O.F.M., to Charles Lusk, 27 January 1918, Lucy Jobin, PF NPRC.

113 Abner wrote this while resigning from the position of seamstress at the Albuquerque Indian School. She added, "I have been connected with the above school for nearly thirteen years. . . . Since my father is getting old I feel it my duty to obey the call. If for any reason or reasons I can not be of help on the reservation, I ask of you, as head of the Indian Department to aid me in getting work elsewhere. . . . I therefore thank you Honorable Commissioner for giving words of encouragement to those who are striving to better themselves and so help those about them." AA to CIA, 18 June 1915, Annie K. Abner, PF NPRC.

114 Salena Kane to CIA, 11 April 1913, John A. Buntin, PF NPRC.

115 Assistant Superintendent to CIA, 23 December 1914; and Efficiency Report, 1 April 1911, in Julia Wheelock [Metoxyn], PF NPRC.

116 Superintendent Allen to CIA, 2 September 1919; and CIA to AC, 12 September 1919, in Alice Cornelius, PF NPRC. Laura, one of the founders of the Society of American Indians, had advocated for Alice in the past. See Laura Cornelius Kellogg to CIA, 23 July 1912, Alice Cornelius, PF NPRC.

117 Meyer, *The White Earth Tragedy*, 178, 182, 200. For a discussion of other tensions within Native communities, especially those based on class or status, see Mihesuah, *Indigenous American Women*, 62–80.

118 Meyer, *The White Earth Tragedy*, 189.

119 Personnel Record Blank, n.d.; Resolution of the Tribal Business Committee, Standing Rock Reservation, 17 February 1912; and Superintendent of Standing Rock to CIA, 13 July 1912, all in Agnes B. Reedy, PF NPRC. Jane Gray described a similar divide on the Nez Perce reservation, where allotting agent Alice Fletcher could only find willing assistance among the returned students, "that much-maligned class on the reservation." Gray, *With the Nez Perce*, 56.

120 Horne, *Essie's Story*, 64. Italics in original.

121 Wilson, *Ohiyesa*; Iverson, *Carlos Montezuma*; Tong, *Susan La Flesche Picotte*; and Waggoner, *Fire Light*.

CHAPTER SIX

1 ARCIA 1906, 64; see also 42–63.

2 The rhetoric of family also became an important way to facilitate new working relationships in the business world at this time. See Kwolek-Folland, *Engendering Business*. For more on leisure and work, see Peiss, *Cheap Amusements*; Murphy, *Mining Cultures*; and Rosenzwieg, *Eight Hours for What We Will*.

3 *Rules for Indian Schools*, 27.

4 Efficiency Report, 1 November 1914, Allie Busby, PF NPRC. See also Andrew Spencer to CIA, 12 April 1893, LR #13592; and Jenkins, *Girl from Williamsburg*, 40.

5 Golden, *Red Moon Called Me*, 96; Estelle Aubrey Brown, *Stubborn Fool*, 68; Iliff, *People of the Blue Water*, 259–63; Patricia A. Carter, "'Completely Discouraged.'"

6 Woodruff, *Indian Oasis*, 30–31.

7 Inspection Report, Special Agent L. A. Dorrington, 20–27 October 1916, section 5, 1, 3, Hoopa File, Dorrington Records, box 5, NARA SB.

8 FK to CIA, 28 January 1929, Frank Kyselka, PF NPRC.

9 Thisba Hutson Morgan, "Reminiscences of My Days in the Land of the Ogallala Sioux," 46.

10 Golden, *Red Moon Called Me*, 16, 70; Riney, *The Rapid City Indian School*, 183.

11 MK to CIA, 11 July 1916, Minnie C. King, PF NPRC. Australian scholars have suggested that white and Indigenous women sharing work experiences and living in interracial hierarchical communities could develop interracial friendships. Haskins and Schedlich-Day, "My Mate Ellen."

12 Woodruff, *Indian Oasis*, 30–31; Golden, *Red Moon Called Me*, 16. See Riney, *The Rapid City Indian School*, 183–84.

13 *Regulations of Indian Office, Indian Schools*, 22. See also the employee club ledger from Mount Pleasant at NARA GLR.

14 Golden, *Red Moon Called Me*, 30; and Iliff, *People of the Blue Water*, 258.

15 SBFP 109; ARCIA 1906, 203; and SBFP 453. For other examples, see NMHP, 25 December 1901; and Inspection Report, Special Agent L. A. Dorrington, 20–27 October 1916, Hoopa File, Dorrington Records, box 5, NARA SB.

16 Horne, *Essie's Story*, 62, 66.

17 Ruckman, "Indian Schooling in New Mexico," 49–50.

18 Woodruff, *Indian Oasis*, 33–37. Employees were also required to serve as Sunday school teachers at the schools.

19 Inspection Report, Special Agent L. A. Dorrington, 20–27 October 1916, Section I, 17, Hoopa File, Dorrington Records, box 5, NARA SB. See also SBFP 37.

20 *Rules and Regulations Governing the Department of the Interior* 1907, 24.

21 Minnie Braithwaite was asked to stop hosting an evening social hour because a coworker worried all the employees would be required to do so. Jenkins, *Girl from Williamsburg*, 285–86.

22 Holidays served important pedagogical purposes in the schools. See Adams, *Education for Extinction*, 191–206.

23 *Rules for Indian Schools*, 22; and ARCIA 1902, 173.

24 Iliff, *People of the Blue Water*, 245–46, 249. See also Golden, *Red Moon Called Me*, 44.

25 Ellicott and Arnold, *Land of Grasshopper Song*, 201.

26 Iliff, *People of the Blue Water*, 252–53.

27 SBFP 442; ibid.; HVAD, 15 March 1919; Kneale, *Indian Agent*, 63; and SBFP 105. Sometimes Native people appropriated these new holidays and celebrations as their own or used them to mask Indigenous activities. See Iverson, *When Indians Became Cowboys*; Ellis, Lassiter, and Dunham, *Powwow*; and Bracken, *The Potlatch Papers*, 221.

28 Iliff, *People of the Blue Water*, 44–46, 182; Horne, *Essie's Story*, 65. See also Golden, *Red Moon Called Me*, 73; and HVAD, 10 August 1919.

29 Ruckman, "Indian Schooling in New Mexico," 53.

30 Those communities could just as easily be split by resentment and jealousy as they could provide entertainment and companionship. Peterson, "'Holy Women' and Housekeepers," 258.

31 Kneale, *Indian Agent*, 44.

32 Ibid., 59.

33 Duncan, *Blue Star*, 176, 184. Both Holmes and Fellows were white women married to Native men. *Official Register of the United States* (1891), 700.

34 Hedgpeth temporarily worked as boy's matron in 1903. SBFP 447.

35 NMHP, 20 June 1901.

36 NMHP, 22 June, 30 June, and 2 July 1901.

37 NMHP, 5, 9, 13, 16, 24 July 1901; 22 August 1901; 2, 19, 25, 26 September 1901; 22 October 1901; 30 November 1901; 31 December 1901; 13, 14, 22, 25 January 1902. Many of Hedgpeth's photographs are available in the Phoebe Hearst Collection at University of California, Berkeley, and several are included in this book. See images 2.3, 6.3. and 7.2.

38 If they were close enough to local towns, the white employees often found entertainment there. See Golden, *Red Moon Called Me*, 96; Iliff, *People of the Blue Water*, 229; and Lomawaima and McCarty, *To Remain an Indian*, 54–55.

39 Horne, *Essie's Story*, 57.

40 Superintendent Tidwell to CIA, 31 March 1922; Superintendent Tidwell to CIA, 9 November 1921; and MK to CIA, 21 December 1927, all in Maggie Keith, PF NPRC. One employee was chastised for a party thrown by his son. See Riney, *Rapid City Indian School*, 181.

41 CIA to West, 6 June 1921, Ada Rice, PF NPRC. See also Lomawaima and McCarty, *To Remain an Indian*, 54–55

42 ARCIA 1900, 19; ARCIA 1895, 9.

43 ARCIA 1905, 43.

44 Thisba Hutson Morgan, "Reminiscences of My Days in the Land of the Ogal-lala Sioux," 46. See also Peterson, "'Holy Women' and Housekeepers," 258; and Patricia A. Carter, "'Completely Discouraged,'" 67.

45 Kneale, *Indian Agent*, 54 and 72.

46 NMHP, 30 November 1901. See also NMHP, 8 August 1901.

47 Golden, *Red Moon Called Me*, 63. See also Iliff, *People of the Blue Water*, 248.

48 Iliff, *People of the Blue Water*, 220–23. See also Duncan, *Blue Star*, 191–92.

49 Golden, *Red Moon Called Me*, 32–34, 39–41. White employees were sometimes horrified by what they witnessed. See Iliff, "The Medicine Man at Work."

50 The Tuells were at Lame Deer on the Northern Cheyenne Reservation from 1906 to 1912. Grinnell later used Tuell's photographs to illustrate his book, *The Cheyenne Indians*. Aadland, *Women and Warriors*, xiii.

51 Aadland, *Women and Warriors*, 6. After he retired from the Indian Service, Thomas Marquis moved to Hardin, Montana, and became the historian for a number of his Native friends. For example, he edited Wooden Leg's (Northern Cheyenne) autobiography, *A Warrior Who Fought Custer* (1931). Krupat, *Native American Autobiography*, 171–72.

52 Kneale, *Indian Agent*, 48–49, 53. For other white employees who spoke Native languages, see Duncan, *Blue Star*, 166–67; Efficiency Report, 1914, Timothy J. Burbank, PF NPRC; and Chief Clerk Hauke to the Secretary of the Interior, 30 August 1909, Charles M. Buchanan, PF NPRC.

53 Golden, *Red Moon Called Me*, 81; and Aadland, *Women and Warriors*, 64–71.

54 During the Cold War, however, new concerns arose about tribal communities being communistic. See Rosier, "'They Are Ancestral Homelands.'"

55 Iliff, *People of the Blue Water*, 6, 271; see also 53, 245, 255, and 263. But Iliff's earlier writings were much less celebratory. See Iliff, "The Medicine Man at Work."

56 Estelle Aubrey Brown, *Stubborn Fool*, forward.

57 For a discussion of similar antimodern attitudes, see Jacobs, *Engendered Encounters*; and Lears, *No Place of Grace*.

58 Golden, *Red Moon Called Me*, 34.

59 Ibid., 10.

60 Kneale, *Indian Agent*, 67.

61 The incident occurred while the Kneales were stationed at the Unitah and Ouray Reservation between 1914 and 1923. Kneale, *Indian Agent*, 306–7.

62 ARCIA 1902, 43. Kneale's tenure in the Indian Service overlapped with the Collier administration, and it may be that he was influenced by the ideas of cultural relativism prevalent in that administration.

63 Kneale, *Indian Agent*, 41, 105.

64 On changing courtship patterns, see Rothman, *Hands and Hearts*.

65 Ruckman, "Indian Schooling in New Mexico," 47–48. See also Estelle Aubrey Brown, *Stubborn Fool*, 66; and Iliff, *People of the Blue Water*, 258.

66 SBFP 109. Corabelle Fellows remembered another couple hosting her wedding reception at their day school. Duncan, *Blue Star*, 204.

67 SBFP 356; SBFP 55.

68 Francis Colegrove, disciplinarian, and Nellie Burill Colgrove, assistant seamstress, HVEL, 102a, 103a.

69 Esther Burnett was actually in an outing program when they married but joined the Indian Service soon after. Horne, *Essie's Story*, 58. See also Vuckovic, *Voices from Haskell*, 256.

70 See *The Native American*, 3 February 1906, 39; and *The Native American*, vol. 10, no. 42 (December): 1909, 426.

71 See also Personnel Blank, 31 May 1911, Annie Abner, PF NPRC. According to the Indian Census of 1904, Abner's husband, Joseph, was Oneida. The 1938 Indian census lists him as Mohawk but enrolled at United Pueblo Agency. The federal census of 1900 lists Joseph Abner as being from New York and working as an engineer at Albuquerque Indian School. National Archives Microfilm Publication M595, 1938, roll M595_626, United Pueblos, 1; National Archives Microfilm Publication M595, 1904, roll M595_1, "Casa Blanca Band of Pueblo Indians," 2; and U.S. Census 1900, "Duranes, Bernalillo County, New Mexico," Schedule 1, Supervisor's District 199, Enumeration District 171. Retrieved from Ancestry.com (accessed 21 August 2008). For other examples, see Principal to CIA, 16 June 1911, Jessie Morago, PF NPRC; Superintendent McGregor to CIA, 6 September 1927, Katie Brewer, PF NPRC; and Industrial Survey, Jack St. Germain, Lac Du Flambeau Agency, NARA GLR, 1922 (digital version accessed on Arc catalog, 27 August 2008).

72 Allen, "Does Euro-think Become Us?," 10. Other scholars have argued that intertribal marriage weakens tribal ties. See Gonzalez, "Ojibwa Women and Marriage." Much of the literature on Native intermarriage focuses on interracial marriage, and the discussions of intertribal marriage that do exist tend to focus on the twentieth-century urban Indian experience. See, for example, Paredes, "Chippewa Townspeople"; Ritzenthaler and Sellers, "Indians in an Urban Situation"; Willard, "Outing, Relocation, and Employment Assistance"; and Weibel-Orlando, *Indian Country, L.A.*, 34–38.

73 Horne, *Essie's Story*, 74.

74 Conversation with Jack Norton Jr., 13 December 2008, Albuquerque, N.M.

75 Efficiency Report, 1 May 1926; Superintendent McGregor to CIA, 6 September 1927; O. H. Lipps, District Supt. in Charge, to CIA, 14 October 1930; and Personnel Blank, 11 May 1912, all in Katie Brewer, PF NPRC.

76 Schubnell, *N. Scott Momaday*, 15–18; and Momaday, *Conversations with N. Scott Momaday*, 217–18.

77 In 1934, for example, 149 of the 1,575 married couples (9 percent) on Rosebud Reservation were composed of white men married to Lakota women, and sixty-eight (4 percent) were composed of white women married to Lakota men. Biolsi, *Deadliest Enemies*, 5.

78 See Perdue, *"Mixed Blood" Indians*; Smits, "'Squaw Men,'"; and Hagan, "Squaw Men."

79 Lottie Horne was the aunt of Bob Horne (Essie's husband). SBFP 431 and 344.

80 See especially Superintendent, Crow Agency to CIA, 25 April 1925; and Memo, Chief of Education Division to Mr. Merritt n.d., both in Harriet H. Kyselka, PF NPRC.

81 Autta Nevitt (Delaware) married Ray Parrett, superintendent at Bishop School in California. Harriet Holliday (Chippewa) married Frank Kyselka, who served as superintendent at Hoopa Valley. See Autta Nevitt, PF NPRC; and Frank Kyselka, PF NPRC. Autta Nevitt wrote that she was a Delaware from Kansas. Like Addie Molzahn, she may have phenotypically appeared white, since the census enumerator listed both women as white but the Indian Service employed them as Indians. Personnel Blank, n.d., Autta Nevitt, PF NPRC. See also Efficiency Report, 21 January 1910, Ida Lewis, PF NPRC; and Rand, "Red, White, and Black."

82 The employee lists in the ARCIA reveal that many Native men and white women—William and Rebecca Holmes and J. B. and A. M. Freeland, for example—taught in the day schools. A more in-depth examination of these employee lists would probably also reveal similar couples in the boarding schools and agency service, such as Theodore and Ella Branchaud, who worked together as janitor and cook at the White Earth Boarding School. ARCIA 1895, 530–31, 542. See also William Holmes to CIA, 20 June 1891, LR #23892. Katherine Ellinghaus has identified three other couples at the Hampton School, and Glenda Riley also notes two white teachers who chose to marry Native men. Ellinghaus, "Assimilation by Marriage," 285; and Riley, Women and Indians on the Frontier, 201. In 1893 William Howard commented on interracial marriage at the Dawes Institute (later the Santa Fe Indian School): "I don't doubt that they love each other. But that is not all that should be considered." Ruckman, "Indian Schooling in New Mexico," 57.

83 Smits, "'Squaw Men,'" 42; Ellinghaus, "Assimilation by Marriage"; and Biolsi, Deadliest Enemies, 5–6.

84 Harper's Weekly, 15 August 1895, 531; and Elaine Goodale Eastman, Pratt, 198.

85 Stephen R. Riggs to John Eaton, 27 August 1877, quoted in Smits, "'Squaw Men,'" 46.

86 For a detailed discussion of the men's heritage, see Cahill, "You Think It Strange," 112–13 and n. 33.

87 This finding confirms Katherine Ellinghaus's conclusions about similar couples who met in the eastern boarding schools of Carlisle and Hampton. See Ellinghaus, Taking Assimilation to Heart.

88 Samuel Campbell, Joseph Estes, and Charles Eastman, all Dakota men, had attended missionary schools during their early years.

89 Joseph Estes, PF NPRC. On Campbell, see New York Times, 29 April 1888.

90 See Wellington Salt, PF NPRC; Application form of Richard Smith, 9 July 1894, LR #25547; M. M. Lemmond to CIA, 24 October 1893, LR #25547; and Wilson, Ohiyesa, 20–26, 32–33.

91 In 1890, 3.49 percent of all seventeen-year-olds were high school graduates; by 1900 that had risen to 6.38 percent. Susan B. Carter, Historical Statistics of the United States, 393, 421.

92 On the ordination of Native men, see Bonnie Sue Lewis, Creating Christian Indians, 67–90.

93 Pilling, Bibliography of Siouan Languages, 21.

94 Brudvig, Hampton Normal and Agricultural Institutes American Indian Students,

1878–1923. See Joseph Estes, Hampton Institute Alumni student files. Many thanks to Bert Ahern for generously sharing his notes on Estes with me.

95 Wilson, *Ohiyesa*, 83.

96 Application, n.d., and Efficiency Report, 1 April 1912, Wellington Salt, PF NPRC.

97 See Prucha, *The Churches and the Indian Schools*; and Bonnie Sue Lewis, *Creating Christian Indians.*

98 See Record of Employees in Indian Service application for Edith Salt, n.d., Wellington Salt, PF NPRC.

99 Personnel Record, n.d., and AE to CIA, 15 April 1918, Anna Estes, PF NPRC.

100 It may be that Hoffman's father was born in England and emigrated through Canada, but that is unclear. See Charlotte S. Hoffman in U.S. Census 1900, "Fort Berthold Agency, McLean County, North Dakota," Schedule 1, Supervisor's District 199, Enumeration District 261B; U.S. Census 1910, "Fort Berthold Agency, McLean County, North Dakota," Indian Population, Supervisor's District 2, Enumeration District 241; and U.S. Census 1920, "McLean County, North Dakota," Supervisor's District 247, Enumeration District 114. Retrieved from Ancestry.com (accessed 24 May 2007).

101 Duncan, *Blue Star*, 52; Minnie E. Dickson to CIA, Washington, D.C., 25 April 1893, LR #15208; Application, 14 March 1924, Edith Salt, PF NPRC.

102 Elaine Goodale Eastman, *Sister to the Sioux*, 3.

103 The records for Salt and Hoffman commence after their marriages. Fellows, Dickson, Goodale, and Johnson were all employed before their marriages. Anna Johnson was working as a cook at the Lower Brule School in South Dakota when she met Joseph Estes, who was a day-school teacher on the reservation. AE to CIA, 15 April 1918, PF NPRC. It is possible that William and Rebecca Holmes initially met while he was a student and she was a matron at the Santee Boarding School. Application for Appointment of William and Rebecca Holmes, LR #23892.

104 Fellows was remarkably strict in her support of the ideology of total assimilation, as we saw in chapter 3; but after hours, she enjoyed learning about Dakota culture and often spent her vacations traveling across the reservation with Dakota families. Duncan, *Blue Star*, 157, 166–67, 187, 191–92.

105 Ibid., 183.

106 Bliss-Isely Collection, box 4, MS 91-2, folder 2.

107 Duncan, *Blue Star*, 183, 200–201. A newspaper article asserted that Campbell was "employed by the bureau of Indian Affairs and is stationed at Fort Bennett." *Bismarck Daily Tribune*, 27 March 1888, 1.

108 Wilson, *Ohiyesa*, 41.

109 Elaine Goodale Eastman, *Sister to the Sioux*, 43.

110 Ibid., 153.

111 Charles A. Eastman, *From Deep Woods*, 86–89.

112 See Alfred Dickson, U.S. Bureau of the Census, U.S. Census 1870, "Chautauqua County, New York," Schedule 1, 9; and U.S. Census 1880, "Chautauqua County, New York," Schedule 1, 14, Supervisor's District 11, Enumeration District 62. Retrieved from Ancestry.com (accessed 24 May 2007).

113 Minnie E. Dickson to CIA, 25 April 1893, LR #15208.

114 Minnie E. Dickson to CIA, 26 July 1892, LR #27123.

115 Andrew Spencer to Acting CIA, 14 April 1893, LR #13592.

116 Mrs. Samuel Campbell to CIA, 12 July 1888, LR #17909.

117 Elaine Goodale Eastman, *Sister to the Sioux*, 172.

118 Joseph Escalanti was married to a Yuma woman who also worked at the school. After an Indian Office investigation of Escalanti and Miss Rachel for having an affair, he tragically shot and killed himself. See Estelle Aubrey Brown, *Stubborn Fool*, 125–30; and Golden, *Red Moon Called Me*, 99–100. See also Charles L. Davis, Supervisor Ft. Yuma School, to CIA, 11 April 1910; and Report of Harwood Hall, Supervisor of Indian Schools, 10 April 1910, both in Joseph Escalanti, PF NPRC.

119 Rev. Suate Ocol and R. H. Smith to Secretary of the Interior, 26 April 1893, LR #16041.

120 See Connell-Szasz, *Between Indian and White Worlds*.

121 For example, Richard Smith's mother was a white woman married to a Cherokee man, and Charles Eastman's grandfather was a white man who had a relationship with a Dakota woman. Mooney, "Myths of the Cherokee," 178.

122 Charles A. Eastman, *From Deep Woods*, 105–6. See also Elaine Goodale Eastman, *Sister to the Sioux*, 43; and Wilson, *Ohiyesa*, 43–47.

123 *Washington Post*, 26 February 1888; and *New York Times*, 24 March 1888. Fellows never referred to Campbell as Chaska. It is possible that the press conferred the name as a way to refer back to another "civilized" Indian who saved a white woman by pretending to be her husband during the Minnesota "Sioux Uprising" or Dakota War of 1862. That first Chaska was hanged for his participation in the event despite the woman's efforts to defend him. See Namias, *White Captives*, 204–61.

124 See "A Social Sensation: A Former Washington Girl to Wed a Sioux Indian," *Washington Post*, 26 February 1888; and Auntie May to Corabelle Fellows, Sunday, February 26, 1887, and Maria to Corabelle Fellows, 24 March 1885, Bliss-Isely Collection, MS 91-2, box 4, folder 6. See also Duncan, *Blue Star*, 201–2.

125 *Lincoln Evening News*, 4 August 1891.

126 *Middletown Daily Argus*, 2 April 1894.

127 *Lorain County Reporter*, 25 January 1896. Apparently warnings were necessary because young white women kept marrying Indian men. In 1893 the *Sioux Valley News* ran an article titled "Wedded an Indian: Fellows-Chaska Case Duplicated at Sisseton Agency," which was about a white missionary who married her coworker at the mission. Correctionville (Iowa) *Sioux Valley News*, 1 June 1893. See also *Lincoln Evening News*, 4 August 1891; *Freeborn County Standard*, 7 March 1894; *Manitoba Morning Free Press*, 20 February 1894; and *Lorain County Reporter*, 7 May 1898.

128 *Ogden Standard*, 21 February 1894.

129 *Newark Daily Advocate*, 23 April 1894.

130 The public was fascinated by pairings of white women and Indian men. See "An Indian Marriage," *New York Times*, 21 March 1888; "Virginian Wins Indian Bride," *New York Times*, 6 March 1904; "Indian Weds White Girl," *New York Times*, 20 February 1905; "Indian Weds White Girl," *Washington Post*, 3 January 1907; "White Girl Weds Indian," *Washington Post*, 28 December 1907; "Denver Girl

Weds Indian," *New York Times*, 28 December 1907; and "White Girl Weds Indian," *Washington Post*, 5 November 1907. See also Phil Deloria's analysis of the way in which this theme was handled in early twentieth-century film in *Indians in Unexpected Places*, 94–103.

131 Duncan, *Blue Star*, 204–5.

132 *Washington Post*, 7 May 1888.

133 *New York Times*, 6 October 1888, 5; and "Chaska's Marriage to Cora B. Fellows: Dime Show Earnings Wasted," *New York Times*, 26 December 1888.

134 "Their Marriage a Failure," *Frederick News*, 26 December 1888.

135 For a discussion of the way race and consumption were interlinked, see Bederman, *Manliness and Civilization*, 1–44.

136 Duncan, *Blue Star*, 204.

137 Elaine Goodale Eastman, *Sister to the Sioux*, 169. In his memoir, Charles also mentioned the Reverend Charles Smith Cook—"a Yankton Sioux graduate of Trinity College and Seabury Divinity School"—and his white wife, a young New York woman. They may have been the couple to whom Elaine was referring. See Charles Eastman, *From Deep Woods*, 85–86.

138 Both of the memoirs are refracted through editors. Goodale's was published posthumously; Fellows, who was blind, told her story to Kunigunde Duncan, who then edited it for publication. It is unclear who chose the titles for the two memoirs.

139 Aron, *Working at Play*, 64.

140 *Daily Mitchell Republican*, 21 August 1891. While Fellows is quoted as calling her husband "Sam Chaska," I suspect that the reporter took this liberty so that his readers would know to whom she was referring.

141 For example, the *Waukesha Freeman* reported: "Mrs. Cora Fellows Chaska is bringing suit for divorce from her husband, Sam Chaska. . . . Probably the matrimonial venture of Mrs. Elaine Goodale Eastman will result likewise." *Waukesha Freeman*, 27 June 1891.

142 See *Lincoln Evening News*, 4 August 1891; *Freeborn County Standard*, 7 March 1894; *Manitoba Morning Free Press*, 20 February 1894; and *Lorain County Reporter*, 7 May 1898.

143 Improper relationships with the opposite sex were often used in this way. Ellen Rothman, a historian of courting, has described this period as a transition in gender relations when "men's and women's separate spheres were contracting and overlapping, but the boundary lines were still highly charged and difficult to approach." Adding race to the mixture made those dangerous lines more volatile still. Rothman, *Hands and Hearts*, 192. Apparently, this also sometimes happened to white men, although it was rare. Gordon Lillie, later know by the stage name Pawnee Bill, was accused of sexual misconduct with his female Indian students during a heated political struggle on the Pawnee reservation. See Shirley, *Pawnee Bill*, 79.

144 Golden, *Red Moon Called Me*, 26–27.

145 For example, in 1906 at the Wittenberg Agency in Wisconsin, Ida F. Clayton, the white field matron, was dismissed after marrying a Native man. Her superintendent, S. A. M. Young, wrote to the Office of Indian Affairs and recommended

that her position be discontinued until "it is possible to secure the services of a woman with a little more dignity." In 1909 Superintendent Wise of the Chilocco School charged that Miss Mary Broad, a white teacher, was lacking in morals because "she is indiscreet in her attitude toward some of the older Indian boys." The following year, she resigned to marry one of them. Quoted in Emmerich, "'To Respect and Love,'" 181; and Superintendent Wise to CIA, 1 November 1909, Miss Mary Broad, PF NPRC.

146 Andrew Spencer to CIA, 12 April 1893, LR #13592.

147 A. Spencer to Acting CIA, 14 April 1893, LR #13592.

148 Minnie E. Dickson to CIA, 22 May 1893, LR #18969.

149 Minnie E. Dickson to CIA, 24 July 1893, LR #27599.

150 The Eastern Cherokee presented a particular case because they had only recently come under federal supervision and had a history of self-determination. They had even been allowed to vote in state elections. Because of North Carolina's refusal to recognize them as full citizens, they looked to federal supervision to provide protection—especially the right to sue to recover their land. Also, because the federal government believed that the Eastern Cherokee would eventually join their relatives in Indian Territory, they had not been recognized as a separate tribe, nor had they received federal supervision until 1869 or an agent until 1875. Finger, *The Eastern Band of Cherokee*, 113, 125, 139.

151 R. H. Smith to CIA, 29 July 1893, LR #28336.

152 R. H. Smith to CIA, April 1893, LR #15883.

153 R. H. Smith to CIA, 29 July 1893, LR #28336. Emphasis in original.

154 Although the couples primarily defended their relationships in terms of behavior, when those arguments were rejected, they did sometimes fall back on the language of race as a last resort. Smith's joke here, and both Fellows's and Dickson's description of their husbands as being of mixed-race heritage, illustrate their desperate efforts to curtail the criticism they encountered, even at the expense of undermining their own previous arguments. See *New York Times*, 9 April 1888; and Dickson to CIA, 24 July 1893, LR #27599.

155 Smith was the son of Nimrod Smith (Tsaladihi) and a white woman. Virginia Carney, who has studied the life of Smith's sister, Lottie, asserts that they were enrolled in the tribe despite their mother's white heritage and the Cherokee matrilineal system of descent. Carney, *Eastern Band Cherokee Women*, 199 n. 42; and Perdue, *"Mixed Blood" Indians*, 35.

156 Joseph Estes to CIA, 7 August 1897, LR #33364; Joseph F. Estes to Dr. Wm. Hailmann, 6 October 1897, LR #42328; and Joseph Estes to Superintendent of Indian Schools, 3 December 1900, LR #60135.

157 JE to CIA, 13 March 1901, Joseph Estes, PF NPRC.

158 AE to CIA, 20 March 1901, Anna Estes, PF NPRC. A similar incident seems to have taken place at Western Shoshone in 1911. See George H. Paul to Senator F. H. Warren, 11 February 1911, Michael H. Brown, PF NPRC.

159 AE to CIA, 20 March 1901, Anna Estes, PF NPRC.

160 Acting Comm. Abbott to Chas. Hoffman, letter #75144–1912, Charles Hoffman, PF NPRC.

161 Efficiency Report, 1 November 1913, Wellington Salt, PF NPRC.

162 Efficiency Report, 8 November 1910, Wellington Salt, PF NPRC. Salt himself recorded his "race" as "Canadian" or "English [and] Indian," but his supervisors had difficulty pinning down his identity. Over the years, whites described him variously as "Indian," "mixed-blood," "half-breed," "Mixed Blood Chippewa," and "Indian ¹⁄₁₆ or ¹⁄₃₂"; as having "a very slight amount of Indian blood"; and, by the end of his career, as "white." See Wellington Salt, PF NPRC. At least once, Mrs. Salt was misidentified as "Indian." See ARCIA 1896, 582. It is possible that having grown up in Canada, Wellington Salt felt more comfortable with a mixed or Métis heritage than did white Americans, who understood race in terms of a dichotomy. See Thorne, *The Many Hands of My Relations*.

163 Charles Eastman had several clashes with his white superiors; in one of them, the agent charged Eastman with having an extramarital affair with a white female employee and of inappropriate relations with a white patient. Wilson, *Ohiyesa*, 70–77; 111–16.

164 Biolsi, *Deadliest Enemies*, 5

165 More work remains to be done on how Native communities responded to those relationships.

CHAPTER SEVEN

1 The tribal designation is Hupa, while the geographic term is Hoopa.

2 Of the irregular Indian employees, 11,479 were men and 941 were women. There were 2,516 regular Indian employees, of whom 1,995 were men and 521 were women. ARCIA 1912, 164–65. Those numbers were based upon the reports of supervisors but do not correlate the salary lists that report 2,033 Indian employees and 3,632 regular white employees. ARCIA 1912, 307.

3 This chapter relies heavily on Nelson, *Our Home Forever*.

4 The Hupa and their neighbors tended to use the flow of water to describe directions. See Kroeber, *Handbook of the Indians of California*, 15; and Goddard, *Life and Culture of the Hupa*, 13–18. See also David Rich Lewis, *Neither Wolf nor Dog*, 79–80, 90; Bell, *Karuk*, 7; Norton, *Genocide in Northwestern California*, 11–12; and Steinberg, Dunk, and Comet, *In Hoopa Territory*, 12.

5 The Hupa heard about the Spanish and traded for European goods with neighbors, but they did not actually see whites until the 1820s. David Rich Lewis, *Neither Wolf nor Dog*, 71, 82–83.

6 Nelson, *Our Home Forever*; David Rich Lewis, *Neither Wolf nor Dog*, 82–83.

7 David Rich Lewis, *Neither Wolf nor Dog*, 83; Norton, *Genocide in Northwestern California*, 40.

8 Cited in Norton, *Genocide in Northwestern California*, 38.

9 Norton describes other massacres in the areas around Hoopa Valley including the Hayfork Massacre of 1852, the killing of over 150 Tolowa people at Yontoket on the Smith River in 1853 and another attack in 1854, the 1860 annihilation of an entire village of Wiyot on Indian Island in Humboldt Bay, and the 1863 massacre of a Mattole village at Squaw Creek. Norton, *Genocide in Northwestern California* 26, 41–43, 47–50, 65, 82–85, 96 and David Rich Lewis, *Neither Wolf nor Dog*, 85.

10 Norton, *Genocide in Northwestern California*, 66.

11 These conflicts were much more complicated than described here; see Nelson, *Our Home Forever*, 47–89.

12 Norton, *Genocide in Northwestern California*, 99–100, 111; David Rich Lewis, *Neither Wolf nor Dog*, 84–88. Many California tribes negotiated treaties with the U.S. government, which were not ratified. Unlike many of the Southern California tribes, however, the Hupa tribe's distance from white communities helped it retain its land base. See Lee Davis, "California Tribes," in *Encyclopedia of North American Indians*, 94–98.

13 Nelson, *Our Home Forever*, 88–90, 181–88. The Hupa and Yurok reservations were separated in 1988. For more on the Yurok tribe, see Buckley *Standing Ground*, 40–49.

14 HVEL, 97.

15 Kroeber, *Handbook of the Indians of California*, 130. In 1888 the population was given as 650, in 1900 as 430, and in 1905 as 412. David Rich Lewis, *Neither Wolf nor Dog*, 79.

16 "50 Years of Progress."

17 ARCIA 1902, 170.

18 Reed and Arnold, *In the Land of Grasshopper Song*, 21.

19 SBFP 37.

20 ARCIA 1912, 164–65.

21 HVEL.

22 ARCIA 1887, 7.

23 Mortsolf to CIA, 13 December 1911 [i], folder 5, box 130, series 52, HVA.

24 Nelson, *Our Home Forever*, 18.

25 In this paragraph, I depend heavily on Nelson, *Our Home Forever*. See also, David Rich Lewis, *Neither Wolf nor Dog*, 79; Bell, *Karuk*, 84–107; and Goddard, *Life and Culture of the Hupa*.

26 Norton, *Genocide in Northwestern California*, 6–7.

27 *Acorn*, 28 October 1899, in SBFP 48. Injuries were common. Policeman Arthur Saxton resigned in 1908 because of "injuries rec'd thrown from horse." HVEL, 158.

28 ARCIA 1883, 11. See also ARCIA 1902, 171.

29 ARCIA 1885, 4–5; ARCIA 1887, 7; ARCIA 1884, 12. Nelson makes a similar argument in *Our Home Forever*, 102–8.

30 ARCIA 1887, 7.

31 Berryman Lack held this position for the first part of the 1887–88 year for $360. James Marshall served for the second half of the year and also received $360. ARCIA 1888, 394.

32 The white employees were born in Virginia, Iowa, Illinois, Nova Scotia, Ireland, and Germany.

33 Three Native men were paid ten dollars per month, but no distinction as to their work was made.

34 ARCIA 1888, 9.

35 A total of thirty-eight Indian men worked in both regular and irregular positions during the second quarter of 1888. According to the agent's report, there were 134 males over the age of eighteen on the reservation. HVEL, 16–18; and ARCIA 1888, 9.

36 HVEL, 17; Nelson lists these men as reservation leaders in *Our Home Forever*, 108.

37 ARCIA 1896, 539–51.

38 ARCIA 1887, 8–9; and 50th Congress, 1st Session, H.R. Ex. Doc. No. 44, 2. See also David Rich Lewis, *Neither Wolf nor Dog*, 97

39 This figure was derived using the consumer price index converter at ⟨eh.net/ hmit/⟩ (accessed 14 June 2010).

40 ARCIA 1892, 228–29. The exact balance of paid and unpaid road labor is unclear. In 1892 the government was paying men to work on the road. Subsequent discussions in the ARCIA indicate that the government attempted to institute corvée labor, but it was difficult to get good men to work without wages. See ARCIA 1902, 174; ARCIA 1905, 187; *Reports of the Department of the Interior for the Fiscal Year Ended June 30, 1913*, 13; and ARCIA 1916, 19.

41 50th Congress, 1st Session, H.R. Ex. Doc. No. 44, 44; and ARCIA 1887, 9.

42 ARCIA 1892, 228–29. See also ARCIA 1889, 124; ARCIA 1879, 9; and ARCIA 1885, 6

43 ARCIA 1903, 140.

44 ARCIA 1903, 143; ARCIA 1905, 186. See also ARCIA 1916, 21.

45 SBFP 90. McGowan was the senator from the fifth district; see *Journal of the Senate during the Thirty-first Session of the Legislature of the State of California* (Sacramento, 1895), 981.

46 SBFP 51

47 SBFP 52. See also, ARCIA 1905, 29.

48 Very few Native women appear among the long lists of men in the first years of the ledger. The first, temporary seamstress Louisa Piban, appeared in the employee ledger in 1888. HVEL1888, 14. In the fourth quarter of 1890, Piban and Mary Marshall were employed as seamstresses; HVEL 30. In 1892 Susie Lack, Josie Glen, and Sarah Sherman, all Native, worked as temporary cooks, Lack for twenty-three days and Glen and Sherman for eleven days for 75 cents per day. HVEL 1892, 41–42.

49 ARCIA 1896, 126.

50 HVEL, 83. The U.S. Census describes her as "Wishoskan" (now Wiyot), from Humboldt Bay, and white. 12th U.S. Census, Carlisle, Cumberland, Pennsylvania; roll T623_1401, Enumeration District, 167. Retrieved from Ancestry.com (accessed 9 January 2008).

51 Lottie Horne was listed as Klamath (now Yurok) and white. U.S. Census 1900, "Hoopa Valley Indian Reservation, Humboldt, California," roll T623_87, 10B, Enumeration District 207. Retrieved from Ancestry.com (accessed 9 January 2008).

52 HVEL, 83. Although the ledger lists her as Indian, in the federal census she was listed as white—with the exception of the 1880 census taker, who noted that her mother was ½ white and Jessie was ¾ white. No tribal affiliation was listed. U.S. Census 1880, "Redwood, Humboldt, California," roll 65, Family History Film, 1254065, 319D, Enumeration District 27. Retrieved from Ancestry.com (accessed 9 January 2008).

53 All of the nonlocal Native employees appear to be employed at the school rather than the agency, with two exceptions: August Lucien and Harriet Kyselka,

both of whom started in school service and transferred to agency service while at Hoopa. The nonlocal employees were Sarah Cliffe from Washington State, assistant matron, HVEL 1897, 98; Emma Robart from Wisconsin, assistant matron, HVEL 1898, 100; Herbert Thorton from Oregon, baker, HVEL 1898, 102, 104; Joseph Teaba from Washington State (former pupil at Chemawa, Oregon), baker, HVEL 1899, 108; Carrie Cornelius from Wisconsin, assistant laundress, HVEL 1899, 108, 117, 119, 121, 125, 127; Perry Tsamanwa from Laguna, New Mexico, shoe and harness maker, former Carlisle student, HVEL 1899, 110, 117, 121, 125, 127, 135; George F. Hazlett from Montana, assistant industrial teacher, former Carlisle student, HVEL 1900, 117, 119; Matilda Kruger from Vancouver, Washington, seamstress, HVEL 1900, 117, 121, 125, 127, 135, 138, 142, 146, 153, 159; Ella P. Dennis from Illinois, HVEL 1900, 119, 121, 123; Rosa Lucier from Oregon, assistant cook, HVEL 1900, 121, 127; August Lucier from Oregon (he transferred to the agency first as a temporary painter and then as a farmer in second quarter of 1901), HVEL 1901, 123, 125, 128; Sara L. Kennedy from Gowanda, New York, HVEL 1901, 125, 127; Martha Owl from North Carolina, Eastern Band of Cherokee, assistant cook, HVEL 1901, 127; Harriet H. Kyselka from Michigan (most likely L'Anse band of Chippewa), teacher, assistant matron, matron, clerk (she also briefly served in the agency as financial clerk), HVEL 1902, 135, 138, 142, 146, 148, 156, 159, 160; Alonzo Spieche from Arizona, former Carlisle student, shoe and harness maker, HVEL, 1903, 138; Delia Randell from Washington state, nurse, HVEL 1903, 138 (according to SBFP, she "is a full blood Idaho Indian lady, a graduate of the Carlisle Indian school and of the famous new Haven School for nurses," SBFP 450); Sam Oitema (Hopi) from Arizona, shoe and harness maker, former Phoenix Indian School student, HVEL 1906, 149, 153, 156, 159; and Mary Crook from Washington state, assistant matron, HVEL 1909, 159.

54 Harriet Kyselka, the wife of Superintendent Kyselka, was an exception. She often filled temporary positions, fitting the pattern for wives of superintendents.

55 SBFP 450 and 99.

56 Nelson, *Our Home Forever*, 140; ARCIA 1906, 203; and Horne, *Essie's Story*, 58.

57 Inspection Report, Special Agent L. A. Dorrington, 20–27 October 1916, section 5, 2, Hoopa File, Dorrington Records, box 5, NARA SB.

58 I have supplemented the entries with information from throughout the diary and with identifying information from the federal censuses of 1900, 1910, 1920, and 1930 as well as the California Indian Census records, all retrieved from Ancestry.com. For other examples of multiple internal transfers, see Superintendent to CIA, 21 July 1915, Violetta Nash, PF NPRC; and LB to CIA, 25 October 1921, Leo Bonnin, PF NPRC.

59 HVAD, 24 May 1919 to 4 June 1919.

60 U.S. Census 1920, "Klamath, Humboldt, California," roll T625_98, 5A, Enumeration District 57.

61 HVAD, 10, 19, 22, and 26 March 1919; 16 and 21 July 1919; 12 and 31 August 1919; and 1 September 1919.

62 HVEL, 159; HVAD, 2 January, 8 July, 11 August, and 31 October 1919; "List of

Employees on rolls of the Interior Department for Hoopa Valley," 5 August 1925, folder: Civil Service Commission, box 56, series 51, HVA.

63 U.S. Census 1920, "Klamath, Humboldt, California," roll T625_98, 1A, Enumeration District 57; and HVAD, 5, 21, and 24 May 1919.

64 Mrs. Moses had worked as a seamstress at Oregon's Warm Springs Agency in 1908. See letter, 25 July 1908, Emily Hunt, PF NPRC; and U.S. Census 1920, "Klamath, Humboldt, California," roll T625_98, 1A, Enumeration District 57.

65 HVEL.

66 HVEL.

67 Information on Tonini from U.S. Census 1900, "Hydesville, Humboldt, California," roll T623_87, 12A, Enumeration District 27; and U.S. Census 1930, "Honolulu, Honolulu, Hawaii Territory," roll 2633, 1A, Enumeration District 16. On Preston: U.S. Census 1910, "Union, Humboldt, California," roll T624_77, 6A, Enumeration District 29; and U.S. Census 1920, "Eureka Ward 3, Humboldt, California," roll T625_98, 6A, Enumeration District 52.

68 Daisy Hill was the laundress for the agency hospital in 1925. "List of Employees on rolls of the Interior Department for Hoopa Valley," 5 August 1925, folder: Civil Service Commission, box 56, series 51, HVA.

69 Invasive species including wild mustard, Canadian thistle, and blackberry also entered the valley. David Rich Lewis, *Neither Wolf nor Dog*, 91–97. In 1887 a salmon cannery was opened at the Yurok village of Requa by whites who disregarded the Yurok and Hupa concerns about the health of their fisheries. Agent Dougherty supported the tribes, but the canneries continued unregulated until 1933, when the state banned commercial fishing on the river. Conservative estimates suggest that at a peak in 1912, the canneries harvested 141,000 salmon (over 1.384 million pounds canned), which does not include the offshore commercial harvest of approximately 200,000 fish originating in the Klamath River. Steinberg, Dunk, and Comet, *In Hoopa Territory*, 78.

70 Hupa men did not leave for outside wage work in great numbers until 1923, when the new road made it easier to travel back and forth. David Rich Lewis, *Neither Wolf nor Dog*, 107.

71 The memo indicated that there was great demand from Indians for Service positions across the country. Reports of Returned Students, 13 June 1913, Inspection and Investigation Reports, box 131, folder no. 9 [i], Returned Students 1914–17, series 53, HVA.

72 Whiteley, "Why Anthropology Needs More History." Rand notes the importance of being able to participate in everyday routines in *Kiowa Humanity*, 7.

73 In 1902 some Hupa men worked for salmon canneries, in the lumber industry, and at shingle mills, while others hired on with sheep and cattle ranchers. ARCIA 1902, 174.

74 George Nelson, IIS, box 17, Hoopa Valley; and HVAD, 15, 19, and 22 November 1919.

75 Letter, Supt. Asbury to CIA, n.d. 1924, NARA SB; Inspection and Investigation Reports, box 131, folder no. 9 [i], Returned Students 1914–17, series 53, HVA. An inspector in 1916 noted that many of the Lower Klamath (Yurok) Indians worked for the canneries. The Annual Report of the Superintendent concurred, adding

that Hupa who wanted work could get it on road crews and small mills in the area "if they are willing to leave their homes." Inspection Report, Special Agent L. A. Dorrington, 20–27 October 1916, section 2, 1, Hoopa File, Dorrington Records, box 5, HVA.

76 HVEL and "Indian Census Rolls, 1885–1940," National Archives Microfilm Publication M595, 1893, roll M595_182, Hoopa Valley Agency, 5. Retrieved from Ancestry.com (accessed 14 November 2008).

77 The clerk between 1905 and 1909 faithfully recorded reasons for resignation. See HVEL: David Matsen, 1904, 144; Arthur Saxton, 1903, 141; Imogene Marshall, 1908, 156; and George Latham, 1907, 155. See also HVEL: Dora Saxon, 1909, n.p.; Matilda Kruger, 1909, n.p.; Robert Ferry, 1909, 156; Chas. Finch, 1904, 144, and 1909, 161; Jerry Horne, 1909, 161; Ned Jackson, 1908, 158; George Latham, 1908, 158; Sherman Roberts, 1909, 161; and Robert Jake, 1909, 161.

78 Nelson, *Our Home Forever*, 131.

79 ARCIA 1892, 228.

80 SBFP 94.

81 ARCIA 1897, 498–99; ARCIA 1900, 206. The federal government often filled the role of consumer. Between 1889 and 1905, the ARCIA presented statistics for "Indian Lands, Crops, Stock, and Labor." The numbers indicate that while the government did not purchase the majority of Indian produce, it was a substantial customer. The Indian Office took on this role to teach the lessons of equal exchange but also as a way to avoid the giving of rations.

82 They also earned $1,280 "labor for wages for Government," $2,300 "labor for others," and sold $6,066.06 worth of products to the government and $7,879.50 to others. While the report mentions a revival of basket making, the agent did not include basket sales in his "estimate of the products of Indians," though he did include agricultural produce, butter, and wood cordage. ARCIA 1901, 193.

83 ARCIA 1902, 171.

84 ARCIA 1916, 19–20.

85 See HVEL 157, 145, and 138.

86 ARCIA 1903, 140.

87 See also SBFP 45 and 48–49; ARCIA 1900, 206; and Steinberg, Dunk and Comet, *In Hoopa Territory*, 7.

88 Lomawaima and McCarty, *To Remain an Indian*, 56–58.

89 One weaver, Peachy, was married to Thomas Todi, who worked as irregular laborer for the Indian Service throughout the 1890s. U.S. Census 1920, "Klamath, Humboldt, California," roll T625_98, 1B; Enumeration District 57. Accessed 2 December 2008. See also HVEL.

90 M. E. Chase to C. Taber, 12 February 1907; Minnie G. Randolph to C. Taber, 15 May 1908; Marie Johnson to C. Taber, 2 October 1907; Marie Johnson to C. Taber, 31 October 1907; Marie Johnson to C. Taber, 6 December 1907; and Sophie R. Miller to C. Tabor, 11 August 1906, all in CTC. On the role of basket weaving in Indigenous women's economic strategies in Central California, see Barrett, *Pomo Indian Basketry*; Sarris, *Mabel McKay*; and McLendon, "Pomo Baskets."

91 See IIS, box 17, Hoopa Valley, for J. Brett, P. Freddie, C. Beaver, T. Marshall, and

G. Latham. 2 March 1926 letter on traders gives information about the Beavers; RG 75, NARA SB.

92 The survey of households at Hoopa Valley was incomplete. Only sixty-eight families were surveyed, possibly skewing the sample toward those who worked for the government. IIS, box 17, Hoopa Valley.

93 F. Colegrove, IIS, box 17, Hoopa Valley. Francis Colegrove had worked as an irregular and regular employee for the Indian Office and served as judge on the Indian Court of Offenses. HVEL, 35, 59, 127, 72, 141, and 145.

94 Despite the agent's pronouncement of Marshall as "progressive," his status was listed as that of "ward," not citizen. J. Marshall, IIS, box 17, Hoopa Valley.

95 ARCIA 1888, 9; SBFP 40. Before working for the Indian Service, he had been a packer, probably for the Brizard Company. In the employee ledger, he appears in multiple quarters: 1888:1 "Industrial Teacher (previously packer"; 1888:2 "Industrial Farmer"; 1889:1–2 "Industrial Teacher"; 1890:2–3 "Additional farmer"; 1890:4 "Asst. Farmer"; 1891:1 "Additional farmer"; 1892:4 "Irregular laborer"; 1895:3 and 1895:4 "Assistant foreman, wagon road." See HVEL, 15, 16, 19, 20, 26, 28, 30, 33, 47, 76, 79. It was most likely James that the agent was describing in 1900 when he wrote: "One of these [Indian] men supplies beef to the school and agency, the quantity furnished last year being 40,000 pounds. The supply is brought in twice or thrice weekly, dressed, and in excellent condition. This man keeps up his herd largely by purchases from white men in the surrounding country." ARCIA 1900, 206. See also SBFP, 53.

96 There are only a few years for which detailed information about Native employees is available for Hoopa Valley after 1911, but when there is, members of the Marshall family appear. Several of James and Mary's children appear in the 1919 agency diary working for the Indian Service: Mahlon Marshall was disciplinarian 1 January 1919, road-chainman 5 April 1919, and axeman 7 April 1919 and 5 August 1919. Earnest Marshall was doing road work on 11 February 1919, as were Edward (17 and 30 January 1919) and Mahlon (7 and 11 February 1919 and 22 March 1919). Edward also appeared as a farmer on 11 and 28 April 1919; 14 and 20 May 1919; 16 June 1919; 7, 9, 29, and 31 July 1919; and 6 August 1919. James Marshall Jr. worked in the hospital (he was mentioned on 12 April and 10 June 1919), while Julius hauled freight on 5 June 1919. Two of his daughters-in-law—Matilda Marshall, Edward's wife (30 June 1919), and Imogene (née Masten), Julius's wife (8 and 22 July 1919 and 11 August 1919)—also worked for the Indian Service. In 1925 three of his daughters-in-law were employed: Imogene was the cook; Lizzie (née Beaver), James Jr.'s wife, worked as a laundress; and Matilda was a temporary cook. Incidentally, none of the women were receiving retirement deductions, either because as Indian laborers they were exempt or because as temporary laborers they were ineligible. See "List of Employees on rolls of the Interior Department for Hoopa Valley," 5 August 1925, folder: Civil Service Commission, box 56, series 51, HVA.

97 Quoted in Lewis and McLester, *Oneida Lives*, 112–13.

98 Julius Marshall, IIS, box 17, Hoopa Valley.

99 HVEL 114; SBFP 280; HVAD, 2 January 1919 and 31 October 1919.

100 J. Marshall, IIS, box 17, Hoopa Valley.

101 "List of Employees on rolls of the Interior Department for Hoopa Valley," 5 August 1925, folder: Civil Service Commission, box 56, series 51, HVA.

102 J. Marshall, IIS, box 17, Hoopa Valley.

103 E. Marshall, IIS, box 17, Hoopa Valley; HVAD, 20 October, 29 November, and 22 December 1919; "World War I Draft Registration Cards, 1917–1918; Miscellaneous County, California"; roll 2022331, Draft Board: 0. Retrieved from Ancestry.com (accessed 10 June 2010).

104 SBFP 380.

105 Nelson, *Our Home Forever*, 145. Thanks to Jude Marshall for generously sharing information about his great-grandfather, Edward.

106 Edward Marshall was a council member representing the tribe at the 1934 Northwest Indian Conference discussing the Wheeler-Howard Act at Chemewa, Oregon. Vine Deloria, *The Indian Reorganization Act*, 135.

107 For a discussion of the council's actions, see Nelson, *Our Home Forever*, 174–78.

108 Earnest Jr. was James Sr.'s grandson. James Sr.'s children served on the council until 1964. The seven elected officials of the council represent the seven fields or districts that correspond to traditional village sites and make up the Hoopa Valley. See Council History PDF available on the Hupa Tribe's website, 〈http://www.hoopa-nsn.gov/government/council.htm〉 (accessed 2 February 2010).

109 Quoted in Nelson, *Our Home Forever*, 145–46. Kyselka added: "Progress along material lines has been much greater, proportionately, than along mental and spiritual ones." ARCIA 1902, 171.

110 Not all Hupa used this economic strategy. David Risling Sr. and his family do not appear in any government employment records. Risling played an important role in keeping Hupa cultural traditions alive, and during the 1950s and 1960s, he and his son, David Jr., traveled throughout California helping to revive Native dances. Trafzer, *As Long as the Grass Shall Grow and Rivers Flow*, 375.

111 ARCIA 1883, 11–13. Emphasis in original. Agent Beers made similar complaints. See ARCIA 1891, 220; and ARCIA 1892, 229.

112 See also Hagan, *Indian Police and Judges*, 69–81.

113 Nelson, *Our Home Forever*, 147–48.

114 Ibid., 214 n. 15.

115 On Masten, see HVAD, 22 July 1919. SBFP 269–71.

116 Nelson writes of Mortsolf, who served as superintendent in 1908–12 and 1915–24: "The longer he stayed in the valley, the more he objected to the Hupa's way of life." Nelso, *Our Home Forever*, 159.

117 Latham began as an industrial teacher in 1888 and became a policeman in 1893. He moved back and forth between Service positions and managing his hotel. A trustee of the Methodist church, Latham appears to have angered both white administrators and tribal members at different times. Mortsolf reported that he had been discharged from the position of chief of police for taking bribes. From these scraps of evidence, Latham appears as neither "progressive" nor "traditional" but at the center of numerous loyalties. HVEL; Latham, IIS, box 17, Hoopa Valley; SBFP 269–71.

118 Jacob Hostler, IIS box 17, Hoopa Valley; Ed Pratt served as police private from

1904 to 1906, but by 1922 the agent wrote that he was "not to be considered a progressive Indian." HVEL; E. Pratt, IIS, box 17, Hoopa Valley.

119 Nelson, *Our Home Forever*, 147; R. Hayden, IIS, box 17, Hoopa Valley; HVEL 1905 and 1907.

120 ARCIA 1900, 207.

121 ARCIA 1903, 141.

122 The Hupa "enthusiastically responded" to Superintendent Mortsolf's suggestion that they hold an election to create a tribal business council to oversee "roads, irrigation projects, and other community services." Nelson, *Our Home Forever*, 152. Two other members of the five-person council, Oscar Brown and John Campbell, had also worked for the Indian Service.

123 On Colegrove, see Norton, *Genocide in Northwestern California*, 122. Administrators later described another judge, James Jackson, as "one of the most prosperous Indians on the reservation." J. Jackson, IIS, box 17, Hoopa Valley. Jackson had represented the tribe on a trip to the Round Valley Reservation in 1877 when the government contemplated sending the Hupa there. Both men's sons served on the tribal council. Council History PDF available on the Hupa Tribe's website, ⟨http://www.hoopa-nsn.gov/government/council.htm⟩ (accessed 2 February 2010). Lewis argues that during the 1890s, "Profit or accumulation in the traditional Hupa sense was important, but only when it could be used in ways that brought power and status to the owner. And during this period when white agents usurped most of the political power from traditional leaders, that outlet became the group activities and rituals which, in themselves, required wealth and time away from the fields." David Rich Lewis, *Neither Wolf nor Dog*, 99.

124 ARCIA 1903, 141.

125 Goddard, *Hupa Texts*, 237, 265, 319.

126 Ibid., 93. Oscar Brown, described by Nelson as a "prominent" tribal member, worked as a laborer and an industrial teacher in 1894 and 1895 and again in 1905. Nelson, *Our Home Forever*, 174. Sam Brown served as a laborer in 1900 and as an assistant industrial teacher in 1905 and 1906. David Masten, whose wife collaborated with Goddard, held multiple posts between 1897 and 1908. James Anderson worked as a laborer at the agency during 1891, 1893–95, and 1901. See HVEL; and D. Masten, 1922, IIS, box 17, Hoopa Valley.

127 Julius Marshall's son, Earnest Jr., became a photographer and historian whose work was recently exhibited for the first time in 2009 at the Marin Museum of the American Indian in the exhibit *Hoopa Valley Tribe: People, Places, and Culture, 1930–1960*. See ⟨http://www.moremarin.com/more_culture/2009/04/cargo.html⟩ (accessed 2 February 2010). Earnest's grandson Bradley Marshall is a regalia maker and Tribal Liaison for UC Berkeley's Phoebe Hearst Museum of Anthropology. He very generously shared his thoughts about his grandfather and family history with me.

128 Superintendent Mortsolf to CIA, 15 October 1915, folder: Carpenter, box 56, series 51, HVA; and *Indian Census Rolls, 1885–1940*, National Archives Microfilm Publication M595, 1919, roll M595_183, Hoopa Valley Agency, 20. Retrieved from Ancestry.com (accessed 25 June 2010). On Norton's appointment, see Superintendent to CIA, 24 February 1913; Superintendent Holden to CIA, 26 March

1914; and Sherman Norton to CIA, 17 June 1913, all in folder: Carpenter, box 56, series 51, HVA.

129 Sherman Norton to CIA, 17 June 1913; and Superintendent Holden to CIA, 4 September 1913; Superintendent Holden to CIA, 26 March 1914, all in folder: Carpenter, box 56, series 51, HVA. Norton had a lot of work. Superintendent Kyselka had complained about the conditions of the school buildings in 1904, when they were roughly half a century old. By 1924 they were in such bad shape that the floor of one of the school buildings collapsed. In response to Holden's letter, the Indian Office did increase the salary from $540 to $660, but that was not as much as Holden had requested or Norton desired. Nelson, *Our Home Forever*, 145, 160; Assistant CIA Meritt to Superintendent Holden, 15 April 1914; Superintendent Mortsolf to the CIA, 17 October 1915; and Superintendent Mortsolf to CIA, 18 June 1918, folder: Carpenter, box 56, series 51, HVA. Like Sherman Norton, Charles Eastman encountered similar tactics when agents disagreed with him. Wilson, *Ohiyesa*, 115.

130 Superintendent Holden to CIA, 26 March 1914; and Superintendent Holden to CIA, 6 May 1914, folder: Carpenter, box 56, series 51, HVA.

131 Norton to CIA, 18 June 1918, folder: Carpenter, box 56, series 51, HVA. Both positions were temporary and without retirement deductions. "List of Employees on rolls of the Interior Department for Hoopa Valley," 5 August 1925, folder: Civil Service Commission, box 56, series 51, HVA.

132 Superintendent Mortsolf to CIA, 17 October 1915, folder: Carpenter, box 56, series 51, HVA.

133 Several other employees had also signed the petition, including Robinson Shoemaker, William Quimby, and Robert Hostler. For the list of signers, see Nelson, *Our Home Forever*, 154, 215 n. 51.

134 Nelson, *Our Home Forever*, 146, 172. Norton was a member of the tribal council in 1935, 1938, and 1941. See Council History PDF available on the Hupa Tribe's website, ⟨http://www.hoopa-nsn.gov/government/council.htm⟩ (accessed 2 February 2010).

135 S. Norton and J. Carpenter, IIS, box 17, Hoopa Valley.

136 Superintendent to CIA, 18 June 1918, folder: Carpenter, box 56, series 51, HVA.

137 Superintendent Holden reported that Norton was "willing to fill the carpenter position and do carpenter work for the salary of $660, but he does not feel that he should be asked to continue to do any longer, the electrical and plumbing work for this small salary." Superintendent Holden to CIA, 6 May 1914, folder: Carpenter, box 56, series 51, HVA.

138 Superintendent to CIA, 17 October 1915, folder: Carpenter, box 56, series 51, HVA.

139 Ibid.; Sherman Norton to CIA, 18 June 1918, folder: Carpenter, box 56, series 51, HVA. On the 1918 reallotment of the valley, see David Rich Lewis, *Neither Wolf nor Dog*, 182–83.

140 Mortsolf wrote: "There are no local Indians that I can recommend at this time, as all who are enterprising and energetic enough to fill such a place are already at work, earning double the wages this position pays. Owing to the demand for all classes of mechanics, and especially here on the Coast, where there is an immense activity in shipbuilding, the salary is not sufficient to command the ser-

vices of a really capable man." Superintendent Mortsolf to CIA, 14 July 1918; and Assistant CIA to Superintendent Mortsolf, n.d., both in folder: Carpenter, box 56, series 51, HVA.

141 Norton, *Centering in Two Worlds*, 14–18, 27, 29–30.

142 Ibid., 14.

143 The Rupert Costo chair, established in 1986, was the first endowed academic position in American Indian History in the University of California system. Norton was not the only Hupa to play an important role in the field of Native American Studies. David Risling Jr. became the first director of Native American Studies at the University of California, Davis, and helped found D-Q University. The Risling family, however, had a slightly different trajectory. See note 110 in this chapter. Trafzer, *As Long as the Grass Shall Grow and Rivers Flow*, 375.

144 Many thanks to Jack Norton for reading this section and sharing his family history. Norton, *Centering in Two Worlds*, 27, 29–30.

145 Bauer, *We Are All Like Migrant Workers Here*, 1–7, 130–36. See also Meyer, *The White Earth Tragedy*.

CHAPTER EIGHT

1 Holm, *The Great Confusion*, xi–xvii.

2 The Philippines, however, were administered by the War Department, not the Department of the Interior.

3 See Freer, *The Philippine Experiences of an American Teacher*, 275–76; ARBIC 1900, 7; LMC 1904; SBFP 209, 218; and Report of the United States Philippine Commission, "Home Addresses of American Teachers in the Philippines," Appendix CC, 518. See also Williams, "United States Indian Policy and the Debate over Philippine Annexation."

4 Jenkins, *Girl from Williamsburg*, 81–82, 317. See also Request for Transfer, 24 June 1912, Eva Greenwood, PF NPRC. Puerto Rican students were admitted to the Indian boarding school at Carlisle after the Spanish-American War. "Richard Henry Pratt," *Dictionary of American Biography*, 175–76. Wilson Gill first worked as general supervisor of moral and civic training in Cuba for the War Department before taking the position of supervisor at large of Indian Schools. See Gill, *A New Citizenship*, 3, 8, 198–204. Native people also used territorial possessions in their arguments. See *Report of the Executive Council on the Proceedings of the First Annual Conference of the Society of American Indians*; and Hertzberg, *The Search for American Indian Identity*, 118–19. Although he acknowledges the similarities with Indian policy, Julian Go emphasizes its differences from Philippine policy. Both he and Paul Kramer explore the strategies the United States shared with other imperial nations. Philippine policy differed from Indian policy in terms of territorial status and program funding, but the motivating ideology of wardship and the connections created by personnel also need to be explored. Indeed, the latter answers Go's call to explore "circuits of exchange" of information about colonial governance. Go, "Global Perspectives on the U.S. Colonial State"; and Kramer, *Blood of Government*, 10–12, 25–27.

5 Howard, *The Autobiography of General O. O. Howard*, 203.

6 ARCIA 1901, 3–4

7 An indefinite timeline for sovereignty, what Kramer calls "calibrated colonial-ism," was used to legitimate imperial rule in the Philippines as well. Kramer, *Blood of Government*, 19, 191–98.

8 Wiebe, *The Search for Order*; Rodgers, "In Search of Progressivism"; Rodgers, *Atlantic Crossings*; Ross, *The Origins of American Social Science*.

9 In a sample of twenty-three teacher, principal teacher, and superintendent applications from 1889 from white men and women who subsequently appear on the employee lists in the ARCIA, seventeen included previous teaching experience in common schools, with an average of 12.87 years (from a low of one year to a high of thirty). If we assume that those not listing teaching experience had none, the average for all twenty-three applicants is 8.9 years. Many of them listed college or normal school experience beyond common school education, including one who had attended one of the nation's leading teacher-training schools at Oswego, New York. Others listed the University of Michigan, Baylor Female College (Texas), Delaware Literary Institute (New York), and Magginouess College (Kentucky). The least educated had attended high school until sixteen before teaching in public school for four years. See Applications #211 E. Hoyt, #212 F. Hoyt, #1734 L. Freer, #1594 C. Mason, #1597 G. Whitacre, #3715 C. Davis, #3714 J. McCain, #3437 F. McNeill, #3607 J. Collins, #3713 J. Garrett, #4384 A. Simpson, #4425 E. Taylor, #4423 Mollie Gaither, #4424 L. Gordon, #4595 L. Evans, #4836 L. Hughes, #4836 H. Vernon, #5084 G. Nock, #5086 M. Nock, #1607 Millard Fouteh, #1601 William Beadle, #1590 William Thomas Calmis, #1599 Albert Kalb, all in LR 1889.

10 Elaine Goodale Eastman, *Sister to the Sioux*, 127. For more on Eastman's appointment and the increasing institutionalization of the Indian Service, see Stuart, *The Indian Office*, 145.

11 Elaine Goodale Eastman, *Sister to the Sioux*, 127. ARCIA 1890, 277–79; ARCIA 1893, 360–61.

12 ARCIA 1890, 277–79; ARCIA 1893, 360–61; ARCIA 1895, 360.

13 ARCIA 1900, 45. Agencies may have sponsored smaller conferences as well. See Dorrington to Mortsolf, 11 December 1917, Hoopa File, Dorrington Records, box 5, NARA SB.

14 ARCIA 1906, 75.

15 Golden, *Red Moon Called Me*, 48.

16 Jenkins, *Girl from Williamsburg*, 115–17. These conferences, as well as the detailed updates about employees in school newsletters such as the Phoenix School's *Native American*, kept employees connected in their far-flung posts across the country and helped to create a unified identity as Service employees.

17 Wesley, *NEA*, 289–91. See also *National Education Association Annual Report*, 1899, 35–36. Twenty-five of the NEA's prominent members also signed the petition.

18 ARCIA 1900, 44–45.

19 Wesley, *NEA*, 17.

20 Assistant Secretary Laylin to JB, 11 February 1914, John Brown, PF NPRC.

21 National Education Association Annual Report, 1901, vi–vii.

22 Ibid., 893.

23 ARCIA 1902, 387–95.

24 ARCIA 1903, 27, 386.

25 DeCora claimed that an exhibit of Indian children's art at an NEA meeting inspired her ideas about Native art. See A. DeCora Dietz, "Native Indian Art," in *Report of the Executive Council*, 84.

26 Jenkins, *Girl from Williamsburg*, 115.

27 Aug. 24, 1912, 37 Stat. L., 519, as reenacted Aug. 24, 1922, 42 Stat. L., 829; quoted in Schmeckebier, *The Office of Indian Affairs*, 482.

28 See Supt. H. J. McQuigg to J. F. House, 16 May 1922, Edith Salt, PF NPRC; and Superintendent Dickens to CIA, 4 April 1930, Lavinia Cornelius, PF NPRC.

29 *Regulations of the Indian Office, Indian Schools*, 20.

30 See Efficiency Report, 1 April 1931, Edgar Bates, PF NPRC; and Efficiency Report, 1 April 1931, Mary Baird, PF NPRC.

31 LC to Eleanor Gregg, 12 August 1930, Lavinia Cornelius, PF NPRC. Emphasis in original.

32 While this generally benefited employees and supervisors were usually encouraging, this was not always the case. For instance, Jennie Burton's supervisor reprimanded her because he believed her correspondence courses were interfering with her classroom work. Burton was trying to better her options for a transfer to clerkship through the course. Efficiency Report, 26 November 1909, Jennie L. Burton, PF NPRC.

33 Efficiency Report, 1 November 1912, Mary H. Baird, PF NPRC.

34 MB to Supt. Hart, 26 August 1919; and Superintendent Hart to CIA, 17 June 1919, both in Mary H. Baird, PF NPRC.

35 Efficiency Report, 1 April 1931, Mary H. Baird, PF NPRC.

36 Roosevelt, *An Autobiography*, 399–400, 401. See also Hagan, *Theodore Roosevelt and Six Friends of the Indian*. Political scientist Stephen Skowronek describes the period between 1900 and 1920 as a "reevaluation" of government operations resulting in the "construction and control of new administrative systems." Skowronek also argues that this period represented an ongoing struggle between the executive and legislative branches to control the civil service administration. Skowronek, *Building a New American State*, 178.

37 Roosevelt, *An Autobiography*, 394; ARCIA 1907, 9–15. Leupp said of his friendship with Roosevelt: it "had survived so many years of storm and stress, such differences of opinion, and so much plain speech on both sides." Leupp, *The Man Roosevelt*, v.

38 Pinkett, "Investigations of Federal Record-Keeping," 165.

39 Mrs. Emily Tunison to Hoke Smith, Secretary of the Interior, 3 August 1893, LR #29367.

40 Pinkett, "Investigations of Federal Record-Keeping," 176, 178; Kraines, "The President versus Congress," 7.

41 Kraines, "The President versus Congress," 8.

42 Pinkett, "Investigations of Federal Record-Keeping," 311–12.

43 See the letters from President Roosevelt and Secretary Garfield, ARCIA 1907, 13–14. Prucha attributes the Indian Office's efforts at reorganization solely to the

enthusiasm of the commissioners of Indian Affairs. See Prucha, *The Great Father*, 779–83.

44 ARCIA 1907, 10.

45 ARCIA 1907, 15.

46 Pinkett, "Investigations of Federal Record-Keeping," 190; see also Pinkett, "The Keep Commission," 307–8.

47 ARCIA 1907, 9–15. Instead of letter books organized chronologically, the Indian Office began to keep files organized by topic or person. In 1912 the commissioner reported that the bureau had hired three historians to organize the old correspondence. ARCIA 1912, 70–71.

48 Kraines, "The President versus Congress," 53; Pinkett, "The Keep Commission," 312.

49 Prucha, 763 and 780.

50 ARCIA 1912, 5.

51 *Regulations of the Indian Office, Indian Schools*, 7.

52 Efficiency Reports, May 1914, November 1915, and May 1926, Katie Brewer, PF NPRC.

53 Efficiency Report, 2 May 1916, Sophie Picard, PF NPRC; Efficiency Report, 1 November 1914, Jessie Morago, PF NPRC; and Efficiency Report, 14 May 1914, Naomi Dawson, PF NPRC.

54 Efficiency Reports, 31 December 1920, 1 May 1923, and 1 May 1925, Agnes Fredette, PF NPRC.

55 Jenkins, *Girl from Williamsburg*, 156, 302. See also Hedgepeth Diary, 28 July and 17 August, NMHP; and Efficiency Report, 1 November 1923, in Dollie Johnson, PF NPRC.

56 Efficiency Report, 1 April 1913, Autta Parrett, PF NPRC; Efficiency Report, 1 November 1915, Katie Brewer, PF NPRC; Efficiency Report, 1 May 1914, Violetta Nash, PF NPRC.

57 Efficiency Report, 1 May 1921, Lucy Jobin, PF NPRC.

58 Efficiency Report, 2 May 1923 and 1 January 1919, Addie Molzahn, PF NPRC; and Efficiency Report, 1 April 1917, Jessie Morago, PF NPRC.

59 Efficiency Report, 2 May 1923, Addie Molzahn, PF NPRC; Efficiency Report, 1 April 1917, Jessie Morago, PF NPRC; Efficiency Report, 1 May 1914, Katie Brewer, PF NPRC; and Efficiency Report, 31 December 1920, Agnes Fredette, PF NPRC.

60 Vocational Reading Report, 27 March 1915, Agnes Fredette, PF NPRC.

61 Report on Supervision of Individual Instructors, 22 December 1915; and Efficiency Report, 1 May 1918, in Agnes Fredette, PF NPRC.

62 ARBIC 1914, 7.

63 The staggering proportion of disease in the boarding schools is illustrated by one historian's use of a school graveyard as a primary source. Child, *Boarding School Seasons*, 112–15. See also Trennert, *The Phoenix Indian School*, 101–9; Holm, *The Great Confusion*, 175–77; and Prucha, *The Great Father*, 852–63.

64 Emmerich, "'Save the Babies!'"

65 See ARCIA 1912, 13. On this shift, see Emmerich, "'To Respect and Love.'"

66 *American Journal of Nursing* 12, no. 1 (October 1911): 57; *The Trained Nurse and*

Hospital Review, 44 (see also 35–37, 199, 205); *The World Almanac and Encyclopedia 1916*, 167.

67 By 1928 Gregg's report of the nursing service for the Indian Office was included along with those of the Army Nurse Corps, Navy Nurse Corps, Veteran's Bureau, and Public Health Service in the "News" section of the journal. These reports indicated the number of new hires as well as open positions. *American Journal of Nursing* 28, no. 1 (January 1928): 81–84. In an article, Gregg described the fictionalized journey of a woman maneuvering through the process of taking a civil service exam and receiving an appointment in the Indian Service. Another emphasized the exoticness of nursing work in Alaska. Gregg, "The Government Hires a Nurse"; Gregg, "A Federal Nursing Service above the Arctic Circle"; and Gregg, *The Indians and the Nurse*, 82–89.

68 Cox-Richardson, *The Death of Reconstruction*; Hoxie, *A Final Promise*, 83–187; Fredrickson, *The Black Image in the White Mind*, especially chapter 8; and Bederman, *Manliness and Civilization*. Hoxie argues that abolition offered "pleasant memories" but was toothless. I see the free labor ideal as a greater influence in that early period, with a shift to Social Darwinist ideas by the turn of the century. Hoxie, *A Final Promise*, 8. On multiple influences, see Adams, "Fundamental Considerations."

69 ARCIA 1902, 5.

70 Cook, "Frontier Savages," 7.

71 Westerners looked to multiple sources for labor in this period. See Sanchez, *Becoming Mexican American*; Gordon, *The Great Arizona Orphan Abduction*; Deutsch, *No Separate Refuge*; Ngai, *Impossible Subjects*; and Meeks, *Border Citizens*. See also Gordon, "Internal Colonialism and Gender."

72 Hoxie, *A Final Promise*, 147–210.

73 Hoxie argues that beginning with Estelle Reel's tenure as superintendent of Indian Schools, but especially under Commissioner Leupp, the government shifted away from the nineteenth-century ideas of equality and toward "lowered expectations for Indian students, increased emphasis on vocational training, and the consignment of Native Americans to marginal roles in society." Hoxie, "Redefining Indian Education," 13.

74 For a longer discussion of how ideas of gradual assimilation affected the shape of the School Service, see Adams, *Education for Extinction*, 306–33.

75 Hoxie, "Redefining Indian Education," 11. Hoxie points out that the 1916 curriculum was developed exclusively by Indian Office bureaucrats without input by missionaries and reformers, the "friends of the Indian" who had had a say in these things in the past. Hoxie, "Redefining Indian Education," 17. On Reel, see Lomawaima and McCarty, *To Remain an Indian*, 51–52.

76 LMC 1902, 89. See also ARCIA 1903, 6–7.

77 ARCIA 1904, 44. Edwin Chalcraft, a special inspector, reported from the Siletz Agency that Indians had "received patents in fee, to assume their own responsibility as fully as possible and realize that they were citizens in fact, as well as in name, and must look to the State laws for protection and relief in the same manner as their white neighbors." Local county officials, he continued, "have accepted the situation and been providing for the care of insane Indians, incor-

rigible boys and girls, furnishing support from the County pauper fund for Indigent citizen Indians, and paying widows pensions under the State law." These changes—Indians as hard-working land owners and state officials taking up their obligations—signaled to Chalcraft that "the time had about come when Siletz Agency could be abolished and the little unfinished work put in charge of the Salem Indian School at Chemawa." Chalcraft, *Assimilation's Agent*, 289, 287, 284.

78 Prucha, *The Great Father*, 823–25; ARCIA 1912, 11–12; and ARCIA 1914, 5–8. See also ARCIA 1912, 11. Congress first appropriated $20,000 for public school tuition in 1914 and continued to increase that appropriation. Indian students listed as enrolled in public schools were often nonattendants, however, because of racial prejudice.

79 ARCIA 1912, 11–12.

80 ARCIA 1914, 7.

81 In 1912 the Indian Office ended funding for Indian students at the Hampton Institute, and all Indian students were gone by 1923. Adams, *Education for Extinction*, 321–28. In the 1890s, the federal government had policed enrollment to ensure that Indian students attended the public schools that received federal money. See Hoxie, "Redefining Indian Education," 16–17.

82 Quoted in Meeks, "The Tohono O'odham." Commissioner Leupp did not see all aspects of Native culture as a problem, but he argued: "Our aboriginal brother brings, as his contribution to the common store of character, a great deal which is admirable, and which only needs to be developed along the right line." Hoxie notes that the emphasis on day schools helped Native communities retain their cohesion, especially because children were not taken from home. Quoted in Hertzburg, *The Search for American Indian Identity*, 17–18; and Hoxie, "Redefining Indian Education."

83 Quoted in Hoxie, "Redefining Indian Education," 14–15. On Indians as members of the "child races" and similar to blacks, see ibid., 10; as similar to the deaf and dumb, see ibid., 11; and as similar to Filipinos, see ibid., 12. Leupp noted that Hampton and Tuskegee were good examples for Indian education. ARCIA 1906, 69. See also Lomawaima and McCarty, *To Remain an Indian*, 62–63; and Holm, *The Great Confusion*, 172.

84 Hoxie, *A Final Promise*, 83–187.

85 ARCIA 1905, 3; ARCIA 1908, 29.

86 ARBIC 1905, 10–11.

87 The Board of Indian Commissioners lasted into the 1920s but with much less influence. The Lake Mohonk Conference expanded its concerns after the Spanish-American War to include "other dependant peoples," but the death of founder Albert Smiley in 1912 severely affected it, and the last consecutive conference was held in 1916. See Prucha, *The Great Father* (abridged), 267.

88 See Mackay, "Warrior into Welder," especially chapter 3.

89 Leupp, *The Indian and His Problem*, 110–11.

90 Ibid., 111. One page later, he wrote that the difficulty of life in the Indian Service "accounts for the frequency with which the Commissioner is besieged by his field subordinates"—presumably white—"for transfers." Leupp, *The Indian and His Problem*, 112.

91 ARCIA 1905, 15.

92 The outing system also emphasized the placement of Native girls as domestic servants. See Jacobs, "Working on the Domestic Frontier."

93 Emmerich, "Right in the Midst of My Own People," 201, 203.

94 The percentage of Native employees in regular positions dipped from a high of 43 percent of Service personnel in 1892 to 40 percent in 1909. Commissioner Leupp and other officials also worried that Indians were relying too heavily on Indian Service careers. Steven J. Novak, "Real Takeover," 646–47. A study of the position of boys' adviser in 1931–32 urged the employment of more highly trained personnel. In his conclusion, the author acknowledged that because this position was exclusively filled by Indian men, his "attempts to raise the standards and qualifications for these positions will be construed in many quarters as deliberate attempts to force the Indians out of these positions." As a remedy, he suggested creating a fellowship at Haskell Institute to train them to fit his recommendations. McCaskill, *The Boys' Adviser*, 94–95.

95 Prucha, *The Great Father*, 875. As with the Dawes Act, the Burke Act resulted in millions of acres of land leaving Indian control.

96 This is not to say that tribal identities disappeared or stopped mattering but that Natives found an intertribal identity to be useful in their efforts to influence federal policies. *Report of the Executive Council on the Proceedings of the First Annual Conference of the Society of American Indians*, 3–5. Emphasis in original. For previous organizations, see D. Anthony Tyeeme Clark, "At the Headwaters," 70–90.

97 There were white members, but only Natives were allowed to be voting members of the society. D. Anthony Tyeeme Clark, "Representing Indians," 10–11. See also Hertzberg, *The Search for American Indian Identity*, 27, 73; Maddox, *Citizen Indians*; and Hoxie, *Talking Back to Civilization*, 1–27

98 Hertzberg, *The Search for American Indian Identity*, 19, 43. Gertrude Bonnin held several positions, including clerk and teacher, at the Uintah and Ouray Agency and School as well as clerk at Standing Rock. Sworn Statement, Gertrude Bonnin, 17 June 1912, Raymond A. Bonnin, PF NPRC.

99 D. Anthony Tyeeme Clark, "Representing Indians," 56–58; and *Quarterly Journal of the Society of American Indians* (1914), 176. The addresses of a number of other members listed under "Active members present at the first conference of the Society of the American Indians" were often Indian schools or agencies, suggesting that many members were employees or students. *Report of the Executive Council on the Proceedings of the First Annual Conference of the Society of American Indians*, 178–79.

100 D. Anthony Tyeeme Clark, "Representing Indians," 12; Hertzberg, *The Search for American Indian Identity*, 85–98, 135–54.

101 Tribal identity still mattered. *American Indian Magazine* reported that during an exchange about the loyalty of Native Indian Service employees, "His [Rev. Sherman Coolidge's] replies seemed to fire the blood of the Apache. Montezuma jumped to his feet, waving his arms wildly. 'I am an Apache,' he shouted to Mr. Coolidge, 'and you are an Arapahoe. I can lick you. My tribe has licked your tribe before.'" *American Indian Magazine* 4, no. 3 (July–September 1916): 266–67; see also 265.

102 *Report of the Executive Council on the Proceedings of the First Annual Conference of the Society of American Indians*, 1912, 123–124.

103 *American Indian Magazine* 4 no. 1 (January–March 1916): 28–31. Redbird offered a similar talk to the Lake Mohonk Conference in 1908 entitled "An Indian's View of the Indian Problem." For Redbird's biography, see *LMC* 1908, 47.

104 Quoted in Hertzberg, *Search for American Indian Identity*, 148, 332. Emphasis in original. Rev. Coolidge also used his work experience to criticize the Indian Service. See *Report of the Executive Council on the Proceedings of the First Annual Conference of the Society of American Indians*, 127. See also the articles "Are Your Officers Traitors?" and "Open Debate on the Loyalty of Indian Employees in the Indian Service," *American Indian Magazine* 4, no. 3 (July–September 1916): 15–18, 252–56.

105 Quoted in Hertzberg, *The Search for American Indian Identity*, 98; see also 88 and 94.

106 Quoted in ibid., 148.

107 Zitkala-Sa, *American Indian Stories*. On Bonnin and Montezuma's relationship and ideological differences, see Johnson and Wilson, "Gertrude Simmons Bonnin," 29–30. Other Native authors such as Charles Eastman made similar charges in their writings. See Charles A. Eastman, *From Deep Woods*.

108 Hertzberg, *The Search for American Indian Identity*, 106. See also Standing Bear, *Land of the Spotted Eagle*, 252–54 and Wilson, *Ohiyesa*, 92–103.

109 Montezuma Papers, *Wassaja*, 2 June 1917, 4.

110 Hertzberg, *The Search for American Indian Identity*, 136–37, 147; and *American Indian Magazine* (1916): 32.

111 Quoted in Hertzberg, *The Search for American Indian Identity*, 79, 97, 98, 126. By the sixth annual conference in 1916, however, the issue came to a head in an intense debate over the question of the loyalty of government employees—although, Hertzberg argues, the ongoing debate over their loyalty "had already eliminated [Indian Service employees] from active participation" in the organization. Hertzberg, *The Search for American Indian Identity*, 153.

112 Ibid., 43.

113 Iverson, *Carlos Montezuma*, 63–115; Hertzberg, *The Search for American Indian Identity*, 118–19.

114 Montezuma Papers, *Wassaja* 1 (April 1916): 1. Hertzberg, *The Search for American Indian Identity* 136–37, 147; and American Indian Magazine (1916): 32.

115 Montezuma christened the paper with his Apache name, Wassaja, and created dual editorial personalities: "Dr. Montezuma," the well-educated, polite writer, and "Wassaja," the angrier, louder personality. He represented this dualism in the masthead of the paper, which portrayed two Native figures. One, wearing a headdress, stands next to a tepee sending smoke signals. The other, dressed in a suit, stands next to the Statue of Liberty. The urban Indian holds a paper that reads, "Let my people go." The caption states: "Ed. by Wassaja (Dr. Montezuma's Indian name, meaning 'Signaling') An Apache Indian." Montezuma Papers, *Wassaja* 3 (January 1919): 1.

116 Quoted in Hertzberg, *The Search for American Indian Identity*, 142.

117 Montezuma Papers, *Wassaja* 4 (April 1919): 1.

118 Montezuma Papers, *Wassaja* 1 (January 1917): 4.

119 Montezuma Papers, *Wassaja* 2 (June 1917): 4.

120 Montezuma Papers, *Wassaja* 3 (March 1919): 1–2.

121 *Quarterly Journal of the Society of American Indians*, 176; *American Indian Magazine* 4, no. 3 (July–September 1916): 253.

122 Hertzberg, *The Search for American Indian Identity*, 97.

123 Lomawaima and McCarty note that despite the pressure by students, parents, and boarding school administrators to add high school grades in off-reservation schools, the Indian Office refused. After the publication of the Meriam Report, however, which suggested that the off-reservation boarding schools should function as high schools, the higher grades were slowly added. But the authors fault the Collier administration with undoing that accomplishment. They report "that in 1936 there were 13 high schools in the federal school system for Indians, none of them accredited." Lomawaima and McCarty, *To Remain an Indian*, 69–73.

CHAPTER NINE

1 Efficiency Report, 1 November 1909, Anna B. Bowman, PF NPRC. Bowman received similar criticism in her Efficiency Report of 1912: "She has hardly kept abreast with the progress made by other teachers. I have had a talk with Miss Bowman and advised her of the necessity on her part of attending some professional school next summer, and otherwise keeping abreast with the best thought and practice in classroom work." Efficiency Report, 1 October 1912, Anna B. Bowman, PF NPRC. See also Efficiency Report, 6 December 1914, Anna L. Bowlder, PF NPRC; and Superintendent Crandall to CIA, 2 April 1912, Nora Buzzard, PF NPRC. On rising ideas of professionalism, see Stage and Bincenti, *Rethinking Home Economics*.

2 Efficiency Report, n.d. (circa 1930), Madeline Jacker, PF NPRC. See also Superintendent Roberts to CIA, 9 January 1929, Madeline Jacker, PF NPRC; Efficiency Report, 1 April 1931; and Efficiency Report, 1 April 1933, Lavina Cornelius, PF NPRC; Charles Shell to CIA, 23 January 1909, Naomi Dawson, PF NPRC; and Efficiency Report, 1 April 1934, Rose Dougherty, PF NPRC.

3 Chief of Education Division, OIA, to LB, 30 December 1909, Lewis L. Brink, PF NPRC. See also VB to CIA, 17 January 1910; Assistant CIA Abbott to William L. Beldon, 3 February 1910; and Superintendent Charles Davis to CIA, 4 June 1910, all in Victor E. Brown, PF NPRC.

4 AB to CIA, 21 February 1921, Allie B. Busby, PF NPRC.

5 On the characteristics desired in employees, see Thomas Jefferson Morgan, "The Education of American Indians," 3–14, 20; and ARCIA 1899, 10, 29.

6 Applicants between the ages of twenty-five and forty-five received full credit on the civil service exam for age, while those above and below those years were docked "proportionately." Matrons were required to be over the age of twenty, but wives of superintendents were exempt from this requirement. Civil Service Commission, *Manual of Examinations* (1899), 66, 73.

7 Efficiency Report, 6 May 1910; CIA to Superintendent Scott, 18 May 1916; Superintendent Scott to CIA, 7 June 1916; CIA to Superintendent Scott, 16 June 1916;

Superintendent Scott to CIA, 19 June 1916; and Efficiency Report, 1 May 1918, all in Jennie Brown, PF NPRC.

8 Efficiency Report, 1 November 1918; and Superintendent Allen to CIA, 4 March 1920, in Otis F. Badger, PF NPRC.

9 See also Superintendent Haggett to CIA, 28 August 1912, Michael H. Brown, PF NPRC.

10 ARCIA 1921, 36.

11 Clark, Craig, and Wilson, *A History of Public Sector Pensions*, 158.

12 Efficiency Report, 1 May 1924, Rose Dougherty, PF NPRC.

13 *Federal Employee* 1, no. 1 (July 1916): 12, 28; *Federal Employee* 1, no. 4 (October 1916): 151, 155. See also Increased Compensation, 1919 Hearings before Subcommittee of House Committee on Appropriations, 65th Cong., 2nd Session, GPO, 1918, 29–35.

14 FERA was amended in 1926 and again in 1930. There does not appear to be a substantial history of FERA, nor do many scholars discuss it in depth. See Clark, Craig, and Wilson, *A History of Public Sector Pensions*, 154–66; Skowronek, *Building a New American State*, 208; Van Riper, *History of the United States Civil Service*, 276–77; Others do not mention the act; see Maranto and Schultz, *A Short History of the United States Civil Service*; Fishback and Kantor, *A Prelude to the Welfare State*; Orloff, *The Politics of Pensions*; and Costa, *The Evolution of Retirement*.

15 *Congressional Record*, 66th Cong., 2nd sess., 1920, 6359, 6369, 6370, 6371.

16 Ibid., 6372; see also 6370. Supporters also contended that every other "civilized" nation provided a pension plan for civil servants. They pointed to the example of business retirement plans and the successful state teacher retirement systems to demonstrate the practicality of the federal retirement plan. *Congressional Record*, 66th Cong., 2nd sess., 1920, 2443, 3393, 3395, 3396, and 6366. By 1924 there were some 500 retirement systems in the country, mostly state governments and about 100 public schoolteacher retirement systems. Baish, "Retirement Systems and Moral in Public Service," 339.

17 Skocpol, *Protecting Soldiers and Mothers*; Linda Gordon, *Pitied but Not Entitled*; Gordon, *Women, the State, and Welfare*; Jensen, *Patriots, Settlers*.

18 *Congressional Record*, 66th Cong., 2nd sess., 1920, 5132. See also Doyle, "The Federal Civil Service Retirement Law."

19 *Congressional Record*, 66th Cong., 2nd sess., 1920, 6377.

20 Ibid., 5141.

21 Ibid., 5133.

22 Ibid., 1920, 5141.

23 Ibid., 6376; see also 6372.

24 Ibid., 3397–98.

25 Ibid., 6373.

26 This conclusion is based on the initial assessment of the 1920 debates and needs more investigation.

27 *Congressional Record*, 66th Cong., 2nd sess., 1920, 6369.

28 Ibid., 6364, 6357.

29 Baish, "Retirement Systems and Moral in Public Service," 344; and Clark, Craig, and Wilson, *A History of Public Sector Pensions*, 163–64.

30 Prucha, *The Great Father*, 771.

31 ARBIC 1918, 12.

32 Prucha, *The Great Father*, 854–55.

33 ARBIC 1920, 5–6.

34 Prucha, *The Great Father*, 794, 759–62, 790–95; Holm, *The Great Confusion*, xvi, 153–81. The postwar years were characterized by shrinking budgets and pressure from Congress to economize. See Prucha, *The Great Father* (abridged), 272.

35 See Interior Department Appropriation bill, 1924, Hearing before the Subcommittee of House Appropriations (GPO, 1922), 131–32, 136, 139; Prucha, *The Great Father* (abridged), 272; and Lomawaima and McCarty, *To Remain an Indian*, 69–70.

36 The survey report for each family consisted of a single sheet with a picture of the family's house on it. The survey taker also recorded the details that allowed officials to place the family within the organization of the reservation: the name of the allottee and his or her allotment number, age, amount of Indian blood, wardship status, and the number of family members who also lived in the house. Assistant Commissioner Merrit to Mr. Barnd, 29 May 1922, Camp Verde, box 1, IIS. See also Assistant Commissioner Merritt to M. Parrett, Bishop Agency, 31 October 1925, CA, box 1, IIS; and 21 August 1928, Colville, box 6, IIS. Colonial theorists argue that states govern by collecting knowledge about populations, ordering that knowledge into particular categories, and redeploying it in a manner that facilitates governance. Scott, *Seeing Like a State*.

37 ARCIA 1922, 11. See also *Interior Department Appropriation Bill, 1924*, 140.

38 CIA to Superintendent Belden, 23 June 1910, Agnes Reedy, PF NPRC.

39 Superintendent Asbury to CIA, 9 December 1920, Harriet Kyselka, PF NPRC; Supervisor of Farming Davis to CIA, 28 January 1913, John Buntin, PF NPRC; and Efficiency Report, 20 December 1921, Agnes Fredette, PF NPRC. See also Superintendent Haggett to CIA, 28 August 1912, Michael H. Brown, PF NPRC.

40 *Interior Department Appropriation Bill for 1923* (GPO, 1922), 205–6.

41 CIA to John B. Brown, 17 September 1925; and CIA to John B. Brown, 17 October 1921, both in Mary E. Brown, PF NPRC. See also CIA to Charles Burton, 7 December 1914, Ella Burton, PF NPRC; and Superintendent Duclos to CIA, 19 October 1925, Artie Peacore, PF NPRC.

42 CIA to John B. Brown, 17 September 1925, Mary E. Brown, PF NPRC; CIA to Jessie Scott, 26 January 1931, Jessie Morago, PF NPRC.

43 On Collier, see Philip, *John Collier's Crusade*; Lawrence C. Kelly, *The Assault on Assimilation*; Denby, *Battle for the BIA*; and Wenger, *We Have a Religion*. On wider reformers, see Deloria and Lytle, *The Nations Within*, 38–53.

44 Prucha, *The Great Father*, 808. The researchers and their fields included Ray A. Brown, assistant professor of law, University of Wisconsin (legal aspects of Indian problems); Henry Roe Cloud (Winnebago), president of the American Indian Institute, Wichita, Kansas (Indian adviser); Edward Everett Dale, professor of history, University of Oklahoma (economic conditions); Emma Duke (conditions of Indian migrants to urban communities); Herbert R. Edwards, medical field secretary of the National Tuberculosis Association (health); Fayette A. McKenzie, professor of sociology, Juniata College, Huntington, Pennsylvania

(existing material relating to Indians); Mary Louis Mark, professor of sociology, Ohio State University (family life and activities of women); W. Carson Ryan Jr., professor of education, Swarthmore College (education); and William J. Spillman, agricultural economist, U.S. Department of Agriculture (agriculture). The composition of the committee indicates the social shifts in women's roles that had occurred since the 1880s. Two of the ten experts were women, included not for their innate female qualities but for their scientific expertise. While Mary Louis Mark's field certainly retained the focus on the family that the women of the WNIA had emphasized, her approach was that of a professional sociologist, not of a female moral reformer. Prucha, *The Great Father*, 808–9 n. 37. In 1923 the Indian Office had appointed the Committee of One Hundred to undertake its own internal study. Five Indian Service employees or former employees (all men) sat on the Committee of One Hundred. Four of them were Native men who had served in the Indian Service—Charles Eastman, Rev. Sherman Coolidge, Rev. Fr. Philip Gordon, and Dennison Wheelock—but were most likely chosen for their connections to the SAI rather than their work experience. John W. Clark, a former Indian agent, seems to have been the only white employee on the committee. Arthur C. Parker, the president of the SAI for many years, was elected as chair of the Committee of One Hundred. Their participation illustrates how the SAI's concerns were incorporated into the criticisms of the Indian Office. See D. Anthony Tyeeme Clark, "Representing Indians," especially chapter 4.

45 McKenzie had left the Indian Service and become a sociology professor, first at the historically black Fisk University and then Juniata College. See Prucha, *The Great Father*, 809.

46 The Meriam Report's solutions echoed those put forth by reformers in the 1880s—in particular, the advocacy of cooperation with missionaries. See *The Problem of Indian Administration*, 812–47; Prucha, *The Great Father*, 809–10; and Critchlow, "Lewis Meriam, Expertise, and Indian Reform."

47 The Brookings Institution conducted another study specifically examining the position of boys' adviser for the Indian Service in 1931–32 and came to similar conclusions. McCaskill, *The Boys' Adviser*, 81–88.

48 *The Problem of Indian Administration*, 15, 27–28, 378. Indian Service employees were aware of the criticisms and discussed them. Frustrated by the report's negative assessment of their work, one even volunteered to write a response from an employee's point of view. The Indian Office ultimately appointed three superintendents based on their "knowledge and expertise" to write an official response. Efficiency Report, n.d. (circa 1928), Leo Bonnin, PF NPRC; Frank Kyselka, private letter to CIA, 28 January 1929; and Frank Kyselka, official letter to CIA, 28 January 1929, Frank Kyselka, PF NPRC; Roy O. West, Interior Secretary, to John Buntin, 22 October 1928, John Buntin, PF NPRC.

49 *The Problem of Indian Administration*, 28.

50 Estelle Aubrey Brown, *Stubborn Fool*, 92; Application for Retirement from the Civil Service on Account of Total Disability Form, n.d., Allie (Alice) B. Busby, PF NPRC. Clark, Craig, and Wilson, *A History of Public Sector Pensions*, 154–66

51 Leo Bonnin to CIA, 14 September 1926, Robert Burns, PF NPRC.

52 ARCIA 1921, 36.

53 Superintendent Goodman to CIA, 19 February 1912; Indian Application for Employment Form, 14 March 1912; NS to CIA, 14 March 1912; CIA to Superintendent Goodman, 25 April 1912; and Acting CIA to Superintendent Goodman, 31 May 1912, all in Nellie Santeo, PF NPRC. See also Acting Commissioner to AG, 10 April 1913, Alice Gorman, PF NPRC.

54 ARCIA 1900, 734; Personal Information Blank, 1 March 1910, and Superintendent McGregor to CIA, 6 September 1927, both in Katie Brewer, PF NPRC.

55 Efficiency Report, 1 May 1926, Katie Brewer, PF NPRC.

56 O. H. Lipps, District Superintendent in Charge, to CIA, 30 December 1927, Katie Brewer, PF NPRC.

57 For example, her efficiency report of 1914 described her as "one of the best of women." Efficiency Report, 1 May 1914, Katie Brewer, PF NPRC.

58 Superintendent Hall to CIA, 13 May 1921, Katie Brewer, PF NPRC.

59 CIA to Senator McNary, 17 April 1922, Katie Brewer, PF NPRC. See also HK to CIA, 28 October 1928, Harriet Kyselka, PF NPRC; and SD to CIA, 18 March 1927; Memorandum for Secretary of Interior from Assistant CIA, 18 March 1927; and Chief Clerk, Department of the Interior to Civil Service Commission, 10 June 1927, all in Susie McDougal, PF NPRC

60 Chief of the Division of Appointments, Mails and Files to Superintendent, 23 September 1927, Katie Brewer, PF NPRC.

61 Assistant CIA to District Superintendent, 8 February 1929, Katie Brewer, PF NPRC.

62 ARCIA 1928, 2, 21. President Coolidge issued Executive Order #4948 on 14 August 1928 limiting the number of positions for which Native people were eligible upon passing a noncompetitive exam. See Vogt, "Eligibility for Indian Employment Preference," 32–33.

63 Chapman had held two temporary positions in 1924, but they did not factor into her eligibility. CIA to Superintendent Dorrington, 9 December 1929; HC to Mr. Roosevelt, 31 October 1934; and CIA to HC, 30 November 1934, all in Harriet Chapman, PF NPRC. See also Mary Barnes to CIA, 19 November 1934; and Lillian Kriloff to Civil Service Commission, 31 January 1939, both in Mary Paquette, PF NPRC.

64 John Doyle to the Secretary of the Interior, 11 May 1929; CIA to Superintendent Dorrington, 9 December 1929; HC to CIA, 14 October 1934; and CIA to HC, 21 March 1941, all in Harriet Chapman, PF NPRC.

65 Acting Superintendent McCowen to CIA, 12 April 1932, Dollie Johnson, PF NPRC. Deductions from Johnson's salary began in 1930, but in order to qualify for a full pension, employees were required to pay a lump sum that would cover the amount that would have been deducted from their paychecks over the course of their careers. Johnson had not done so before she died (and probably could not afford to do so).

CONCLUSION

1 Horne, *Essie's Story*, 83, 86, 163.

2 Collier had a long history of agitation against the Indian Office. He had been a social worker in New York's downtown ethnic neighborhoods, where he became

enamored by the regenerative possibilities of communitarian and traditional societies for industrial society. Introduced to Pueblo cultures by Mabel Dodge Luhan on a visit to New Mexico in 1920, he learned about their struggle with the Indian Office over of its ban on their ceremonial dances. In the pueblos, Collier believed he had found an ideal form of community and took up activism on the Natives' behalf. First working with the General Federation of Women's Clubs, he founded the American Indian Defense Association in 1923. Although Collier was extremely outspoken against the Indian Office, President Roosevelt appointed him to lead it. Previously a thorn in the side of officials, he now held the reins of power. See Lawrence C. Kelly, *The Assault on Assimilation*; Philip, *John Collier's Crusade for Indian Reform*; and Denby, *Battle for the BIA*.

3   Collier's emphasis on day schools, for example, had a different motivation but similar consequences as his predecessor's policies. While his policy was ostensibly meant to safeguard the cohesion and traditions of Native communities, the Indian Office continued to cut back on the resources for off-reservation boarding schools without making up for the loss of advanced educational opportunities with new high schools on the reservations. Thus the end result of Collier's educational policy was still a decline in opportunities for Native children. Lomawaima and McCarthy, *To Remain an Indian*. Historians also point to the Collier administration's well-intentioned but disastrous livestock-reduction policies on the Navajo reservation as the continuation of federal paternalism. See White, *The Roots of Dependency*; and Weisiger, *Dreaming of Sheep*. On the other hand, Collier supported Native people's right to practice their religions and also helped pass the Indian Arts and Crafts Board Act in 1935 that was designed to help foster Native arts and provide a source of income in Native communities. Wenger, *We Have a Religion*; and Meyn, "Fighting for Indian Artisans: John Collier, René d'Harnoncourt, and the Indian Arts and Crafts Board," 57.

4   The bill as passed by Congress was shorter and less radical than what Collier had proposed. Taylor, *The New Deal*, 18–29.

5   25 U.S.C. § 472.

6   See Prucha, *The Great Father*, 963.

7   In 1933 the funds allotted through the Public Works program for Indian reservations were $19 million, while the Indian Office's total budget that year was approximately $22 million. Connell-Szasz, *Education and the American Indian*, 42. Like other New Deal programs, the Indian Civilian Conservation Corps was based on a male breadwinner. Only 7 percent of the jobs went to Native women. O'Neill, "Charity or Industry?"; Kessler-Harris, *In Pursuit of Equity*, 76; Mettler, *Dividing Citizens*. At Hoopa, the tribal council also complained that New Deal programs only hired married men. Nelson, *Our Home Forever*, 177. But many of the CCC programs were also designed to keep Native men near their families. Taylor, *The New Deal*, 18.

8   Scott, *Weapons of the Weak*.

9   While not all schools or reservations were in the trans-Mississippi West, the majority were.

10 The phrase is Richard White's; see *It's Your Misfortune and None of My Own*, 58. See also William J. Novak, "The Myth of the 'Weak' American State"; West, "Re-

constructing Race"; Merrill, "In Search of the 'Federal Presence'"; and Johnston, "Beyond 'The West.'"

11 Stoler, *Carnal Knowledge and Imperial Power*, 60. See also Kramer, *Blood of Government*, 25–27; and Jacobs, "Working on the Domestic Frontier."

12 Concerns about rape almost never appear in the Indian Office records. In fact, in one unusual case where the commissioner reported the rape of a white teacher, he casually passed to the next item without any comment on possible wider implications for other female employees. ARCIA 1896, 22–23. Accusations of the sexual violation of white women had elicited violence against Native men in Minnesota just two decades earlier after the Minnesota "Sioux uprising" or Dakota War of 1862, and during the antebellum period, whites threatened violence over the Boudinot cousins' marriages to white women in New England. See Namias, *White Captives*, 204–61; and the introduction of Gaul, *To Marry an Indian*. See also Riley, *Women and Indians on the Frontier*, 204.

13 Kramer, *The Blood of Government*, 229–84; Ngai, *Impossible Subjects*, 96–126; Findlay, *Imposing Decency*; Lui, *The Chinatown Trunk Mystery*; Hodes, *White Women, Black Men*.

14 Billions as measured in current dollars.

15 In 1974 the Supreme Court ruled in *Morton v. Mancari*, 417 U.S. 535 (1974), that preferential hiring of Native people in the Indian Service was allowable because it was based on political basis, not race: "The preference is not directed towards a 'racial' Group consisting of 'Indians'; instead, it applies only to members of 'federally recognized' Tribes. This operates to exclude many individuals who are racially to be classified as 'Indians.' In this sense, the preference is political rather than racial in nature." Quoted in Garroutte, *Real Indians*, 18, 170 n. 18.

16 If we include the Indian Health Service, which is housed in the Health and Human Services Department, we see similar numbers. Its total employees is 15,487 (71 percent are Indian) ⟨http://info.ihs.gov/Profile08.asp⟩ (accessed 5 January 2009); *Indian Affairs, U.S. Department of the Interior 2007 Performance & Accountability Report*, 8. PDF file, ⟨http://www.doi.gov/bia/whats_hot.html⟩ (accessed 4 August 2008). The Indian Health Service, for example, is the largest employer of Native nurses, ⟨http://www.minoritynurse.com/features/nurse_emp/09-01-03.html ⟩ (accessed 5 January 2009).

17 As of December 2008, the Walmart Corporation claimed to employ 16,000 American Indian and Alaskan Native associates. see "American Indian and Alaskan Native Fact Sheet," downloaded from ⟨http://walmartstores.com/FactsNews/FactSheets/⟩ (5 January 2009).

18 For an overview of the case and a longer history of mineral leases, see Thorne, *The World's Richest Indian*, 215–26.

19 "Secretary Salazar, Attorney General Holder Announce Settlement of Cobel Lawsuit," press release, 8 December 2009; PDF file, ⟨www.bia.gov⟩ (accessed 28 June 2010).

Bibliography

MANUSCRIPT SOURCES

Chicago, Ill.

Wassaja: Freedom's Signal for the Indian, Carlos Montezuma Papers, Microfilm,
    Reel 5, "Correspondence, Continued," Newberry Library

Eureka, Calif.

Susie Baker Fountain Papers, vol. 34, Hoopa/Goodard/Indians, Humboldt County
    Library

Humboldt County, Calif.

"50 Years of Progress: A Memorial of the 50th Anniversary of the Establishment of
    the Business of A. Brizard Inc. at Arcata, Humboldt County, California, June
    1913." Folder: Commerce—Dept. Stores—Newsletter,
    Brizard Ink, vol. 2, no. 4, January 1954, Humboldt County Historical Society.

Northampton, Mass.

Eastman-Goodale-Dayton Family Papers, Sophia Smith Collection, Smith College

Pasadena, Calif.

Weinland Correspondence, Huntington Library

Philadelphia, Pa.

*Testimony of the Society of Friends on Indian Civilization Submitted to the Commission
    Appointed to Consider the Transfer of the Indian Bureau to the War Department*,
    Friends' Book Association, 1878

Redlands, Calif.

Redland Indian Association Minute Books, 1894–1924, 2 vols., California
    Collection, A. K. Smiley Public Library

St. Louis, Mo.

Personnel Folders, National Personnel Records Center

San Anselmo, Calif.

Nellie McGraw Hedgpeth Papers, Graduate Theological Union

San Bruno, Calif.

Records of the Hoopa Valley Agency, Record Group 75, National Archives and
    Records Administration

Hoopa Valley Agency Diary, vol. 1 (1 January 1919 to 30 June 1919), Record Group
    75, National Archives and Records Administration

Hoopa Valley Employee Ledger, 1883–1911, Hoopa Valley Agency, Record Group 75,
    National Archives and Records Administration

Inspection Report, Special Agent L. A. Dorrington, 20–27
  October 1916, Dorrington Records, Box 5, Hoopa File, National Archives and
    Records Administration
Records of the Hoopa Valley Agency, Record Group 75, National Archives and
    Records Administration
San Francisco, Calif.
  Cornelia Taber Collection, 1906–1926, California Historical Society
Washington, D.C.
  General Records, Letters Received 1824–1907, General Records of the Bureau of
    Indian Affairs, Record Group 75, National Archives Building
  Reports of Indian Industry Surveys, 1922–29, Record Group 75, Entry 762,
    National Archives Building
Wichita, Kansas
  Bliss-Isely Collection, Wichita State University Special Collections

NEWSPAPERS

Bismarck Daily Tribune
Daily Mitchell Republican (South Dakota)
Frederick News (Maryland)
Freeborn County Standard (Minnesota)
Lincoln Evening News (Nebraska)
Lorain County Reporter (Elyria, Ohio)
Manitoba Morning Free Press

Middletown Daily Argus (New York)
Newark Daily Advocate (Ohio)
New York Times
Ogden Standard (Utah)
Sioux Valley News (Correctionville, Iowa)
Washington Post
Waukesha Freeman (Wisconsin)

PRIMARY SOURCES: SERIALS AND
GOVERNMENT PUBLICATIONS

American Indian Magazine. Published as the *Quarterly Journal of the Society of American
    Indians*. Washington, D.C., 1914–16.
American Journal of Nursing. Philadelphia: J. B. Lippincott Company, 1911–39.
Annual Meeting and Report of the Women's National Indian Association. Philadelphia,
    1883–94.
Annual Reports of the War Department, vol. 7, *Report of the Philippine Commission*.
    Washington, D.C.: Government Printing Office, 1904.
Board of Indian Commissioners. *Annual Report*. Washington, D.C.: Government
    Printing Office, 1869–1927.
Commissioner of Indian Affairs. *Annual Report*. Washington, D.C.: Government
    Printing Office, 1869–1927.
Congressional Globe, part 2, 3rd session, 41st Congress, 1870–71.
*Congressional Record: Proceedings and Debates of the Second Session of the Sixty-sixth
    Congress of the United States of America*. Vol. 59. Washington, D.C.: Government
    Printing Office, 1920.
*Congressional Record Containing the Proceedings and Debates of the Fifty-First U.S.
    Congress, First Session. Also Special Session of the Senate*. Vol. 21, part 2. Washington,
    D.C.: Government Printing Office, 1889.
Department of the Interior. *Regulations of the Indian Office, Indian Schools*. Washington,
    D.C.: Government Printing Office, 1928.

————. *Regulations of the Indian Service: Duties and Conduct of Superintendents and Other Employees.* Washington, D.C.: Government Printing Office, 1929.

————. *Rules for the Indian School Service.* Washington, D.C.: Government Printing Office, 1913.

Department of the Interior, Office of Indian Affairs. *Routes to Indian Agencies and Schools with Their Post Office and Telegraphic Addresses and Nearest Railroad Stations.* Washington, D.C.: Government Printing Office, 1915.

Federal Employee. Washington, D.C.: National Federation of Federal Employees.

First Annual Report of the United States Civil Service Commission. Washington, D.C.: Government Printing Office, 1884.

Indian Appropriation Bill Hearings before the Committee of Indian Affairs, United States Senate. 64th Congress, 2nd session. Washington, D.C.: Government Printing Office, 1917.

Indian Office. *Regulations of the Indian Office.* Washington, D.C.: Government Printing Office, 1904.

Indian Rights Association. *Annual Report.* Philadelphia, 1883–1900.

The Indian's Friend: The Organ of the Women's National Indian Association. Philadelphia, 1890–1911.

Interior Department Appropriation Bill, 1923: Hearing before Subcommittee of House Committee on Appropriations. 67th Congress, 4th session. Washington, D.C.: Government Printing Office, 1922.

Interior Department Appropriation Bill, 1924: Hearing before Subcommittee of House Committee on Appropriations. 67th Congress, 4th session. Washington, D.C.: Government Printing Office, 1922.

Jessie Short et al. v. the United States. United States Court of Claims Cases, vol. 202, 870.

Journal of the Senate during the Thirty-First Session of the Legislature of the State of California. Sacramento, 1895.

National Education Association Annual Report. Washington, D.C.: Government Printing Office, 1899–1907.

The Native American. Phoenix: Phoenix Indian School, 1906–9.

Nursing World 48 (March 1912): 184–85.

Office of Indian Affairs, *Rules for the Indian School Service.* Washington, D.C.: Government Printing Office, 1898.

The Official Register of the United States Containing a List of the Officers and Employees in the Civil, Military, and Naval Service on the First of July, 1893, Together with a List of Vessels Belonging to the United States. Vol. 1, *Legislative, Executive, Judicial.* Compiled under the direction of the Secretary of the Interior by J. G. Ames, Superintendent of Documents. Washington, D.C.: Government Printing Office, 1869–1905.

Proceedings of the Annual Meeting of the Lake Mohonk Conference of Friends of the Indian. N.p.: The Lake Mohonk Conference, 1883–1916.

Register of Officers and Agents, Civil, Military, and Naval, in the Service of the United States. Washington, D.C.: Government Printing Office, 1870-1906.

Report of the Executive Council on the Proceedings of the First Annual Conference of the Society of American Indians. Washington, D.C., 1912.

Report of the Secretary of Interior: Being Part of the Message and Documents Communicated to the Two Houses of Congress at the Beginning of the Second Session of the Fiftieth Congress. Vol. 2. Washington, D.C.: Government Printing Office, 1888.

Report of the United States Philippine Commission to the Secretary of War. Vol. 1, part 9. Washington, D.C.: Government Printing Office, 1901.

Reports of the Department of the Interior for the Fiscal Year Ended June 30, 1913. Vol. 2. Washington, D.C.: Government Printing Office, 1914.

Rules for Indian Schools with Course of Study, List of Text-Books, and Civil Service Rules. Washington, D.C.: Government Printing Office, 1892.

Science 18 (1903): 413.

Trained Nurse and Hospital Review. Vols. 31–32. New York, July 1903–June 1904.

United States Civil Service Commission. Manual of Examinations for the Classified Civil Service of the United States. Washington, D.C.: Government Printing Office, 1899.

———. Manual of Examinations for the Spring of 1915. Washington, D.C.: Government Printing Office, 1915.

PRIMARY SOURCES: BOOKS AND ARTICLES

Abair, Sister Saint Angela Louise. "'A Mustard Seed in Montana': Recollections of the First Indian Mission in Montana: Ursuline Nuns on the Northern Cheyenne Indian Reservation." Edited by Orlan J. Svingen. Montana: The Magazine of Western History 34 (Spring 1984): 16–31.

Arnold, Mary Ellicott, and Mabel Reed. In the Land of Grasshopper Song: Two Women in the Klamath River Indian Country in 1908–09. New York: Vantage Press, 1957; repr., Lincoln: University of Nebraska Press, 1980.

Bailey, E. H. "Practical Friendly Visiting." Lend a Hand: A Record of Progress (July 1895): 60–63.

Battey, Thomas C. The Life and Adventures of a Quaker among the Indians. Introduction by Alice Marriott. Boston: Lee and Shepard, 1875; repr., Norman: University of Oklahoma Press, 1968.

Beecher, Catharine, and Harriet Beecher Stowe. The American Woman's Home, or Principles of Domestic Science; Being a Guide to the Formation and Maintenance of Economical, Healthful, Beautiful and Christian Homes. Introduction by Joseph Van Why. Hartford, Conn.: Stowe-Day Foundation, 1991.

Brown, Estelle Aubrey. Stubborn Fool: A Narrative. Caldwell, Idaho: Caxton Printers, 1952.

Chalcraft, Edwin L. Assimilation's Agent: My Life as a Superintendent in the Indian Boarding School System. Edited and with an introduction by Cary C. Collins. Lincoln: University of Nebraska Press, 2005.

Cook, Joseph. "Frontier Savages, White and Red." Indian Rights Association Pamphlet. Philadelphia, n.d.

Corey, Elizabeth. Bachelor Bess: The Homesteading Letters of Elizabeth Corey, 1909–1919. Edited by Philip L. Gerber. Iowa City: University of Iowa Press, 1990.

Duncan, Kunigunde. Blue Star: The Story of Corabelle Fellows, Teacher at Dakota Missions, 1884–1888. With an introduction by Bruce Forbes. Caldwell, Idaho: Caxton Printers, 1938; repr., St. Paul: Minnesota Historical Society Press, 1990.

Eastman, Charles A. From Deep Woods to Civilization: Chapters in the Autobiography of an Indian. With an introduction by Raymond Wilson. Boston: Little, Brown, 1936; repr., Lincoln: University of Nebraska Press, 1977.

Eastman, Elaine Goodale. *Pratt, the Red Man's Moses*. Norman: University of Oklahoma Press, 1935.

———. *Sister to the Sioux: The Memoirs of Elaine Goodale Eastman, 1885–91*. Edited by Kay Graber. Lincoln: University of Nebraska Press, 1978.

Fisk, Clinton B. *Plain Counsels for Freedmen: In Sixteen Brief Lectures*. American Tract Society, 1866.

Freer, William B. *The Philippine Experiences of an American Teacher: A Narrative of Work and Travel in the Philippine Islands*. New York: Scribner's Sons, 1918.

Gay, E. Jane. *With the Nez Perces: Alice Fletcher in the Field, 1889–92*. Edited and with an introduction by Frederick E. Hoxie and Joan T. Mark. Lincoln: University of Nebraska Press, 1981.

Gill, Wilson Lindsley. *A New Citizenship: Democracy Systemized for Moral and Civic Training*. Philadelphia: American Patriotic League, 1913.

Golden, Gertrude. *Red Moon Called Me: Memoirs of an Indian Service School Teacher*. Edited by Cecil Dryden. San Antonio, Tex.: Naylor Company Book Publishers, 1954.

Gregg, Elinor D. "A Federal Nursing Service above the Arctic Circle." *American Journal of Nursing* 36, no. 2 (February 1936): 128–34.

———. "The Government Hires a Nurse." *American Journal of Nursing* 39, no. 5 (May 1939): 524–28.

———. *The Indian and the Nurse*. Norman: University of Oklahoma Press, 1965.

Heizer, Robert F., ed. *Federal Concerns about Conditions of California Indians, 1853 to 1913: Eight Documents*. New Mexico: Ballena Press, 1979.

Horne, Esther Burnett. *Essie's Story: The Life and Legacy of a Shoshone Teacher*. Lincoln: University of Nebraska Press, 1998.

Howard, O. O. *The Autobiography of General O. O. Howard*. Vol. 2. New York, 1907.

Hoxie, Frederick E., ed. *Talking Back to Civilization: Indian Voices from the Progressive Era*. Boston: Bedford/St. Martins, 2001.

Iliff, Flora Gregg. "The Medicine Man at Work." *Southern Workman* 47, no. 11 (1918): 544–47.

———. *People of the Blue Water: My Adventures among the Walapai and Havasupai Indians*. New York: Harper & Brothers, 1954.

Institute for Government Research. *The Problem of Indian Administration*. Edited by Lewis Meriam. Baltimore: Johns Hopkins University Press, 1928.

Jackson, Helen Hunt. *A Century of Dishonor: A Sketch of the United States Government's Dealings with Some of the Indian Tribes*. Forward by Valerie Sherer Mathes. New York: Harper & Brothers, 1885; repr., Norman: University of Oklahoma Press, 1995.

Jenkins, Minnie Braithwaite. *Girl from Williamsburg*. Richmond, Va.: Dietz Press, 1951.

Kneale, Alfred. *Indian Agent*. Caldwell, Idaho: Caxton Printers, 1950.

Leupp, Francis E. *The Indian and His Problem*. New York: Scribner's Sons, 1910.

———. *The Man Roosevelt: A Portrait Sketch*. New York: D. Appleton and Company, 1915.

———. "Woman in the Indian Service: Sometimes She Is a Nurse, Sometimes a Pottery Worker, Sometimes a Detective, but Always an Efficient Aid." *Delineator* 75 (June 1910): 484–85.

McCaskill, Joseph C. *The Boys' Adviser in the Government Boarding Schools for Indians*. Lawrence, Kans.: Haskell Institute, 1934.

McLaughlin, James. *My Friend the Indian*. Boston: Houghton Mifflin, 1910.

Mooney, James. "Myths of the Cherokee." In *Nineteenth Annual Report of the Bureau of American Ethnology to the Secretary of the Smithsonian Institution, 1897–98*, edited by J. W. Powell. Washington, D.C., 1900.

Morgan, Thisba Hutson. "Reminiscences of My Days in the Land of the Ogallala Sioux." *South Dakota Historical Collections* 29 (1958): 21–46.

Morgan, Thomas Jefferson. "The Education of American Indians." N.p., n.d.

Nabokov, Peter, ed. *Native American Testimony: An Anthology of Indian and White Relations from Prophecy to the Present, 1492–1992*. New York: Penguin, 1992.

Nienburg, Bertha M. "Status of Women in the Government Service in 1925." *Bulletin of the Women's Bureau*, no. 53. Washington, D.C.: Government Printing Office, 1926.

Nock, George W. "Teacher to the Mojaves: The Experiences of George W. Nock, 1887–1889, Part I." Edited by Henry P. Walker. *Arizona and the West* 9 (Summer 1967): 143–66.

Pilling, James Constantine. *Bibliography of Siouan Languages*. Washington, D.C.: Government Printing Office, 1887.

Pratt, Richard Henry. *Battlefield and Classroom: An Autobiography*. Edited by Robert M. Utley. Tulsa: University of Oklahoma Press, 2003.

Proctor, Arthur W. *Principles of Public Personnel Administration*. Institute for Government Research. New York: D. Appleton & Company, 1921.

Qoyawayma, Polingaysi [Elizabeth Q. White]. *No Turning Back: A Hopi Indian Woman's Struggle to Live in Two Worlds*. As told to Vada F. Carlson. Albuquerque: University of New Mexico Press, 1964.

Ramona Mission and the Mission Indians. N.p.: Publications of the WNIA, May 1889.

Ronan, Mary. *Frontier Woman: The Story of Mary Ronan as Told to Margaret Ronan*. Edited by H. G. Merriam. Missoula: University of Montana Press, 1973.

Roosevelt, Theodore. *An Autobiography*. New York: The MacMillan Co., 1913.

Ruckman, Jo Ann. "Indian Schooling in New Mexico in the 1890s: Letters of a Teacher in the Indian Service." *New Mexico Historical Review* 56 (January 1981): 37–69.

Schmeckebier, Laurence F. *The Office of Indian Affairs: Its History, Activities, and Organization*. Institute for Government Research Service Monographs of the United States Government, no. 48. Baltimore: John Hopkins University Press, 1927.

Scoville, Annie Beecher. "The Field Matron's Mission." *Outlook* 68 (August 1901).

Soulé, J. H. *The United States Blue Book: A Register of Federal Offices and Employments in Each Territory and the District of Columbia with Their Salaries and Emoluments*. 6th ed. Washington, D.C.: J. H. Soulé Publisher, 1893.

Sparhawk, Francis C. *Report of the Committee on Indian Libraries*. N.p.: Publications of the WNIA, November 1891.

Standing Bear, Luther. *Land of the Spotted Eagle*. Foreword by Richard N. Ellis. New York: Houghton Mifflin, 1933; repr., Lincoln: University of Nebraska Press, 1978.

———. *My People, the Sioux*. Foreword by Richard N. Ellis. New York: Houghton Mifflin, 1928; repr., Lincoln: University of Nebraska Press, 1975.

Stewart, Irene. *A Voice in Her Tribe: A Navajo Woman's Own Story*. Edited by Lowell John Bean and Thomas C. Blackburn. Socorro, N.Mex.: Ballena Press Anthropological Papers, No. 17, 1980.

Taber, Cornelia. *California and Her Indian Children*. N.p., 1911.

Tatum, Laurie. *Our Red Brothers and the Peace Policy of Ulysses S. Grant*. Foreword by Richard Ellis. Philadelphia: J.C. Winston, 1899; repr., Lincoln: University of Nebraska Press, 1970.

Tilson, Laura E. *Report on Hospital Work*. N.p.: Publications of the WNIA, 1891.

U.S. Bureau of the Census. *Historical Statistics of the United States, Colonial Times to 1970*. Bicentennial Edition, pt. 2. Washington, D.C., 1975.

———. *Twelfth Census of the United States*. Washington, D.C.: National Archives and Records Administration, 1900.

Ward, Alice May. "Red Tragedies: The Experiences of a Field Matron on the Cheyenne Reservation in Montana." *Sunset Magazine* 50 (1923): 23.

Warren, Charles. *Answers to Inquiries about the U.S. Bureau of Education, Its Work and History: Prepared, under the Direction of the Commissioner*. Washington, D.C.: Government Printing Office, 1883.

Welsh, Herbert. *A Dangerous Assault upon the Integrity of the Civil Service Law in the Indian Service*. Philadelphia: Indian Rights Association, 1893.

White, E. E. *Experiences of a Special Indian Agent*. Introduction by Edward Everett Dale. Little Rock, Ark.: Diploma Press, 1893; repr., Norman: University of Oklahoma Press, 1965.

Woehlke, Walter V. "The Filipino and the Indian: Why Has America Uplifted the One and Slaughtered the Other?" *Sunset Magazine* 50 (April 1923): 25.

Woodruff, Janette. *Indian Oasis*. Edited by Cecil Dryden. Caldwell, Idaho: The Caxton Printers, Ltd., 1939.

Woodworth-Ney, Laura. "The Diaries of a Day-School Teacher: Daily Realities on the Pine Ridge Indian Reservation, 1932–1942." *South Dakota History* 24 (Fall/Winter 1994): 194–211.

The World Almanac and Book of Facts. N.p., 1899.

The World Almanac and Encyclopedia 1916. New York: Press Publishing Co., 1915.

Wright, A. O. "Contributions: An Indian School." *Wisconsin Journal of Education* 30, no. 4 (April 1900): 83–85.

Wyaco, Virgil. *A Zuni Life: A Pueblo Indian in Two Worlds*. Transcribed and edited by J. A. Jones, with a historical sketch by Carroll L. Riley. Albuquerque: University of New Mexico Press, 1989.

Zitkala-Sa. *American Indian Stories*. Forward by Dexter Fisher. Washington, D.C.: Hayworth Publishing House, 1921; repr., Lincoln: University of Nebraska Press, 1985.

SECONDARY SOURCES

Aadland, Dan. *Women and Warriors of the Plains: The Pioneer Photography of Julia E. Tuell*. New York: Macmillan, 1996.

Adams, David Wallace. *Education for Extinction: American Indians and the Boarding School Experience, 1875–1928*. Lawrence: University Press of Kansas, 1995.

———. "Education in Hues: Red and Black at Hampton Institute, 1878–1893." *Southern Atlantic Quarterly* 76 (Spring 1977): 159–76.

———. "Fundamental Considerations: The Deep Meaning of Native American Schooling, 1880–1900." *Harvard Educational Review* 58, no. 1 (February 1988): 1–28.

Ahern, William. "An Experiment Aborted: Returned Indian Students in the Indian School Service." *Ethnohistory* 44 (Spring 1997): 263–304.

Albers, Patricia, and Beatrice Medicine, eds. *The Hidden Half: Studies of Plains Indian Women.* Washington, D.C.: UP of America, 1983.

Alexander, Ruth Ann. "Gentle Evangelists: Women in Dakota Episcopal Missions, 1867–1900." *South Dakota History* 24 (Fall/Winter 1994): 175–93.

———. "'The Perfect Christian Gentleman': Women and Bishop William Hobart Hare in South Dakota Missions." *Anglican and Episcopal History* 63 (September 1994): 335–62.

Allen, Paula Gunn. "Does Euro-think Become Us?" In *Daughter of Mother Earth: The Wisdom of Native American Women*, edited by Barbara Alice Mann, 1–28. Westport, Conn.: Praeger, 2006.

American Journal of Nursing.

Anderson, Benedict. *Imagined Communities: Reflections on the Origin and Spread of Nationalism.* London: Verso, 1983, 1991.

Anderson, Douglas Firth. "Protestantism, Progress, and Prosperity: John P. Clum and 'Civilizing' the U.S. Southwest, 1871–1886." *Western Historical Quarterly* 33 (Autumn 2002): 315–36.

Andrews, Thomas G. "Turning the Tables on Assimilation: Oglala Lakotas and the Pine Ridge Day Schools, 1889–1920s." *Western Historical Quarterly* 33 (Winter 2002): 407–30.

Aron, Cindy. *Ladies and Gentlemen of the Civil Service.* New York: Oxford University Press, 1987.

———. *Working at Play: A History of Vacations in the United States.* New York: Oxford University Press, 1999.

Baish, H. H. "Retirement Systems and Moral in Public Service." *Annals of the American Academy of Political and Social Science*, vol. 113, *Competency and Economy.* In *Public Expenditures* (May 1924): 338–50.

Baker, Paula. "The Domestication of Politics: Women and American Political Society, 1780–1920." In *Women, the State, and Welfare*, edited by Linda Gordon, 55–91. Madison: University of Wisconsin Press, 1990.

Bannan, Helen M. "Newcomers to Navajoland: Transculturation in the Memoirs of Anglo Women, 1900–1945." *New Mexico Historical Review* 59 (April 1984): 165–86.

———. "'True Womanhood' on the Reservation: Field Matrons in the United States Indian Service." Working Paper 18, Southwest Institute for Research on Women. Tucson: University of Arizona Press, 1984.

Barrett, Samuel A. *Pomo Indian Basketry.* Introduction by Sherri Smith-Ferri. Berkeley: Phoebe Hearst Museum of Anthropology, 1996.

Basch, Norma. *Framing American Divorce: From the Revolutionary Generation to the Victorians.* Berkeley: University of California Press, 1999.

Bauer, William, Jr. *We Are All Like Migrant Workers Here: Work, Community, and Memory on California's Round Valley Reservation, 1850–1941.* Chapel Hill: University of North Carolina Press, 2009.

Bederman, Gail. *Manliness and Civilization: A Cultural History of Gender and Race in the United States, 1880–1917.* Chicago: University of Chicago Press, 1995.

Bell, Maureen. *Karuk: The Upriver People.* Happy Camp, Calif.: Naturegraph Publishers, 1991, 2002.

Bensel, Richard Franklin. *Yankee Leviathan: The Origins of Central State Authority in America, 1859–1877.* New York: Cambridge University Press, 1990.

Benson, Susan Porter. *Counter Cultures: Saleswomen, Managers, and Customers in American Department Stores, 1890–1940.* Champaign: University of Illinois Press, 1988.

Berkhofer, Robert F. *Salvation and the Savage: An Analysis of Protestant Missions and American Indian Responses, 1787–1862.* New York: Antheneum, 1965, 1976.

Berthrong, Robert. "Jessie Rowlodge: Southern Arapaho Political Intermediary." In *Between Indian and White Worlds: The Cultural Broker,* edited by Margaret Connell-Szasz, 217–22. Norman: University of Oklahoma Press, 1994.

Biolsi, Thomas. *Deadliest Enemies: Law and Race Relations on and off Rosebud Reservation.* Berkeley: University of California Press, 2007.

Bordin, Ruth. *Woman and Temperance: The Quest for Power and Liberty, 1873–1900.* Philadelphia: Temple University Press, 1981.

Boydston, Jean. *Home and Work: Housework, Wages, and the Ideology of Labor in the Early Republic.* New York: Oxford University Press, 1990.

Boyer, Paul. *Urban Masses and Moral Order in America, 1820–1920.* Cambridge: Harvard University Press, 1978.

Bracken, Christopher. *The Potlatch Papers: A Colonial Case History.* Chicago: University of Chicago Press, 1997.

Bredbenner, Candice L. *A Nationality of Her Own: Women, Marriage, and the Law of Citizenship.* Berkeley: University of California Press, 1998.

Brown, Richard Maxwell. "Violence." In *The Oxford History of the American West,* edited by Clyde Milner, Carol A. O'Connor, and Martha A. Sandweiss, 393–426. New York: Oxford University Press, 1994.

Brudvig, Jon L. *Hampton Normal and Agricultural Institutes American Indian Students, 1878–1923.* 1994; 1996. ⟨http://www.twofrog.com/hamptonmale1.txt⟩. 9 September 2007.

Brumberg, Joan J. *Mission for Life: The Story of the Family of Adoniram Judson, the Dramatic Events of the First American Foreign Mission and the Course of Evangelical Religion in the Nineteenth Century.* New York: Free Press, 1980.

Buckley, Thomas C. T. *Standing Ground: Yurok Indian Spirituality, 1850–1990.* University of California Press, 2002.

Buffalohead, W. Roger, and Paulette Fairbanks Molin. "'A Nucleus of Civilization': American Indian Families at Hampton Institute in the Late Nineteenth Century." *Journal of American Indian Education* 35, no. 3 (May 1996): 59–94.

Burgess, Larry E. "The Lake Mohonk Conferences on the Indian, 1883–1916." Ph.D. diss., Claremont Graduate University, 1972.

———. *Mohonk, Its People and Spirit: A History of One-Hundred Years of Growth and Service.* New York: Smiley Brothers, 1980.

Cahill, Cathleen D. "'Only the Home Can Found a State': Gender, Labor, and the United States Indian Service, 1869–1928." Ph.D. diss., University of Chicago, 2004.
———. "'You Think It Strange That I Can Love an Indian': Native Men, White Women, and Marriage in the Indian Service." *Frontiers: A Journal of Women Studies* 29, nos. 2 and 3 (2008): 106–45.

Calloway, Colin G. *Our Hearts Fell to the Ground: Plains Indian Views of How the West Was Lost.* Boston: Bedford Books, 1996.

Carby, Hazel V. *Reconstructing Womanhood: The Emergence of the Afro-American Woman Novelist.* New York: Oxford University Press, 1987.

Carney, Virginia Moore. *Eastern Band Cherokee Women: Cultural Persistence in Their Letters and Speeches.* Knoxville: University Tennessee Press, 2005.

Carter, Patricia A. "'Completely Discouraged': Women Teachers' Resistance in the Bureau of Indian Affairs Schools, 1900–1910." *Frontiers* 15 (1995): 53.

Carter, Susan B., ed. *Historical Statistics of the United States: Earliest Times to the Present.* Vol. 2, *Work and Welfare.* New York: Cambridge University Press, 2006.

Carter, Thomas, Edward Chappell, and Timothy McCleary. "In the Lodge of the Chickadee: Architecture and Cultural Resistance on the Crow Indian Reservation, 1884–1920." *Perspectives in Vernacular Architecture* 10 (2005): 97–111.

Child, Brenda J. *Boarding School Seasons: American Indian Families, 1900–1940.* Lincoln: University of Nebraska Press, 1998.

Clark, D. Anthony Tyeeme. "At the Headwaters of a Twentieth-Century 'Indian' Political Agenda: Rethinking the Origins of the Society of American Indians." In *Beyond Red Power: American Indian Politics and Activism since 1900,* edited by Daniel M. Cobb and Loretta Fowler, 70–90. Santa Fe: School for Advanced Research, 2007.
———. "Representing Indians: Indigenous Fugitives and the Society of American Indians in the Making of Common Culture." Ph.D. diss., University of Kansas, 2004.

Clark, Elizabeth B. "'The Sacred Rights of the Weak': Pain, Sympathy, and the Culture of Individual Rights in Antebellum America." *Journal of American History* 82 (September 1995): 463–93.

Clark, Neil M. "Dr. Montezuma, Apache: Warrior in Two Worlds." *Montana: The Magazine of Western History* 23 (April 1973): 56–65.

Clark, Robert L., Lee A. Craig, and Jack W. Wilson. *A History of Public Sector Pensions in the United States.* Philadelphia: University of Pennsylvania Press, 2003.

Clemmons, Linda. "'Our Children Are in Danger of Becoming Little Indians': Protestant Missionary Children and Dakotas, 1835–1862." *Michigan Historical Review* 25 (Fall 1999): 69–90.

Clifford, Geraldine Jonçich. "Man/Woman/Teacher: Gender, Family, and Career in American Educational History." In *American Teachers: Histories of a Profession at Work,* edited by Donald Warren, 293–343. New York: Macmillan, 1989.

Coleman, Michael C. *American Indian Children at School, 1850–1930.* Jackson: University Press of Mississippi, 1993.
———. "Not Race, but Grace: Presbyterian Missionaries and American Indians, 1837–1893." *Journal of American History* 67 (June 1980): 41–60.

Comaroff, Jean, and John Comaroff. *Of Revelation and Revolution: Christianity, Colonialism, and Consciousness in South Africa.* Vol. 1. Chicago: University of Chicago Press, 1991.

Connell-Szasz, Margaret. *Education and the American Indian: The Road to Self-Determination since 1928.* Albuquerque: University of New Mexico Press, 1974, 1999.

———, ed. *Between Indian and White Worlds: The Cultural Broker.* University of Oklahoma Press, 1994.

Costa, Dora. *The Evolution of Retirement: An American Economic History, 1880–1990.* Chicago: University of Chicago Press, 1998.

Cott, Nancy. *The Bonds of Womanhood: "Woman's Sphere" in New England, 1780–1835.* New Haven: Yale University Press, 1987.

———. *Public Vows: A History of Marriage and the Nation.* Cambridge: Harvard University Press, 2000.

Cox-Richardson, Heather. *The Death of Reconstruction: Race, Labor, and Politics in the Post–Civil War North, 1865–1901.* Cambridge: Harvard University Press, 2001.

———. *West from Appomattox: The Reconstruction of America after the Civil War.* New Haven: Yale University Press, 2007.

Cremin, Laurence A. *American Education: The Metropolitan Experience.* New York: Harper & Row, 1988.

Critchlow, Donald T. "Lewis Meriam, Expertise, and Indian Reform." *Historian* 43 (May 1981): 325–44.

Danziger, Edmund Jefferson. *Indians and Bureaucrats: Administering the Reservation Policy during the Civil War.* Urbana: University of Illinois Press, 1974.

Davis, Lee. "California Tribes." In *Encyclopedia of North American Indians,* edited by Frederick E. Hoxie. Boston: Houghton Mifflin Company, 1996.

Deloria, Philip J. *Indians in Unexpected Places.* Lawrence: University Press of Kansas, 2004.

———. *Playing Indian.* New Haven: Yale University Press, 1998.

Deloria, Vine, *Custer Died for Your Sins.* Norman: University of Oklahoma Press, 1988.

———, ed. *The Indian Reorganization Act: Congresses and Bills.* Norman: University of Oklahoma Press, 2002.

Deloria, Vine, and Clifford M. Lytle. *The Nations Within: The Past and Future of American Indian Sovereignty.* Austin: University of Texas Press, 1998.

DeMallie, Raymond. "Male and Female in Traditional Lakota Culture." In *The Hidden Half: Studies of Plains Indian Women,* edited by Patricia Albers and Beatrice Medicine, 237–66. Washington, D.C.: University Press of America, 1983.

Denby, David. *Battle for the BIA: G. E. E. Lindquist and the Missionary Crusade against John Collier.* Tucson: University of Arizona Press, 2004.

Densmore, Frances. *Chippewa Customs.* Bureau of American Ethnology, Bulletin 86. Washington, D.C.: Government Printing Office, 1929.

———. "Use of Plants by the Chippewa Indians." In *The Annual Report of the Bureau of American Ethnology, 1926–1927,* 275–398. Washington, D.C.: Government Printing Office, 1928.

———. "The Words of Indian Songs as Unwritten Literature." *Journal of American Folklore* 63, no. 250 (October–December 1950): 450–58.

Deutsch, Sarah. *No Separate Refuge: Culture, Class, and Gender on an Anglo-Hispanic Frontier in the American Southwest, 1880–1940.* New York: Oxford University Press, 1987.

———. *Women and the City: Gender, Space, and Power in Boston, 1870–1940.* New York: Oxford University Press, 2000.

Dippie, Brian W. *The Vanishing America: White Attitudes and U.S. Indian Policy*. Middletown, Conn.: Wesleyan University Press, 1982.

Dorsey, Bruce. *Reforming Men and Women: Gender in the Antebellum City*. Ithaca, N.Y.: Cornell University Press, 2002.

Douglas, Ann. *The Feminization of American Culture*. New York: Knopf, 1977.

Doyle, John T. "The Federal Civil Service Retirement Law." *Annals of the American Academy of Political and Social Science* 113 (May 1924): 330–38.

Dublin, Thomas. *Transforming Women's Work: New England Lives in the Industrial Revolution*. Ithaca, N.Y.: Cornell University Press, 1994.

Dyk, Walter. "Preface." In *Left Handed, Son of Old Man Hat: A Navajo Autobiography*. Lincoln: University of Nebraska Press, 1967. Originally published as *Son of Old Man Hat: A Navajo Autobiography* by Harcourt, Brace & World, 1938.

Edmunds, R. David. *The New Warriors: Native American Leaders since 1900*. Lincoln: University of Nebraska Press, 2001.

Edney, Matthew H. *Mapping an Empire: The Geographical Construction of British Indian, 1765–1843*. Chicago: University of Chicago Press, 1997.

Edwards, Laura F. *Gendered Strife and Confusion: The Political Culture of Reconstruction*. Urbana: University of Illinois Press, 1997.

Elben, Jack E. *The First and Second United States Empires: Governors and Territorial Government, 1784–1912*. Pittsburgh: University of Pittsburgh Press, 1968.

Ellinghaus, Katherine. "Assimilation by Marriage: White Women and Native American Men at Hampton Institute, 1878–1923." *Virginia Magazine of History and Biography* 108, no. 3 (2000): 279–303.

———. *Taking Assimilation to Heart: Marriages of White Women and Indigenous Men in the United States and Australia, 1887–1937*. Lincoln: University of Nebraska Press, 2006.

Ellis, Clyde. *To Change Them Forever: Indian Education at the Rainy Mountain Boarding School, 1893–1920*. Norman: University of Oklahoma Press, 1996.

———. "'We Had a Lot of Fun, but of Course That Wasn't the School Part': Life at Rainy Mountain Boarding School, 1893–1920." In *Boarding School Blues: Revisiting American Indian Educational Experiences*, edited by Clifford E. Trafzer, Jean A. Keller, and Lorene Sisquoc, 65–98. Lincoln: University of Nebraska Press, 2006.

Ellis, Clyde, Luke Eric Lassiter, and Gary H. Dunham. *Powwow*. Lincoln: University of Nebraska Press, 2005.

Ellis, Mark R. "Reservation Akicitas: The Pine Ridge Indian Police, 1879–1885." *South Dakota History* 29 (Fall 1999): 185–210.

Emmerich, Lisa. "The Field Matron Program and Cross-Cultural Contact." *American Indian Culture and Research Journal* 15, no. 4 (1991): 33–48.

———. "Marguerite LaFlesche Diddock: Office of Indian Affairs Field Matron." *Great Plains Quarterly* 13 (Summer 1993): 162–71.

———. "'Right in the Midst of My Own People': Native American Women and the Field Matron Program." *American Indian Quarterly* 15 (Spring 1991): 201–16.

———. "'Save the Babies!': American Indian Women, Assimilation Policy, and Scientific Motherhood, 1912–1918." In *Writing the Range: Race, Class, and Culture in the Women's West*, edited by Elizabeth Jameson and Susan Armitage, 393–411. Norman: University of Oklahoma Pres, 1997.

————. "'To Respect and Love and Seek the Ways of White Women': Field Matrons, the Office of Indian Affairs, and Civilization Policy, 1890–1938." Ph.D. diss., University of Maryland, 1987.

Engs, Robert F. *Educating the Disfranchised and Disinherited: Samuel Chapman Armstrong and Hampton Institute, 1839–1893*. Knoxville: University of Tennessee Press, 1999.

Epstein, Barbara Leslie. *The Politics of Domesticity: Women, Evangelism, and Temperance in Nineteenth-Century America*. Middletown, Conn.: Wesleyan University Press, 1981.

Farragher, John Mack. *Women and Men on the Overland Trail*. New Haven: Yale University Press, 1979.

Fear-Segal, Jacqueline. "'Use the Club of White Man's Wisdom in Defense of Our Customs': White Schools and Native Agendas." *American Studies International* 40 (October 2002): 6–32.

————. *White Man's Club: Schools, Race, and the Struggle of Indian Acculturation*. Lincoln: University of Nebraska Press, 2007.

Findlay, Eileen. *Imposing Decency: The Politics of Sexuality and Race in Puerto Rico, 1870–1920*. Durham, N.C.: Duke University Press, 1999.

Finger, John R. *The Eastern Band of Cherokee, 1819–1900*. Knoxville: University of Tennessee Press, 1984.

Fishback, Price V., and Shawn Everett Kantor. *A Prelude to the Welfare State: The Origins of Workers' Compensation*. Chicago: University of Chicago Press, 2006.

Flanagan, Maureen A. *Seeing with Their Hearts: Chicago Women and the Vision of the Good City, 1871–1933*. Princeton: Princeton University Press, 2002.

Flores, Dan. "Bison Ecology and Bison Diplomacy: The Southern Plains from 1800 to 1850." *Journal of American History* 78 (September 1991): 465–85.

Foner, Eric. *Reconstruction: America's Unfinished Revolution, 1863–1877*. New York: Harper & Row, 1988.

Foucault, Michel. *Discipline and Punish: The Birth of the Prison*. Translated by Alan Sheridan. New York: Pantheon Books, 1977.

————. "Governmentality." In *The Foucault Effect: Studies in Governmentality with Two Lectures by and an Interview with Michel Foucault*, edited by Graham Burchell, Colin Gordon, and Peter Miller, 87–104. Chicago: University of Chicago Press, 1991.

Fowler, Loretta. *Tribal Sovereignty and the Historical Imagination: Cheyenne-Arapaho Politics*. Lincoln: University of Nebraska Press, 2002.

Fox-Genovese, Elizabeth. *Within the Plantation Household: Black and White Women of the Old South*. Chapel Hill: University of North Carolina Press, 1988.

Franchot, Jenny. *Roads to Rome: The Antebellum Protestant Encounter with Catholicism*. Berkeley: University of California Press, 1994.

Fredrickson, George M. *The Black Image in the White Mind: The Debate on Afro-American Character and Destiny, 1817–1914*. New York: Harper & Row, 1971.

Frye-Jackobson, Matthew. *Barbarian Virtues: The United States Encounters Foreign Peoples at Home and Abroad, 1876–1917*. New York: Hill and Wang, 2001.

Garroutte, Eva Marie. *Real Indians: Identity and the Survival of Native America*. University of California Press, 2003.

Gaul, Theresa Strouth, ed. *To Marry an Indian: The Marriage of Harriet Gold and Elias Boudinot in Letters, 1823–1839*. Chapel Hill: University of North Carolina Press, 2005.

Genetin-Pilawa, Joseph C. "Confining Indians: Power, Authority, and the Colonialist Ideologies of Nineteenth-Century Reformers." Ph.D. diss., Michigan State University, 2008.

Gibbon, Guy. *The Sioux: The Dakota and Lakota Nations*. Oxford, UK: Blackwell Publishing, 2003.

Ginzberg, Lori D. "Pernicious Heresies: Female Citizenship and Sexual Respectability in the Nineteenth Century." In *Women in the Unstable State in Nineteenth-Century America*, edited by Alison M. Parker and Stephanie Cole, 139–62. With an introduction by Sarah Barringer Gordon. College Station, Tex.: Texas A&M Press, 2000.

———. *Women and the Work of Benevolence: Morality, Politics, and Class in the Nineteenth-Century United States*. New Haven: Yale University Press, 1990.

Go, Julian. "Global Perspectives on the U.S. Colonial State in the Philippines." In *The American Colonial State in the Philippines: Global Perspectives*, edited by Julian Go and Anne Foster, 1–22. Durham, N.C.: Duke University Press, 2003.

Goddard, Pliny Earle. *Life and Culture of the Hupa*. Berkeley: The University Press, 1903.

Gonzalez, Penny. "Ojibwa Women and Marriage from Traditional to Modern Society." *Wicazo Sa Review* 8, no. 1 (Spring 1992): 31–34.

Gordon, Linda. *The Great Arizona Orphan Abduction*. Cambridge: Harvard University Press, 2001.

———. "Internal Colonialism and Gender." In *Haunted By Empire*, edited by Anne Stoler, 427–51. Durham, N.C.: Duke University Press, 2006.

———. *Pitied but Not Entitled: Single Mothers and the History of Welfare, 1890–1935*. Cambridge: Harvard University Press, 1994.

———, ed. *Women, the State, and Welfare*. Madison: University of Wisconsin Press, 1990.

Gordon, Sarah Barringer. *The Mormon Question: Polygamy and Constitutional Conflict in Nineteenth-Century America*. Chapel Hill: University of North Carolina Press, 2002.

Gray, Susan. *The Yankee West: Community Life on the Michigan Frontier*. Chapel Hill: University of North Carolina Press, 1996.

Greenwald, Emily. *Reconfiguring the Reservation: The Nez Perces, Jicarilla Apaches, and the Dawes Act*. Albuquerque: University of New Mexico Press, 2002.

Gustafson, Melanie Susan. *Women in the Republican Party, 1854–1924*. Urbana: University of Illinois Press, 2001.

Hagan, William T. *Indian Police and Judges: Experiments in Acculturation and Control*. Lincoln: University of Nebraska Press, 1966, 1980.

———. *The Indian Rights Association: The Herbert Welsh Years*. Tucson: University of Arizona Press, 1985.

———. "Squaw Men on the Kiowa, Comanche, and Apache Reservations: Advance Agents of Civilization or Disturbers of the Peace?" In *The Frontier Challenge: Responses to the Trans-Mississippi West*, edited by John G. Clark, 171–202. Lawrence: University Press of Kansas, 1971.

———. *Theodore Roosevelt and Six Friends of the Indian*. Norman: University of Oklahoma Press, 1997.

Harlan, Louis R. *Booker T. Washington: The Making of a Black Leader, 1856–1901*. New York: Oxford University Press, 1972.

Hartog, Hendrik. *Man and Wife in America: A History*. Cambridge: Harvard University Press, 2000.

Haskell, Thomas L. *The Emergence of Professional Social Science: The American Social Science Association and the Nineteenth-Century Crises of Authority*. Urbana: University of Illinois Press, 1977.

Haskins, Victoria, and Shannon Schedlich-Day. "My Mate Ellen: Cross-Cultural Friendship between Women in a 'Pioneer Memoir.'" In "Indigenous Victorians: Repressed, Resourceful and Respected," edited by Lynette Russell and John Arnold. Special issue, *La Trobe Journal* 85 (May 2010): 70–82.

Hayden, Dolores. *The Grand Domestic Revolution: A History of Feminist Designs for American Homes, Neighborhoods, and Cities*. Cambridge: MIT Press, 1981.

Herr, Elizabeth. "Women, Marital Status, and Work Opportunities in 1880 Colorado." *Journal of Economic History* 55 (June 1995): 339–66.

Herring, Rebecca. "Their Work Was Never Done: Women Missionaries on the Kiowa-Comanche Reservation." *Chronicles of Oklahoma* 64 (Spring 1986): 69–83.

Hershberger, Mary. "Mobilizing Women, Anticipating Abolition: The Struggle against Indian Removal in the 1830s." *Journal of American History* 86, no. 1 (June 1999): 15–40.

Hertzberg, Hazel W. *The Search for American Indian Identity: Modern Pan-Indian Movements*. Syracuse, N.Y.: Syracuse University Press, 1971.

Hewitt, Nancy. *Women's Activism and Social Change: Rochester, New York, 1822–1872*. Ithaca, N.Y.: Cornell University Press, 1984.

Hill, Patricia. *The World Their Household: The American Woman's Foreign Missionary Movement and Cultural Transformation, 1870–1920*. Ann Arbor: University of Michigan Press, 1985.

Hodes, Martha. *White Women, Black Men: Illicit Sex in the Nineteenth-Century South*. New Haven: Yale University Press, 1997.

———, ed. *Sex, Love, Race: Crossing Boundaries in North American History*. New York: New York University Press, 1999.

Hoganson, Kristin L. *Fighting for American Manhood: How Gender Politics Provoked the Spanish-American and Philippine-American War*. New Haven: Yale University Press, 1999.

Holliday, J. S., and William Swain. *The World Rushed In: The California Gold Rush Experience*. Norman: University of Oklahoma Press, 2002.

Holm, Tom. *The Great Confusion in Indian Affairs: Native Americans and Whites in the Progressive Era*. Austin: University of Texas Press, 2005.

Hoogenboom, Ari. *Outlawing the Spoils: A History of the Civil Service Reform Movement, 1865–1883*. Urbana: University of Illinois Press, 1961.

Hosmer, Brian C. *American Indians in the Marketplace: Persistence and Innovation among the Menominees and Metlakatans, 1870–1920*. Lawrence: University Press of Kansas, 1999.

Hosmer, Brian C., and Colleen M. O'Neill, eds. *Native Pathways: American Indian Culture and Economic Development in the Twentieth Century*. Boulder: University Press of Colorado, 2004.

Houston, Robert B., Jr. *Two Colorado Odysseys: Chief Ouray Porter Nelson*. iUniverse, 2005.

Hoxie, Frederick E. *A Final Promise: The Campaign to Assimilate the Indians, 1880–1920*. Lincoln: University of Nebraska Press, 1984.

———. *Parading through History: The Making of the Crow Nation in America, 1805–1935.*
New York: Cambridge University Press, 1995.

———. "Redefining Indian Education: Thomas J. Morgan's Program in Disarray."
Arizona and the West 24, no. 1 (Spring 1982): 5–18.

———, ed. *Encyclopedia of North American Indians.* Boston: Houghton Mifflin
Company, 1996.

Hunter, Jane. *The Gospel of Gentility: American Women Missionaries and Turn-of-the-
Century China.* New Haven: Yale University Press, 1984.

Hurt, R. Douglass. *Indian Agriculture in America: Prehistory to the Present.* Lawrence:
University Press of Kansas, 1987.

Hutchinson, William. *Errand unto the World: American Protestant Thought and Foreign
Missions.* Chicago: University of Chicago Press, 1987.

Ingersoll, Thomas N. *To Intermix with Our White Brothers: Indian Mixed Bloods in the
United States from Earliest Times to the Indian Removals.* Albuquerque: University of
New Mexico Press, 2005.

Iverson, Peter. *Carlos Montezuma and the Changing World of American Indians.*
Albuquerque: University of New Mexico Press, 1982.

———. *When Indians Became Cowboys: Native Peoples and Cattle Ranching in the
American West.* Norman: University of Oklahoma Press, 1997.

Jacobs, Margaret D. *Engendered Encounters: Feminism and Pueblo Cultures, 1879–1934.*
Lincoln: University of Nebraska Press, 1999.

———. *White Mother to a Dark Race: Settler Colonialism, Maternalism, and the Removal
of Indigenous Children in the American West and Australia, 1880–1940.* Lincoln:
University of Nebraska Press, 2009.

———. "Working on the Domestic Frontier: American Indian Domestic Servants
in White Women's Households in the San Francisco Bay Area, 1920–1940." In
"Domestic Frontiers: The Home and Colonization." Special issue, *Frontiers: A Journal
of Women Studies* 28, nos. 1–2 (2007): 165–99.

Jensen, Laura. *Patriots, Settlers, and the Origins of American Social Policy.* Cambridge,
UK: Cambridge University Press, 2003.

Johnson, Allen, ed. *Dictionary of American Biography.* Vols. 6, 14, and 15. New York:
Charles Scribner's Sons, 1928.

Johnson, David L., and Raymond Wilson. "Gertrude Simmons Bonnin, 1876–1938:
'Americanizing the First America.'" *American Indian Quarterly* 10 (Winter 1988):
27–40.

Johnson, Walter. "On Agency." *Journal of Social History* 37, no. 1 (Fall 2003): 113–24.

Johnston, Robert D. "Beyond 'The West': Regionalism, Liberalism, and the Evasion of
Politics in the New Western History." *Rethinking History* 2, no. 2 (1998): 239–77.

Jones, Jacqueline. *Soldiers of Light and Love: Northern Teachers and Georgia Blacks,
1865–1873.* Chapel Hill: University of North Carolina Press, 1980.

Josephy, Alvin M., Jr. *Nez Perce Country.* Lincoln: University of Nebraska Press, 2007.

Kaplan, Amy. "'Left Alone with America': The Absence of Empire in the Study of
American Culture." In *Cultures of United States Imperialism*, edited by Amy Kaplan
and Donald E. Pease, 3–21. Durham, N.C.: Duke University Press, 1993.

Katz, Michael B. *In the Shadow of the Poorhouse: A Social History of Welfare in America.*
New York: Basic Books, 1986.

Keller, Jean A. *Empty Beds: Indian Student Health at Sherman Institute, 1902–1922.* Ann Arbor: University of Michigan Press, 2002.

Keller, Morton. *Regulating a New Society: Public Policy and Social Change in America, 1900–1933.* Cambridge: Harvard University Press, 1994.

Keller, Robert H., Jr. *American Protestantism and United States Indian Policy, 1869–1882.* Lincoln: University of Nebraska Press, 1983.

Kelly, Lawrence C. *The Assault on Assimilation: John Collier and the Origins of Indian Policy Reform.* Albuquerque: University of New Mexico Press, 1983.

Kelly, Patrick. *Creating a National Home: Building the Veterans' Welfare State, 1860–1900.* Cambridge: Harvard University Press, 1997.

Kelsey, Harry. "A Dedication to the Memory of Annie Heloise Abel-Henderson, 1837–1947." *Arizona and the West* 15 (Spring 1973): 1–4.

Kerber, Linda K. "The Abolitionist Perception of the Indian." *Journal of American History* 62 (September 1975): 271–95.

Kessler-Harris, Alice. *In Pursuit of Equity: Women, Men, and the Quest for Economic Citizenship in Twentieth-Century America.* New York: Oxford University Press, 2001.

King, Charles R. "Indian Service Physician on the Northern Plains: Dr. James L. Neaves at Ft. Berthold, 1878–1885." *North Dakota History* 58 (Fall 1991): 20–34.

Klibard, Herbert M. *Schooled to Work: Vocationalism and the American Curriculum, 1876–1946.* New York: Teachers College Press, 1999.

Knack, Martha C. "Philene T. Hall, Bureau of Indian Affairs Field Matron: Planned Culture Change of Washakie Shoshone Women." *Prologue* 22 (Summer 1990): 151–67.

Koven, Seth, and Sonya Michel, eds. *Mothers of a New World: Maternalist Politics and the Origins of Welfare States.* New York: Routledge, 1993.

Kraines, Oscar. "The President versus Congress: The Keep Commission, 1905–1909: First Comprehensive Presidential Inquiry into Administration." *Western Political Quarterly* 23, no. 1 (March 1970): 5–54.

Krainz, Thomas A. *Delivering Aid: Implementing Progressive-Era Welfare in the American West.* Albuquerque: University of New Mexico Press, 2005.

Kramer, Paul A. *The Blood of Government: Race, Empire, the United States, and the Philippines.* Chapel Hill: University of North Carolina Press, 2006.

Kroeber, Alfred Louis. *Handbook of the Indians of California.* Berkeley: California Book Company, 1953. Reprint of Bureau of American Ethnology of the Smithsonian Institution Bulletin no. 78, 1925.

Krupat, Arnold, ed. *Native American Autobiography: An Anthology.* Madison: University of Wisconsin Press, 1994.

Kvasnicka, Robert M., and Herman J. Viola, eds. *The Commissioners of Indian Affairs, 1824–1977.* Lincoln: University of Nebraska Press, 1979.

Kwolek-Folland, Angel. *Engendering Business: Men and Women in the Corporate Office, 1870–1930.* Baltimore: Johns Hopkins University Press, 1994.

Lears, Jackson. *No Place of Grace: Anti-Modernism and the Transformation of American Culture.* New York: Pantheon Books, 1981.

Leuchtenburg, William E. "The Pertinence of Political History: Reflections on the Significance of the State in America." *Journal of American History* 73 (December 1986): 585–600.

Lewis, Bonnie Sue. *Creating Christian Indians: Native Clergy in the Presbyterian Church.* Norman: University of Oklahoma Press, 2003.

Lewis, David Rich. *Neither Wolf nor Dog: American Indians, Environment, and Agrarian Change.* New York: Oxford University Press, 1994.

Lewis, Herbert S., and L. Gordon McLester. *Oneida Lives: Long-Lost Voices of the Wisconsin Oneidas.* Lincoln: University of Nebraska Press, 2005.

Lindsey, Donal F. *Indians at Hampton Institute, 1877–1923.* Urbana: University of Illinois Press, 1995.

Littlefield, Alice. "Indian Education and the World of Work in Michigan, 1893–1933." In *Native Americans and Wage Labor: Ethnohistorical Perspectives,* edited by Alice Littlefield and Martha C. Knack, 100–121. Norman: University of Oklahoma Press, 1996.

Littlefield, Alice, and Martha C. Knack, eds., *Native Americans and Wage Labor: Ethnohistorical Perspectives.* Norman: University of Oklahoma Press, 1996.

Lomawaima, K. Tsianina. "Estelle Reel, Superintendent of Indian Schools, 1898–1910: Politics, Curriculum, and Land." *Journal of American Indian Education* 35 (May 1996): 5–32.

———. *They Called It Prairie Light: The Story of Chilocco Indian School.* Lincoln: University of Nebraska Press, 1994.

Lomawaima, K. Tsianina, and Teresa L. McCarty. *To Remain an Indian: Lessons in Democracy from a Century of Native American Education.* New York: Teachers College Press, 2006.

Lui, Mary Ting Li. *The Chinatown Trunk Mystery: Murder, Miscegenation, and Other Dangerous Encounters in Turn of the Century New York.* Princeton: Princeton University Press, 2005.

Mackay, Kathryn L. "Warrior into Welder: A History of Federal Employment Programs for American Indians, 1878–1972." Ph.D. diss., University of Utah, 1987.

Maddox, Lucy. *Citizen Indians: Native American Intellectuals, Race, and Reform.* Ithaca, N.Y.: Cornell University Press, 2006.

Maranto, Robert, and David Schultz. *A Short History of the United States Civil Service.* Lanham, Md.: University Press of America, 1991.

Marchand, Roland. *Advertising the American Dream: Making Way for Modernity, 1920–1940.* Berkeley: University of California Press, 1985.

Mardock, Robert Winston. *The Reformers and the American Indian.* Columbia: University of Missouri Press, 1971.

Marino, Cesare. "Reservations." In *Native Americans in the Twentieth Century: An Encyclopedia,* edited by Mary B. Davis. London: Garland, 1994.

Markowitz, Harvey. "Luther Standing Bear." In *Encyclopedia of North American Indians,* edited by Frederick E. Hoxie, 608. Boston: Houghton Mifflin Company, 1996.

Mathes, Valerie Sherer. "Forward." In *A Century of Dishonor: A Sketch of the United States Government's Dealings with Some of the Indian Tribes,* by Helen Hunt Jackson. New York: Harper & Brothers, 1885; repr., Norman: University of Oklahoma Press, 1995.

———. *Helen Hunt Jackson: Her Indian Reform Legacy.* Austin: University of Texas, 1990.

———. "Nineteenth-Century Women and Reform: The Women's National Indian Association." *American Indian Quarterly* 14 (Winter 1990): 1–18.

————. "Parallel Calls to Conscience: Reformers Helen Hunt Jackson and Harriet Beecher Stowe." *Californians* 1 (Summer 1983): 32–40.

Mathes, Valerie Sherer, and Richard Lowitt. *The Standing Bear Controversy: Prelude to Indian Reform*. Urbana: University of Illinois Press, 2003.

Mattingly, Carol. *Well-Tempered Women: Nineteenth-Century Temperance Rhetoric*. Carbondale: Southern Illinois University Press, 1998.

McAfee, Ward. *Religion, Race, and Reconstruction: The Public School in the Politics of the 1870s*. New York: State University of New York Press, 1998.

McAnulty, Sarah. "Angel DeCora: American Artist and Educator." *Nebraska History* 57, no. 2 (Summer 1976): 143–99.

McCarthy, Robert. "The Bureau of Indian Affairs and the Federal Trust Obligation to American Indians." *Brigham Young University Journal of Public Law* 19, no. 1 (2004): 1–160.

McClintock, Anne. *Imperial Leather: Race, Gender, and Sexuality in the Colonial Contest*. New York: Routledge, 1995.

McFeely, William S. *Yankee Stepfather: General O. O. Howard and the Freedmen*. New York: Norton, 1994; first published by Yale University Press, 1968.

McKee, Elizabeth A. "Civilizing the Indian: Field Matrons under Hoopa Valley Agency Jurisdiction, 1898–1919." M.A. thesis, California State University, Sacramento, 1982.

McLendon, Sally. "Pomo Baskets: The Legacy of William and Mary Benson." *Native Peoples: The Art and Lifeways* 4 (Fall 1990): 26–33.

McPherson, James. *The Abolitionist Legacy: From Reconstruction to the NAACP*. Princeton: Princeton University Press, 1975.

Meeks, Eric V. *Border Citizens: The Making of Indians, Mexicans, and Anglos in Arizona*. Austin: University of Texas Press, 2007.

————. "The Tohono O'odham, Wage Labor, and Resistant Adaptation, 1900–1930." *Western Historical Quarterly* 34 (Winter 2003): 469–90.

Meinig, Donald W. *The Shaping of America: Transcontinental America, 1850–1915*. New Haven: Yale University Press, 1998.

Merrill, Karen. "In Search of the 'Federal Presence' in the American West." *Western Historical Quarterly* 30 (Winter 1999): 449–74.

Mettler, Suzanne. *Dividing Citizens: Gender and Federalism in New Deal Public Policy*. Ithaca, N.Y.: Cornell University Press, 1998.

Meyer, Melissa L. *The White Earth Tragedy: Ethnicity and Dispossession at a Minnesota Anishinaabe Reservation, 1889–1920*. Lincoln: University of Nebraska Press, 1994.

Meyerowitz, Joanne. *Women Adrift: Independent Wage Earners in Chicago, 1880–1930*. Chicago: University of Chicago Press, 1988.

Meyn, Susan Labry. "Fighting for Indian Artisans: John Collier, René d'Harnoncourt, and the Indian Arts and Crafts Board." In *Politics and Progress: American Society and the State since 1865*, edited by Andrew E. Kersten and Kriste Lindenmeyer, 55–70. Westport, Conn.: Praeger, 2001.

Mihesuah, Devon A. *Cultivating the Rosebuds: The Education of Women at the Cherokee Female Seminary, 1851–1909*. Urbana: University of Illinois Press, 1993.

————. *Indigenous American Women: Decolonization, Empowerment, Activism*. Lincoln: University of Nebraska Press, 2003.

Miller, Jay. "Families." In *Encyclopedia of Native American Indians*, edited by Frederick E. Hoxie, 192–97. New York: Houghton Mifflin Company, 1999.

Miller, Randall M. "The Freedmen's Bureau and Reconstruction: An Overview." In *The Freedmen's Bureau and Reconstruction: Reconsiderations*, edited by Paul A. Cimballa and Randall M. Miller, xiv–xix. New York: Fordham University Press, 1999.

Mills, Sara. *Discourses of Difference: An Analysis of Women's Travel Writing and Colonialism.* London: Routledge, 1991.

Milner, Clyde A., II. *With Good Intentions: Quaker Work among the Pawnees, Otos, and Omahas in the 1870s.* Lincoln: University of Nebraska Press, 1982.

———. "With Good Intentions: Quaker Work and Indian Survival; The Nebraska Case, 1869–1882." Ph.D. diss., Yale University, 1979.

Mink, Gwendolyn. "The Lady and the Tramp: Gender, Race, and the Origins of the American Welfare State." In *Women, the State, and Welfare*, edited by Linda Gordon, 55–91. Madison: University of Wisconsin Press, 1990.

———. *The Wages of Motherhood: Inequality in the Welfare State, 1917–1942.* Ithaca, N.Y.: Cornell University Press, 1995.

Momaday, N. Scott. *Conversations with N. Scott Momaday.* Edited by Matthias Schubnell. Oxford: University Press of Mississippi, 1987.

Monmonier, Mark. "The Rise of the National Atlas." *Cartographica* 31 (1994): 1–15.

Moses, L. G. *Wild West Shows and the Image of American Indians, 1883–1933.* Albuquerque: University of New Mexico Press, 1999.

Moulton, Candy. *Chief Joseph: Guardian of the People.* New York: Forge Books, 2005.

Murphy, Mary. *Mining Cultures: Men, Women, and Leisure in Butte, 1914–1941.* Urbana: University of Illinois Press, 1997.

Nabokov, Peter, and Robert Easton. *Native American Architecture.* New York: Oxford University Press, 1989.

Namias, June. *White Captives: Gender and Ethnicity on the American Frontier.* Chapel Hill: University of North Carolina Press, 1993.

Nelson, Byron, Jr. *Our Home Forever: The Hupa Indians of Northern California.* Edited by Laura Bayer. Salt Lake City: Howe Brothers, 1988.

Ngai, Mae M. *Impossible Subjects: Illegal Aliens and the Making of Modern America.* Princeton: Princeton University Press, 2004.

Norton, Jack. *Centering in Two Worlds: Essays on Native Northwestern California History, Culture and Spirituality.* Gallup, N. Mex.: Center for the Affirmation of Responsible Education, 2007.

———. *Genocide in Northwestern California: When Our Worlds Cried.* San Francisco: Indian Historian Press, 1979.

Novak, Steven J. "The Real Takeover of the BIA: The Preferential Hiring of Indians." *Journal of Economic History* 50 (Fall 1990): 639–54.

Novak, William J. "The Myth of the 'Weak' American State." *American Historical Review* 113, no. 3 (June 2008): 752–72.

———. *The People's Welfare: Law and Regulation in Nineteenth-Century America.* Chapel Hill: University of North Carolina Press, 1996.

O'Brien, Sharon. "Bureau of Indian Affairs." In *Encyclopedia of North American Indians*, edited by Frederick E. Hoxie, 85–88. Boston: Houghton Mifflin Company, 1996.

Oetelaar, Gerald A. "Stone Circles, Social Organization, and Special Places: Forbis' Skepticism Revisited." In *Archaeology on the Edge: New Perspectives from the Northern Plains*, edited by Brian Kooyen and Jane Kelly. Calgary: University of Calgary Press, 2004.

Officer, James E. "The Bureau of Indian Affairs since 1945: An Assessment." *Annals of the American Academy of Political and Social Science* 436 (March 1978): 61–72.

O'Neill, Colleen. "Charity or Industry? American Indian Women and Work Relief in the New Deal Era." In *Women at Work: A Transnational Study of Aboriginal and Native American Women's Labor from the Late Nineteenth Century to the Modern Era*, edited by Carol Williams and Joan Sangster. Urbana: University of Illinois Press, forthcoming.

Onuf, Peter. *Statehood and Union: A History of the Northwest Ordinance*. Bloomington: Indiana University Press, 1987.

Orloff, Ann. *The Politics of Pensions: A Comparative Analysis of Britian, Canada, and the United States, 1880–1940*. Madison: University of Wisconsin Press, 1993.

Osburn, Katherine. *Southern Ute Women: Autonomy and Assimilation on the Reservation, 1887–1934*. Albuquerque: University of New Mexico Press, 1998.

Ostler, Jeffrey. *The Plains Sioux and U.S. Colonialism from Lewis and Clark to Wounded Knee*. Cambridge, UK: Cambridge University Press, 2004.

Paredes, J. Anthony. "Chippewa Townspeople." In *Anishinabe: Six Studies of Modern Chippewa*, edited by J. Anthony Paredes, 343–46. Tallahassee: University Presses of Florida, 1980.

Pascoe, Peggy. *Relations of Rescue: The Search for Female Moral Authority in the American West, 1874–1939*. New York: Oxford University Press, 1990.

Paul, Rodeman W. *Mining Frontiers of the Far West, 1848–1880*. New York: Holt, Rinehart and Winston, 1963.

Peacock, Ronnie. "Clara Davis True: Timeline." 26 July 2001. Copy in author's possession.

Peiss, Kathy. *Cheap Amusements: Working Women and Leisure in Turn-of-the-Century New York*. Philadelphia: Temple University Press, 1986.

Perdue, Theda. *"Mixed Blood" Indians: Racial Construction in the Early South*. Athens: University of Georgia Press, 2005.

Peterson, Susan. "'Holy Women' and Housekeepers: Women Teachers on South Dakota Reservations, 1885–1910." *South Dakota History* 13 (Fall 1983): 245–69.

Petrik, Paula E. *No Step Backward: Women and Family on the Rocky Mountain Mining Frontier, Helena, Montana, 1865–1900*. Helena: Montana Historical Society Press, 1987.

Philip, Kenneth R. *John Collier's Crusade for Indian Reform, 1920–1954*. Forward by Francis Paul Prucha. Tucson: University of Arizona Press, 1977.

———, ed. *Indian Self-Rule: First-Hand Accounts of Indian-White Relations from Roosevelt to Reagan*. Logan: Utah State University Press, 1995.

Pinkett, Harold T. "Investigations of Federal Record-Keeping, 1888–1906." *American Archivist* 21 (April 1958): 163–94.

———. "The Keep Commission, 1905–1909: A Rooseveltian Effort for Administrative Reform." *Journal of American History* 52, no. 2 (September 1965): 297–312.

Pomeroy, Earl S. *The Territories and the United States, 1861–1890: Studies in Colonial Administration*. Philadelphia: University of Pennsylvania Press, 1974.

Powell, Peter J. "Foreword." In *Women and Warriors of the Plains: The Pioneer Photography of Julia Tuell*, by Dan Aadland. New York: Macmillan, 1996.

Pratt, Mary Louise. *Imperial Eyes: Travel Writing and Transculturation*. London: Routledge, 1992.

Priest, Loring Benson. *Uncle Sam's Stepchildren: The Reformation of United States Indian Policy, 1865–1887*. New Brunswick: Rutgers University Press, 1942.

Prucha, Francis Paul. *American Indian Policy in Crisis: Christian Reformers and the Indian, 1865–1900*. Norman: University of Oklahoma Press, 1964.

———. *The Churches and the Indian Schools, 1888–1912*. Lincoln: University of Nebraska, 1979.

———. *The Great Father: The United States Government and the American Indians*. Lincoln: University of Nebraska Press, 1984.

———. *The Great Father: The United States Government and the American Indians*. Abridged edition. Lincoln: University of Nebraska Press, 1986.

———, ed. *Americanizing the American Indians: Writings by the 'Friends of the Indian,' 1880–1900*. Cambridge: Harvard University Press, 1973.

———, ed. *Documents of United States Indian Policy*. 2nd ed. Lincoln: University of Nebraska Press, 1990.

Rai, Kul B., and John W. Critzer. *Affirmative Action and the University: Race, Ethnicity, and Gender in Higher Education Employment*. Lincoln: University of Nebraska Press, 2000.

Rand, Jacki Thompson. *Kiowa Humanity and the Invasion of the State*. Lincoln: University of Nebraska Press, 2008.

———. "Red, White, and Black: A Personal Essay on Interracial Marriage." *Frontiers: A Journal of Women Studies* 29, nos. 2 and 3 (2008): 51–58.

Reyhner, Jon Allen, and Jeanne Eder. *American Indian Education: A History*. Norman: University of Oklahoma Press, 2004.

Riley, Glenda. *Women and Indians on the Frontier, 1825–1915*. Albuquerque: University of New Mexico Press, 2004. Originally published in 1984.

Riney, Scott. *The Rapid City Indian School, 1898–1933*. Norman: University of Oklahoma Press, 1999.

Ritzenthaler, Robert E., and Mary Sellers. "Indians in an Urban Situation." *Wisconsin Archeologist* 36, no. 4 (1955): 147–61.

Rockwell, Stephen J. "Building the Old American State: Indian Affairs, Politics, and Administration from the Early Republic to the New Deal." Ph.D. diss., Brandeis University, 2001.

———. *Indian Affairs and the Administrative State in the Nineteenth Century*. Cambridge, UK: Cambridge University Press, 2010.

Rodgers, Daniel T. *Atlantic Crossings: Social Politics in a Progressive Age*. Cambridge: Harvard University Press, 1998.

———. "In Search of Progressivism." *Reviews in American History* 10 (December 1982): 113–32.

Rohrbough, Malcom. *The Land Office Business: The Settlement and Administration of American Public Lands, 1789–1837*. New York: Oxford University Press, 1968.

Rose, Willie Lee. *Rehearsal for Reconstruction: The Port Royal Experiment*. New York: Oxford University Press, 1976.

Rosenzweig, Roy. *Eight Hours for What We Will: Workers and Leisure in an Industrial City, 1870–1920*. Cambridge and New York: Cambridge University Press, 1983.

Rosier, Paul C. "'They Are Ancestral Homelands': Race, Place, and Politics in Cold War Native America, 1945–1961." *Journal of American History* 92, no. 4 (March 2006): 1300–1326.

Ross, Dorothy. *The Origins of American Social Science*. Cambridge, UK: Cambridge University Press, 1991.

Rothman, Ellen. *Hands and Hearts: A History of Courtship in America*. New York: Basic Books, 1984.

Rubenstein, Bruce. "To Destroy a Culture: Indian Education in Michigan, 1855–1900." *Michigan History* 60 (Summer 1976): 137–60.

Ryan, Mary P. *Cradle of the Middle Class: The Family in Oneida County, New York, 1790–1869*. New York: Cambridge University Press, 1981.

———. *Women in Public: Between Banners and Ballots, 1825–1880*. Baltimore: John Hopkins University Press, 1990.

Sanchez, George. *Becoming Mexican American: Ethnicity, Culture, and Identity in Chicano Los Angeles, 1900–1945*. New York: Oxford University Press, 1993.

Sandoval-Strausz, Andrew K. *Hotel: An American History*. New Haven: Yale University Press, 2007.

Sarris, Greg. *Mabel McKay: Weaving the Dream*. Berkeley: University of California Press, 1994.

Schackel, Sandra. *Social Housekeepers: Women Shaping Public Policy in New Mexico, 1920–1940*. Albuquerque: University of New Mexico Press, 1992.

Scharf, John Thomas, and Thompson Westcott. *History of Philadelphia, 1609–1884*. Vol. 2. Philadelphia, 1884.

Schubnell, Matthias. *N. Scott Momaday: The Cultural and Literary Background*. Norman: University of Oklahoma Press, 1985.

Schwantes, Carlos. *Hard Traveling: A Portrait of Work Life in the New Northwest*. Lincoln: University of Nebraska Press, 1994.

Scott, James C. *Seeing Like a State: How Certain Schemes to Improve the Human Condition Have Failed*. New Haven: Yale University Press, 1998.

———. *Weapons of the Weak: Everyday Forms of Peasant Resistance*. New Haven: Yale University Press, 1987.

Sedlak, Michael W. "Let Us Go and Buy a School Master." In *American Teachers: Histories of a Profession at Work*, edited by Donald Warren, 257–90. New York: Macmillan, 1989.

Shirley, Glenn. *Pawnee Bill: A Biography of Major Gordon W. Lillie, White Chief of the Pawnees, Wild West Showman, Last of the Land Boomers*. Albuquerque: University of New Mexico Press, 1958.

Simonsen, Jane E. *Making Home Work: Domesticity and Native American Assimilation in the American West, 1860–1919*. Chapel Hill: University of North Carolina Press, 2006.

Simpson, Brooks D. "Ulysses S. Grant and the Freedmen's Bureau". In *The Freedmen's Bureau and Reconstruction: Reconsiderations*, edited by Paul A. Cimballa and Randall M. Miller, 1–28. New York: Fordham University Press, 1999.

Sklar, Kathryn Kish. *Catharine Beecher: A Study in American Domesticity*. New Haven: Yale University Press, 1973.

Skocpol, Theda. *Protecting Soldiers and Mothers: The Political Origins of Social Policy in the United States*. Cambridge: Harvard University Press, 1992.

Skowronek, Stephen. *Building a New American State: The Expansion of National Administrative Capacities, 1877–1920*. New York: Cambridge University Press, 1982.

Smith, Burton M. "Thomas Jefferson Morgan and Anti-Catholicism." *Canadian Journal of History* 22 (August 1988): 213–33.

Smith, Jason Scott. "New Deal Public Works at War: The WPA and Japanese American Internment." *Pacific Historical Review* 72, no. 1 (February 2003): 63–92.

Smits, David D. "'Squaw Men,' 'Half-Breeds,' and Amalgamators: Late Nineteenth-Century Anglo-American Attitudes toward Indian-White Race-Mixing." *American Indian Culture and Research Journal* 15, no. 3 (1991): 29–61.

Stage, Sarah, and Virginia B. Bincenti, eds. *Rethinking Home Economics: Women and the History of a Profession*. Ithaca, N.Y.: Cornell University Press, 1997.

Stamm, Henry Edwin. *People of the Wind River: The Eastern Shoshones, 1825–1900*. Norman: University of Oklahoma Press, 1999.

Stanley, Amy Dru. "Beggars Can't Be Choosers: Compulsion and Contract in Post-bellum America." *Journal of American History* 78 (March 1999): 1265–93.

———. *From Bondage to Contract: Wage Labor, Marriage, and the Market in the Age of Slave Emancipation*. New York: Cambridge University Press, 1998.

Steinberg, Sabra L., Jeffrey R. Dunk, and TallChief A. Comet. *In Hoopa Territory: A Guide to Natural Attractions and Human History of the Hoopa Valley Indian Reservation and Surrounding Areas*. Hoopa, Calif.: Hoopa Valley Tribal Council, 2000.

Sterett, Susan Marie. *Public Pensions: Gender and Civic Service in the States, 1850–1937*. Ithaca, N.Y.: Cornell University Press, 2003.

Stewart, James B. *Holy Warriors: The Abolitionists and American Slavery*. New York: Hill & Wang, 1996.

Stoler, Ann Laura. *Carnal Knowledge and Imperial Power: Race and the Intimate in Colonial Rule*. Berkeley: University of California Press, 2002.

———. "Empires and Intimacies: Lessons from (Post) Colonial Studies: A Round Table." *Journal of American History* 88, no. 3 (December 2001): 829–97.

———. "Matters of Intimacy as Matters of State: A Response." *Journal of American History* 88, no. 3 (December 2001): 895.

———, ed. *Haunted by Empire: Geographies of Intimacy in North American History*. Durham: Duke University Press, 2006.

Stuart, Paul. *The Indian Office: Growth and Development of an American Institution, 1865–1900*. Ann Arbor: University of Michigan Press, 1979.

Summers, Carol. "Intimate Colonialism: The Imperial Production of Reproduction in Uganda, 1907–1925." *Signs* 16, no. 4 (Summer 1991): 787–807.

Svingen, Orlan J. *The Northern Cheyenne Indian Reservation, 1877–1900*. Niwot, Colo.: University Press of Colorado, 1993.

Swint, Henry L. *The Northern Teacher in the South, 1862–1970*. Nashville: Vanderbilt University Press, 1941.

Taylor, Graham D. *The New Deal and American Indian Tribalism: The Administration of the Indian Reorganization Act, 1934–45*. Lincoln: University of Nebraska Press, 1980.

Thorne, Tanis C. *The Many Hands of My Relations: French and Indians on the Lower Missouri*. Columbia: University of Missouri Press, 1996.

————. *The World's Richest Indian: The Scandal over Jackson Barnett's Oil Fortune*. New York: Oxford University Press, 2003.

Tong, Benson. *Susan La Flesche Picotte, M.D.: Omaha Woman Leader and Reformer*. Foreword by Dennis Hastings. Norman: University of Oklahoma Press, 1999.

Torpey, John C. *The Invention of the Passport: Surveillance, Citizenship, and the State*. Cambridge, UK: Cambridge University Press, 2000.

Trachtenberg, Alan. *The Incorporation of America: Culture and Society in the Gilded Age*. New York: Hill and Wang, 1982.

Trafzer, Clifford F. *As Long as the Grass Shall Grow and Rivers Flow: A History of Native Americans*. Fort Worth: Hartcourt College Publishers, 2000.

Trennert, Robert A., Jr. *The Phoenix Indian School: Forced Assimilation in Arizona, 1891–1935*. Norman: University of Oklahoma Press, 1988.

————. "Selling Indian Education at Worlds Fairs and Expositions, 1893–1904." *American Indian Quarterly* 11 (Fall 1987): 203–33.

Utley, Robert M. *Frontier Regulars: The United States Army and the Indian, 1866–1891*. New York: Macmillan, 1974.

Utley, Robert M., and Barry Mackintosh. *The Department of Everything Else: Highlights of Interior History*. National Park Service, 1989, ⟨http://www.nps.gov/history/history/online_books/utley-mackintosh/index.htm⟩. 20 October 2010.

Van Riper, Paul. *History of the United States Civil Service*. Evanston, Ill.: Row and Peterson, 1958.

Varon, Elizabeth R. "Patriotism, Partisanship, and Prejudice: Elizabeth Van Lew of Richmond and Debates over Female Civic Duty in Post–Civil War America." In *Women and the Unstable State in Nineteenth-Century America*, edited by Alison M. Parker and Stephanie Cole, 113–38. College Station, Tex.: Texas A&M Press, 2000.

Vogt, Anita. "Eligibility for Indian Employment Preference in the Bureau of Indian Affairs." *Indian Law Reporter* 1, no. 6 (June 1974).

Vuckovic, Myriam. *Voices from Haskell: Indian Students between Two Worlds, 1884–1928*. Lawrence: University Press of Kansas, 2008.

Waggoner, Linda M. *Fire Light: The Life of Angel DeCora, Winnebago Artist*. Norman: University of Oklahoma Press, 2008.

Walls, Wendy. "Gender and the 'Citizen Indian.'" In *Writing the Range: Race, Class, and Culture in the Women's West*, edited by Elizabeth Jameson and Susan Armitage, 202–29. Norman: University of Oklahoma Press, 1997.

Wanken, Helen M. "'Woman's Sphere' and Indian Reform: The Women's National Indian Association, 1879–1901." Ph.D. diss., Marquette University, 1981.

Warren, Donald, ed. *American Teachers: Histories of a Profession at Work*. New York: Macmillan, 1989.

Waugh, Joan. *Unsentimental Reformer: The Life of Josephine Shaw Lowell*. Cambridge: Harvard University Press, 1997.

Weibel-Orlando, Joan. *Indian Country, L.A.: Maintaining Ethnic Community in a Complex Society*. Urbana: University of Illinois Press, 1999.

Weisiger, Marsha. *Dreaming of Sheep in Navajo Country*. Seattle: University of Washington Press, 2009.

Welke, Barbara. "When All the Women Were White, and All the Blacks Were Men: Gender, Class, Race, and the Road to Plessy, 1855–1914." *Law and History Review* 13 (Fall 1995): 261–316.

Wenger, Tisa Joy. *We Have a Religion: The 1920s Pueblo Indian Dance Controversy and American Religion.* Chapel Hill: University of North Carolina Press, 2009.

Wesley, Edgar B. *NEA: The First Hundred Years: The Building of the Teaching Profession.* New York: Harper Brothers, 1957.

West, Elliot. *Growing up with the Country: Childhood on the Far Western Frontier.* Albuquerque: University of New Mexico Press, 1989.

————. "Reconstructing Race." *Western Historical Quarterly* 34 (Spring 2003): 7–26.

White, Richard. *It's Your Misfortune and None of My Own: A History of the American West.* Norman: University of Oklahoma Press, 1991.

————. *The Roots of Dependency: Subsistence, Environment, and Social Change among the Choctaws, Pawnees, and Navajos.* Lincoln: University of Nebraska Press, 1983.

————. "The Winning of the West: The Expansion of the Western Sioux in the Eighteenth and Nineteenth Centuries." *Journal of American History* 65 (Fall 1978): 319–43.

Whiteley, Peter M. "Why Anthropology Needs More History." *Journal of Anthropological Research* 60, no. 4 (Winter 2004): 487–514.

Wiebe, Robert H. *The Search for Order, 1877–1920.* New York: Hill and Wang, 1967.

Wilkins, David, and K. Tsianina Lomawaima, *Uneven Ground: American Indian Sovereignty and Federal Law.* Norman: University of Oklahoma Press, 2001.

Willard, William. "Outing, Relocation, and Employment Assistance: The Impact of Federal Indian Population Dispersal Programs." *Wicazo Sa Review* 12, no. 1 (Spring 1997): 29–46.

Williams, Walter L. "United States Indian Policy and the Debate over Philippine Annexation: Implications for the Origins of American Imperialism." *Journal of American History* 66 (March 1980): 810–31.

Wilson, Raymond. *Ohiyesa: Charles Eastman Santee Sioux.* Urbana: University of Illinois Press, 1983, 1999.

Wishart, David. *An Unspeakable Sadness: The Dispossession of the Nebraska Indians.* Lincoln: University of Nebraska Press, 1994.

Wissler, Clark. *Material Culture of the Blackfoot Indians.* Anthropological Papers of the American Museum of Natural History, vol. 5, pt. 1. New York: The Trustees, 1910.

Wright, Gwendolyn. *Moralism and the Model Home: Domestic Architecture and Cultural Conflict in Chicago, 1873–1913.* Chicago: University of Chicago Press, 1980.

Yellin, Jean Fagan. *Women and Sisters: The Antislavery Feminists in American Culture.* New Haven: Yale University Press, 1989.

Yellin, Jean Fagan, and John C. Van Horne, eds. *The Abolitionist Sisterhood: Women's Political Culture in Antebellum America.* Ithaca, N.Y.: Cornell University Press, 1994.

Young, Mary E. "Gertrude Bonnin." In *Notable American Women, 1607–1950: A Biographical Dictionary,* edited by Edward T. James, Janet Wilson, and Paul S. Boyer, 199–200. Cambridge: Belknap Press of Harvard, 1971.

Zaeske, Susan. *Signatures of Citizenship: Petitioning, Antislavery, and Women's Political Identity.* Chapel Hill: University of North Carolina Press, 2003.

Index

Page numbers in italics indicate illustrations

employee role models and, 7, 55, 145, 223, 259; Indian Service employees' resistance to, 104, 113, 116, 120, 128, 134, 170–71, 197–205, 260, 261; influences on, 11; land use and, 41–42, 45–46; marriage and, 39–40, 41, 87, 248; men's role and, 39–40, 50, 106, 162, 178; Native community's resistance to, 40–41, 76–77, 79, 81, 209, 259; origins of, 7, 24, 32; parents' displacement under, 6, 39, 52–55, 79; roads and, 180, 181; women policy makers' importance to, 259; women role models and, 65, 66, 80, 228; women's role and, 40, 41, 65–67, 80, 228, 259. *See also* Home and family life

Assimilation policy, contradictions of: interracial contact and, 136, 137, 145, 148–49, 150–51, 154, 158–66, 168–69, 264; Native employees and, 130, 165–66, 177–78, 203, 261; women and, 71–76, 78, 80–81, 83–84, 90–92, 259

Atkins, John, 70

Badger, Otis F., 239
Baird, Mary, 216
Baldwin, Marie (Chippewa/French), 229, 230, 277 (n. 8)
Baptist Home Missionary Society, 27
Barstow, A. C., 28
Bauer, William J., 206, 287 (n. 55)
Beard, A. F., 28
Beaulieu, C. H. (Chippewa), 121
Beaver, Charles (Hupa), 193
Beaver, Jessie, 183, 193
Betts, David U., 99
"B.I.A." (song), 1
BIC. *See* Board of Indian Commissioners
Bigmouth Tom (Hupa), 180
Biolsi, Thomas, 153
Blackfeet (tribe), 38
Blackfeet Reservation, 94
Blackhawk's War, 9
Blacks. *See* African Americans
Blish, William, 97

Blue Lake Advocate, 191
Blue Star. *See* Fellows, Corabelle
Boarding schools, 79, 83, 91, 96, 97, 138; children's experiences at, 100–101, 183; couples and, 85; health conditions at, 222, 249–50; at Hoopa Valley Reservation, 152, 182–86, 191, 195, 201, 209; Indian Service employees as graduates of, 109, 111–12, 227, 228; nurse training at, 112; overview of, 54, 55–58; phasing out of, 224–25, 227, 244–45; social life at, 147. *See also specific schools*

Board of Indian Commissioners, 29, 31, 32, 40, 209, 234; colonies and, 209; creation of, 19, 20; family and, 38, 44, 50; freedpeople and, 26, 28; Indian Service issues and, 221–22, 243, 244; Lake Mohonk Conference and, 25; Progressives and, 226, 228

Bonney, Mary, 22–23, 24
Bonnin, Gertrude (Yankton Sioux), 118, 131, 229, 230–31
Bonnin, Jerdine (Wyandot/m), 99
Bonnin, Leo (Yankton Sioux), 99, 131, 250
Bonnin, Raymond (Yankton Sioux), 121, 126, 131
Boston Indian Citizenship Commission, 28
Bowdler, Anna, 237
Bowman, Anna, 237
Braithwaite, Minnie, 63–64, 68, 92, 98, 209, 213, 215, 221
Branchaud, Theodore and Ella, 296 (n. 82)
Brehaut, Charlotte, 152
Brett, John (Hupa), 193
Brewer, David (Puyallup), 153, 252
Brewer, Katie (Native Alaskan/m), 153, 251–53, 251
Brink, Lewis L., 237
Broad, Mary, 300 (n. 145)
Bronson, Ruth Muskrat (Cherokee), 104
Brookings Institution, 98
Brooks, Erastus, 271 (n. 37)

Democratic Party, 10, 44, 70

Densmore, Frances, 37

Dependency, 29, 30, 32, 39, 49; federal pensions and, 242

Dickson, Minnie, 155, 157, 158, 159, 164–65, 167

Dix, Dorothea, 273 (n. 67)

Domesticity. *See* Home and family life; Women's role

Dorchester, Merial, 47, 65

Dorrington, L. A., 138

Dougherty, William, 178, 179, 180, 181

Douglas, Belle, 143

Douglas, George, 143

Dows, Willie (Hupa), 186

D-Q University, 311 (n. 143)

Dwellings, 36, 37, 38, *246*

Eastern Cherokee (tribe), 300 (n. 150)

Eastern Cherokee Agency, 158; school, 95

Eastern Navajo Agency, 115

Eastman, Charles (Santee Sioux), 155–60, 229, 296 (n. 88), 322 (n. 44)

Eastman, Elaine Goodale, 70, 74, 118; background of, 157–58; interracial marriage of, 155, 157–60, 161, 163, 164; *Sister to the Sioux* (memoir), 163; teacher training and, 212

Education. *See* Indian School Service; Native education; *specific schools and types of schools*

Ellinghaus, Katherine, 269 (n. 14), 296 (nn. 82, 87)

Ellis, Mark, 109

Emmerich, Lisa, 227, 314 (n. 65)

Escalanti, Joseph (Quechan), 159

Estes, Anna Johnson, 101, 155, 156, 157, 166–67, 297 (n. 103)

Estes, Joseph (Yankton Sioux), 101–2, 130–31, 134, 296 (n. 88), 297 (n. 103); interracial marriage of, 155, 157, 166–67

Etheridge, Florence, 240

Family life. *See* Home and family life

Farming, 45–46, 53, 226

Faurote, Mary, 209

Federal Employee (newsletter), 240

Federal Employee Retirement Act of 1920, 240, 241, 242–43, 245, 250–51, 252, 254

Federal Employees Union, 240–42

Federal government: Indian Service staffing direction by, 44; Meriam Report critique of Indian policy and, 248–49; perceived obligation to Native Americans of, 15–20, 23, 26, 32–33, 255–56, 262–63; program rationales of, 210, 241–42, 255–56, 262–63; tribal sovereignty and, 2–3, 17, 264–65; West and development of, 3, 18, 80, 262; women and, 7, 71, 73, 74–78, 80–81, 87–88, 259. *See also* Civil service; Congress, U.S.; Treaties; *specific agencies, bureaus, departments, and policies*

Fellows, Corabelle, 68, 76–77, 143; adopted Dakota name of, 163; interracial marriage of, 155, 157, 158–59, 160–64, *160*

Field matrons, 89, 94–96; Native women as, 111, 129–30, 227–28; professional nurse replacements of, 223; role of, 45, 46–47, 91

Finch, Charles (Hupa), 198

Fisk, Clinton B., 26–27

Fisk University, 27, 31

Five Civilized Tribes, 23

Fletcher, Alice, 30, 64

Fond du Lac School, 131

Forest Grove Indian School. *See* Chemawa (Forest Grove) Indian School

Fort Berthold Training School, 131, 167

Fort Defiance School, 79

Fort Gaston, 173, 177, 182, 189, 191

Fort Humboldt, 173

Fort Laramie, treaty of (1868), 21–22

Fort Lewis School, 154, 225

Fort Marion, 24

Fort Simcoe School, 95

Fort Yates, 120–21

Foss, Mary, 92

Fowler, Loretta, 119

Indian commissioners. *See* Board of
    Indian Commissioners
Indian Education Department, 213, 214
Indian Health Service, 325 (n. 16)
Indian Leader (periodical), 221
Indian removal policy, 9, 23
Indian Reorganization Act of 1934
    (Wheeler-Howard Act), 257–58,
    264–65
Indian Rights Association, 24, 25, 28, 38,
    43, 232, 234
"Indian Rings," 19
Indians. *See* Native Americans; *specific
    tribal groups*
Indian School Service: female employees
    of, 57, 64–65, 90, 112, 263; female
    Native employees of, 112–22; origins
    of, 44–45; personnel requirements
    of, 93, 121; program of, 52–56; school
    types/operations and, 55–57; seen as
    temporary, 53, 224; staffing by sex, *64*;
    staffing by race, *110*; traditional values
    of, 236. *See also* Native education
Indian Service, 187, 189; activists' cri-
    tique of, 230, 232–33; administrative
    reform and, 42–44, 220, 221–22, 248;
    aging workforce of, 236–40; as catchall
    department, 52; civil service control
    of, 44, 70–71, 73, 89, 90, 93, 222, 259,
    262; contemporary critics of, 216–17;
    cutbacks imposed on, 245; efficiency
    measures and, 220–21; employee
    discontent and, 96–98, 103, 132–33,
    243–44, 248–49; employee families
    and, 93–102; employee isolation and,
    137–39; employee racial classification
    and, 125–26, 128; employee social
    life and, 136–51, 168, 259; employees'
    policy influence on, 10–11, 59, 102,
    257, 258–59; employee turnover and,
    89, 103, 227, 249; field experience vs.
    theory and, 58–59, 103; inefficiency of,
    217–18; interracial relationships and,
    164–65, 167–68; "intimate colonial-
    ism" and, 6, 98–99, 154; job benefits
    of, 115–16; jobs held by, *110*; as model

for U.S. overseas colonial administra-
    tions, 209; motives for joining, 85–87;
    Native dwelling survey of, 194; Na-
    tives' influence on, 145–51; paperwork
    and, 50–51; pensions and retirement
    and, 239–40, 249–56; personnel
    requirements of, 95; positions under,
    50–51; professionalization movement
    and, 212–23; racism of, 126, 128–32,
    134–35, 139, 149, 230, 261–62; roads
    and, 180, 181; salary practices of, 69,
    86, 88, 133, 179, 180–81, 183, 200,
    201, 245, 254; spending on, 2; spousal
    hiring policy and, 55, 82–103, 245,
    247–48, 259; staffing and recruiting by,
    42–43, 44, 69–71, 87, 222–23; teaching
    institutes and, 212–13, 216; temporary
    workers and, 170, 179, 260; troubles of,
    209, 243–44, 248–49; women's influ-
    ence on, 259
Indian Service Native employees: as-
    similation resistance of, 104, 113, 116,
    120, 125, 128, 134, 170–71, 197–205,
    260, 261; assimilation role of, 51–52,
    105–6, 126, 259; assimilation's limits
    and, 130, 165–66, 177–78, 203, 261; bu-
    reaucratic maneuvering and, 132–33,
    168, 260; Bureau of Indian Affairs and,
    265; civil service and, 111, 251, 254,
    255, 258; community critics of, 104,
    230–34; community loyalties and,
    117–20, 134, 201; education of, 109,
    111–12; family and, 85, 101–2, 115–17,
    152–53; free-labor ideology and, 51,
    105–6; Hoopa Valley Reservation and,
    175–81, 206; importance of, 105, 175,
    187, 255, 260; intertribal identity and,
    7, 123–25, 135, 144, 152–53, 183–84,
    230, 233, 262; motives of, 109, 113,
    115–18, 134, 201, 261; numbers of, 2, 7,
    51–52, 106, 228, 259; pay of, 106, 107,
    119, 133, 179, 180–81, 254; pensions
    and, 250–56; posts held by, 105, 106–7,
    110, 112–13, 130–31, 134, 187, 226–28,
    254; professionalization and, 211, 215,
    220–21; racial classification of, 126,

128, 129, 261–62; Society of American Indians and, 229–34; supervisory positions and, 130–31; as temporary, 170, 260; tensions with white colleagues and, 122–35, 139; tribal identity and, 120–22; white-collar jobs and, 112, 260, 261; women's experiences as, 85, 112–13, 123–24, 129–30, 260, 261

Indian Service Teachers' Association, 232–33

Indian Service women employees, 2, 6–7, 63–81, 83–84, 89–92, 103, 186–87, 259, 263; aging and, 237, 254–55; as boarding-school staff, 57, 182; demands on, 137; federal role vs. traditional role of, 71–78, 80–81; firing and disciplining of, 164–65, 166; high posts held by, 64–65; job seeking by, 69–71, 80; motives for joining, 68–69; Natives as, 112–13, 123–24, 129–30

Indian's Friend (newsletter), 271 (n. 40)

Indian Territory, 9, 21–22, 53–54, 300 (n. 150)

Indian Treaty-Keeping and Protective Association, 23, 30

Infant mortality, 223

Institute for Government Research, 248

Interior Department, 9, 219, 248, 265

Interracial marriage, 153–69; of Native men and white women, 24, 154–68, 169; of Native women and white men, 153–54; racist condemnation of, 160–64, 165, 168

Interstate Commerce Commission, 43

Intertribal identity, 124–25, 229, 233–34, 289 (n. 84)

"Intimate colonialism," 11, 58, 83, 137; complications of, 79, 98–99, 103, 154, 168; definition of, 6; social provision and, 263; U.S. variety of, 264

Jacker, Madeline (Chippewa/German), 117, 237

Jackson, Andrew, 9

Jackson, Helen Hunt, *A Century of Dishonor*, 23, 30, 64; as Indian advocate, 24, 30; Indian Service and, 64–65, 67; *Ramona*, 65

Jackson, James (Hupa), 199, 200

Jacobs, Margaret, 6, 269 (nn. 9, 12, 14), 273 (nn. 3, 5)

Jarnaghan, William (Hupa), 185, 186

Jemez Pueblo, 101

Jobin, Lucy (Chippewa/m), 98–99, 125; racism and, 126, 128, 131–32

Johnie, Minnie (Hupa), 185, 186

Johnson, Anna. *See* Estes, Anna Johnson

Johnson, Dollie (Chinook), 97, 123, 124, 125, 256

Johnson, Emma D. (Pottawatomi), 230, 289 (n. 88)

Johnson, Marie, 74–75, 193

Jones, William, 106, 210–11, 214, 215, 223, 224–25

Joseph, Chief (Nez Perce), 21

Jump Dance, 199

Kane, Salena (Pottawatomie), 94, 132–33

Karuk (tribe), 75, 141, 171

Keep Commission, 217, 219, 220

Keith, Maggie Goulette (Yankton Sioux), 144–45

Keshena School, 129, 133

Kickapoo School, 131

King, Minnie C. (Cherokee/m), 139

Kinney, Abbott, 67

Kinney, Sarah, 47

Kiowa (tribe), 24, 36

Kiowa Agency, 123

Klamath Reservation, 125; school, 145

Kneale, Albert, 86, 87, 91–92, 143, 147–51; *Indian Agent*, 149–51

Kneale, Edith, 86, 87, 91, 148, 150

Kneale, Etta, 91–92, 150

Kohpay, Henry (Osage), 229

Koontz, Charles H., 214

Kouni, Annie (Laguna Pueblo), 152, *152*. *See also* Abner, Annie

Kroeber, Alfred L., 176

Kyselka, Frank, 138, 141, 154, 247; Hoopa Reservation and, 175, 191, 197–99

McKenzie, Fayette A., 229, 248, 321–22 (nn. 44, 45)

McLaughlin, James, 18

Memoirs, 148–51

Men. *See* Gender; Male role; Native men

Menominee (tribe), 121

Menominee School, 214

Meriam, Lewis, 248

Meriam Report (1928), 98, 248–49

Merrill, Karen, 3

Mesket, Anderson (Hupa), 186, *196*

Metoxyn, Julia Wheelock (Oneida), 129–30, 133

Mexican War, 9

Meyer, Melissa, 133

Meyers, Annie, 151–52

Midwest, U.S., 8–9

Military action, 18–19, 20–21, 22, 173–74

Miller, Emily C., 49

Mills, Cyrus H., 152, 191

Missionaries, 72, 87, 193, 199, 233; Indian Service employees and, 63, 68, 156; Lake Mohonk Conference and, 25

Mission Indians, 65

Mohonk Mountain House. *See* Lake Mohonk Conference for the Friends of the Indian

Mojave (tribe), 100

Momaday, Al (Kiowa), 153

Momaday, Natachee (Cherokee/m), 153

Momaday, N. Scott (Kiowa/Cherokee), 101, 153; *House Made of Dawn*, 101

Montezuma, Carlos (Yavapai Apache), 104, 229, 231–32

Morago, Jessie, 117

Morgan, Thisba Huston, 96

Morgan, Thomas Jefferson, 27, 44, 65, 226

Mormon Wives (novel), 24

Morrill Act of 1862, 31

Morton v. Mancari (1974), 325 (n. 15)

Mortsolf, Jesse, 185, 186, 198, 201, 202, 203

Nash, Violetta (Winnebago), 111

National Education Association, 212, 213–15

Native American (periodical), 221

Native Americans: activism of, 211, 229–34, 265; citizenship and, 27, 28–29, 228, 234; coercion of, 18–19, 76–79; divisions among, 133–34; employed outside Indian Service, 113–14; federal mistreatment of, 15–17, 210, 248–49; freedpeople parallel with, 28–29; intertribal identity and, 229, 233–34; removal policy and, 9, 23; tribal sovereignty of, 2–3, 17, 264–65; ward status of, 6, 11, 20, 26, 32–33, 53, 71, 210, 229, 255, 262, 263. *See also* Allotment policy; Assimilation policy

Native American Studies, 204, 311 (n. 143)

Native culture, 3–4, 246, 257–58; activist embracement of, 211; ceremonies and, 176, 199–200, 202, 204–5; crafts and, 146, 192–93, 324 (n. 3); dance and, 144–45, 144, 147–48; dwellings and, 36, 37, 38, 246; games and, 196; shared resources and, 49

Native education: for adults, 44–47; downplaying of higher education and, 211, 224–25, 235, 244–45; early experiments in, 24–25; funding of schools and, 96; Indian Service employees and, 109, 211, 260; reformer advocates of, 30–31; student abuse and, 79; teaching institutes and, 112, 212–13, 216; vocational training focus of, 224–25, 235, 244–45; white children and, 96–97. *See also* Boarding schools; Contract schools; Day schools; Indian School Service

Native men: assimilation policy and, 39–40, 44, 46, 50, 106, 162, 178; authority positions and, 130–31; farming and, 45–46; interracial marriage and, 24, 153–69. *See also* Indian Service Native employees

Native women: allotment policy and, 41; crafts and, 192–93; as field matrons, 111, 129–30, 227–28; field matrons and, 46–47; Hoopa Reservation and, 182,

Redwood (tribe), 173, 174
Reed, Isaiah (Oneida), 195
Reed, Mabel, 69, 75–76, 141, 175
Reedy, Agnes (Minnesota Sioux/m), 133–34
Reel, Estelle, 39–40, 65, 192–93; as higher education opponent, 224, 225
"Rehearsal for Reconstruction" (Pierce), 27–28
Religion: Christian values and, 49, 50; contract schools and, 43–44, 68; Indian Service staffing and, 43. *See also* Missionaries
Rennett, Francis (Hupa), 179
Republican Party, 10, 44, 130
Requa, Calif., 74, 75, 186
Reservation agents, 50
Reservation system, 20, 223, 265; adult education and, 45; boundaries of, 9, 18; dependency blamed on, 29, 30; Indian Reorganization Act and, 258; jobs and, 115, 116, 118, 260; slavery analogy with, 29; U.S. map of, 4. *See also* Allotment policy; *specific reservations*
Retirement. *See* Pensions and retirement
Rhoads, James E., 28
Rice, Ada (Winnebago), 120, 125
Riggs, Thomas, 34, 39
Riggs Institute, 68, 130, 156, 157
Riley, Glenda, 296 (n. 82)
Risling, David, Jr. (Hupa), 311 (n. 143)
Road building, 180–82, 183, 185, 186, 187, 192
Robertson, Alice, 53–54
Roman Catholic Church, 43–44, 276 (n. 86)
Roosevelt, Theodore, 217, 218, 219, 225
Rosebud Reservation, 100, 106–7, 117
Rosenkrang, Dr., 186
Round Valley Reservation, 129, 206
Rules for Indian Schools (1892), 53, 93
Rupert Costo chair (University of California), 311 (n. 143)

Sacramento Agency, 254
Salem School, 123

Salt, Edith, 155, 156, 157, 163, 167
Salt, Wellington (Chippewa/m), 155–56, 157, 163, 167
Salt River Reservation, 117
Sambo (Hupa), 181
San Juan Pueblo (New Mexico), 116
Santa Fe Indian School, 140, 151
Santee Agency Boarding School, 130, 166, 297 (n. 103)
Santeo, Nellie (Papago), 111, 117, 251
Sauk and Fox (tribe), 9
Saxon, Arthur (Hupa), 108, 198
Schools. *See* Indian School Service; Native education; *specific schools and school types*
Scott, Superintendent, 120, 238, 239
Sells, Cato, 2, 224, 225
Senate, U.S.: Committee on Indian Affairs, 15, 41; debate on treatment of Native Americans, 15–17
Seneca School, 116
Shawnee (tribe), 9
Shawnee Agency, 125; Indian school, 132
Sherman, John (Hupa), 180
Shoemaker, Robinson (Hupa), 190, 199
Shoshone (tribe), 144
Siletz Agency, 315–16 (n. 77); school, 86
Simmons, Isabella C., 70
Simonsen, Jane, 275 (n. 58)
Simpson, Albert, 154
Sioux (tribe), 73, 121, 159, 178. *See also* Lakota Sioux; Oglala Lakota Sioux
Sioux Reservation, 24, 70
Sisseton Reservation, 100
Sister to the Sioux (E. Eastman), 163
Skocpol, Theda, 6, 25, 241
Slavery, 22, 23; emancipation and, 11, 26; reservation policy analogy with, 29. *See also* Abolitionism
Smiley, Albert, 25
Smith, Nimrod (Cherokee), 158
Smith, Richard (Cherokee/m), 155, 156, 157, 158, 159; Indian Office critique of, 165–66
Smits, David, 155
Snyder, Frederick, 152

Wage labor. *See* Free-labor ideology
Wahpeton Boarding School, 125, 140, 142, 184
Walker, Francis A., 10
Walmart Corporation, 325 (n. 17)
Ward, William Hays, 28
War Department, 9, 19, 21, 311 (n. 2)
Warm Springs Reservation, 187; school, 69
Washington, Booker T., 225
Wassaja (newspaper), 104, 232, 232–33
Water Drops (novel), 24
Weitchpec, Calif., 75, 185, 186
Welsh, Herbert, 24, 43, 109
West, Elliot, 3
West (U.S.): federal power and, 3, 80, 262; political influence of, 224; views of, 10, 223–24
Westerman, Floyd Red Crow (Sisseton-Wahpeton), 1
Wheeler-Howard Act of 1934. *See* Indian Reorganization Act
Wheelock, Dennison (Oneida), 229, 322 (n. 44)
Whilkut (tribe), 173
Whipple, Henry, 23
White, Richard, 3, 272 (n. 70)
White-collar jobs, 112, 183, 260, 261
White Deerskin Dance, 199
White Earth Boarding School, 296 (n. 82); reservation, 111, 121, 133
White Horse Camp, 143
White women: in federal bureaucracy, 87–88; Hoopa Reservation and, 187; Indian policy reform and, 22–24; Indian Service influence of, 259; interracial marriage and, 24, 154, 156–68, 169; political mobilization by, 23–24; as superintendents' wives, 89, 98–99, 247. *See also* Gender; Indian Service women employees; Maternalism; Women's role

Wigwams, 37, 38
Willow Creek, 182
Wind River, 134
Winnebago (tribe), 7, 120, 125
Winnebago Reservation, 91–92
Wittenberg Agency, 299–300 (n. 145)
Wiyot massacre (1860), 301 (n. 9)
Women. *See* Gender; Native women; White women; Women's role
Women's Bureau, 7, 17–18, 65, 262
Women's National Indian Association, 193, 199, 276 (n. 86); Indian Service employees and, 68, 69; Mohonk reformers and, 25, 29, 34; Native homes as focus of, 46, 47, 48; origins of, 23, 24, 30
Women's role, 36, 40, 41, 65–67, 80, 228, 259; domestic skills and, 90–92, 103; moral authority and, 157. *See also* Maternalism
Women writers, 23–24
Woodruff, Janette, 137, 139, 140
Work, Hubert, 248
World War I, 243–44, 247
Wounded Knee Day School, 143
Wounded Knee Massacre (1890), 158
Wyaco, Virgil (Zuni), 115
Wyman, Sarah (Anishinabe), 115–16

Yankton School, 99
Yankton Sioux, 125, 145
Yellow Hat, 77
Yellow Robe, Chauncey (Dakota), 229
Yellowstone National Park, 21
Young, P. L., 185
Young Men's Christian Association, 156
Yuma School, 63, 92, 159
Yurok (tribe), 171, 173, 191–92, 193, 206

Zitkala-Sa. *See* Bonnin, Gertrude
Zuni Day School, 84; reservation, 115